Current Perspectives:
Readings from InfoTrac® College Edition

White Collar Crime

NICOLE PIQUERO
John Jay College of Criminal Justice

THOMSON
™
WADSWORTH

Australia • Brazil • Canada • Mexico • Singapore • Spain
United Kingdom • United States

THOMSON
TM
WADSWORTH

Current Perspectives: Readings from InfoTrac® College Edition
White Collar Crime

Executive Editor: *Marcus Boggs*
Acquisitions Editor: *Carolyn Henderson-Meier*
Assistant Editor: *Meaghan Banks*
Marketing Manager: *Terra Schultz*
Marketing Communications Manager: *Tami Strang*
Project Manager, Editorial Production: *Samen Iqbal*
Creative Director: *Rob Hugel*
Art Director: *Maria Epes*

Print Buyer: *Becky Cross*
Permissions Editor: *Mardell Glinski Schultz*
Production Service: *Ruchika Vij, ICC Macmillan Inc.*
Copy Editor: *Heather Mann*
Cover Designer: *Larry Didona*
Cover Image: *Photolibrary.com/Photonica*
Compositor: *ICC Macmillan Inc.*

Library of Congress Control Number:
2007934468

Student Edition:
ISBN-13: 978-0-495-10385-1
ISBN-10: 0-495-10385-3

For more information about our products, contact us at:
Thomson Learning Academic Resource Center
1-800-423-0563

For permission to use material from this text or product, submit a request online at
http://www.thomsonrights.com.
Any additional questions about permissions can be submitted by e-mail to
thomsonrights@thomson.com.
Thomson Higher Education
10 Davis Drive
Belmont, CA 94002-3098 USA

Contents

Preface   v

The Discovery of White Collar Crime   1

1. Primary Definitions of Crime and Moral Panic: A Content Analysis
    of Experts' Quotes in Feature Newspaper Articles on Crime   3
    MICHAEL WELCH, MELISSA FENWICK, AND MEREDITH ROBERTS

Studying White Collar Crime and Assessing Its Costs   23

2. Organizational Crime in NASA and Among Its Contractors:
    Using a Newspaper as a Data Source   25
    JURG GERBER AND ERIC FRITCH

Occupational Crime and Avocational Crime   39

3. Investor Reaction to Disclosures of Employee Fraud   41
    JAMES M. LUKAWITZ AND PAUL JOHN STEINBART

Governmental Crime: State Crime and Political White Collar Crime   53

4. Democratization and Political Corruption in the Philippines and
    South Korea: A Comparative Analysis   55
    JON S.T. QUAH

State-Corporate Crime, Crimes of Globalization, and Finance Crime   75

5. Risky Business Revisited: White-Collar Crime and the Orange
    County Bankruptcy   77
    SUSAN WILL, HENRY N. PONTELL, AND RICHARD CHEUNG

6. The Parliamentary Enquiry on Fraud in the Dutch Construction Industry Collusion as Concept Between Corruption and State-Corporate Crime   97
   GRAT VAN DEN HEUVEL

7. Globalization and the Federal Prosecution of White Collar Crime   115
   ELLEN S. PODGOR

Enterprise Crime, Contrepreneurial Crime, and Technocrime   141

8. Protect Yourself Against Identity Theft: Here's How to Guard Against the Nation's Fastest-Growing White-Collar Crime   143
   MARCY TOLKOFF

Explaining White Collar Crime: Theories and Accounts   147

9. Control Fraud as an Explanation for White-Collar Crime Waves: The Case of the Savings and Loan Debacle   149
   W. BLACK

Policing and Regulating White Collar Crime   177

10. Investigative Planning: Creating a Strong Foundation for White-Collar Crime Cases   179
    ARTHUR L. BOWKER

11. Firm Self-Regulation Through International Certifiable Standards: Determinants of Symbolic versus Substantive Implementation   185
    PETRA CHRISTMANN AND GLEN TAYLOR

Prosecuting, Defending, and Adjudicating White Collar Crime   217

12. In Enron's Wake: Corporate Executives on Trial   219
    KATHLEEN F. BRICKEY

13. Prison Time, Fines, and Federal White-Collar Criminals: The Anatomy of a Racial Disparity   249
    MAX M. SCHANZENBACH AND MICHAEL L. YAEGER

14. Prosecutions Drop for US White-Collar Crime; They're Down 28 Percent from Five Years Ago, as Homeland Security Cases Rise in Priority   285
    ALEXANDRA MARKS

InfoMarks: Make Your Mark   289

Preface

The study of white-collar crime is as frustrating as it is exciting. The frustration often arises because of the lack of agreement as to what exactly constitutes white-collar crime. The definitional debate is as old as the study of white-collar crime itself, and still can be found in the intellectual conversations of today. The confusion over the definition began when Edwin Sutherland first introduced the term "white collar criminal" in 1939 during his presidential address to the American Sociological Society. Much of his focus was on introducing a type of crime not commonly studied at the time, namely calling attention to the fact that the poor were not the only ones committing crime, rather than developing a definitive definition. However, he did note that white-collar crimes should be considered as "crimes committed by a person of respectability and high social status in the course of his occupation" (Sutherland, 1983: 7).

Even today, a precise definition of white-collar crime is not easily agreed upon. Some scholars favor the use of an offender-based definition, such as the one proposed by Sutherland. Others reject the use of offender characteristics (e.g., social and employment status) in defining what constitutes this crime type, and thereby prefer an offense-based definition. Former federal prosecutor Herbert Edelhertz (1970: 3) provided an offense-based definition of white-collar crime stating that it is "an illegal act or series of illegal acts committed by nonphysical means and by concealment or guile to obtain money or property, to avoid the payment or loss of money or property, or to obtain business or personal advantage." The use of an offense-based definition allows for a broader range of offenses to be included under the purview of white-collar crime but does little to differentiate the crimes committed by the poor and those of the upper-classes, the distinction originally laid out by Sutherland. Regardless of definitional preference, one distinct feature that has emerged is the existence of a distinct category of crimes and criminals that are substantially different from street crimes and criminals (Weisburd and Waring, 2001: 9).

Once you move beyond the definitional debate, the study of white-collar crime is an exciting area to research. Much like the larger study of crime and criminality, the study of white-collar crime is multidisciplinary, drawing from several different disciplines including (but not limited to): criminology and criminal justice, business, sociology, psychology, economics, ethics, and law. The multidisciplinary approach allows for endless research questions and possibilities from a variety of different angles and perspectives to be tackled, investigated, and acted upon. Since each disciplinary focus has its own unique approach to addressing research problems and issues, it allows for diversity in not only the way white-collar crime is defined, but also how it is studied. This diversity pulls together the various intellectual environments from the represented disciplines to give the study of white collar crime a well-rounded balance. It is precisely because of this balance that researchers are provided with the framework in which they can study the issues of crime, law, and justice that are commonly asked or need to be asked regarding white-collar crime and white-collar criminals.

While the study of white-collar crime is exciting, it is also a challenging area to study. On the one hand, the multidisciplinary approach offers endless possibilities for areas of study; but on the other hand, the sheer span of disciplines that contribute to the intellectual knowledge base requires scholars to keep up to date with the latest research from a variety of disciplinary areas, many of which they may have no formal training in. As such, scholars must be well versed in a variety of different areas and understand how the related disciplinary foci intersect with one another. Similarly, globalization of the economy and marketplace is also requiring students of white-collar crime scholarship to look beyond their own national borders to understand the crimes and atrocities that are occurring at the hands of those in power—both in terms of governmental and business leadership—from around the world. This requires scholars to understand the laws, definitions, and even customs of countries other than their own.

Access (or lack thereof) to data also poses a problem for researchers studying white-collar crime. While it is not an insurmountable challenge, it is one that requires creativity and patience on the part of the researcher. To this end, those who study white-collar crime have used a variety of different methodological approaches, both qualitative and quantitative, to address the research issues and questions at hand. Gaining access to official data, such as that provided by criminal justice and regulatory agencies, is less problematic than trying to obtain data dealing with motivations for offending. Lack of easy access has not hampered scholars from addressing motivational issues; rather, they have turned to other sources such as interviews or scenario-based surveys in order to address motivational issues of offending. Scholars working in this area have gone a long way to advance what is known and understood about white-collar criminality; however, there is still a long way to go. Because the study of white-collar crime is still in its infancy—its introduction to social science was less than seventy years ago—there are probably more unanswered questions than there are answered ones on topics and issues surrounding white-collar crime and its criminals. There are, without a doubt, many challenges that have faced and will continue to face researchers working in this area, but this is an area of research that has much to offer.

These readings were selected from Wadsworth InfoTrac College Edition. This compilation is designed to be as diverse as the perspectives which contribute to the study of white-collar crime and criminality.

REFERENCES

Edelhertz, H. (1970). *The nature, impact, and prosecution of white-collar crime.* Washington, DC: U.S. Government Printing Office.

Sutherland, E. H. (1983). *White collar crime: The uncut version.* New Haven, CT: Yale University Press.

Weisburd, D., & Waring, E. (2001). *White-collar crime and criminal careers.* New York: Cambridge University Press.

The Discovery of White Collar Crime

1

Primary Definitions of Crime and Moral Panic: A Content Analysis of Experts' Quotes in Feature Newspaper Articles on Crime

Michael Welch, Melissa Fenwick, and Meredith Roberts

Research on crime news continues to generate scholarly interest, particularly in the realm of social constructionism. From this perspective, researchers have documented the process by which crime is shaped into news—especially the pivotal role played by law enforcement officials. In this study, the authors contribute to this area of inquiry by administering a content analysis of 105 feature articles on crime published in four national newspapers between 1992 and 1995. In addition to exploring the topics of crime, they systematically examined the nature of quotes offered by two groups of experts, namely, state managers (e.g., police and politicians) and intellectuals (e.g., professors). Their findings support previous research demonstrating the media's heavy reliance on law enforcement officials in formulating primary definitions of crime. The significance of primary definitions of crime within the context of the dominant ideology and moral panic is discussed at length.

"Primary definitions of crime and moral panic: A content analysis of experts' quotes in feature newspaper articles on crime," by Michael Welch, Melissa Fenwick, and Meredith Roberts from *Journal of Research in Crime and Delinquency*, 34(4): 474–494 (1997). Reprinted by permission of Sage Publications.

Research on crime news continues to generate scholarly interest, particularly in the realm of social constructionism. From this perspective, researchers have documented the process by which crime is shaped into news—especially the pivotal role played by law enforcement officials. In this study, the authors contribute to this area of inquiry by administering a content analysis of 105 feature articles on crime published in four national newspapers between 1992 and 1995. In addition to exploring the topics of crime, they systematically examined the nature of quotes offered by two groups of experts, namely, state managers (e.g., police and politicians) and intellectuals (e.g., professors). Their findings support previous research demonstrating the media's heavy reliance on law enforcement officials in formulating primary definitions of crime. The significance of primary definitions of crime within the context of the dominant ideology and moral panic is discussed at length.

Drawing from the sociology of knowledge, mass communication, organizations and occupations, social stratification, and especially social constructionism, research on crime news—also known as news-making criminology (Barak 1988, 1994)—continues to generate valuable scholarly interest. In pursuit of understanding the process and production of crime news, researchers have grown to appreciate the macro-, meso-, and microsociological forces that contribute to its form, content, and scope, as well as its significance in American culture. At its most basic level:

> Crime, then, is "news" because its treatment evokes threat to, but also reaffirms, the consensual morality of the society: a modem morality play takes place before us in which the "devil" is both symbolically and physically cast out from the society by its guardians—the police and the judiciary. (Hall et al. 1978:66)

Reaching beyond the importance of Durkheimian perspectives of crime news, however, recent research tends to focus on the social construction processes dictating how crime events become crime news. In doing so, critical investigations have explored the relationship between the media and the primary definers of crime—namely, law enforcement officials—in locating answers about the role that police play in shaping the public image of crime (Barak 1994; Chermak 1994; Kasinsky 1994; Kidd-Hewitt and Osborne 1995; Surette 1992; also see the classic works of Fishman 1978; Hall et al. 1978; Humphries 1981). Indeed, a major consequence of primary definitions of crime in news remains profoundly evident:

> What is most striking about crime news is that it very rarely involves a first-hand account of the crime itself, unlike the "eyewitness" report from the battle-front of the war correspondent. Crime stories are almost wholly produced from the definitions and perspectives of the institutional primary definers. (Hall et al. 1978:68; also see Ericson, Baranek, and Chan 1987, 1989, 1991)

It is argued that primary definitions of crime are largely shaped by the dominant ideology (Abercrombie, Hill, and Turner 1980; Hall et al. 1978; Herman and Chomsky 1988; Sahin 1980). Moreover, because such definitions are imposed early in the defining stage of the social construction of crime news—by public officials whose credibility typically rests in their positions of power and prestige—these ideological perspectives command the field. As a result, primary definers (i.e., law enforcement officials) succeed in establishing the terms of reference from which all discussion of crime emanates; in fact, even dissenters must at the very least acknowledge the dominant ideology's prominence at the center of discourse.

In a companion article (Welch, Fenwick, and Roberts forthcoming), we examined evidence of ideology in crime news by administering a content analysis of quoted statements offered by experts in feature newspaper articles on crime. In examining the quotes of two groups of experts—namely, state managers (i.e., politicians and criminal justice practitioners) and intellectuals (i.e., professors and nonacademic researchers)—we found that statements offered by state managers were significantly more ideological (in both the causes of crime and the commands of what to do about crime) insofar as they distorted (or neglected) the causal connection between social conditions and crime. Furthermore, we also confirmed that politicians and law enforcement officials serve as the primary definers of crime, whereas professors and nonacademic researchers function as secondary definers of crime.

In this article, we continue our examination of quoted statements offered by different types of crime experts (i.e., state managers versus intellectuals)—a rarely studied aspect of crime news. Thus, by identifying the principal themes of quoted statements about crime, we illuminate how the media image of crime is shaped and from whose perspective. Whereas particular attention is directed at the significance of primary definitions of crime (including topics of crime), evidence of moral panic is also discussed. In sum, this project endeavors to contribute to the growing body of research on crime news by documenting key patterns among experts' statements.

RESEARCH METHOD

The Sample of Feature Articles on Crime

The sample of feature newspaper articles in this study was drawn from four major newspapers: The New York Times, the Washington Post, the Los Angeles Times, and the Chicago Tribune. These newspapers were selected because of their large circulation, their reputation for offering readers a national coverage of news, and because together they contribute to a sense of geographic representation. A total of 105 feature newspaper articles about crime were published in these selected newspapers between 1992 and 1995; specifically, 42 feature articles were published in The New York Times, 24 in the Washington Post, 23 in the Los Angeles Times, and 16 in the Chicago Tribune. It should be noted that the greatest number of feature articles about crime appeared in 1994 (n = 38) followed by 1993 (n = 31), 1992 (n = 0), and 1995 (n = 16) (see Table 1).

TABLE 1   Number of Feature Articles on Crime per Year by Newspaper

Newspaper	1992	1993	1994	1995	Totals
The New York Times	7	12	15	8	42
Washington Post	7	6	6	5	24
Los Angeles Times	3	7	12	1	23
Chicago Tribune	3	6	5	2	16
Total	20	31	38	16	N = 105

For the purposes of this study, our sample of newspaper articles about crime includes only those articles indexed as features and containing at least one quote from a crime expert. Obviously, there are perhaps hundreds of articles about crime incidents published each year by these newspapers. However, feature articles on crime were selected because they typically offer focused discussions of crime in which experts' quotes are particularly relevant. With this in mind, the objective of our research was to examine the content of experts' quotes within the context of feature articles on crime.

Groups of Experts: State Managers and Intellectuals

Two major groups of experts (N = 179) were constructed for this study. The first group of experts—state managers (n = 112)—includes 62 law enforcement officials (and officers), 23 politicians (i.e., elected and appointed officials), 13 criminal justice organization advocates (e.g., New York City's Citizen Crime Commission), 5 prosecutors (e.g., United States attorneys and district attorneys), and 2 defense lawyers. In addition, this group of state managers includes a judge, a criminal justice service administrator, a corrections official, a juvenile services official, a poll taker, a chief economist at a security firm, and a forensic psychologist. The rationale for grouping politicians with criminal justice practitioners is based on their similar roles as state managers; also in our previous study, we found that the content of their quotes were consistently similar in terms of ideological statements (Welch et al. forthcoming) (see Table 2).

The second group of experts—intellectuals (n = 67)—includes 58 professors and 9 nonacademic researchers (e.g., analysts at the RAND Corporation). The rationale for grouping professors and nonacademic researchers is based on their roles as intellectuals; moreover, in our previous study we also found that the content of their quotes was consistently similar in terms of ideological statements (Welch et al. forthcoming) (see Table 2).

It should be noted that the unit of analysis in this study was the specific quote offered by a crime expert. Therefore, even though 179 experts were quoted within 105 feature articles, we enumerated 267 total quotes for our analysis. Expectedly, some experts appeared in several feature articles and were quoted numerous times. Overall, however, the prevalence of oft-quoted experts—as measured by the number of articles they appeared in and the number of times they were quoted—was indeed limited. For example, among the

TABLE 2 Types of Experts among State Managers and Intellectuals Quoted in Feature Newspaper Articles on Crime (N = 179)

State Managers	Number (Percentage)	Intellectuals	Number (Percentage)
Law enforcement	62 (55)	Professors	58 (87)
Politicians	23 (21)	Nonacademic	
Advocates	13 (12)	researchers	9 (13)
Prosecutors	5 (4)		
Defense lawyers	2 (1.7)		
Judge	1 (.89)		
Corrections	1 (.89)		
Juvenile services	1 (.89)		
Criminal justice services	1 (.89)		
Forensic psychologist	1 (.89)		
Chief economist at security firm	1 (.89)		
Poll taker	1 (.89)		
Total	n = 112		n = 67

NOTE: The pool of state managers includes 98 men and 14 women. The pool of intellectuals includes 56 men and 11 women.

group of state managers in our sample, the most oft-quoted expert was Louis J. Freeh (Director of the Federal Bureau of Investigation [FBI]), appearing in five articles and quoted seven times. Nevertheless, of the 112 state managers in our sample, most appeared in only one article and rarely were they quoted more than once or twice.

A similar pattern was found among the group of intellectuals. For instance, Professor James Alan Fox (Northeastern University) was the most oft-quoted expert, appearing in five articles and quoted nine times. Of the 67 intellectuals in our sample, most appeared in one to three articles and rarely were they quoted more than three times. Overall, our sample contained a relatively wide representation of quoted experts, meaning this pool included those with national reputations as well as those considered regional and local figures. Once again, aside from the oft-quoted figures mentioned (i.e., Louis J. Freeh and James Alan Fox), the pool of quoted experts was remarkably varied.

Although not surprising (given the enormous representation of men employed in criminal justice and academics), the vast majority of experts quoted in our sample are men; of the 179 experts, there are 154 men (86 percent) and 25 women (14 percent). Specifically, the pool of state managers includes 98 men and 14 women, whereas the pool of intellectuals includes 56 men and 11 women. As Table 2 indicates, the highest represented segment of experts is the group of male politicians and practitioners, comprising 55 percent (n = 98) of the pool of experts quoted. Conversely, the least represented segment of experts is the group of female professors (and nonacademic researchers), including six percent (n = 11) of the pool of experts. Indeed, the gender imbalance in this sample of experts suggests an androcentric worldview of crime, thereby reproducing a male perspective of crime (see Daly 1994; Messerschmidt 1986; Simpson 1989). Moreover, there also appears to be a racial bias within this pool of experts insofar as the overwhelming numbers of experts quoted are White. (Admittedly, however, this finding is not based on a systematic examination of race but rather a cursory review of the list of quoted experts. An exhaustive search to identify the race of 179 experts was deemed too costly in terms of time and effort for the purpose and scope of this study.)

FINDINGS

In addition to revealing notable themes among quoted experts (i.e., state managers and intellectuals), our content analysis also exposes key dimensions of crime news, including biases in topical coverage. In this section, we present the study's chief findings, patterns, and related items of interest.

Topics in Crime News

In our sample, 47 separate topics are represented among 105 feature articles about crime, thus suggesting a seemingly diverse range of crime issues. The most common topic was crime rates/trends (n = 15), followed by the crime drop in New York City (n = 8); youth crime and juvenile delinquency (n = 8); and politicians discussing crime (n = 7). Furthermore, the remaining articles offered a varied assortment of issues, including the growth in prison population, "3 strikes" laws, firearms, carjacking, genetics, gangs, DNA, stalking, urban violence, women offenders, and the war on drugs.

It is important to acknowledge, however, the disproportionate emphasis on street crime in our sample. Despite 47 different topics, only one of these articles went beyond street crime to focus on white-collar offenses. Indeed, the media bias toward street crime (especially offenses committed by individuals) to the exclusion of white-collar, corporate, governmental, military, and political crime (especially offenses committed by groups and organizations) is clearly evident. In sum, this particular finding suggests that the topics selected for these feature newspaper articles might be ideologically filtered or screened. Consequently, these selected issues reproduce a public image of lawlessness that disproportionately focuses on street crime (particularly property offenses committed by low-income individuals). As we shall discuss later, the media's preoccupation with these types of offenses could be indicative of moral panic against street crime.

Similarly, this pattern of selected topics within the framework of moral panic also supports the assertion that crime news is commodified—for public consumption—according to the dominant ideology. A principal aspect of the dominant ideology of crime is its insinuation that street offenses are the most costly, dangerous, and threatening form of crime (see Barlow, Barlow, and Chiricos 1995a, 1995b; Welch 1996a, 1996b). Financial assessments of the costs attached to different types of offenses, however, contradict the dominant ideology's image of crime. It is estimated that the cost of street crime hovers around 4 billion dollars per year, whereas the expense of white-collar and corporate crime exceeds that figure 50 times—reaching 200 billion dollars per year (Albrecht, Wernz, and Williams 1995; Mokhiber and Wheat 1995:9). Furthermore, about 24,000 homicides were committed in the United States in, for example, 1995. By contrast, during the same period, more than 56,000 workers died as a result of injuries or diseases caused by unsafe working conditions—that is more than 300 fatalities per day (since 1970 when the Occupational Safety and Health Act was enacted, thus enabling the agency to record these fatalities) (Mokhiber and Wheat 1995:9; also see Reiman 1995; Serrin 1991:80; Welch 1996a:21–24).

Themes of Experts' Quotes

Besides serving exploratory and heuristic purposes, our content analysis of experts' quotes reveals several distinct themes, including (1) statements confirming that crime (and fear) is a problem, (2) statements serving as technical remarks, (3) statements criticizing popular perceptions of crime, (4) statements criticizing official statistics and trends, and (5) statements conveying alarmist reactions to crime. It should be noted that these categories were treated as mutually exclusive even though many experts' quotes (particularly lengthy quotes) included several different statements. (For example, a lengthy quote could include both a statement confirming crime as a problem in addition to a separate statement serving as a technical remark; see Table 3.)

STATEMENTS CONFIRMING CRIME
(AND FEAR) AS A PROBLEM

This thematic category includes the largest number of quoted statements, accounting for 37 percent (n = 100) of all quotes (N = 267). It is worth noting that state managers offered 72 statements, comprising almost half (48 percent) of all quoted statements from that group. By contrast, intellectuals offered 28 quoted statements confirming crime (and fear) as a problem, accounting for only about one-quarter (24 percent) of their statements (see Table 3). Therefore, this finding suggests that nearly half of the time, journalists rely on state managers (especially, politicians and law enforcement officials) to confirm crime (and fear) as a problem. As we shall discuss later, this reliance on state managers has significant relevance to primary definitions of crime.

TABLE 3   Number of Quoted Statements about Crime per Theme by Politicians and Practitioners Compared with Professors and Nonacademic Researchers (a)

Themes of quotes	Politicians and Practitioners Number (Percentage)	Professors and Nonacademic Researchers Number (Percentage)
Confirm crime, problem, fear	72 (48)	28 (24)
Technical remark	42 (28)	35 (30)
Critical of popular perception of crime	17 (11)	19 (16)
Critical of official statistics and trends	9 (6)	21 (18)
Alarmist	11 (7)	13 (11)
Total	151	116

Themes of quotes	Total Number (Percentage)
Confirm crime, problem, fear	100 (37)
Technical remark	77 (29)
Critical of popular perception of crime	36 (13)
Critical of official statistics and trends	30 (11)
Alarmist	24 (9)
Total	N = 267

(a) Quoted statements are drawn from 105 feature newspaper articles about crime in the New York Times, the Los Angeles Times, the Chicago Tribune, and the Washington Post from 1992 to 1995.

The following quoted statements drawn from our sample illustrate how experts confirm crime (and fear) as a problem:

> There is a definite increase in self-defense shootings . . . I don't know . . . whether its [sic] because more people are arming themselves in anticipation of something happening or the direct result of people being more and more afraid. (Melanie Shaw, chief of homicide and narcotics division of the Prince George's County state attorney's office, Washington Post, March 23, 1995, p. 1)

> The crime rate has gone down and that's good, but unfortunately it is still at a very high level. . . . A generation ago there were 300 murders a year on average (in New York City), a fourth committed with guns. Today we rejoice when the number of murders goes below 2,000. (Thomas A. Repetto, president of Citizens Crime Commission, nonprofit research group, The New York Times, April 2, 1994, p. 24)

TECHNICAL STATEMENTS

Accounting for 29 percent (n = 77) of all quoted statements (N = 267), this thematic category includes the second largest number of experts' quotes. Of these 77 technical remarks, 42 statements were offered by state managers, accounting for more than one-quarter (28 percent) of all quoted statements from that group. Similarly, intellectuals offered 35 technical remarks, constituting almost one-third (30 percent) of their statements. This particular finding suggests that journalists turn to both state managers (especially, politicians and law enforcement officials) as well as intellectuals for the purposes of clarifying terms, concepts, and criminal justice procedures. Although technical remarks may appear ideologically "neutral," they are, however, presented in a context previously defined by state managers (see the Discussion section for additional elaboration). The following quoted statements serve as technical remarks in crime news:

> While crack is a stimulant, heroin is a depressant. (Jeffrey Fagan, Columbia University criminologist, The New York Times, July 23, 1995, p. 4)

> The F.B.I. doesn't do a test unless the person has been arrested, and unless they've had a court order for the person to give a blood test. (Peter Neufeld, co-chairman of the National Association of Criminal Defense Lawyers DNA Task Force, Chicago Tribune, February 21, 1995, p. 1)

STATEMENTS CRITICAL OF POPULAR
PERCEPTIONS OF CRIME

As a category, statements criticizing popular perceptions of crime include the third fewest number of quotes, representing 13 percent (n = 36) of all quotes (N = 267). Of these statements, state managers and intellectuals offer a comparable number of critical remarks about popular perceptions of crime: 17 and 19 statements, respectively. It is worth noting that quoted statements that are critical of popular perceptions of crime are relatively few in number; even among the group of intellectuals, such criticisms account for only 16 percent of all their quoted statements (see Table 3). The implication is that these critical statements appear tangential to the already established context of crime. Thus, the popular perception of crime parallels (or is a function of) the dominant ideology and continues to be reproduced, in large part, because the voice of dissent is minimal. Consider the following critical remarks about popular perceptions of crime:

> It is not surprising that crime is declining, even though the fact contradicts the national hysteria that we're in the midst of a crime wave. (Peter Greenwood, acting director of RAND Corporation's criminal justice program, Los Angeles Times, March 16, 1994, p. 3)

> Although dramatic slayings, resulting from an increase in firepower, may be only a small portion of total murders, they capture, a large portion of attention. (Marcus Felson, USC professor of sociology, Los Angeles Times, May 2, 1994, p. A-16)

STATEMENTS CRITICAL OF OFFICIAL
CRIME STATISTICS AND TRENDS

This thematic category includes the second fewest number of quoted statements (n = 30) accounting for 11 percent of all quotes (N = 267). Although relatively few in number, the bulk of criticism of official crime statistics and trends is offered by intellectuals (n = 21); nevertheless, these remarks make up only 18 percent of the quoted statements from this group. From the perspective of the dominant ideology thesis, the public image of crime is largely constructed and perpetuated by "official" measures of lawlessness (which, in turn, are also used as "official" measures of "effectiveness" of the criminal justice system). Hence, it is not surprising to find very little dissent among state managers, who incidentally offered a mere nine critical remarks (accounting for 6 percent of quoted statements from this group) (see Table 3). The following quoted statements drawn from our sample illuminate how some experts remained critical of official statistics and trends:

> I'm not persuaded, because crime rates have gone up and down. (Freda Adler, president of the American Society of Criminology, The New York Times, November 19, 1995, p. 43)

> The figures wiggle from year to year, like the stock market.... Crime has been up so high, you'd expect it to go back down. (Howard Snyder, director of systems research at the National Center for Juvenile Justice in Pittsburgh, The New York Times, May 23, 1995, p. A-14)

ALARMIST REACTIONS TO CRIME
AND MORAL PANIC

Although relatively few in number (n = 24, 9 percent of all quoted statements), alarmist reactions to crime are remarkably significant because by their very nature (perhaps as products of sensationalism), they are emotionally driven. Moreover, because these reactions alarm the public, they remain instrumental in generating fear of crime. In this vein, alarmist reactions to crime are indicative of moral panic—"a turbulent, excited, or exaggerated response to deviance or a social problem" (Mann 1984:255; see also Chiricos 1996; Cohen 1972; Fishman 1978; Hall et al. 1978; Hickman 1982; Jenkins 1992).

Similarly, alarmist reactions to crime—as a type of moral panic—pronounced by state managers (especially politicians and law enforcement officials) often take the form of demagoguery. Indeed, such alarmist reactions are intended to appeal to citizens' (particularly voters) fears often for the purpose of advancing a political agenda (e.g., increased expenditures in the criminal justice system). Likewise, our sample included several inflammatory proclamations emblematic of demagoguery and moral panic.

> These are not the Cleaver kids soaping up some windows. These are middle school kids conspiring to hurt their teacher, teenagers shooting people and committing rapes, young thugs running gangs and terrorizing neighborhoods and showing no remorse when they get caught. (Zell Miller, Georgia governor, The New York Times, January 24, 1994, p. A-12)

> And there is a growing uneasiness among city officials about the number of youths carrying weapons to school and walking the corridors with guns and knives. (Clyde A. Isley, Mount Vernon police commissioner, The New York Times, January 30, 1994, p. 1)

> Our streets are being stained with the blood of our children, and it's going to stop. Damn it. It has got to stop. (Pete Wilson, California governor, The New York Times, January 24, 1994, p. A-14)

Alarmist reactions to crime offered by state managers further contribute to moral panic because their messages are delivered by seemingly credible authorities and political leaders (i.e., moral entrepreneurs). Furthermore, state managers not only confirm crime as a problem but add a heightened sense of anxiety and urgency to an emerging moral panic. Taken together, alarmist reactions to crime advance the dominant ideology because they create the demand for greater expenditure in the criminal justice apparatus aimed at street crime. Certainly, the following items resonate with moral panic:

> The ominous increase in juvenile crime coupled with the population trends portend future crime and violence at nearly unprecedented levels. (Louis Freeh, FBI director, Chicago Tribune, November 19, 1995, p. 3)

> This [drop in crime] is also the lull before the storm. (John J. Dilulio, professor of politics and public affairs at Princeton University, The New York Times, November 19, 1995, p. 18)

> Unless we act now, while our children are still young and impressionable, we may indeed have a bloodbath of teen violence by the year 2005. (James Alan Fox, dean of the College of Criminal Justice at Northeastern University in Boston, The New York Times, May 23, 1995, p. A-14)

Even though the alarmist statements in this study account for only 9 percent of all quotes, evidence of moral panic becomes perceptibly larger if we combine the categories "alarmist reactions to crime" (n = 24) and "statements confirming crime (and fear) as a problem" (n = 100). Together, these categories comprise

124 remarks or 46 percent of all quoted statements. To justify collapsing these categories, it could be argued that alarmist reactions to crime are manifest expressions of moral panic, whereas statements that confirm crime (and fear) as a social problem represent a subtle—or even latent—form of moral panic. For example, the following declarations could be interpreted as mild, subtle, or latent forms of moral panic.

> It's no wonder crime is America's No. 1 concern. We've become a society of victims or people afraid of becoming victims. (Charles E. Schumer, Brooklyn Democrat who heads the House Judiciary Subcommittee on Crime and Criminal Justice, The New York Times, October 31, 1994, p. A-20)

> I describe it as a boa constrictor phenomenon . . . noting that the number of Americans under the age of 18, now 60 million, will increase to more than 70 million by the turn of the century. We can see that bulge of youth population coming. (William J. Bratton, New York City police commissioner, The New York Times, November 13, 1994, p. A-14)

Admittedly, there are methodological and theoretical risks in characterizing all statements that confirm crime (as a problem) as moral panic generated by moral entrepreneurs. Simply put, crime is indeed a social problem, and aside from its artifacts of social constructionism, crime has material consequences producing social and personal harm. Nevertheless, the term moral panic does not necessarily mean that "there's nothing there" but rather that the state-sponsored strategies designed to deal with such problems are "fundamentally inappropriate" (Cohen 1972:204). The following statements clearly address the problem of serious juvenile offenses, but they also endorse a state-sponsored intervention that many criminologists would find inappropriate:

> The laws were written when kids were committing juvenile crimes, but now they're committing adult crimes like rape and murder. The laws are anachronistic and need to be changed. (Andrew J. Stein, chairman of the New York City Commission on Juvenile Offenders, The New York Times, June 25, 1994, p. 27)

> Punishment has to be swift and certain. When children commit adult crimes, they should be prosecuted as adults. We can't coddle criminals because they are young. We're not just talking about gang members. What we are seeing is total disregard for pain and human life among the young. It's scary, and I predict it will only get worse. (Jeanine Ferris Pirro, Westchester [NY] County district attorney, The New York Times, January 30, 1994, p. 15)

By contrast, critics of hard control in criminal justice (e.g., harsher penalties, the proliferation of prisons, and expansion of law enforcement) insist that moral panics contribute to the escalating vocabulary of punitive motives. Moreover, these punitive motives are used to justify inappropriate strategies of dealing with crime, especially those neglecting the root causes of crime and violence (Barlow et al. 1995a, 1995b; Chiricos 1996; Melossi 1985; Welch 1996a, 1996b).

With this in mind, scholars should continue to cast a critical eye on what types of unlawful activity the media (via its primary definers, namely, law enforcement officials) portray as crime and ask, what is the relative harm caused by each particular form of lawlessness? Our sample of 47 crime topics certainly encompasses several serious forms of harm, such as assault, robbery, and urban violence. Conversely, our sample also reveals the inclusion of novelty issues of crime presented under the guise of serious crimes, for instance, proposals for youth curfews, "3 strikes" laws, closed (fortressed) communities, trading cards featuring infamous criminals such as Jeffrey Dahmer and Al Capone, genetics and crime, the criminal mind, as well as the war on drugs (for analyses on the social construction of the war on drugs in the news media, see Chermak 1996; Chiricos 1996; Orcutt and Turner 1993). Indeed, the inclusion of these novelty issues also contributes to alarmist reactions to crime and moral panic. In addition, our sample of topics also includes several revised social constructions of previously existing forms of crime (see Best 1995; Binder 1993; Gamson et al. 1992; Johnson 1995; Sacco 1995; Surette 1992). Consider, for instance, the revised social construction of carjacking presented with fervor commonly found in moral panic.

> Carjacking is a crime that affects all of us—a huge population. It's not something you can protect yourself from by building a moat or locking a door. (Gerald M. Caplan, dean of the McGeorge School of Law in Sacramento and former attorney general counsel of Washington's Metropolitan Police Department, Los Angeles Times, September 16, 1992, p. A-9)

Interestingly, even some law enforcement officials remain skeptical of the emerging crisis of carjacking:

> We don't even like to say "carjacking." . . . Its robbery and its [sic] been going on for a long time. There's a lot of hype going on right now. (Billy Davis, spokesman for the Chicago Police Department, The New York Times, December 9, 1992, p. A-18)

It should be mentioned that our sample of quoted statements also included remarks that did not fit into any of the established thematic categories (including 11 statements offered by state managers and 14 offered by intellectuals). Nevertheless, many of these quotes are noteworthy because they reveal additional evidence of moral panic attached to, among other things, fear and condemnation of so-called urban and youth culture.

> It's kids from New York City and the Bronx bringing new ways to town, their city ways. . . . It's almost a gangster attitude, a disrespect for authorities and adults. (Vincent D. Schiavone, lieutenant police officer, Hastings-on-the-Hudson, The New York Times, January 30, 1994, p. 15)

> Mindless violence belongs to New York, to Los Angeles, to Miami—not to Toronto and Ottawa. Our robbers and our teen-agers aren't supposed to behave that way. (Michael Valpy, columnist Toronto Globe & Mail, the nation's leading newspaper, Los Angeles Times, April 9, 1994, p. A-17)

Conversely, the following retort contests moral panic by offering the public an alternative view of blaming urban culture:

> Those least at risk are sometimes the most fearful. He [Webb] attributed the phenomenon to a tendency by the media to hype crime coverage, a strong word-of-mouth network in tightly knit neighborhoods that amplifies reports of incidents and a latent racism about "those people down there" in the inner city. "In the extremely rural areas north of the city, there's a widespread belief that Omaha is a hotbed of criminal activity and vice." (Vincent Webb, chairman of the University of Nebraska's criminal justice department, Los Angeles Times, June 26, 1992, p. A-24)

Finally, and perhaps revealingly, of the 105 articles in our sample, only one feature was devoted to the media and crime. That particular article included four critical statements about the media offered by intellectuals and one by a state manager. The following thought sheds additional light on the role of the media in promoting moral panic:

> People come to think they're in great danger because the media tend to spotlight middle-class victims. (James Fyfe, professor of criminal justice at Temple University, Washington Post, July 4, 1993, p. A-20)

DISCUSSION AND CONCLUSION

Obviously, our sample of 105 feature articles on crime represents only a fraction of the crime news stories published each year by the print media. Nevertheless, our findings reveal that the two most common themes among experts' quotes are statements that confirm crime (and fear) as a problem (37 percent of all quoted statements, N = 267) followed by technical remarks (29 percent). Moreover, the two critical categories remained clearly underrepresented, namely, statements that were critical of popular perceptions of crime (13 percent) and comments that were critical of official statistics and trends (11 percent).

In addition to these findings, it is important to draw attention to the media's heavy reliance on state managers as experts, and more significantly as primary, definers of crime. Of the 179 experts quoted in our sample, nearly 63 percent are state managers, whereas 37 percent are intellectuals. Furthermore, of the 112 state managers quoted, 62 (55 percent of state managers) are law enforcement officials and 23 (nearly 21 percent) are political and government leaders (elected and appointed officials). It is worth noting that several other types of experts are underrepresented, especially defense lawyers (n = 2, or 1.7 percent). In fact, the near absence of defense lawyers raises questions of whether the media ignore them because of their inherent adversarial role within the criminal justice apparatus, thereby preserving the dominant ideology.

Among the group of intellectuals, we identified 58 professors and nine nonacademic researchers. Admittedly, it could be argued that there is not much numerical difference between the 62 law enforcement officials and

58 professors; however, as we noted previously—and shall elaborate further—journalist tend to rely on law enforcement officials for primary and "official" definitions of crime. Thus, even though professors are interviewed and quoted, the definitional context—arguably situated within the dominant ideology—is already established. Consequently, professors' critical insights (of which there were many, n = 40) are typically presented as secondary and "nonofficial" interpretations of crime. In light of its central importance to this study, let us discuss the significance of primary definitions of crime and their roles in reproducing the dominant ideology.

Primary Definitions of Crime
and the Dominant Ideology

In the realm of primary definitions of crime, our findings support previous research on the relationship between print journalism and law enforcement (Chermak 1994; Ericson 1995; Ericson et al. 1987, 1989, 1991; Fishman 1978; Hall et al. 1978; Kasinsky 1994; Schlesinger and Tumber 1994). Conversely, efforts to expose and explain the complex relationship between the media and law enforcement are subject to criticism—at times, informally denounced as conspiracy theory. In brief, conspiracy theory suggests that because the media are capitalist owned, journalists simply—and uncritically—reproduce the dominant ideology of the political (and economic) elite in their news coverage. This conspiratorial view of the media prompts many scholars to disagree, insisting that the relationship between journalists and the political elite as it pertains to the production of news is far more complex (Barak 1994; Fishman 1978; Hall et al. 1978; Henry 1994; Kasinsky 1994; Surette 1992). Among the principal components of news production—particularly crime news—is the media's reliance on primary definers of crime. Moreover, the relationship between the media and the primary definers of crime is not the result of a conspiracy; rather, the media's dependence on the primary definers is a product of structure.

It is through this structured relationship that the dominant ideology of crime is filtered—often giving the public the impression that journalists are more autonomous than they actually are in conducting their tasks of reporting crime. Thus, researchers contend that the media do not autonomously select news topics but, according to Hall et al. (1978:57), journalists are "cued in" to "specific new topics by regular and reliable institutional sources" who serve as primary definers within a hierarchy of credibility (i.e., law enforcement officials and politicians) (Becker 1967, 1973; Cohen and Young 1981). As evidence, our sample reveals that the second leading topic (n = 8) among feature articles was the crime rate drop in New York City, perhaps suggesting that local law enforcement officials were "cueing" journalists for the purpose of publicizing police "effectiveness" in reducing crime.

It is also important to keep in mind that the relationship between the media and the institutional sources serving as primary definers of crime is also structured, in large part, around the organizational needs and routines of journalists.

The media as an organization operates under incessant time restrictions. Consequently, journalists must rely on institutional resources not only for the purpose of meeting, unreasonable deadlines but also to assure the public that the crime news is "officially" confirmed and "validated" by credible sources—namely, law enforcement officials and political leaders (Benedict 1992:10). As previously noted, our study found that Louis J. Freeh (director of the FBI) was the most oft-quoted state manager in our sample, appearing in five articles and quoted seven times.

It should be noted that the relationship between the media and law enforcement agencies is mutually rewarding insofar as police officials help journalists produce their product—that is, crime news. According to this relation of reciprocity, law enforcement agencies also benefit because as primary definers of crime they not only have the luxury of interpreting events first but also enjoy the opportunity to promote their institutional objectives and needs (e.g., financial funding, the hiring of additional manpower, and the acquisition of equipment) (Chermak 1994,1996; Kasinsky 1994). Numerous statements in our sample reveal this type of fiscal and ideological posturing by state managers.

> In short term, the expenditure of money has to increase. We need more and better cops, more prosecutors. (Eric H. Holder, Jr., U.S. attorney, Washington Post, July 5, 1994, p. A-6)

> Each one you catch, evidence shows they have committed a host of other crimes. If you take them out of society, these are cost savings never calculated into what we spend on new prisons. (Bill Jones, secretary of state, California, former assemblyman and author of the "Three Strikes Law," Washington Post, March 8, 1995, p. A-14)

Researchers also continue to document how police officials present initial definitions of crime that, in turn, promote their public image (Barak 1994; Chermak 1994, 1996; Fishman 1978; Hall et al. 1978; Humphries 1981; Kasinsky 1994; Surette 1992). Included in our sample are several statements offered by law enforcement officials that demonstrate this form of organizational self-promotion:

> The modest decreases in crime are, in large part, attribute to the men and women in law enforcement who daily risk their lives for the public's safety. (Louis J. Freeh, FBI director, The New York Times, November 19, 1995, p. 18)

> I'm here tonight to play the role of the resident gadfly. I'm here to tell you that police make a difference, and we do take offense at some of your colleagues saying otherwise. We are changing behavior in New York City. (William J. Bratton, The New York Times, November 19, 1995, p. 43)

From a Marxian perspective, the dominance of the ruling class extends beyond the ownership and control of the means of material production but also exerts influence over the means of mental production. In this context, primary definitions of crime presented by state managers are crucial forms of mental production. Thus, these mental products (i.e., primary definitions of crime) are transformed, transmitted, and reproduced according to the imperatives of the dominant ideology, thereby determining what is socially thinkable.

Likewise, the dominant ideology serves the interests of the ruling class by protecting and reproducing their "way of life." Just as important though, the dominant ideology also offers universal qualities that ensure that their worldview is shared to some degree by the subordinate classes of the society (see Gramsci 1971; Larrain 1983; Marx 1978; Sahin 1980). Drawing from our sample, the following proclamations presented by state managers are significant because they project compelling messages rooted in universality.

> We must get guns out of the hand of children. (Evan Bayh, governor of Indiana, The New York Times, January 24, 1994, p. 1)

> Americans are finally fed up with violence that cuts down another citizen with gunfire every 20 minutes. (President Bill Clinton, Washington Post, December 4, 1993, p. D-1)

> The nation must find ways to achieve large crime reductions that are permanent. (Louis J. Freeh, FBI director, Los Angeles Times, May 2, 1994, p. A-16)

Despite the dominance of state managers in defining crime, however, this article also sheds light on an emerging window of opportunity for intellectuals—especially professors—to educate the public about crime (see Barak 1994; Cohen 1985; Fox and Levin 1993; Greek 1994; Henry 1994; Israel 1996). Consider the following thoughts that challenge the dominant ideology of crime:

> The get-tough movement has made punishment the only growth industry in government today. (Todd Clear, professor of criminal justice, Rutgers University, The New York Times, May 28, 1993, p. B-7)

> It'll go away. It's called a moral panic. Moral panic is almost completely unrelated to underlying reality. I've seen them come and go. There was carjacking. Hate crime. Gold chain snatching. Remember gold chains? (Dan Lewis, criminologist, Northwestern University, Los Angeles Times, February 13, 1994, p. A-16)

Although clearly riding against the prevailing current of "official" definitions of crime, it seems that print journalists are becoming increasingly receptive to alternative interpretations. Accordingly, Barak (1994) suggests that "journalists' values and practices are not fixed rigidly but are rather fluid" (p. 260). In this vein, perhaps intellectuals should take the initiative to cue journalists into the importance of looking beyond street crime (e.g., white collar, corporate, and political crime) and becoming critical of the dominant strategies of crime control (see Welch et al., forthcoming, for an in-depth discussion of the role of intellectuals in news-making criminology).

REFERENCES

Abercrombie, N., S. Hill, and B. S. Turner. 1980. The Dominant Ideology Thesis. London: Allen & Unwin.

Albrecht, Steve, G. W. Wernz, and T. L. Williams. 1995. Fraud: Bringing Light to the Dark Side of Business. Burr Ridge, IL: Irwin.

Barak, Gregg. 1988. "Newsmaking Criminology: Reflections on the Media, Intellectuals, and Crime." Justice Quarterly 5 (4): 565–87.

_____. 1994. Media, Process, and the Social Construction of Crime. New York: Garland.

Barlow, Melissa H., D. E. Barlow, and T. G. Chiricos. 1995a. "Economic Conditions and Ideologies of Crime in the Media: A Content Analysis of Crime News." Crime & Delinquency 41 (1): 3–19.

_____. 1995b. "Mobilizing Support for Social Control in a Declining Economy: Exploring Ideologies of Crime Within Crime News." Crime & Delinquency 41 (2): 191–204.

Becker, Howard S. 1967. "Who's Side Are We On?" Social Problems 14:239–47.

_____. 1973. Outsiders: Studies in the Sociology of Deviance. New York: Free Press.

Benedict, Helen 1992. Virgin or Vamp: How the Press Covers Sex Crimes. New York: Oxford University Press.

Best, Joel. 1995. Images of Issues: Typifying Contemporary Social Problems. New York: Aldine de Gruyter.

Binder, Amy. 1993. "Constructing Racial Rhetoric: Media Depictions of Harm in Heavy Metal and Rap Music." American Sociological Review 58 (December): 753–67.

Chermak, Steven. 1994. "Crime in the News Media: A Refined Understanding of How Crimes Become News." Pp. 95–130 in Media, Process, and the Social Construction of Crime, edited by G. Barak. New York: Garland.

_____. 1996. "The Presentation of Drugs in the News Media: The News Sources Involved in Social Problem Construction." Indiana University, Bloomington. Unpublished manuscript.

Chiricos, Theodore. 1996. "Moral Panic as Ideology: Drugs, Violence, Race and Punishment in America." Pp. 19–48 in Justice with Prejudice: Race and Criminal Justice in America, edited by M. Lynch and E. B. Patterson. New York: Harrow & Heston.

Cohen, Stanley. 1972. Fulk Devils and Moral Panics. The Creation of the Mods and Rockers. London: MacGibbon & Kee.

Cohen, Stanley. 1985. Visions of Social Control. Cambridge, MA: Polity.

Cohen, Stanley and J. Young. 1981. The Manufacture of News. Beverly Hills, CA: Sage.

Daly, Kathleen. 1994. Gender, Crime, and Punishment. New Haven, CT: Yale University Press.

Ericson, Richard V. 1995. Crime and the Media. Aldershot, VT: Dartmouth.

Ericson, Richard V., P. M. Baranek, and J.B.L. Chan. 1987. Visualizing Deviance: A Study of News Organizations. Toronto: University of Toronto Press.

_____. 1989. Negotiating Control: A Study of News Sources, Toronto: University of Toronto Press.

_____. 1991. Representing Order: Crime, Law, and Justice in the News Media. Toronto: University of Toronto Press.

Fishman, Mark. 1978. "Crime Waves as Ideology." Social Problems 25:531–43.

Fox, James and Jack Levin. 1993. How to Work with the Media. Newbury Park, CA: Sage.

Gamson, William, D. Croteau, W. Hoynes, and T. Sasson. 1992. "Media Images and the Social Construction of Reality." Annual Review of Sociology 18:373–93.

Gramsci, Antonio. 1971. Selections from the Prison Notebooks. New York: International.

Greek, Cecil. 1994. "Becoming a Media Criminologist: Is 'Newsmaking Criminology' Possible?" Pp. 265–86 in Media, Process, and the Social Construction of Crime, edited by G. Barak. New York: Garland.

Hall, Stuart, C. Critcher, T. Jefferson, J. Clarke, and B. Roberts. 1978. Policing the Crisis: Mugging, the State and Law and Order. New York: Holmes & Meiser.

Henry, Stuart. 1994. "Newsmaking Criminology as Replacement Discourse." Pp. 287–318 in Media, Process, and the Social Construction of Crime, edited by G. Barak. New York: Garland.

Herman, E. H., and N. Chomsky. 1988. Manufacturing Consent: The Political Economy of the Mass Media. New York: Pantheon.

Hickman, Melissa. 1982. "Crime in the Streets —. A Moral Panic: Understanding 'Get Tough' Policies in the Criminal Justice System." Southern Journal of Criminal Justice 8:7–22.

Humphries, D. 1981. "Serious Crime, News Coverage, and Ideology." Crime & Delinquency 27:191–205.

Israel, Michael. 1996. "Should ACJS Join COSSA?" ACJS Today 14(4): 1, 12.

Jenkins, P. 1992. Intimate Enemies: Moral Panics in Contemporary Great Britain. New York: Aldine de Gruyter.

Johnson, John M. 1995. "Horror Stories and the Construction of Child Abuse." Pp. 17–31 in Images of Issues: Typifying Contemporary Social Problems, edited by J. Best. New York: Aldine de Gruyter.

Kasinsky, R. G. 1994. "Patrolling the Facts: Media, Cops, and Crime." Pp. 203–36 in Media. Process, and the Social Construction of Crime, edited by G. Barak. New York: Garland.

Kidd-Hewitt, David and R. Osborne. 1995. Crime and the Media: The Postmodern Spectacle. East Haven, CT: Pluto.

Larrain, Jorge. 1983. Marxism and Ideology. London: Macmillan.

Mann, Michael. 1984. The Encyclopedia of Sociology. New York: Continuum.

Marx, Karl. 1978. "The German Ideology." Pp. 146–200 in The Marx Engels Reader. 2d ed., edited by R. D. Tucker. New York: Norton.

Melossi, Dario. 1985. "Punishment and Social Action: Changing Vocabularies of Punitive Motive within a Political Business Cycle." Current Perspectives in Social Theory 6:169–97.

Messerschmidt, James W. 1986. Capitalism, Patriarchy, and Crime: Toward a Socialist; Feminist Criminology. Totowa, NJ: Rowman & Littlefield.

Mokhiber, Russell and Andrew Wheat. 1995. "Shameless: 1995's 10 Worst Corporations." Multinational Monitor December: 9–16.

Orcutt, James D., and J. B. Turner. 1993. "Shocking Numbers and Graphic Accounts: Quantified Images of Drug Problems in the Print Media." Social Problems 40:190–206.

Reiman, Jeffrey. 1995. The Rich Get Richer and the Poor Get Prison: Ideology, Class and Criminal Justice. 4th ed. Boston: Allyn & Bacon.

Sacco, Vincent. 1995. "Media Constructions of Crime." Annals 539:141–54.

Sahin, H. 1980. "The Concept of Ideology and Mass Communication." Journal of Communication Inquiry 61:3–12.

Schlesinger, Philip and H. Tumber. 1994. Reporting Crime: The Media Politics of Criminal Justice. Oxford: Clarendon.

Serrin, William. 1991. "The Wages of Work." The Nation, January 28, pp. 80–82.

Simpson, Sally. 1989. "Feminist Theory, Crime, and Justice." Criminology 27 (4): 605–32.

Surette, Ray. 1992. Media, Crime & Criminal Justice: Images and Realities. Pacific Grove, CA: Brooks/Cole.

Welch, Michael. 1996a. Corrections: A Critical Approach. New York: McGraw-Hill.

———. 1996b. "Critical Criminology, Social Justice, and an Alternative View of Incarceration." Critical Criminology: An International Journal 7 (2): 43–58.

Welch, Michael, Melissa Fenwick, and Meredith Roberts. Forthcoming. "State Managers, Intellectuals, and the Media: A Content Analysis of Ideology in Experts' Quotes in Feature Newspaper Articles on Crime." Rutgers University, New Brunswick. New Jersey. Justice Quarterly.

Studying White Collar Crime and Assessing Its Costs

2

Organizational Crime in NASA and Among Its Contractors: Using a Newspaper as a Data Source

Jurg Gerber and Eric Fritch

Investigative research can use periodicals as [a] data source. In investigating organizational crime in a government institution, NASA, the regional paper 'The Houston Post' proved a rich source of information in spite of the fact that regional news media usually under-report allegations of criminal activities committed by institutions.

INTRODUCTION

Despite being less of a problem today than it was in the past, information on the extent of corporate and organizational crime is still difficult to find. The most commonly used and cited measure of the extent of crime in the United States, the Crime Index, includes only street crimes, and thus by definition

"Organizational crime in NASA and among its contractors: Using a newspaper as a data source," by Jurg Gerber and Eric Fritch from *Social Justice,* 22(1): 75 (1995). Reprinted by permission.

excludes both white-collar and corporate crimes. Therefore, only a segment of all crimes is compiled in the Crime Index. Without such ready access, researchers are forced to collect their own data sets from a variety of sources. Commonly used sources include the records of federal agencies such as the Federal Trade Commission (e.g., Simpson, 1986). In some instances, researchers may obtain access to court-related documents such as pre-sentence investigation reports (e.g., Weisburd et al., 1991).

Previously, we contributed to this process by suggesting the use of newspapers as a data source (Gerber and Fritsch, 1993). Using The Wall Street Journal as our information base, we traced the corporate activities of General Electric (GE) throughout the 1980s. We were particularly interested in determining the value of GE's defense-related contracts, which violations it had allegedly been engaged in, the sanctions received for these violations (e.g., fines), and the consequences of such sanctions in terms of obtaining future contracts. Relying on what must be one of the most conservative records of white-collar crime, we were able to show that GE obtained defense contracts worth at least $43 billion during the 1980s, was accused of numerous unethical and illegal practices, admitted to having engaged in many of these practices, but suffered virtually no negative consequences. The fines it was required to pay were minimal (they represented .17% of the value of GE's contracts during the 1980s) and the company continued to receive contracts, even while nominally "banned" from new contracts.

Furthermore, we showed that GE was able to mitigate the negative publicity it received partially by nominating to its board of directors individuals who had extensive ties to the Pentagon and various branches of the federal government. Thus, we documented the participation of GE's directors in what had been termed the "power elite" by Mills (1956) and studied subsequently in detail by Domhoff (1983) and Useem (1984). In particular, we were able to show the existence of a "revolving door" that lets individuals move freely within the executive branch of government, the military, and corporate leadership.

The present project represents an extension of our earlier study by focusing on another agency, the National Aeronautics and Space Administration (NASA), which has the ability to award large sums of money to contractors who provide defense-related goods and services. However, although the GE study focused on a single corporation that had obtained contracts from one agency of the federal government, the Department of Defense, the current study is more ambitious in three important ways. First, we study all corporations that deal with a federal agency, NASA. Second, though our earlier study focused on the wrongdoing of the corporation alone, this study will also examine the illegal practices of the agency itself. Third, although the Pentagon is a national governmental agency whose interactions with corporations can easily be monitored through a national newspaper such as The Wall Street Journal, NASA has several regional centers. Hence, we decided that the regional press is of importance for this study. The current project will therefore demonstrate the feasibility of using the regional press as a data source for corporate and organizational crime.

METHODS

One goal of our earlier study had been the development of a research technique that relies on an unusual source of white-collar crime data: The Wall Street Journal. This newspaper is the leading source of business news and maintains one of the most complete indexes of all major newspapers, yet it has been underutilized as a research tool for social scientists interested in white-collar crime. We further develop this research technique here by using a regional paper instead of a national newspaper. Our selection of The Houston Post was influenced by two factors. First, the publication had to be of regional significance. Since Houston is the location of the Johnson Space Center, which houses mission control for NASA, a newspaper from this city was a natural choice. Second, the newspaper must also have a detailed indexing system. The other major paper in Houston, The Houston Chronicle, does not and was thus eliminated from consideration.

For this study, we selected all articles published in the Post during the 1980s that dealt with NASA's budgets, its contractors, problems, allegations, and claims made against both the agency and the corporations involved with the agency. Excluded from the analysis were articles that did not deal with any of the above topics, but instead reported developments during individual space missions.

As we indicated previously, our research technique results in a conservative estimate of contracts awarded to corporations. It is unlikely that all the contracts NASA awarded during the 1980s were recorded by The Houston Post. Smaller contracts are likely to have been omitted, but major projects awarded to corporations are likely to have been reported. Similarly, allegations of unethical or criminal behavior by either the agency or the contractors are likely to be under-reported by the regional news media. In an analysis of newspaper coverage of an oil spill in Santa Barbara, Molotch and Lester (1974) found that the activities most covered by the press were those that best suited the interests of oil companies and the executive branch of the federal government; environmentalists had much less access to the media. Given the importance of NASA and its contractors to the Houston economy, we would expect that local newspapers would be conservative in their reporting of organizational misconduct. Findings from this study are therefore likely to be biased in favor of the organizations involved.

To supplement our information, we consulted other sources of data. Such sources included governmental documents (e.g., Subcommittee on Space, 1991) that focus on NASA expenditures and its relationship with contractors, and secondary analyses of the agency (e.g., Vaughan, 1990).

WHITE-COLLAR CRIME, NASA, AND
ITS CONTRACTORS

Whenever the focus of a study is on what is loosely called "white-collar crime," controversy arises over the nature and definitions of the acts to be analyzed. Unfortunately, definitions of what constitutes white-collar crime differ widely. While Sutherland (1940), the intellectual father of the concept, used a definition that was relatively broad and involved acts in violation of many different forms of law, his critics argued that only acts that violated the criminal law should be studied (Tappan, 1947). The problem with the second approach is that individuals who engage in white-collar criminal activities often have the power to affect legal definitions. Restricting the field of study to criminal violations eliminates behaviors of politically powerful perpetrators. It is thus necessary to study behaviors that are not legally crimes. Although such a procedure leads to some conceptual ambiguity, ignoring these behaviors would be more problematic. Instead of white-collar crime, concepts such as white-collar illegality (Shapiro, 1980) or white-collar law breaking (Reiss and Biderman, 1980) might have to be used by researchers.

We will use a definition of white-collar crime that is broad enough to allow for the violation of several forms of law, not only criminal law. Following Coleman (1994: 5) we will focus on behaviors that represent a "violation of the law committed by a person or group of persons in the course of an otherwise respected and legitimate occupation or financial activity." More specifically, since our primary focus is on the wrongdoing of organizational entities, we will study "crimes committed with the support and encouragement of an organization whose goals it is intended to advance" (Ibid.: 12).

CLAIMS AGAINST NASA

NASA is accused of many things that can be construed as indications of white-collar crime: lack of fiscal responsibility, unethical practices, and general incompetence that borders on criminal negligence, to name a few. A claim that is raised repeatedly against NASA deals with cost overruns and fiscal irresponsibility. As can be seen from Table 1, NASA budget outlays for the 1980s totaled about $72 billion. Perhaps not surprisingly, numerous claims have been made that NASA has administered its funds in questionable ways. For instance, NASA's estimates for the total development costs of several projects have been much lower than later estimates. Table 2 shows some of the more spectacular underestimates of several projects. By 1992, the estimate for developing the Hubble Space Telescope was nearly four times the original amount, while that for the Mars Observer was about 50% higher than the original estimate.

TABLE 1   NASA Budgets for Fiscal Years 1980–1989
(in Millions of Dollars)

FY 1980	4,852
FY 1981	5,426
FY 1982	6,035
FY 1983	6,664
FY 1984	7,048
FY 1985	7,318
FY 1986	7,403
FY 1987	7,592
FY 1988	9,092
FY 1989	11,051
Total	72,481

SOURCE: Subcommittee on Space (1991: 24).

TABLE 2   Estimated Total Project Cost of Several NASA Projects
(in Millions of Dollars)

	Original Development Estimate		1992 Estimate
	Date	Range	
Hubble Space Telescope	1/78	435–470	1,545
Gamma Ray Observatory	1/80	180–225	555–565
Ulysses	1/83	120–140	169
Tethered Satellite	1/83	40–50	145–150
Magellan	1/84	320–350	463
Advanced Communications Technology Satellite	1/84	325–425	499
Mars Observer	1/84	300–375	450–500

SOURCE: Table is adapted from Subcommittee on Space (1991: 20).

Why were these estimates so far off the mark? It is conceivable that they were low due to unforeseen or unforeseeable circumstances. Conversely, the estimates may have been intentionally too low from the outset. It is possible that NASA officials perceived a need to underestimate the costs of various projects for them to be approved; true estimates might have led to a failure in obtaining funding for the project. Finally, estimates might have been initially correct, but turned out to be too low due to mismanagement and graft.

We have no data that would let us examine the possibility that estimates were intentionally low at the outset. However, claims are made repeatedly that NASA has financial problems due to incompetence, mismanagement, and graft, rather than to unforeseen circumstances. A relatively minor example is illustrated by the following claim in the The Houston Post (1983a: 13A):

> NASA also used a 5-passenger aircraft to ferry officials between Washington and Wallops Island, VA, where the space agency operates a research station, although the average passenger load was only 2.7 per flight, and it subsequently replaced this aircraft with a 9-passenger model.

As some critics point out, such waste may be the rule at NASA rather than the exception. According to a Miami Herald investigative report, one-third of NASA's budget is wasted. Examples of such waste include the following:

> the space agency routinely paid $30 for pins that should cost 3 cents, paid $159,000 for a $5,000 cooling fan and paid $256 to fly a contractor's dogs coast to coast (The Houston Post, 1986a: 11A).

Along similar lines, the agency has also been criticized for its lavish hosting of VIPs during shuttle launches. For instance, it has been reported that NASA spent $1.5 million on VIPs for the first nine launches (The Houston Post, 1986b: 5A).

Undoubtedly the most spectacular example, and also the most tragic, of NASA malfeasance of the 1980s involved the explosion of the Challenger space shuttle in 1986. It is unquestioned today that the immediate technical problem that led to the tragedy was the faulty design of the O-rings in the solid rocket booster (Presidential Commission, 1986). From a social science perspective, and specifically from the perspective of white-collar crime, it is noteworthy that the explosion was not an "accident," but rather an event that could have been anticipated and to some extent predicted. In fact, problems with the O-rings were known as early as 1977 (Vaughan, 1990), and the press reported within days after the explosion on memos that circulated around NASA at least a year prior to the explosion that the shuttle and its crew were in jeopardy in the future (The Houston Post, 1986c: 3A). In addition, the press also reported that astronauts were not adequately informed of these dangers (Talley and Asker, 1986: 20A).

What made this tragedy possible when NASA apparently knew for years that accidents were bound to happen? Part of the explanation may lie in Perrow's (1984) concept of normal accidents—accidents that involve advanced technologies and the way we handle them. Some technologies are so complex that their mere existence poses risks. Accidents are bound to happen, regardless of how careful we may be; given these technologies, and their potential organizational and systemic problems, the question is not if an accident will happen, but when.

An alternate explanation of the Challenger disaster, advocated by Vaughan (1990), may lie in NASA's organizational structure and decision-making processes. Although NASA was aware of technological problems with the O-rings, it did not extensively sanction its supplier, Morton Thiokol, since doing so would have been detrimental to the agency as it was dependent on the company. Furthermore, monitoring panels internal and external to NASA were not autonomous from the agency and thus could not meaningfully carry out their supervisory capacities.

NASA has largely been able to avoid monetary punishments stemming from its questionable practices. The federal government, as the party ultimately responsible, agreed to settle the claims of families of four of the members who died in the Challenger explosion. It contributed 40% of the approximately $750,000 paid to family members of the four victims (Simmon, 1986). Several more claims were filed against the government as a result of the Challenger, but they had not been settled by the end of the decade. According to our review of the press, at least $33.2 million were sought from NASA and the federal government in these suits. Considering that NASA's budget for the 1980s totaled more than $72 billion, even if the government were to pay the full $33.2 million sought by the plaintiffs, and even if this money were to come out of NASA's budget, the monetary settlement would be inconsequential (representing .04% of the budget for the decade).

It is possible that the negative publicity following the Challenger explosion might have had an adverse effect on subsequent funding decisions by Congress. However, even if that were true, the direct monetary consequences of NASA's organizational misconduct were negligible. The agency appears to have evaded negative sanctions to a large extent.

CLAIMS AGAINST CONTRACTORS

Like any governmental agency, NASA not only receives money from tax revenues, but it also passes some of it on to contractors. Other agencies, such as the Pentagon, award many more contracts, for larger dollar amounts, than does NASA. However, as one of the agencies that is tied to national defense, the money NASA can award is substantial. As can be seen from Table 3, the agency awarded at least 24 contracts during the 1980s to private corporations, with a total value of over $12 billion. Most of this money was awarded in a relatively small number of contracts. The first award announced in The Houston Post during the 1980s was on September 8, 1983, when Lockheed received a two billion dollar contract to handle all space shuttle launch and landing activities for a six-year period. Lockheed, working with several subcontractors, replaced Rockwell, which had held the previous contract. However, only two years later, Rockwell received a $685 million award to handle "most day-to-day activities in the space shuttle program in Houston" (Asker, 1985: 1).

Throughout the rest of the decade, the same few companies continued to receive the lion's share of contract money made available to private industry. Pratt and Whitney received a $182 million contract in 1986 for the development of "safer turbopumps for the space shuttle main engines" (Asker, 1986a: 9). Lockheed landed a $655 million contract in 1987 to provide engineering

TABLE 3 **Contracts Awarded by NASA to Private Corporations**
              (in Millions of Dollars)

Year	Number of Contracts	Value of Contracts
1980	0	0
1981	0	0
1982	0	0
1983	1	2,000.0
1984	0	0
1985	3	1,011.5
1986	7	725.0
1987	8	8,846.0
1988	3	89.1
1989	2	134.0
Totals	24	12,805.6

SOURCE: The Houston Post, 1980–1989.

support at the Johnson Space Center in Houston (Asker, 1987a: 15), while later that year Morton Thiokol had its contract for space shuttle solid rocket boosters renewed in a contract worth $1.8 billion, despite its problems in the Challenger explosion (The Houston Post, 1987a: 1). Finally, through the remainder of 1987, five companies combined in a joint venture to land a contract that was worth a combined total of $6.25 billion. The corporations involved were Gruman Aerospace (Laws, 1987a), McDonnell Douglas, Boeing Aerospace, General Electric, and Rockwell (Laws, 1987b).

There is little doubt that private industry receives huge contracts from NASA. The question remains as to whether NASA, and thus taxpayers, receive fair value for their money. Even a cursory glance over press reports indicates that this is not the case. Repeatedly, claims are made that money has been misappropriated, that technology supplied to NASA has not lived up to promises made, and that contractors cheated in billing procedures. At the same time, it is alleged that contractors have not received any meaningful sanctions.

A specific example of corporate malfeasance includes missing target dates for the completion of contracts. Rockwell committed itself in 1972 to launching the first space shuttle in 1978, but missed that date by about two years. Eventually, it disputed having ever "scheduled" the first launch in 1978 (Maloney, 1980). When such delays occur, a common parallel development is cost overruns. A $18.9 million contract to design space suits for the shuttle was awarded to Hamilton Standard in 1977. At a later date, the contract was estimated to cost at least $236.4 million by 1985, a 12-fold increase (Maloney, 1982b).

Poor design of various parts is another frequent criticism aimed at NASA contractors. At times, the lack of quality may be the result of honest mistakes, while at other times, there is evidence (or at least there are allegations) of corporate wrongdoing. An example of the former includes problems with thermometers that forced an engine shutdown during a launch in 1985 (The Houston Post, 1985a). (1) However, problems with the backpacks of space suits that forced the cancellation of a space walk in 1982 (Maloney, 1982a) and the failure of a space suit during the same mission (Petty, 1982) were later traced to "poor workmanship and inadequate test and assembly procedures" (Petty, 1983: 6). Similarly, NASA was forced in 1988 to ground 25 airplanes "after discovering suppliers may have used falsified strength and reliability data for fasteners used throughout the space program" (Kiely and Laws, 1988: 1). It is at times exceedingly difficult to establish whether it is bad luck, poor design, or outright fraud that leads to problems. For instance, it was announced in 1984 that although it had originally predicted that space shuttle engines would be able to fly 55 missions without overhaul, the engines were "wearing out so fast that they needed repair after almost every flight" (The Houston Post, 1984: 9).

Sometimes there are few doubts as to the culpability of corporate contractors. A Houston federal grand jury indicted ILC Space Systems for "claiming false labor costs on vouchers it submitted for its NASA work" (Manson, 1989: 27). Similarly, Morton Thiokol was accused in 1987 of defrauding NASA when the agency paid for the hiring of 18 quality control and safety personnel for the company, but the money was used "as a slush fund for Thiokol" instead of being used for the hiring of the people (Palomo, 1987b: 1).

NASA, the federal government, and in the case of the Challenger disaster, family members of the crew have sued the corporations for damages and sometimes have sought punitive fines against them. As is usually the case, claims filed against the corporations are initially much larger than what the eventual settlements provide. By far the largest claims made against the corporations were made in conjunction with the Challenger. Family members of the crew sought $2.5 billion from Morton Thiokol in compensatory damages in 1986 and 1987, while the company was sued for $2 billion in a suit filed on behalf of taxpayers for defrauding the government (Palomo, 1987a: 14).

Settlements reached between the plaintiffs and the various corporations are modest by comparison. Although figures were not always precise, and the settlements were at times sealed, Morton Thiokol appears to have agreed to: (1) pay 60% of the approximately $750,000 awarded to each of four crew members' families due to the Challenger disaster (Simmon, 1986), with NASA paying the remaining 40%, (2) pay an undisclosed amount of money to family members of a fifth astronaut (Asker, 1987b), and (3) agreed to a reduction of $10 million in fees from NASA along with performing "$409 million worth of work at no profit" (Asker, 1987c: 1). Similarly, Rockwell International agreed to pay the government $1.5 million for overbilling in 1982 (The Houston Post, 1982: 14), and $1.2 million in 1985 for defrauding the Defense Department, which may have included NASA contracts (Walters, 1985: 3).

All monetary settlements involving NASA contractors combined are almost certainly less than $20 million. Although this figure sounds impressive, it should be kept in mind that NASA awarded contracts worth at least $12.8 billion to private corporations during the 1980s. Fines and settlements therefore represent .15% of the value of these contracts; this represents hardly more than a licensing fee. (2) It is also noteworthy that the fines levied against the corporations and the settlements reached between NASA and the various plaintiffs are similarly minuscule.

CLAIMS AGAINST BOTH CONTRACTORS AND NASA

At times it is virtually impossible to ascertain if problems encountered in space travel are due to contractors' actions, to NASA's activities, a combination thereof, or simply to bad luck. One example of this includes problems with satellite launches in the mid-1980s. In a period of about 29 months, NASA lost five satellites. One satellite was lost in early 1984 when the rocket motors malfunctioned, motors that were described by their manufacturer as "almost fail-safe" (The Houston Post, 1983b: 8). Three more were lost in a five-month period in 1984, again due to problems with the motors and the control systems (Harwood, 1984). Finally, another satellite was lost in April 1985 (Olafson, 1985).

Costs of such losses to taxpayers are difficult to estimate. First, satellites are normally insured through companies such as Lloyd's of London. During one 19-month stretch, insurers lost $600 million (The Houston Post, 1985b). Second, the satellites are often owned by private corporations and thus taxpayers are not directly involved. However, it seems likely that some of the costs will be passed on to taxpayers, either in the form of higher expenditures for NASA, or perhaps in the form of lower corporate income taxes due to higher insurance premiums faced by corporations.

DISCUSSION

Our overview of NASA's activities and its relationship with its contractors has shown a considerable extent of illegal, unethical, and questionable practices. NASA controls billions of dollars and awards large sums to contractors, but there are constantly allegations of questionable activities. Apparently, at least as measured by newspaper coverage, there are few adverse consequences for either the agency, the corporations, or the individuals involved. For instance, corporations caught engaging in fraud appear to continue to receive contracts. Likewise, few if any individuals receive any meaningful sanctions. Indeed, sanctions were most likely to involve fines paid by the corporations—costs that might be passed on to the government in lower tax obligations. Indictments of individuals were rare and, as was the case with James Beggs, the former head of NASA who was included in an indictment of General Dynamics and four individuals associated with that company for fraud, most are eventually thrown out (The Houston Post, 1987b).

The question now is why this happens. Part of the answer may lie in the relationship between individuals in NASA and the corporations that receive contracts. In a discussion of problems encountered by regulatory agencies that attempt to control corporations, Coleman (1994: 177) discussed not only the relative shortage of personnel, but also:

> the fact that government employees receive much lower pay than they would in the corporate sector. . . . The lure of a higher paying job in private industry has led many governmental staffers to cultivate the favor of private interests at the expense of their legal duty.

Professionals at NASA presumably represent their agency, and thus taxpayers, when they monitor contractors. However, newspaper coverage of the careers of NASA officials indicates that many end up in private industry, particularly space-related industry. Several individuals who were involved personally in the fateful decision to launch the Challenger in early 1986 eventually resigned from the agency and ended up working as consultants to NASA contractors or worked for them directly. At least one individual, Judson Lovingood, joined Morton Thiokol following his resignation from NASA (Haederle, 1988).

Closely related to the above is a general mutual dependence between the agency and the contractors. Whenever the agency is adversely affected by an organizational development, the contractors will suffer too. Martin Marietta announced in late 1986 the layoffs of about 700 employees as a result of the moratorium on space shuttle flights (The Houston Post, 1986d). However, the agency becomes likewise dependent on individual contractors. Following the Challenger explosion, Morton Thiokol, which had designed the faulty O-rings, was still eligible for a $75 million bonus for "superior performance" (Asker, 1986c). Maintaining good relationships with specific contractors is a necessity since they may be the only ones to provide specific services. The mutual dependence between the two can become so great that a contractor may even approach the courts to try to keep arrangements between the agency and itself secret. Such secrecy was required if Morton Thiokol was not to be "embarrassed" by documents detailing the relationship (Asker, 1987d).

CONCLUSION

This article is a continuation of a research project that seeks to develop the use of a not frequently used source of data for white-collar crime. In the first project, we used a national newspaper, The Wall Street Journal, to gather information on one corporation involved in national defense. This current study elaborates on this technique by studying all corporations that obtained grants from NASA, the organizational misconduct of the agency itself, and the use of a regional newspaper as the data source.

We are generally satisfied with this regional data source. Relying on The Houston Post for information, we were able to show patterns of mismanagement, incompetence, and graft that were responsible for NASA's financial problems during the 1980s. At the same time, NASA was largely able to avoid paying direct monetary penalties for its organizational misconduct. Similarly, the newspaper documented large contracts that were awarded to various corporations, extensive corporate lawbreaking, but again few meaningful sanctions against the corporations.

It should be reiterated that our research technique is probably biased in favor of NASA and the corporations due to the general tendency of newspapers not to be overly critical of locally dominant economic interests (Molotch and Lester, 1974). Nevertheless, the current study has shown the utility of our research technique; it is possible to study organizational crime using a local newspaper. Future research should be conducted that allows for the evaluation of the extent of the above bias.

Jurg Gerber is an associate professor of Criminal Justice at Sam Houston State University (College of Criminal Justice, Sam Houston State University, Huntsville, TX 77341-2296), where he also serves as Assistant Dean for Undergraduate Studies. His primary research interests involve white-collar crime and comparative criminal justice issues.

Eric J. Fritsch is a doctoral candidate at Sam Houston State University and an assistant professor of Criminal Justice at St. Edward's University in Austin, Texas. He conducts research on juvenile delinquency and drug abuse.

NOTES

1. Delaying a launch is costly for NASA, but it is difficult to estimate what the exact costs are. In a launch that was delayed in 1981 by only a few days, NASA estimated that additional overtime expenditures, "reimbursement to the Department of Defense for launch and landing support," and similar expenses resulted in a total cost of at least $1.5 million (The Houston Post, 1981).

2. In a remarkable coincidence, we found in our earlier study of General Electric's defense contracts that GE's fines represented .17% of the value of their contracts during the 1980s (Gerber and Fritsch, 1993). We therefore have further evidence that relatively little has changed since Geis' (1967) classic study of GE's involvement in the heavy electrical equipment antitrust case of 1961. He concluded that the fine levied against GE was the equivalent of a three dollar fine for an individual with an annual income of $175,000.

REFERENCES

Asker, Jim 1987a "Lockheed Wins NASA Contract." The Houston Post (March 27): 15A.
1987b "McNairs Settle Shuttle Lawsuit with Thiokol." The Houston Post (May 8): 4A.
1987c "Thiokol, NASA Reach Accord." The Houston Post (February 25): 1A.

1987d "Thiokol Says NASA Pacts Are Private." The Houston Post (February 6): 12A.

1986a "NASA Selects Firm to Develop New Turbopumps for Shuttle." The Houston Post (August 14): 9A.

1986b "Shuttle Settlements Anger Attorney in Suit." The Houston Post (December 30): 1A.

1986c "Morton Thiokol to Get $75 Million Bonus." The Houston Post (November 18): 3A.

1985 "Rockwell Wins Pact for Shuttle." The Houston Post (September 13): 1A.

Coleman, James W. 1994 The Criminal Elite: The Sociology of White-Collar Crime. New York: St. Martin's Press.

Domhoff, G. William 1983 Who Rules America Now? A View for the '80s. New York: Touchstone.

Gerber, Jurg and Eric J. Fritsch 1993 "On the Relationship Between White-Collar Crime and Political Sociology: A Suggestion and Resource for Teaching." Teaching Sociology 21: 130–139.

Haederle, Michael 1988 "Major Shuttle Figures Have Left Since Disaster." The Houston Post (September 25): 16A.

Harwood, William 1984 "Satellite's Loss Deals Another Blow to NASA." The Houston Post (June 11): 7E.

Kiely, Kathy and Jerry Laws 1988 "Firms Turning Bad Bolts Loose on U.S.: Report." The Houston Post (July 31): 1A.

Laws, Jerry 1988 "Age Bias Denied at NASA." The Houston Post (March 28): 8A.

1987a "Gruman Awarded Space Station Funds." The Houston Post (July 3): 22A.

1987b "Space Station Jobs a 'Win-Win' for City." The Houston Post (December 1): 1A.

Maloney, Jim 1982a "Backpack Woes Persist in Tests." The Houston Post (November 19): 19A.

1982b "Cost of Failed Spacesuits to Rise 12 Times Above Initial Contract." The Houston Post (November 23): 18A.

1980 "Rockwell Denies 1978 Shuttle Target Date." The Houston Post (December 25): 19A.

Manson, Patricia 1989 "Houston Firm Faces 11 Counts on Overbilling." The Houston Post (July 7): 27A.

Mills, C. Wright 1956 The Power Elite. New York: Oxford University Press.

Molotch, Harvey and Marilyn Lester 1974 "Accidental News: The Great Oil Spill as Local Occurrence and National Event." American Journal of Sociology 81: 235–259.

Olafson, Steve 1985 "$80 Million Shuttle Satellite Fails." The Houston Post (April 14): 1A.

Palomo, Juan R. 1987a "Government Stays Out of Lawsuit over Shuttle." The Houston Post (June 5): 14A.

1987b "Morton Thiokol Employees Accuse Own Company of Fraud." The Houston Post (April 17): 1A.

Perrow, Charles 1984 Normal Accidents: Living with High-Risk Technologies. New York: Basic Books.

Petty, John Ira 1983 "Report Lays Blame for Space Suit Problems." The Houston Post (February 2): 6A.

1982 "Sensor, Missing Locking Devices Stopped Space Walk, Officials Say." The Houston Post (December 3): 12A.

Presidential Commission on the Space Shuttle Challenger Accident 1986 Report of the Presidential Commission on the Space Shuttle Accident, 5 Vols. Washington, D.C.: Government Printing Office.

Reiss, Albert J. and Albert D. Biderman 1980 Data Sources on White-Collar Law Breaking. Washington, D.C.: National Institute of Justice.

Shapiro, Susan P. 1980 Thinking About White-Collar Crime: Matters of Conceptualization and Research. Washington, D.C.: Government Printing Office.

Simmon, Jim 1986 "Details of Shuttle Accord Withheld." The Houston Post (December 31): 3A.

Simpson, Sally S. 1986 "The Decomposition of Antitrust: Testing a Multi-level, Longitudinal Model of Profit-Squeeze." American Sociological Review 51: 859–875.

Subcommittee on Space, House of Representatives, U.S. Congress 1991 1992 NASA Authorization—National Aeronautics and Space Administration Budget Request for Fiscal 1992. Washington, D.C.: Government Printing Office.

Sutherland, Edwin 1940 "White-Collar Criminality." American Sociological Review 5: 1–12.

Talley, Olive and Jim Asker 1986 "NASA Withheld Concerns over Booster Seals." The Houston Chronicle (March 17): 20A.

Tappan, Paul 1947 "Who Is the Criminal?" American Sociological Review 12: 96–107.

The Houston Post 1987a "Playing SRB Monopoly." April 21: 1B.

1987b "Unjust Indictment." June 29: 1B.

1986a "One-Third of NASA Budget Reportedly Wasted." March 17: 11A.

1986b "Agency Spent Almost $1.5 Million on VIPs Attending Shuttle Launches." June 12: 5A.

1986c "NASA Was Told Failure of Seals Was Possibility." 1987. February 9: 3A.

1986d "Space Supplier Jobs Cut by the Hundreds." September 4: 19A.

1985a "Bad Thermometers Caused Shuttle Engine Shutdown." August 13: 6A.

1985b "Destruction of Satellites Puts Insurance Losses Sky-High." September 15: 15A.

1984 "Life of Space Shuttle Engines Proves Much Shorter Than Had Been Hoped." March 26: 9A.

1983a "Agencies Wasting Million in Aircraft Deals, Report Says." July 25: 1A, 13A.

1983b "Boeing Touted Troublesome Rocket as 'Almost Fail-Safe' Before Launch." April 16: 8A.

1982 "Firm to Pay $1.5 Million in Shuttle Overbilling Suit." November 30: 14A.

1981 "Delay Cost at Least $1.5 million, NASA Says." November 11: 1A.

Useem, Michael 1984 The Inner Circle: Large Corporations and the Rise of Business Political Activity in the U.S. and the U.K. New York: Oxford University Press.

Vaughan, Diane 1990 "Autonomy, Interdependence, and Social Control: NASA and the Space Shuttle Challenger." Administrative Science Quarterly 35: 225–257.

Walters, Robert 1985 "Rockwell Caught Again." The Houston Post (November 16): 3B.

Weisburd, David, Stanton Wheeler, Elin Waring, and Nancy Bode 1991 Crimes of the Middle Classes: White-Collar Offenders in the Federal Courts. New Haven, CT: Yale University Press.

Occupational Crime and Avocational Crime

3

Investor Reaction
to Disclosures
of Employee Fraud

James M. Lukawitz and Paul John Steinbart

Fraud is a serious problem facing American businesses, with estimates of the annual losses due to employee theft and embezzlement exceeding $100 billion. Companies have been criticized, however, for failing to report cases of discovered employee fraud. A common rationale for not disclosing such news is the fear of negative publicity. The objective of this study is to determine whether or not such disclosures do indeed create negative publicity for the firm. Investors are one of the important "publics" for any company. Therefore, this study examines investors' reactions to disclosures of employee fraud. Specifically, the stock market's reaction to stories of employee fraud published in the Wall Street Journal was examined to determine whether such disclosures were indeed treated as "bad news." The results indicate that such disclosures are not associated with any negative stock price reactions. Thus, there was no evidence that one important segment of the public, investors, reacted negatively to disclosures of employee fraud.

Employee fraud is a serious problem for American businesses. Estimates of annual losses due to employee theft and embezzlement across all industries exceed $100 billion (Lary, 1989; Wells, 1994). It has been argued that disclosure and subsequent prosecution of all cases of discovered fraud might serve as a deterrent (Albrecht et al., 1994; Dycus, 1991; Richards and Knotts, 1989;

"Investor reaction to disclosures of employee fraud," by James M. Lukawitz and Paul John Steinbart from *Journal of Managerial Issues*, 7(3): 358 (1995). Reprinted from the Journal of Managerial Issues, published by Pittsburgh State University, Pittsburgh, m KS 66762 with permission.

but for an opposing view see Wells, 1990). Management has been criticized, however, for not adequately responding to discovered cases of employee fraud (Dycus, 1991). For example, studies (O'Donoghue, 1987; Richards and Knotts, 1989; Straub and Nance, 1990) have found that less than one-half of the discovered cases of computer-related frauds are ever reported to the authorities. Indeed, it is estimated that less than 20% of all discovered frauds are ever reported (Cushing and Romney, 1993).

A common rationale for management's failure to report discovered cases of fraud is fear of adverse publicity (Richards and Knotts, 1989; Gerlin, 1995). The objective of this paper is to test the validity of that belief. To do so, the reactions of one important segment of the public, investors, are examined. Focusing on investor reactions provides a powerful test of whether any embarrassment or reputational damage to the company arising from disclosure of employee fraud has economic consequences. If disclosure of employee frauds is indeed "bad news," such disclosures should be associated with a negative stock price reaction. The lack of negative market reaction to disclosures of employee frauds would indicate that investors did not perceive any significant long-term financial repercussions arising from the incident.

BACKGROUND AND HYPOTHESES

The word fraud encompasses many types of acts; hence, it is important to carefully define how it is used in this study. The authoritative auditing literature distinguishes two types of irregularities: management fraud and employee frauds (AICPA, 1988). Management fraud refers to such things as fraudulent financial reporting that results in misleading financial statements. The term employee [fraud] refers to the misappropriation of assets, thus including such acts as theft and embezzlement.

This study focuses on the effect of disclosing discovered cases of frauds committed by employees. A recent study by Karpoff and Lott (1993) examined investors' reactions to disclosures of management fraud. They found that the stock market did react negatively to disclosures of management fraud, including such acts as defrauding the government, consumers, and other stakeholders. Karpoff and Lott did not, however, include incidences of fraud by employees in their sample. Therefore, this study extends their research by examining the stock market's reaction to disclosures of employee fraud.

Although Karpoff and Lott found that investors reacted negatively to disclosures of management fraud, there are several reasons to question whether investors react similarly to disclosures of employee fraud. First, the authoritative auditing literature (AICPA, 1988) states that employee frauds are often immaterial in amount. This means that the amounts are too small to seriously affect the company's financial position. Consequently, investors may not react to such disclosures. Second, the disclosure itself indicates that the fraud has been detected and stopped. Therefore, there may be no effect on the company's future performance. Stock prices reflect investors' perceptions of future events; therefore, investors may not react negatively to news of employee fraud that has been detected and stopped. Third, it has been argued that companies publicly disclose cases of employee fraud only when they feel they can recover most or all of the loss (Pae, 1989). If that argument is correct, then any stigma attached to the fraud may be offset by the public's expectation that the loss will be recovered.

On the other hand, the concept of materiality can also be used to support the possibility that there will be a negative stock price reaction to disclosures of employee frauds. The argument is that materiality is not solely a function of the magnitude of the event, but is also affected by the nature of the event. Indeed, Statement of Financial Accounting Concepts No. 2 notes that "items too small to be thought material if they result from routine transactions may be considered material if they arise in abnormal circumstances" (FASB, 1980: paragraph 123). Fraud is (hopefully) an "abnormal" circumstance. Consequently, although employee frauds may be immaterial in size, investors may consider them to be material in nature. Specifically, disclosure of employee frauds may be taken as a signal indicating that weaknesses exist in a company's internal control structure. Investors may believe that the control weaknesses that permitted the disclosed fraud to occur make it likely that other employee frauds exist that have not yet been detected. Therefore, investors may react negatively to such disclosures.

The preceding discussion leads to the first hypothesis to be tested, stated in its alternative form as follows:

H1: There will be a negative stock price reaction to disclosures of employee frauds.

Effect of Required Disclosure: The Banking Industry

Banks are currently required to report all discovered employee frauds in excess of $1,000 to the authorities (12 Code of Federal Regulations, Section 21.11). This prevents bank managers from concealing embarrassing employee frauds or those which they do not want revealed. Other types of companies do not have this mandatory disclosure requirement. Therefore, the probability of disclosure may differ for banks versus other types of companies. Indeed, almost 40% of the fraud disclosures in our sample involve banks. Consequently, we also examine banks and nonbanks separately. Therefore, two additional hypotheses are tested, stated in their alternative form as follows:

H2: There will be a negative stock price reaction to disclosures by banks of employee frauds.

H3: There will be a negative stock price reaction to disclosures by nonbanks of employee frauds.

RESEARCH DESIGN

Sample Selection

The sample was selected by searching the Wall Street Journal Index for the previous decade under the headings of crime, computer crime, white collar crime, fraud, embezzlement and theft. Three screening criteria were used in the search. First, only stories about employee frauds were included in the sample. Stories about fraudulent financial reporting, defense contract or other government fraud, violations of regulations and defrauding of stakeholders were excluded because the information content of such disclosures was already examined by Karpoff and Lott (1993). Second, stories indicating that the company had gone bankrupt were excluded because it would not be possible to separate the information content associated with the fraud story from that associated with bankruptcy. Third, only the first story about a specific fraud was included in the sample. Karpoff and Lott (1993) found that the information content associated with disclosures of management fraud was limited to the first story about that event.

Application of those three criteria yielded a sample of 144 stories about employee frauds. The average number of stories is only 12 each year, indicating that disclosures of employee fraud are relatively rare events. That number was then reduced to the final sample size of 46 stories as follows:

1. The corporate index was searched for other stories about the company within a five-day window centered on the date of the fraud story. If there was a major economic announcement such as earnings, the signing of a major contract, or dividends paid out by the firm during this period, the firm was removed from the sample since it would be impossible to separate the market reaction of the fraud from the other economic news. This led to the elimination of 43 frauds for which there were conflicting events.

2. Only companies that were listed either on the Center for Research in Security Price (CRSP) daily return tape or the Standard and Poors Daily Stock Price Record were retained. This led to the elimination of an additional 53 cases for which stock price data was not readily available.

3. Two cases (Enron, with a loss of $85,000,000 and Chemical Bank, with a loss of $33,000,000) were eliminated because they were disproportionately large compared to the remaining 46 stories, which had an average loss of less than $2,000,000. (1)

Method

Two tests are used to examine investor reactions to disclosures of employee fraud. The first test examines the average standardized cumulative abnormal returns across companies. The abnormal return measures unusual fluctuations in a company's stock prices that differ from its relationship with the average market fluctuation. The abnormal return for company i on day t is calculated as follows:

$$AR_{i,t} = R_{i,t} - (a_i + b_i R_{m,t}) \tag{1}$$

where

$R_{i,t}$ = the return on company i's stock on day t,

a_i, b_i = ordinary least squares (OLS) coefficient estimates from regressing company i's individual daily stock returns on the market returns, and

$R_{m,t}$ = the market return on the CRSP equally-weighted index on day t.

The market model parameters are estimated over a 60-day period from day $t - 61$ through day $t - 2$, where $t = 0$ is the date the story about the employee fraud appears in the Wall Street Journal. The cumulative abnormal returns for each company i (CAR_i) are calculated by summing the abnormal returns across one- and two-day periods to allow sufficient time to serve any reaction to the fraud disclosure. The cross-firm and interval returns are then normalized according to the procedures outlined by Patell (1976).(2) If the abnormal returns for either day $t - 1$, day $t = 0$, or the two-day window are significantly negative, it would provide evidence that investors do indeed treat disclosures of employee frauds as bad news.

The second test examines whether the proportion of companies which experience a negative stock price reaction to disclosures of employee fraud is significantly different from chance. A binomial test is applied to the sign of the abnormal returns experienced by companies that disclose news of employee frauds. A significant test result indicates that companies which make such disclosures are likely to experience a negative stock price reaction to such news. Note, however, that this test is weaker than the first test because it does not examine whether the sizes of the observed negative price reactions are themselves significant.

RESULTS

Table 1 shows that the size of reported frauds in the final sample ranged from $14,500 to $12,000,000, with an average size of slightly less than $2 million. Fifteen (32.6%) of the stories dealt with frauds of less than $1 million and four involved losses of less than $100,000. Although the average size of the frauds at the banks ($2,770,830) was larger than the average size of the fraud at the nonbanks ($1,419,543), the difference in size was not significant (two-tailed $t = 1.63$ p > 10).

TABLE 1 Descriptive Statistics of the Sample

Non Banks

Company	Loss
AMC Entertainment	N/A
AMR	125,000
ARA Services	250,000
American International Group	1,700,000
Anheuser Busch	N/A
Atek Metals	700,000
CNA Financial	3,000,000
Coca Cola	5,000,000
Deere & Company	1,000,000
Dun & Bradstreet	1,500,000
GTE	500,000
Genesco	5,500,000
Global Natural Resources	N/A
Jet Industries	N/A
L.L. Luria & Sons	31,000
LTV (1)(★)	N/A
LTV (2)(★)	14,500
MCA	294,000
Marietta Corp.	385,000
Marriott	150,000
NCR	300,000
Pittston Co. (1)(★)	1,000,000
Pittston Co. (2)(★)	1,000,000
Revlon Group	1,100,000
Tonka	2,000,000
URS	2,500,000
Valley Industries	2,600,000
Woolworth	2,000,000
Avg. Nonbank loss	1,419,543
Avg. Total Loss	1,973,918

Banks

Company	Loss
American Fletcher	4,000,000
American Republican	400,000
Bank of New York (1)(★)	1,200,000
Bank of New York (2)(★)	5,500,000
Bankers Trust NY	1,200,000
Chase Manhattan	900,000
Citicorp	14,800
Comfed Bancorporation	N/A
Crocker National	6,000,000
Financial Corporation of America	N/A
First Chicago	400,000
First City Bancorp TX	18,484
Gibraltar Financial	3,400,000
Harris Bankcorp	1,300,000
Manufacturers Hanover	1,000,000
J.P. Morgan	6,000,000
NCNB	12,000,000
Shawmut National	1,000,000
Avg. Bank loss	2,770,830

★ There were two separate incidents for these three companies.

Hypothesis 1: Investor Reactions (All Firms)

Table 2 presents the data about the stock price reactions to the 46 disclosures of employee frauds in our sample. Hypothesis 1 predicted that disclosures of employee frauds would result in a negative stock price reaction for all firms. The all-companies column in Table 2 provides the results of testing that hypothesis.

Panels A and C show the results of the test involving abnormal returns across companies. Panel A shows the average abnormal returns for each day for companies disclosing news of employee frauds. The data show that the abnormal returns are not significantly less than zero on either day t − 1 or day t = 0. Moreover, Panel C shows that the cumulative abnormal [TABULAR DATA FOR TABLE 2 OMITTED] returns over the two-day window [−1,0] are also not significantly less than zero. Thus, the first method of testing finds no evidence of a negative market reaction to disclosures of employee fraud.

Panels B and D show the results of the test of the proportion of companies experiencing a negative stock price reaction to disclosures of employee fraud. Panel B shows that the proportion of firms experiencing an abnormal negative stock price reaction is not significant on either day t − 1 or day t = 0. Panel D shows that the proportion of firms experiencing negative abnormal stock price reactions across the two-day window [−1,0] is also not significantly different from chance.

In summary, the data presented in Table 2 do not support hypothesis 1. Across all types of firms, there is no evidence of any negative stock market reaction to disclosures of employee frauds.

Hypotheses 2 and 3: Effects of Type of Company

Hypotheses 2 and 3 deal separately with investors' reactions to disclosures of employee frauds by banks and nonbanks, respectively. The column labeled Banks in Table 2 provides data concerning hypothesis 2. Panel A of Table 2 shows that the average abnormal stock returns for banks only were not significantly less than zero on either day t − 1 or day t = 0. Panel C corroborates that finding, showing that the average cumulative stock price returns across both days were not significantly less than zero. Thus, there is no evidence of significant negative market reactions to disclosures of employee fraud by banks.

Panel B of Table 2 shows that the proportion of banks experiencing negative stock price returns on day t − 1 was not significantly different from chance. However, on day t = 0, the day that the story about employee fraud appears in the Wall Street Journal, two-thirds of the banks suffered negative stock price reactions. That proportion is marginally different from chance (p = .08), providing some weak evidence in support of hypothesis 2. Panel D shows that the proportion of banks experiencing cumulative negative stock price returns over the two-day [−1,0] window was not statistically significant.

In summary, there is little evidence that investors reacted negatively to disclosures of employee frauds at banks. Although there was a marginally significant percentage of banks that did experience negative returns on the date such disclosures appeared in the Wall Street Journal, the results in panels A and C indicate that the size of those negative returns was not significantly different from zero.

The column labeled nonbanks in Table 2 provides data concerning hypothesis 3. Panel A shows no evidence of abnormal negative stock price returns on either day t − 1 or day t = 0. Panel C shows no evidence of any negative cumulative stock price returns for the two-day window [−1,0]. Thus, there is no evidence of any significant negative stock price reaction to disclosures of employee frauds by nonbanks.

Panel B shows that the percentage of nonbanks disclosing news of employee frauds which experienced a negative stock price reaction on either day t − 1 or t = 0 was not significant either. Panel D shows similar results for the two-day window [−1,0].

In summary, hypothesis 3 is not supported; there is no evidence of a negative stock price reaction to disclosures of employee frauds at non-banks.

DISCUSSION AND CONCLUSION

Management has been criticized for not disclosing news of discovered employee frauds. It has been argued that one reason management is reluctant to make such disclosures is fear of adverse publicity. This study tested the validity of that belief by examining investor reaction to stories of employee fraud published in the Wall Street Journal. Across all companies, no evidence that investors reacted to such stories as "bad news" was found. There was some weak evidence that a majority of banks that were the victims of employee fraud experienced negative stock price reactions on the day that news of those frauds was published, but the size of the negative price reaction was not statistically significant.

Limitations

Before discussing the implications of these results, several limitations of the study should be noted. The first limitation is that the sample was obtained from only one source, the Wall Street Journal. Investors may have other sources of news about employee frauds. If these other sources are more timely, then disclosure in the Wall Street Journal may not be "news" to these investors. Thus, the failure to find a reaction to such disclosures in this study may be due to investors having become aware of such news from other sources. On the other hand, the Wall Street Journal is the most widely read source of business news and is routinely used by researchers as the source for testing investors' reactions to a variety of disclosures. Moreover, Karpoff and Lott (1993) used the Wall Street Journal as the source in their study and found significant stock market reactions to disclosures of fraud by management (not employees).

The second limitation involves the size of the frauds examined in this study. Most of these frauds were small, especially when considered in terms of total assets or revenues. The failure to find a market reaction may be due to the fact that these employee frauds are immaterial. Market participants may only be concerned with employee frauds when they are large enough to materially affect the firm's financial operations.

Several additional analyses were conducted to test this possibility. First, the size of the fraud in absolute terms, as a percentage of assets, and as a percentage of income, was compared with the company's abnormal returns. None of these measures of size were found to be significantly related to abnormal returns. Second, the analyses were rerun for only those firms for which the size of the fraud was greater than one percent of total assets or one-half of one percent of net income. Again, no significant relationship with abnormal returns was found. Therefore, the results presented in Table 2 appear to indicate that investors do not react negatively to disclosures of employee frauds of the magnitude reported in this study.

Nevertheless, it is important to note that fifty-three firms were lost from the sample due to the inability to gather their stock returns. This exceeds the number retained in the sample, and represents over one-third of all the employee frauds reported during the time period of our study. Most likely, these firms were too small to be a part of the stock return databases. Employee frauds may invoke a market reaction for these small firms where the size of the fraud may be significant in relationship to assets or net income. Further research on whether these small firms are more apt to report employee theft and any market reaction to these reported thefts needs to be undertaken.

The third limitation involves the different requirements for disclosure of employee fraud across companies. Nonbanks are not required to disclose employee frauds, and therefore they may choose which frauds, if any, to disclose. Banks, on the other hand, must disclose all employee frauds that are larger than $1,000. Table 2 did find some weak evidence of a negative stock market reaction to disclosures by banks, but no evidence at all of any reaction to disclosures by other types of companies. It is not possible to tell whether these different results are due to the nature of the disclosure (voluntary versus mandated) or to the type of company (bank versus nonbank). Additional research in this area is needed.

Finally, this preliminary study hypothesized that the report of employee frauds would be "bad news" or "no news" to the firm. We did not examine the potential that such disclosure is "good news" to the firm. The discovery of the fraud may lead to changes in a firm's accounting control system to prevent future frauds which would favorably impact future cash flows. In addition, recovery from insurance or directly from the embezzler may reduce or negate any cost of the initial fraud. Thus, it is possible that some frauds are "bad news" to the company whereas others are "no news" or "good news." Consequently, our failure to find any market reaction may be due to our sample containing a mixture of both types of frauds. This is a topic that also needs to be addressed in future research.

Implications and Conclusion

This study's finding of no evidence that investors react negatively to disclosures of discovered cases of employee fraud has two important policy implications. First, it does not support the common argument that management
should not make such disclosures because they result in negative publicity.
There may be other reasons why management may not want to disclose all
cases of discovered fraud (e.g., fear of being blamed for allowing it to occur
and, therefore, losing one's job), but shareholder welfare does not appear to be
a legitimate concern.

The second implication of our findings concerns the value of requiring
companies to disclose cases of employee fraud. Public concern about fraud is
increasing and there are calls for legislation to increase auditors' responsibility
to find and report fraud (Goldstein and Dixon, 1989; Journal of Accountancy,
1993). Indeed, the public expects auditors to detect and report fraud
(Humphrey et al., 1991). This study, however, finds no evidence that investors
react to such disclosures. This finding suggests that there is no benefit to man-
dating disclosure of employee frauds. The limitations of this study noted above,
however, suggest that additional research on investor reactions to fraud disclosures is warranted.

Future research should also examine whether other user groups (e.g., creditors) react to disclosures of employee fraud. In addition, there may be other
benefits in requiring companies to disclose cases of employee fraud. For example, it has been argued that disclosure has a deterrent effect (Albrecht et al.,
1994; Dycus, 1991; Richards and Knotts, 1989). Research investigating that
possibility is also needed.

James M. Lukawitz Associate Professor of Accountancy University of Memphis

Paul John Steinbart Ernst and Young Distinguished Professor of Accounting Saint
Louis University

NOTES

1.   The analyses were also conducted on the sample of 48 including Enron and Chemical
with no difference in results.

2.   This approach adjusts the abnormal return by the standard error of the regression
equation. Its purpose is to reduce the influence of large abnormal returns for companies
where the regression model provides a poor fit.

REFERENCES

12 Code of Federal Regulations: Banks and Banking. 1992. Washington, D.C.: Office of the
Federal Register National Archives and Records Administration.

Albrecht, W.S., E.A. McDermott, and T.L. Williams. 1994. "Reducing the Loss of Fraud."
Internal Auditor (February): 28–34.

American Institute of Certified Public Accountants. 1988. Statement on Auditing Standards No. 53: The Auditor's Responsibility to Detect and Report Errors and Irregularities. New York: AICPA.

Cushing, B.E., and M.B. Romney. 1993. Accounting Information Systems: A Comprehensive Approach. Reading, MA: Addison-Wesley.

Dycus, D.F. 1991. "Hear No Fraud, See No Fraud, There Is No Fraud." Corporate Controller (January/February): 13–17.

Financial Accounting Standards Board. 1980. Statement of Financial Accounting Concepts No. 2: Qualitative Characteristics of Accounting Information. Stamford, CT: FASB.

Gerlin, A. 1995. "How a Penney Buyer Made Up to $1.5 Million on Vendors' Kickbacks." The Wall Street Journal (February 7): A1, A12.

Goldstein, J.I., and C. Dixon. 1989. "New Teeth for the Public Watchdog: The Expanded Role of the Independent Accountant in Detecting, Preventing, and Reporting Financial Fraud." Business Lawyer 44 (February): 439–502.

Humphrey, C., S. Turley, and P. Mozier. 1991. "An Empirical Dimension to Expectations." Accountancy 108: (October): 30.

Journal of Accountancy. 1993. "Washington Update: AICPA Supports Fraud Detection Bill." (May): 15.

Karpoff, J.M., and J.R. Lott, Jr. 1993. "The Reputational Penalty Firms Bear from Committing Criminal Fraud." Journal of Law and Economics 36: (October): 757–802.

Lary, B.K. 1989. "Why Corporations Can't Lock the Rascals Out." Management Review (October): 51–54.

O'Donoghue, J. 1987. "Strategies Found to be Effective in the Control of Computer Crime in the Forbes 500 Corporations." ACM SIG on Security, Audit & Control (Winter): 1–12.

Pae, P. 1989. "To Catch an Embezzler, Best Be Nimble, Be Quick." The Wall Street Journal (August 3): B1–B2.

Richards, T.C., and R. Knotts. 1989. "Top Management's View of Computer Related Fraud." ACM SIG on Security, Audit & Control (Winter): 34–43.

Straub, D.W., Jr., and W.D. Nance. 1990. "Discovering and Disciplining Computer Abuse in Organizations: a Field Study." MIS Quarterly (March): 45–60.

Wells, J.T. 1990. "Six Common Myths About Fraud." Journal of Accountancy (February): 82–88.

_____. 1994. "The Billion Dollar Paper Clip." Internal Auditor (October): 32–38.

Governmental Crime: State Crime and Political White Collar Crime

4

Democratization and Political Corruption in the Philippines and South Korea: A Comparative Analysis

Jon S.T. Quah

The Philippines and South Korea have long had difficult corruption problems. More recently, both have experienced significant democratization. This article compares the two cases, first developing an analysis of corruption in each country, then laying out their reform strategies and assessing their effectiveness, and finally exploring the contrasting relationships between democratization and corruption that are found in these countries. The Philippines confront reformers with more difficult challenges, beginning with the size and decentralization of the society, but other contrasts are important as well. The political will required to produce successful reform has been lacking in the Philippines, for a variety of reasons, while recent anti-corruption initiatives in Korea have had stronger backing. Recent Korean reforms also emulate the successful approaches of Singapore and Hong Kong in important ways. By itself, democratization will not check corruption in either country, but where

"Democratization and political corruption in the Philippines and South Korea: A comparative analysis," by Jon S.T. Quah from *Crime, Law and Social Change,* 42(1): 61 (2004). Reprinted by permission of Springer Science + Business Media.

reform is accompanied by significant resources and where democratic accountability complements political will—more true of Korea than of the Philippines—significant progress can be made.

INTRODUCTION

In recent years, two important but contradictory trends have affected many countries. The first has been what Huntington (1991) has termed the "Third Wave" of democratization. The second is the tidal wave of corruption scandals around the world, which Moises Naim called the "corruption eruption" (quoted in Leiken, 1996–1997: 56). Coverage of corruption in the Economist, the Financial Times, and the New York Times quadrupled between 1984 and 1995 (Rossant, 1995: 58). There are two reasons for the global exposure of corruption scandals. First is the end of the Cold War and the emergence of civil societies in many countries. Second is the trend toward democracy and markets, which paradoxically has "increased both the opportunities for graft and the likelihood of exposure" (Leiken, 1996–1997: 58).

This article focuses on the experiences of two Asian countries in combating corruption as their political systems became more democratic. In 1986, Corazon Aquino replaced Ferdinand Marcos as President in the Philippines, ending 14 years of martial law and authoritarian rule. South Korea adopted democracy on June 29, 1987, with President Ro Tae Woo's Democratic Declaration. Based on Transparency International's first Corruption Perception Index (CPI) in 1995, Arnold J. Heidenheimer (1996: 338) classified the 41 countries surveyed into three groups: least corrupt, somewhat corrupt, and quite corrupt. South Korea's 27th position and Philippines' 36th position placed both in the "quite corrupt" category. (1) This article has three aims. First, it analyzes the problem of corruption in the "quite corrupt" Philippines and South Korea. Second, it compares and evaluates the effectiveness of the anti-corruption strategies in these two countries. Finally, the article concludes by assessing whether the development of democracy has exacerbated or minimized corruption in these countries. (2)

Before proceeding, it is necessary to define three key concepts: corruption, democracy, and democratization. Heidenheimer (1970: 4–6) has identified three types of social science definitions of corruption: public-office-centered definitions, market-centered definitions, and public-interest-centered definitions. For this article, a public-office-centered definition is most relevant and useful. Corruption refers to "the misuse of public power, office or authority for private benefit—through bribery, extortion, influence peddling, nepotism, fraud, speed money or embezzlement" (UNDP, 1999: 7). Democracy is defined "minimally as a political system in which free and fair elections inclusive of all social groups are held regularly and basic civil and political liberties are respected" (Lipset, 1998: xiii). Democratization is "the process of building a democracy following the collapse of a non-democratic regime" (Sodaro, 2001: 215).

CORRUPTION IN THE PHILIPPINES

Corruption was introduced to the Philippines by the Spanish as the "low salaries and poor working conditions of the bureaucrats and the many opportunities available for corrupt behaviour contributed to the widespread corruption in the colonial bureaucracy" (Quah, 1982: 158). As a public office was viewed as a grant or favor from the King during the Spanish colonial period, "many bureaucrats actually treated the transaction as a business—selling an office at a profit and buying a more lucrative one" (Endriga, 1979: 247–249). In short, graft and corruption were rampant during the Spanish colonial period. The Americans replaced the Spanish in 1898 and the "bureaucracy as a whole was quite clean during this period" because the bureaucrats were paid higher salaries and corrupt civil servants were promptly prosecuted (Quah, 1982: 159).

After World War II, however, the bureaucracy in the Philippines suffered from "low prestige, incompetence, meager resources, and a large measure of cynical corruption" (Corpuz, 1957: 222–223). Bureaucratic corruption became a serious problem during the 1950s, especially during the administration of President Elpidio Quirino (1948–1953), because corruption "permeated the entire gamut of the Philippine bureaucracy, extending from the lowest level of the civil service to the top, excepting the President himself" (Alfiler, 1979: 323). In May, 1950, President Quirino created an Integrity Board consisting of five members to investigate complaints of graft and corruption against civil servants. However, a lack of public support led to its dissolution 5 months later (Quah, 1982: 159).

After winning the 1953 presidential election Ramon Magsaysay established the Presidential Complaints and Action Commission (PCAC) to reduce inefficiency and dishonesty in the civil service, and issued Administrative Order No. 1 to prevent public officials from participating in certain types of official transactions with their real or imaginary relatives. Magsaysay's untimely death in 1957 led to the emergence of the Garcia administration (1957–1962), which abolished the PCAC and replaced it with the Presidential Committee on Administration Performance Efficiency (PCAPE) and the Presidential Fact-Finding Committee (PFFC) in 1958 to implement the government's anti-graft campaign. In February, 1960, Garcia introduced a third agency known as the Presidential Anti-Graft Committee (PAGC) (Alfiler, 1979: 331–337).

President Garcia was succeeded by President Diosdado Macapagal, who served from 1962 to 1965. Macapagal created the Presidential Anti-Graft Committee or PAGCOM. In 1965, Ferdinand Marcos replaced Macapagal as President and replaced PAGCOM with the Presidential Agency on Reforms and Government Operations (PARGO) in January 1966. Three other agencies were set up to assist PARGO: the Presidential Complaints and Action Office (PCAO), the Complaints and Investigations Office (CIO), and the Special Cabinet Committee in Backsliding (Alfiler, 1979: 339–346).

President Marcos's declaration of martial law on September 22, 1972 "ended over a quarter century of robust, if often irresponsible and elitist, democratic politics" (Timberman, 1991: 75). Aquino described the Philippines under Marcos as the "Politics of Plunder":

> His declaration of martial law in 1972 under false pretexts not only protected the fortune he had already acquired, most illicitly over the past two decades. It also served to accelerate the amassing of even more power and wealth for several more years. . . . He lorded it [the economy] over a rapacious team of trusted friends and associates whom he had given lucrative fiefdoms in the economy. Together they stole high and low, from both rich and poor. They treated the Philippine treasury as if it were their personal checking account. The consuming preoccupation with wealth accumulation was abetted by multi-million international loans and massive U.S. foreign assistance packages that were meant for economic development. These resources provided easy opportunities for massive graft. As long as they were available, the stealing by Marcos and his cronies went unabated. . . . In the end, the Philippines had been bled of billions of dollars and had become the "basket case of Asia" by the late 1970s (Aquino, 1987: 116–117).

Similarly, Varela (1995: 174) contended that "graft and corruption reached its all time high" during Marcos's martial law regime as both "had permeated almost all aspects of bureaucratic life and institutions which saw the start of the systematic plunder of the country."

The Philippines has thus relied on 7 laws and 13 anti-graft agencies since it initiated its fight against corruption in the 1950s (Quah, 1999a: 19). The proliferation of anti-graft agencies is the result of the frequent changes in political leadership as these agencies are either created or abolished by the President. From 1950 to 1966, five anti-corruption agencies were formed and dissolved as a result of five changes in political leadership. Similarly, President Marcos created another five anti-graft agencies during his two decades in power. The first three were ineffective and lasted between 8 months and 2 years (Quah, 1982: 168–169). In 1979, President Marcos formed the Sandiganbayan (Special Anti-Graft Court) and the Tanodbayan (Ombudsman) by Presidential Decrees.

When President Aquino assumed office in February, 1986, "there was high expectation that the end of the culture of graft and corruption was near" (Varela, 1995: 174). She established the Presidential Commission on Good Government (PCGG) to identify and retrieve the money stolen by the Marcos family and its cronies. Unfortunately, Aquino's "avowed anti-graft and corruption" stance was viewed cynically by the public as two of her cabinet members and her relatives were accused of corruption. The PCGG itself was also charged with corruption, favoritism and incompetence: by 1988, five of its agents faced graft charges and 13 more were being investigated. In 1987, Aquino created the Presidential Committee on Public Ethics and Accountability (PCPEA) to respond to increasing public criticism. However, the PCPEA was also ineffective as it lacked personnel and funds.

In short, Aquino's "honesty has not been matched by the political will to punish the corrupt" (Timberman, 1991: 235). Her ineffectiveness was manifested in the declining numbers of citizens satisfied with the performance of her administration in tackling corruption—from 72% in March, 1987, to 26% in July, 1989. While Aquino herself had "shared the people's exasperation and despair that she could not achieve the very thing that she wanted to leave as a legacy: a clean and accountable government" (Carino, 1994: 113). According to Reid and Guerrero (1995: 2), Aquino "left behind a mixed legacy. . . . The democratic institutions she struggled to rebuild remained flawed and weak. Corruption prevailed, and Filipinos were increasingly cynical about the state of their nation."

The Tanodbayan or Office of the Ombudsman was "reborn" in 1988 during Aquino's term of office. However, Balgos (1998: 247) notes that "during the first seven years after its rebirth in 1988, the Office of the Ombudsman failed to attract much public scrutiny, the limelight hogged by the more high-profile Sandiganbayan." However, instead of "inspiring confidence in the judicial system," the Ombudsman has elicited "only disappointment—if not contempt—among many of those seeking redress for the wrong done them by public officials. Indeed, the Ombudsman has a notorious reputation for taking a long time in processing the complaints received by it" (Balgos, 1998: 248).

A more serious weakness was caused by a case-quota system introduced by Conrado Vasquez, who was appointed as Ombudsman in 1988. This quota system encouraged inefficiency as investigators "finished the easier cases first to fulfill their quota" and left the more complex ones "untouched for months, or even years." By December, 1994, the Ombudsman had accumulated a backlog of 14,652 cases, or 65% of its total workload. In 1997, the Ombudsman still had pending cases dating back to 1979. The Sandiganbayan's record is worse than the Ombudsman as it completed only 13% of its total caseload in 1996 (Balgos, 1998: 250–251).

In 1992, Fidel Ramos was elected president for a 6-year term. He created the Presidential Commission Against Graft and Corruption (PCAGC) in 1994 to investigate violations of the anti-graft laws by presidential appointees and appointed Eufemio Domingo as its chairman. In 1997, Domingo lamented that

[T]he system is not working. We are not making it work . . . We have all the laws, rules and regulations and especially institutions not only to curb, but to eliminate, corruption. The problem is that these laws, rules and regulations are not being faithfully implemented. . . . I am afraid that many people are accepting (corruption) as another part of our way of life. Big-time grafters are lionised in society. They are invited to all sorts of social events, elected and re-elected to government offices. It is considered an honor—in fact a social distinction—to have them as guests in family and community affairs (Balgos, 1998: 267–268).

Joseph Estrada succeeded Ramos as president, and in his 1998 State of the Nation Address identified the struggle against graft and corruption as his major priority. In early 1999, he requested the World Bank to make recommendations to help his government strengthen its fight against corruption. The World Bank submitted preliminary findings in 1999, recommending "a national strategy for fighting corruption in the Philippines" by "reducing opportunities and motivation for corruption" and making "corruption a high-risk, low-reward activity" (Bhargava, 1999: 1, 5).

During 2000, the Philippine Center for Investigative Journalism (PCIJ) initiated a detailed investigation on the president's wealth, finding that Estrada, his wives and his children were listed as incorporators or board members of 66 companies. In 1999, Estrada had declared in his statement of assets a net worth of P35.8 million and in his income tax return, a net income of only P2.3 million. However, his 1999 official asset declaration could not account for the source of the funds invested in these companies as 14 of them had assets of over P600 million (Coronel, 2000: 42–43).

The Financial Times reported in 2000 that "perceived corruption in the Philippines reached its highest levels in two decades in 1998 and 1999, the first 2 years of the Estrada administration" (Lande, 2001: 92). In October of that year, Senate Minority Leader Teofisto Guingona accused Estrada of receiving "large cash payouts from jueteng, an illegal numbers game." An Estrada crony, Governor Luis Singson, "claimed that he had given the president 400 million pesos (US$ 10 million) from jueteng collections nationwide" (Lande, 2001: 92). Singson's "revelations triggered a major political earthquake" (Magno, 2001: 259).

According to Lande (2001: 92), "it was Estrada's mismanagement of the economy that most decisively turned the upper and middle classes against him." Moreover, the business community did not accept cronyism and its members were disturbed by the preferential treatment given Estrada's friends. However, "the last straw was the revelation that he himself was brazenly corrupt" (Lande, 2001: 92). The minority members of the House of Representatives initiated impeachment proceedings against the president. During the trial, Clarissa Ocampo, senior vice-president of PCI-Equitable Bank, informed the court that Estrada, "under a false identity, was the true owner of several bank accounts holding hundred of millions of pesos" (Magno, 2001: 251). The trial was covered live by the media and "broke all audience records" because it was "a telenovela that outclassed all the others simply because it was real" . . . it became "the single most important educational event on civics and the rule of law in Philippine political history" as it "was a large classroom where the weaknesses of institutions were exposed and the innermost secrets of political corruption revealed" (Magno, 2001: 260, 262).

On January 16, 2001, two pro-Estrada senators prevented "damning evidence" from being revealed in the trial, which "provoked a firestorm of public outrage. The House prosecutors walked out in disgust. Senate president Pimentel resigned. Civil society exploded in nonviolent anger and, acting where the Senate had failed to act, moved over 5 days of massive demonstrations to force the president from office" (Lande, 2001: 94). Four days later, Gloria Macapagal-Arroyo was sworn in as President after Estrada agreed to resign when the military withdrew its support. In her inaugural speech, President Arroyo emphasized that one of four core goals was to "improve moral standards in government and society, in order to provide a strong foundation for good governance." It is, of course, premature to assess President Arroyo's record as she has been in office for only a few years. However, Sheila Coronel, Executive Director of the Philippine Center for Investigative Journalism, observes that Arroyo's government was unlikely to be "reformist" as "I was at her headquarters and I could see the old faces coming out, people who have been accused of corruption in the past" (Sheehan, 2001: 17).

CORRUPTION IN SOUTH KOREA

Corruption is a serious problem in South Korea, judging from the spate of scandals in recent years. According to Young Jong Kim (1994: 215), South Korea has been described as "a ROTC (Republic of Total Corruption) by the people and media." Similarly, Kee Chul Hwang (1996: 107) contends there was "unprecedented corruption" in South Korea as "the symbolic practice of integrity and probity among public employees cannot easily be found."

Historically, corruption was not a serious problem in South Korea during the first half of the Yi Dynasty (1392–1910) as the "internal controls against anti-corruption behavior worked effectively until the beginning of the 16th century" (Rahman, 1986: 117–118). However, the participation of the King's relatives in politics and government from the 16th century onwards led to "increasing nepotism and corruption in administration." Another contributing factor was the relaxation of the civil servants' emphasis on rectitude and thrift and their adoption of a luxurious lifestyle, which compelled them to rely increasingly on "the abuse of power to accumulate wealth illegally" (Rahman, 1986: 119).

After independence in 1945, the South Korean government employed the Criminal Code and administrative prohibitions to tackle the growing problem of corruption. All new presidents, upon taking office, promised to take appropriate measures to eradicate corruption (Kim, 1997: 253). They began in earnest with President Park Chung Hee. Park took office in 1961 after ousting the government of Chang Myon because of its involvement in corruption, its inability to defend the country from communism, and its incompetence in initiating economic and social change (Han, 1989: 273). He created the Board of Audit and Inspection (BAI) in 1963 to act as a direct check on the economic bureaucracy (Hart-Landsberg, 1993: 54). The BAI was thus the first de facto anti-corruption agency in South Korea. (3) In 1975, Park introduced the Seojungshaeshin (General Administration Reform) Movement to curb corruption in the civil service. (4)

Park's assassination in 1979 led to the assumption of power a year later by Chun Doo Hwan. He re-affirmed his government's anti-corruption stance by purging corrupt officials, introducing ethics laws to reward honest officials, and enhancing civil service reforms (Jun, 1985: 63). However, Chun's government lacked legitimacy in the eyes of rival political parties, student leaders, intellectuals, and progressive Christians (Han, 1989: 282–284). Caiden and Kim (1993: 137–139) have criticised the Park and Chun reforms as "sporadic, periodic, episodic, incidental and improvisatory, too cosmetic and lip-serving, and for being implemented quickly and without careful preparation."

The peaceful transfer of power to President Roh Tae Woo in 1988 enabled him to investigate abuses during his predecessor's regime. During parliamentary hearings in November and December, 1988, Chun, his two brothers, and his wife's family were accused of massive corruption. On November 23, 1988, Chun and his wife apologised for their misbehaviour and returned 13.9 billion won (US$ 20 million) to the government. The next year, Chun's brothers were convicted for corruption and imprisoned:

> What became apparent after Chun left office was the depth of corruption and the degree to which it had been quietly tolerated, even expected. The pervasive corruption is another of the ugly legacies bequeathed by the Fifth Republic. Corruption had long been part of the Korean system, but Chun did the country a tremendous disservice by allowing his relatives to prosper. For all his faults, Park had never allowed his family to profit personally from his position. Unfortunately, the Chun and Lee families set an example of egregiously corrupt behavior that still undermines the Korean social contract (Clifford, 1998: 287, emphasis added).

While Roh remained committed to democracy, he was nevertheless plagued by political corruption, as six legislators were found guilty of extorting funds from the business community. The Hanbo scandal of 1992 shocked the country when Chung Tae Soo, chairman of the Hanbo Construction Company, was accused of contributing substantial funds to the ruling and opposition political parties for favors involving land development (FEER, 1992: 138). Roh himself was not immune: it was discovered in 1995 that major business conglomerates and numerous individuals had contributed almost US$ 600 million to his private political fund, which he had used both to reward supporters and for himself and his family (Macdonald and Clark, 1996: 159–160).

When Kim Young Sam became the first civilian President in February, 1993, he launched an intensive anti-corruption campaign. He began with the voluntary declaration of his personal assets and those of his extended family, amounting to 1.77 billion won (or US$2 million) (Oh, 1999: 139). Kim encouraged his cabinet colleagues and ruling party members to follow suit. In 1993, the Public Officials' Ethics Law was revised to institutionalise the disclosure of public officials' assets, and all senior officials were required to register and periodically disclose their assets (Kim, 1997: 255). Kim gave up golf, which had become a symbol of corporate-government cronyism and the exchange of corrupt gifts (Sheridan, 1994: 15).

In 1993, Kim issued an emergency decree establishing a Real-Name Financial Transaction System, which banned the use of anonymous financial accounts and required individuals to use their own names for opening bank accounts. Anonymous or false-name accounts had been the backbone of the black economy and massive fraud, corruption, and tax evasion schemes (Sheridan, 1994: 15; Kim, 1997: 255). The "real-name system" was President Kim's "most potent antidote" to corruption as "the policy dealt a major blow to the prevalent practice of amassing unearned income, and soliciting bribes or political funds through fake or borrowed accounts. By using fake or borrowed accounts, one achieved two goals at once: tax avoidance and the concealment of the trail of recipients of the illicit monies" (Guerrero, 1999: 77).

In 1994, the Election for Public Office and Election Malpractice Prevention Act was enacted to reduce corruption in politics by ensuring transparency in campaign financing, limiting campaign expenditures, preventing electoral irregularities, and imposing heavy penalties for offenders (Kim, 1997: 255). However, the most important reforms introduced by President Kim were the strengthening of the BAI and the creation of the Commission for the Prevention of Corruption, which is an advisory body of private citizens formed to assist the BAI's chairman. The BAI performed three functions: to confirm the closing accounts of the state's revenues and expenditure; to audit a variety of state organisations; and to inspect the work of government agencies and officials. Its chairman was appointed by the president for 4 years with the consent of the National Assembly (Kim, 1994: 218–219).

President Kim's anti-corruption campaign confirmed that corruption was a way of life and exposed its pervasiveness. Indeed, Kim "exposed more dirt than the South Korean people had ever imagined or are comfortable with" (Genzberger et al., 1994: 25). Unlike the earlier efforts of Rhee, Park and Chun, which were ineffective because of the lack of political will (Kim, 1994: 207), Kim demonstrated his commitment by not obstructing the arrest and sentencing of his son. (5) Nevertheless, the Hanbo scandal and his son's arrest and imprisonment had seriously undermined Kim's legitimacy and jeopardised the continued success of his anti-corruption drive (Kim, 1997: 255).

How effective were President Kim's anti-corruption campaigns? The 1996 South Korean Democratization Survey found that 71% of respondents experienced some decrease in political corruption while only 4% reported an increase. However, 49% and 36% of the respondents perceived the level of corruption of Kim Young Sam's government to be "high" or "very high", respectively (Shin, 1999: 212–214). Despite Kim's efforts, "the age-old custom of corruption was not dying at all in the South Korean political marketplace: instead, the informal norms were still overpowering the formal rules of the newly implanted democratic political game" (Shin, 1999: 214).

After assuming office on February 25, 1998, President Kim Dae Jung announced a comprehensive anti-corruption strategy with the objectives of ensuring clean and upright public office, transparent and reliable government, and a just and fair society. The goal was to become a transparent state and to improve South Korea's ranking on Transparency International's CPI from 43rd position in 1998 to 20th position by 2003 (Republic of Korea, 1999: 6). Kim's strategy has six components:

- Creating an Anti-Corruption Committee to co-ordinate programs and activities; and formulating the Anti-Corruption Law to provide protection for whistle-blowers, strengthen citizen participation, and reinforce detection and punishment for corrupt practices.

- Reforming the attitudes and consciousness of public servants by enforcing codes of conduct, education, and increasing the salaries of medium to low level officials to match those in the private sector within 5 years.

- Promoting public awareness of corruption through the schools and other social and cultural centers, the use of mass media to publicize anti-corruption materials, a national movement against corruption, and strengthened international cooperation.

- Forming a social and cultural environment against corruption through the scrutiny and strict control of former government officials, enhancing the transparency of private industries, and eroding collusion among politicians, government officials, and businessmen.

- Improving the reward/protection system for informers, activating citizen watch groups to report corruption, creating a special inspection office to focus on the corruption of senior officials, and increasing financial penalties by retrieving personal gains and government losses.

- Initiating reforms in six corruption-prone areas: tax administration, construction, housing, food and entertainment, environmental management, and police work. More specifically, these reforms focused on implementing deregulation, forming the Online Procedures Enhancement for Civil Applications (OPEN) system, reducing personal contacts between civil servants and the public, and improving overall accountability (Republic of Korea, 1999: 9–22).

Implementation has not been easy. The proposed anti-corruption law met with opposition in the National Assembly and was not enacted until 2001 (Republic of Korea, 2001). In January, 2002, however, the Korean Independent Commission Against Corruption (KICAC) became Korea's de jure anti-corruption agency.

COMPARATIVE ANALYSIS

To compare the effectiveness of anti-corruption strategies in the Philippines and South Korea, it is first necessary to identify major contextual constraints. Table 1 compares the two countries in terms of area, population, GNP per

TABLE 1   Contextual Constraints of the Philippines and South Korea

Country	Philippines	South Korea
Land area	300,000 km^2	99,274 km^2
Population	76.8 million	46.8 million
GDP per capita	US$ 1000	US$ 8690
Unemployment rate	9.4%	6.3%
Size of civil service	1,328,018 (1995)	900,000 (1996)
Civil service as % of population	1.9	2.0

SOURCE: Andrews (2001: 158–159, 178–179), Asian Development Bank (2000: 159, 269), and Burns and Bowornwathana (2001: Table 1.2).

capita, unemployment rate, size of the civil service, and the number of civil servants per 1000 population. The policy context in South Korea is more favorable for anti-corruption action than that in the Philippines for several reasons. The Philippines is three times larger than South Korea in land area, and its population is greater by 30 million people. In addition, the Philippines is an archipelago of 7017 islands; fighting corruption is arduous in the provinces and rural areas as the "boundaries of water and mountain make internal travel and communication difficult" (Carino, 1988: 4–5).

Another advantage of South Korea is that it is more than eight times richer than the Philippines with a GDP per capita of US$8690 in 1999. As the Philippines also has more civil servants than South Korea, it will encounter more difficulty in raising the low salaries of its civil servants. As the unemployment rate in the Philippines in 1999 was 9.4% compared to 6.3% for South Korea, the Philippines would also have more difficulty in downsizing its civil service. Finally, South Korea has a more homogeneous population (99% are Korean) with Korean as the common language, and has given more importance to education; it can thus spread the anti-corruption message more easily throughout the country. Kang (2002: 22) notes other differences and similarities. On one hand, "Korea is ethnically homogeneous, Confucian, and geographically peninsular, whereas the Philippines is multiracial, culturally diverse, and a series of islands." On the other, both countries experienced occupation by the Japanese and by US soldiers after World War II, rely heavily on external finance for their economic activities, and have been capitalist and authoritarian.

COMPARING LEVELS OF CORRUPTION

Any research on corruption faces major problems of measurement. Not only is most corruption furtive by nature; those with knowledge of it may well remain silent. Kee Chul Hwang (1996: 142, 235) found that Korean survey respondents were reluctant to answer questions on the number of times they had offered a bribe to a civil servant, the number of times they had received a bribe when performing their duties, and their reaction if they had received bribes. Thus, survey research methods cannot be used except indirectly. In his study of police corruption in a northeastern city in the United States, Meyer (1973: 39) relied on allegations of police corruption by the citizens and police officers. His caution regarding the incomplete nature of his data should be noted here:

> It must be remembered that these data do not represent the true picture of corruption. They do show the nature and extent of corruption as reported by the various complainants. As such, the data show the picture of corruption as was available to the police chief and his staff. They do not show if, in fact, there was more corruption than was actually reported (emphasis added).

Similarly, Young Jong Kim (1994: 102–103) compiled reports of bureaucratic corruption in two major South Korean newspapers for 6 years (1960–1961, 1970–1971, and 1978–1979). Following Meyer, he warns his readers that:

> . . . the reported incidents do not necessarily reflect the reality of corruption phenomena in Korea, since the dark or hidden area of bureaucratic corruption (i.e., unreported and unknown incidents) might be in existence behind the reported incidents (Kim, 1994: 112).

Such examples show that it is not possible to "measure" the actual level or extent of corruption in a country as scholars usually rely on the reported extent of corruption. Lancaster and Montinola (1997: 16) have recommended the CPI published by Transparency International (TI) as a "robust" index that "captures more than a single indicator" and "combines several measures of political corruption for each country" (Lancaster and Montinola, 1997: 27–28). The CPI is "an attempt to assess the level at which corruption is perceived by people working for multinational firms and institutions as impacting on commercial and social life" (TI, 1996: 5). The 2001 edition ranked 91 countries from 14 different surveys conducted by seven independent institutions among business people, country analysts, and residents. (6) Indeed, the CPI's strength is based on "the concept that a combination of data sources combined into a single index increases the reliability of each individual figure" (Lambsdorff, 2001: 2).

From 1995 to 2001, the CPI ranking for South Korea has consistently been better than that for the Philippines. The rank for the latter declined from 35th least-corrupt in 1995 to 69th in 2000, and improved slightly to 65th in 2001. In South Korea's case, it was ranked 27th in 1995 and declined to 50th in 1999. Its ranking during the last 2 years improved to 48th in 2000, and to 42nd in 2001. In short, South Korea's average ranking from 1995 to 2001 is 39th, which is much higher than the Philippines' average rank of 52nd for the same period. The Philippines also trails South Korea in rankings published by the Hong Kong-based Political Economic Risk Consultancy

(PERC). (7) Between 1995 and 2001, South Korea dropped from fourth to sixth, while the Philippines dropped from eighth to ninth. On average, South Korea ranked sixth out of 12 countries while the Philippines were in seventh position.

EFFECTIVENESS OF THE ANTI-CORRUPTION STRATEGIES

South Korea's higher rankings may well reflect more effective anti-corruption measures, especially since Kim's initiatives of 1999. The effectiveness of anti-corruption measures depends on two factors: "(1) the adequacy of the measures themselves in terms of the comprehensiveness of their scope and powers; and (2) the level of commitment of the political leadership to the goal of eradicating bureaucratic corruption in the country concerned" (Quah, 1982: 175).

There are three patterns of corruption control among the Asian countries (Quah, 1999a: 14–26; Quah, 2001: 457–464). The first exists when there is anti-corruption legislation without an independent agency. The best example of a country with this pattern of corruption control is Mongolia. The Law on Anti-Corruption (LAC) is ineffective; no Mongolian public official has been convicted even though it has been in existence since April, 1996. As there is no independent anti-corruption agency, the task of controlling corruption in Mongolia is shared among the police, the General Prosecutor's Office, and the courts (Quah, 1999b: 19–22). Corruption is a way of life in Mongolia because of the low salaries of public officials, the ample opportunities for corruption, and the low level of LAC enforcement.

The second pattern combines anti-corruption legislation with several agencies, as exemplified in India and the Philippines. In India, the Prevention of Corruption Act (POCA) is implemented by the Central Bureau of Investigation, the Central Vigilance Commission, and anti-corruption bureaus and vigilance commissions at the state level. Similarly, in the Philippines, the anti-graft laws and policies are supplemented by the Sandiganbayan (special anti-corruption court), the Ombudsman, and the PCAGC. This pattern is also ineffective: anti-corruption laws have not been impartially enforced by the agencies because of the lack of political will. Indeed, what is lacking in the Philippines' anti-corruption strategy is not adequate measures but rather the political will to implement these measures and apprehend those found guilty of corruption regardless of their status or position in society.

The third and most effective pattern of curbing corruption involves comprehensive anti-corruption legislation impartially implemented by an independent anti-corruption agency. The best examples are Singapore and Hong Kong; it is not surprising that they are perceived to be the two least corrupt societies in Asia (Quah, 1999a: 22–26).

South Korea has shifted from Pattern 1 to Pattern 3 since 1999. The BAI was created in 1963 to implement the anti-corruption strategy even though it was an audit agency and not an anti-corruption agency. This anomaly was finally rectified in July, 2001 with the enactment of the Anti-Corruption Act, and the creation of the KICAC to implement the Anti-Corruption Act in January, 2002. Korea has sought to reduce both the incentives and opportunities for corruption; in contrast, the Philippines has adopted an incremental strategy since the 1950s, which has been ineffective because of a lack of political will. Successive presidents have chosen to "muddle through" by creating their own agencies to treat the symptoms without attacking the causes of corruption.

CONCLUSION: DEMOCRATIZATION AND CORRUPTION

Has democratization in the Philippines and South Korea minimized, or exacerbated, the problem of corruption? Huntington (1968: 59-61) observed that modernization contributes to corruption for three reasons: (1) it involves a change in the basic values of the society; (2) it creates new sources of wealth and power; and (3) it expands governmental authority and multiplies the activities subjected to governmental regulation. Indeed, "the multiplication of laws thus multiplies the possibilities of corruption" (Huntington, 1968: 62). Harriss-White and White add that "in some contexts . . . the amount of corruption has increased along with and apparently as [a] result of economic liberalization" (quoted in Ghosh et al., 1997: 18).

Economic growth and democratization in South Korea, too, have increased the opportunities for corruption. In 1945, corruption was not a serious problem; it did not become rampant until the country's rapid growth in the 1970s and 1980s. Shin Hae-Nam observes that "Ironically, corruption grew as people became more affluent, and it was probably because of people's new thinking that put material values ahead of moral values" (Straits Times, 1993: 11).

Unlike South Korea, the Philippines is rich in natural resources. Still it declined from being one of Asia's richest countries in the 1950s to one of the poorest in the 1980s (Andrews, 2001: 150). A 1997 World Bank study on the Philippines was sub-titled: "Three Decades of Lost Opportunities" (Kharas, 1997). Many factors are responsible for the country's dismal economic performance, but pervasive graft and corruption, especially during the Marcos regime, resulted in an estimated loss of US$48 billion during the past 20 years (Torrijos, 1999: 4).

The relationship between democratization and corruption is complex and reciprocal. This interaction has been best expressed by Revel (1993: 229): "The best obstacle to corruption is democratic control, and by corollary, corruption is one of the most pernicious ways of subverting democracy." Democracy provides citizens with "an opportunity to punish governments that fail to control corruption" (Ghosh et al., 1997: 20), but as Rose-Ackerman (1996: 376) points out, "in democracies the desire for re-election will deter corruption so long as the electorate disapproves of the practice and has some way of sorting out valid from invalid accusations." If the likelihood of re-election is low (because of a decline in popularity) or zero (if the law prohibits re-election), politicians will have "an incentive to extract as much wealth as possible from their remaining hold on power" as their retirement becomes imminent.

Palmier's (1985: 271–272) comparative study of corruption control in Hong Kong, India, and Indonesia identifies three major causes of corruption: opportunities (which depend on the extent of involvement of civil servants in the administration or control of lucrative activities), salaries, and policing (the probability of detection and punishment). More specifically,

> Bureaucratic corruption seems to depend not on any one of the [three] factors identified, but rather on the balance between them. At one extreme, with few opportunities, good salaries, and effective policing, corruption will be minimal; at the other, with many opportunities, poor salaries, and weak policing, it will be considerable [emphasis added].

If we apply Palmier's analysis to anti-corruption strategies in the Philippines and South Korea, it is obvious that corruption in both countries can be attributed to the low salaries of civil servants, the ample opportunities for corruption, and the low degree of policing. In the Philippines, employees of the Bureau of Immigration are paid "starvation wages," and find it difficult to survive without accepting bribes. Junior policemen are paid such low salaries that they are forced to live in the slums with other criminal elements. Some agencies like the Bureau of Immigration, Customs Department, Department of Education, Culture and Sports, Department of Public Works and Highways, and Bureau of Internal Revenue are more vulnerable to corruption because of their contact with the public and their regulatory functions.

Ineffective policing in the Philippines is reflected in a conviction rate of less than 2% of reported cases in 1997 and 1998. While the ICAC in Hong Kong successfully prosecuted 8.24 corruption cases per 10,000 civil servants in 1997, the comparable figure for the Ombudsman in the Philippines was less than 0.25 cases per 10,000. "The probability that a Hong Kong civil servant will be successfully prosecuted for corruption is almost 35 times greater than his or her counterpart in the Philippines" (Beschel, 1999: 8).

In the case of South Korea, Woo-Cummings (1995: 455–456) has recommended that civil service salaries, which constitute only 70% of private sector wages, should be improved to reduce corruption. Similarly, Jun and Yoon (1996: 107) suggest that while "no one questions the importance of honesty, integrity and dedication in public employees," it is unrealistic to expect them "to show dedication without providing adequate remuneration and changing the administrative culture." Current reforms include the improvement of salaries of middle and junior civil servants to levels found in the private sector within 5 years (Republic of Korea, 1999: 14).

Extensive regulation in South Korea provides ample opportunities for corruption. To build a factory one must prepare an average of 44 documents for the permit application, which then takes several months for approval (Myoungsoo Kim, 1997: 261). In 1998, President Kim formed the Regulatory Reform Committee (RRC) to make the country more business-friendly by eliminating unnecessary regulations. During its first year, the RRC abolished 5326 (or 48%) of the 11,125 administrative regulations (Republic of Korea, 1998).

Finally, the level of policing in South Korea is higher than that in the Philippines. Kim's strategy aims at improved detection and punishment through the following measures:

1. Strengthening the reward system for informers.

2. Activating Citizen Watch for inspecting and auditing of government activities by citizens.

3. Reinforcing detection of corrupt officials by establishing a special inspection office in the Public Prosecutions Administration to focus on the corruption of senior government officials, making property registration of civil servants more systematic, and introducing a law prohibiting money laundering.

4. Strengthening punishment against corrupt public officials by prohibiting them from being employed in the private sector for 5 years and in the civil service for 15 years, punishing both bribe-givers and bribe-takers equally, and increasing the financial penalty (Republic of Korea, 1999: 19–20).

In sum, democratization in the Philippines and South Korea is, by itself, an inadequate deterrent against corruption, especially when the causes for such behavior have not been dealt with. As the critical variable is the political will of the leaders, it is not surprising that South Korea is making much more progress than the Philippines. It is unlikely that South Korea can attain the rank of 20th position soon, given its ranking of 42nd position in 2001. Nevertheless, the adoption of the third pattern of corruption control in South Korea augurs well for the future as long as President Kim Dae Jung's successor remains committed to the eradication of corruption in South Korean society.

Jon S.T. Quah, Department of Political Science, National University of Singapore, 117570 Singapore

NOTES

1. See Table 2 [TABULAR DATA FOR TABLE 2 OMITTED] for details of the CPI rankings for both countries from 1995 to 2001.

2. See the case studies on these two countries in Diamond et al. (1989), Gaerlan (1999), Laothamatas (1997), Leipziger (1997), Lipset (1998), Marsh et al. (1999) and Robinson (1991).

3. For a detailed analysis of the BAI's role, see Kim (1985).

4. For more details on the Seojungshaeshin, see Oh (1982).

5. On May 17, 1997, Kim's son was arrested for bribery and tax evasion in the Hanbo loan scandal and was sentenced to 3 years' imprisonment 5 months later.

6. For more information on the 2001 CPI, see http://www.transparency.org/documents/cpi/2001/cpi2001.html.

7. See PERC, "Corruption in Asia in 2001", http://www.asiarisk.com/l1b10.html.

REFERENCES

Alfiler, Ma. Concepcion, P., "Administrative Measures against Bureaucratic Corruption: The Philippine Experience," Philippine Journal of Public Administration 1979 (23: 3–4) 321–349.

Andrews, J., Pocket Asia, 6th edn. (London: The Economist Newspaper, 2001).

Aquino, B.A., Politics of Plunder: The Philippines under Marcos (Manila: Great Books Trading and College of Public Administration, University of the Philippines, 1987).

Balgos, C.C.A., "Ombudsman," in Sheila S. Coronel (ed.), Pork and Other Perks: Corruption and Governance in the Philippines (Metro Manila: Philippine Center for Investigative Journalism, 1998), pp. 245–271.

Beschel, R.P., "Corruption, Transparency and Accountability in the Philippines," Unpublished Paper (Manila: Asian Development Bank, 1999).

Bhargava, V., "Combating Corruption in the Philippines," (Manila: Philippine Country Management Unit, World Bank, 1999).

Burns, J.P. and B. Bowornwathana, "Asian Civil Service Systems in Comparative Perspective," in John P. Burns and Bidhya Bowornwathana (eds.), Civil Service Systems in Asia (Cheltenham: Edward Elgar, 2001), pp. 1–23.

Caiden, G.E. and J.H. Kim, "A New Anti-Corruption Strategy for Korea," Asian Journal of Political Science 1993 (1: June 1) 133–151.

Carino, L.V., "The Land and the People," in Raul P. de Guzman and Mila A. Reforma (eds.), Government and Politics of the Philippines (Singapore: Oxford University Press, 1988).

Carino, L.V., "Enhancing Accountability in the Philippines: The Continuing Quest," in John P. Burns (ed.), Asian Civil Service Systems: Improving Efficiency and Productivity (Singapore: Times Academic Press, 1994), pp. 106–125.

Clifford, M.L., Troubled Tiger: Businessmen, Bureaucrats, and Generals in South Korea, revised edn. (Armonk: M.E. Sharpe, 1998).

Coronel, Sheila S. (ed.), Investigating Estrada: Millions, Mansions and Mistresses (Metro Manila: Philippine Center for Investigative Journalism, 2000).

Corpuz, O.D., The Bureaucracy in the Philippines (Manila: College of Public Administration, University of the Philippines, 1957).

Diamond, L., J. J. Linz and S. Martin Lipset (eds.), Democracy in Developing Countries: Asia (Boulder: Lynne Rienner Publishers, 1989).

Endriga, J.N., "Historical Notes on Graft and Corruption in the Philippines," Philippine Journal of Public Administration 1979 (23:3–4) 241–254.

Far Eastern Economic Review (FEER), "Korea—South," Asia Yearbook 1992. (Hong Kong: FEER, 1992).

Gaerlan, K.N. (ed.), Transitions to Democracy in East and Southeast Asia (Quezon City: Institute for Popular Democracy, 1999).

Ghosh, A. et al., "Corruption: Reform's Dark Side," Far Eastern Economic Review 1997 (20) 18–20.

Guerrero, D.M., "A Tiger Changing Stripes: Post-Development, Transitions and Democracy in South Korea," in Kristina N. Gaerlan (ed.), Transitions to Democracy in East and Southeast Asia (Quezon City: Institute for Popular Democracy, 1999), pp. 61–103.

Han, S.-J., "South Korea: Politics in Transition," in Larry Diamond et al. (eds.), Democracy in Developing Countries: Asia (Boulder: Lynne Rienner Publishers, 1989), pp. 267–303.

Hart-Landsberg, The Rush to Development: Economic Change and Political Struggle in South Korea (New York: Monthly Review Press, 1993).

Heidenheimer, A.J. (ed.), Political Corruption: Readings in Comparative Analysis (New Brunswick: Transaction Books, 1970).

Heidenheimer, A.J., "The Topography of Corruption: Explorations in a Comparative Perspective," International Social Science Journal 1996 (149) 337–347.

Huntington, S.P., Political Order in Changing Societies (New Haven: Yale University Press, 1968).

Huntington, S.P., The Third Wave: Democratization in the Late Twentieth Century (Norman: University of Oklahoma Press, 1991).

Hwang, K.C., Administrative Corruption in the Republic of Korea, Ph.D. Dissertation, School of Public Administration, University of Southern California (1996).

Jun, J.S., "The Paradoxes of Development: Problems of Korea's Transformation," in Bun Woong Kim et al. (eds.), Administrative Dynamics and Development: The Korean Experience (Seoul: Kyobo Publishing, 1985), pp. 56–75.

Jun, J.S. and J.P. Yoon, "Korean Public Administration at a Crossroads: Culture, Development and Change," in Ahmed S. Huque, Jermain T.M. Lam and Jane C.Y. Lee (eds.), Public Administration in the NICs: Challenges and Accomplishments (Basingstoke: Macmillan Press, 1996), pp. 90–113.

Kang, D.C., Crony Capitalism: Corruption and Development in South Korea and the Philippines (Cambridge: Cambridge University Press, 2002).

Kharas, H.J., "The Philippines: Three Decades of Lost Opportunities," in Danny M. Leipziger (ed.), Lessons from East Asia (Ann Arbor: University of Michigan, 1997), pp. 443–479.

Kim, M.-S., "The Bureau of Auditing and Inspection, and Its Role in Social Development," Administrative Dynamics and Development (1985) 405–418.

Kim, M.-S., "Regulation and Corruption," in Yong Hyo Cho and H. George Frederickson (eds.), The White House and the Blue House: Government Reform in the United States and Korea (Lanham: University Press of America, 1997), pp. 253–269.

Kim, Y.J., Bureaucratic Corruption: The Case of Korea, 4th edn. (Seoul: The Chomyung Press, 1994).

Lambsdorff, J.G., "How Precise are Perceived Levels of Corruption?," 2001 available at http://www.gwdg.de/~uw/2001.html.

Lancaster, T.D. and G.R. Montinola, "Toward a Methodology for the Comparative Study of Political Corruption," Unpublished Paper (1997).

Lande, C.H., "The Return of 'People Power' in the Philippines," Journal of Democracy 2001 (12:2) 88–102.

Laothamatas, A. (ed.), Democratization in Southeast and East Asia (Singapore: Institute of Southeast Asian Studies, 1997).

Leiken, R.S., "Controlling the Global Corruption Epidemic," Foreign Policy 1996–1997 (105: Winter): 55–73.

Leipziger, D.M. (ed.), Lessons from East Asia (Ann Arbor: University of Michigan Press, 1997).

Lipset, S.M. (ed.), Democracy in Asia and Africa (Washington, DC: Congressional Quarterly Inc., 1998).

Macdonald, D.S. and D.N. Clark, The Koreans: Contemporary Politics and Society, 3rd edn. (Boulder: Westview Press, 1996).

Magno, A.R., "Philippines: Trauma of a Failed Presidency," in Southeast Asian Affairs 2001 (Singapore: Institute of Southeast Asian Studies, 2001), pp. 251–262.

Marsh, I., J. Blondel and T. Inoguchi (eds.), Democracy, Governance, and Economic Performance: East and Southeast Asia (New York: United Nations University, 1999).

Meyer, J.C. Jr., "A Descriptive Study of Police Corruption," The Police Chief 1973 (40:8) 38–41.

Oh, J.K.-C., Korean Politics: The Quest for Democratization and Economic Development (Ithaca: Cornell University Press, 1999).

Oh, S.H., "The Counter-Corruption Campaign of the Korean Government (1975–1977): Administrative Anti-Corruption Measures of the Seojungshaeshin," in Bun Woong Kim and Wha Joon Rho (eds.), Korean Public Bureaucracy (Seoul: Kyobo Publishing, 1982), pp. 322–344.

Palmier, L., The Control of Bureaucratic Corruption: Case Studies in Asia (New Delhi: Allied Publishers, 1985).

Quah, J.S.T., "Bureaucratic Corruption in the ASEAN Countries: A Comparative Analysis of their Anti-Corruption Strategies," Journal of South-east Asian Studies 1982 (12:1) 153–177.

Quah, J.S.T., Comparing Anti-Corruption Measures in Asian Countries (Singapore: Centre for Advanced Studies, National University of Singapore) CAS Research Paper Series No. 13 (1999a).

Quah, J.S.T., Combating Corruption in Mongolia: Problems and Prospects (Singapore: Department of Political Science, National University of Singapore), Working Paper No. 22 (1999b).

Quah, J.S.T., "Globalization and Corruption Control in Asian Countries: The Case for Divergence," Public Management Review 2001 (3:4) 453–470.

Rahman, A.T.R., "Legal and Administrative Measures Against Bureaucratic Corruption in Asia," in Ledivina V. Carino (ed.), Bureaucratic Corruption in Asia: Causes, Consequences and Control (Quezon City: JMC Press and College of Public Administration, University of the Philippines, 1986), pp. 109–162.

Reid, R.H. and E. Guerrero, Corazon Aquino and the Brushfire Revolution (Baton Rouge: Louisiana State University Press, 1995).

Republic of Korea, Progress and Prospect of Regulation Reform (Seoul: Office of the Prime Minister, 1998).

Republic of Korea, Korea's Comprehensive Anti-Corruption Programs (Seoul: Office of the Prime Minister, 1999).

Revel, J.-F., Democracy Against Itself: The Future of the Democratic Impulse (New York: The Free Press, 1993).

Robinson, T.W. (ed.), Democracy and Development in East Asia: Taiwan, South Korea, and the Philippines (Washington, DC: The American Enterprise Institute Press, 1991).

Rose-Ackerman, S., "Democracy and 'Grand' Corruption," International Social Science Journal 1996 (149:September) 365–380.

Rossant, J., "Dirty Money," Business Week 1995 (18) 25.

Sheehan, D., "More Power to the Powerful," Far Eastern Economic Review 2001 (1) 16–18 and 20.

Sheridan, G., Tigers: Leaders of the New Asia-Pacific (St. Leonards: Allen and Unwin, 1994).

Shin, D.C., Mass Politics and Culture in Democratizing Korea (Cambridge: Cambridge University Press, 1999).

Shin, P., "South Korean President Laments Corruption Scandals Involving His Sons," Yahoo!News, 15 July, 2002, 1–2. See http://story.news.yahoo.com/news?tmpl=story&u=/ap/20020715/ap_wo_en_po/skorea.

Sodaro, Michael J., Comparative Politics: A Global Introduction, International edn. (Singapore: McGraw-Hill, 2001).

Straits Times, "Special team to root out graft among top S. Korean officials," 12 March, 1993, p. 11.

Timberman, D.G., A Changeless Land: Continuity and Change in Philippine Politics (Singapore: Institute of Southeast Asian Studies, 1991).

Torrijos, E.R., "$48B lost to graft in 20 years—WB," Philippine Daily Inquirer, 2 December 1999, 4.

United Nations Development Programme, Fighting Corruption to Improve Governance (New York: UNDP, 1999).

Varela, A.P., "Different Faces of Filipino Administrative Culture," in Proserpina Domingo Tapales and Nestor N. Pilar (eds.), Public Administration by the Year 2000: Looking Back into the Future (Quezon City: College of Public Administration, University of the Philippines, 1995), pp. 161–177.

Woo-Cummings, M., "Developmental Bureaucracy in Comparative Perspective: The Evolution of the Korean Civil Service," in Hyung-Ki Kim et al. (eds.), The Japanese Civil Service and Economic Development: Catalysts of Change (Oxford: Clarendon Press, 1995), pp. 431–458.

State-Corporate Crime, Crimes of Globalization, and Finance Crime

5

Risky Business Revisited: White-Collar Crime and the Orange County Bankruptcy

Susan Will, Henry N. Pontell, and Richard Cheung

Orange County's bankruptcy is the largest governmental bankruptcy in U.S. history. Initial reports blamed the county's financial difficulties on the county treasurer's gambling with taxpayer dollars in the high-risk derivative market. This article forwards the argument that it was not simply "risky business" that caused the bankruptcy; rather, fraud and other forms of white-collar crime played a significant role in the $2 billion debacle. Using concepts and theories from the literature on white-collar crime and drawing comparisons with other financial scandals, most notably the savings and loan crisis, the authors argue that the financial downfall of Orange County was due to a "criminogenic environment" that allowed for concerted ignorance among officials who were motivated by a fear of falling from their positions of power.

On December 6, 1994, officials of Orange County, California, one of the most affluent and fiscally conservative counties in the nation, declared bankruptcy. It was the largest governmental failure in U.S. history. The once heralded "county investment pool" run by Treasurer Robert Citron, which for years had given investors excellent returns, had taken a

"Risky business revisited: White-collar crime and the Orange County bankruptcy," by
Susan Will, Henry N. Pontell, and Richard Cheung from *Crime and Delinquency*, 44(3): 367
(1998). Reprinted by permission of Sage Publications via Copyright Clearance Center.

dramatic fall in value. Losses were estimated to be between $1.5 and $2 billion. Fearing demands from creditors, county supervisors pulled the plug on the operations of the county investment pool and created years of expensive legal maneuvering. Although the Security and Exchange Commission (SEC) is still investigating the role of Wall Street brokers who sold the county risky interest rate sensitive financial instruments known as "derivatives," (1) and federal and local authorities along with the grand jury have announced civil and criminal indictments against several individuals, (2) the central figure in the debacle is former Treasurer Robert Citron, who has pleaded guilty to fraud charges. (3)

Treasurer for more than 20 years, Citron, the lone Democrat in a staunchly conservative Republican government, was considered a "financial guru" for his ability to make investments that outperformed those of other municipalities throughout the state and the nation. In a county that was hungry for revenues in an antitax environment, Citron played the role well. As former Supervisor Thomas Riley put it, "This is a person who has gotten us millions of dollars. I don't know how the hell he does it, but it makes us all look good" (Martinez 1995, A14). Riley and the other supervisors should have known that the way Citron performed his magic was by taking enormous risks with public funds. Instead, because of the political benefits they reaped, they chose to remain ignorant. They looked the other way, ignoring recommendations for increased oversight for, and reporting from, the treasurers' office. As long as Citron did "whatever he did," elected officials could rest comfortably knowing that they would not have to ask their constituents to pay additional taxes to pay for public services. This "head-in-the-sand" strategy worked well for years, with Citron's portfolio generating an estimated $500 million above what would have been earned using the state's more conservative investment strategy (Brazil, Wilgoren, and Lait 1995).

While Citron's central involvement in the bankruptcy as well as his acknowledged criminal actions cannot be denied, we argue that the extent of white-collar crime goes well beyond the behavior of this single individual. A criminogenic environment that allowed Citron and others to breach their fiduciary responsibilities was central in helping cause the massive loss of public funds in Orange County.

California State Senator Lucy Kallea characterized the process by which county officials sought to raise revenues as a "casino,"

> where billions of dollars of public funds were wagered on risky bets and side bets that were touted as safe ones; where one table in particular—the Orange County investment pool—was paying out record winnings. . . . A casino where one of the dealers claims to have advised the gamblers that he was in too deep, yet at the same time the dealer sold more and more chips—and even helped him borrow more money to keep on gambling. (California Legislature 1995, p. 2)

The same language was used to describe the savings and loan debacle (Calavita, Pontell, and Tillman 1997). Both situations were a result of a casino economy (Bianco 1985) in which profits were made from "fiddling" with money (Trillin 1989). Fiddling in both cases consisted of taking huge risks. In the case of Orange County, it meant immense leveraging and using the failed strategy of betting on interest rates through the use of risky financial instruments sold by Wall Street.

A large white-collar crime literature focuses on high-status individuals who, in the course of their occupation, commit crime for personal gain (Cressey 1953; Quinney 1968; Jesilow, Pontell, and Geis 1993). There is also a substantial literature that focuses on organizational crime, primarily corporate crime (Clinard and Yeager 1980; Geis 1977; Vaughan 1983; Ermann and Lundman 1978; Braithwaite 1984). With the exception of Watergate (Bernstein and Woodward 1974; Archer 1975; Cook 1981), Iran-Contra (Bradley 1988; Draper 1991), and Chambliss's (1993) chapter on state organized crime, relatively few studies examine noncorporate organizational white-collar crime committed by public service officials. Most studies of political whitecollar crime typically involve bribery and other forms of corruption by individuals who use their office for personal gain (Friedrichs 1996, pp. 122–23; Chambliss 1988; Simon and Eitzen 1982; Noonan 1984). However, as Watergate clearly illustrates, some officials betray public trust not for personal economic gain but in the belief that they are acting in the best interest of the organization. They justify illegal activity as being connected to some lofty goal that purportedly benefits citizens or the state, such as protecting democracy or saving special programs. In pursuing such goals, generally their power and prestige increases and personal financial gain is incidental (Geis and Meier 1977, p. 210).

In what follows, we document the events leading up to Orange County's bankruptcy, the county's investment practices, the ineffectiveness of the system of checks and balances, and a description of Merrill Lynch's role in the bankruptcy. The article then reconciles these events with research and theory in white-collar crime to show that the bankruptcy was not simply caused by excessive risk taking but by criminal acts as well.

MAJOR EVENTS LEADING
TO BANKRUPTCY

In 1978, Proposition 13—a citizen-sponsored, antitax initiative that won overwhelming public support—slashed property taxes and forced local governments in California to find new ways of raising revenue (Davis 1995; Hofmeister 1995). Further stress was placed on Orange County's budget when, 10 years later, Proposition 98, which mandated specific levels of spending on education without providing resources to cover the expense, was passed. Compounding the effects of a decrease in the tax rate and public revenues on one hand and an increased demand for services on the other was the fact that between 1990 and 1994, private sector jobs decreased by 55,000 in the county while local government grew, adding 6,000 jobs to the payroll (Hofmeister 1995, p. D1).

"Safe" investments did not appear to provide returns high enough to re-place lost revenues; to cover the rising costs for education, health care, and law enforcement; or to provide for increased citizen demands for services. Begin-ning in 1979, through the lobbying efforts of representatives of local govern-ments, including Orange County's Robert Citron, state regulations governing local government investments were loosened to permit counties to borrow heavily and invest in riskier securities (Morain and Bailey 1994). (4) These legislative changes allowed officials to transform traditionally conservative municipal bonds into much riskier higher yield bonds. Accustomed to the traditional conservative nature of municipal bonds, the public and other pub-lic officials alike seemed oblivious to the fact that as yields increased, so did the risks.

Robert Citron gained a reputation for earning some of the highest returns on investments in the country. Credited with a Midas-like touch, he was con-sidered a financial genius and savior for his ability to rescue popular programs by producing unexpected interest income. Citron's portfolio earned the county 17.7 percent in the last six months of 1981 (Kramer, Kelleher, and Christensen 1994, Special Report 2). In the period 1993 to 1994, the investment fund earned 7.7 percent—$666 million, as compared to the 4.39 percent earned by the state treasurer during the same period. (5) The county soon became de-pendent on this high rate of return on its investments. Citron's reputation as an unbeatable investor helped sell the county's investment program to individ-uals, cities, and other county agencies.

As part of his continuing effort to find new ways to earn high returns, Citron looked for loopholes and pushed the limits of the law. For example, in 1987, Citron—in conjunction with Merrill Lynch Money Market Inc. and First Interstate Public Finance Co.—used a loophole in a section of the 1986 federal tax law to create a new device: a Taxable Arbitrage Investment Portfolio (O'Dell 1987). By using the proceeds from the sale of taxable notes to invest in money market securities that paid higher interest, Citron bypassed federal tax laws that bar local and state governments from making a profit from in-vesting the proceeds of tax-free municipal securities.

> The key element of the new procedure, Citron said, is that he will be able to earn a guaranteed profit for the county during the next year without using any county money. Instead, he'll be investing funds "borrowed" from institu-tional investors who buy the interest-paying taxable notes. (O'Dell 1987, p. D3)

Through a delicate balancing act, Citron built a financial house of cards out of structured notes and reverse repurchase agreements that enabled him to eventually leverage the investment pool by a 2 to 1 ratio (Federal Document Clearing House Congressional Testimony [FDCHT] 1995). (6) He took the $7.5 billion invested by the county and 187 participating agencies (7) to buy securities, used the securities as collateral to borrow more money, and used that money to buy still more securities. This borrowed money, primarily in the form of repurchase agreements, eventually brought the fund's total to more than $20 billion. The strategy of borrowing short and investing long worked fine until interest rates rose, but when they did, Citron's financial house of cards collapsed.

With the aid of hindsight, it is clear that for years there were signs that all was not well with the county's investment pool. "From 1990 through 1993, the portfolio turned over an average of 250% a year" with many of the securities "bought and sold within 30 days" (Jereski 1995, p. A8). The county's inability to hold the fund's long-term securities to maturity should have been an indication that something was wrong.

A 1991 audit conducted by Orange County Auditor Steven Lewis "found that $25 million of medium-term notes were sold on June 28, 1991, and similar amounts and types were purchased on July 2, 1991." The auditor was told "that the department had entered into those transactions at the request of the broker, Merrill Lynch, to help the broker meet financial statement ratios required by the Securities and Exchange Commission" (Orange County 1991, p. 3).

Merrill Lynch and those close to the treasurer's office noted other signs of problems with the investment pool. In 1992, Merrill Lynch expressed concern, in an internal memo, that Orange County's collateral of illiquid volatile securities could expose the brokerage house to a loss of millions. Alarmed that the county had 10 times the leverage in its portfolio than they allow in their own, Merrill Lynch's senior vice president in charge of risk management, Daniel T. Napoli, went to Citron in February 1992 to discourage further leveraging of the county's investment pool (Jereski 1995, p. A1).

Analyses of the county's portfolio later in the year revealed that the $4 billion of derivatives and $2.5 billion of borrowed funds made the fund's coupon income very sensitive to rising interest rates. Merrill's risk team predicted that a "one-percentage point move in key short-term rates would slash the fund's yield by more than two percentage points" (Jereski 1995, p. A8). At that very time, Citron was touting his high yields to entice agencies to invest in the fund. He presented the fund "as a low-risk equivalent of a money-market fund. The county fund's investment guidelines stressed safety and liquidity as a 'foremost primary concern'" (Jereski 1995, p. A8).

By the first quarter of 1993, Orange County's portfolio ballooned to $12 billion, half of which was borrowed money. The county's borrowings had increased by 2.6 times since Merrill Lynch warned its officials in February 1992 that the portfolio was too heavily leveraged (Jereski 1995, p. A8).

Worried that pool investors might suspect that their funds were being used for risky investments if they were paid the actual interest that they were earning, Citron, with the aid of a few other county officials, established an "economic uncertainty fund" in the summer of August 1993 to receive excess profits (Maharaj 1996a). (8) The Los Angeles Times reported that through falsification of records and keeping two sets of books, (9) $85 million that was supposed to be allocated to pool participants was diverted into this account (Wilgoren, Platte, and Vrana 1995). At Budget Director Ronald Rubino's trial, Citron testified that his assistant, Matthew Raabe, claimed that this was necessary because "the pool participants would think something was wrong about obtaining [excessively] high [interest] earnings, and feeling that way, they were liable to withdraw their money" (Maharaj 1996a, p. A12). Therefore, a part of their interest was funneled into the uncertainty fund.

Citron's problems escalated in February 1994 when John Moorlach, his opponent for county tax collector-treasurer, raised questions about Citron's practice of investing public money in risky leveraged securities. Moorlach publicly warned that if interest rates continued to rise, the county would incur major financial losses (Lynch 1994, p. 4). The local press ignored his concerns, but The Wall Street Journal gave them exposure, precipitating an investigation by the SEC (Gottschalk 1994). However, the SEC was persuaded that Citron was complying with state law and that it had no jurisdiction in the matter.

About this time, investors were becoming nervous about the security of their funds. When the city of Tustin withdrew $4 million from the pool in April 1994, Citron accused Moorlach and his supporters of masterminding the withdrawal and of "undermining the county's credit rating" and Citron's chances for reelection (Lynch 1994, p. 6). If additional investors pulled out of the fund, it would hemorrhage. New money was now needed to replace the money withdrawn from the account and to cover the decrease in the fund's market value.

In July 1994, Orange County sold an additional $600 million in taxable notes. The Los Angeles Times speculated that part of the proceeds was invested in the fund and part was used to meet collateral calls. A second mysterious account, "9JJ," was opened in July 1994. This account was "set up in the format of a pool participant's account, but no pool participant was designated for it" (Wilgoren et al. 1995, p. A17). In September, the county issued $320 million in bonds purportedly to finance its pension fund. The proceeds of this issue were put into the investment pool.

During fall 1994, the treasurer's office

> transferred risky securities from a highly leveraged county fund into an invest-ment account shared by more than 130 other investors. Although the securities had lost value, the treasurer's office transferred them at "book" or purchase value instead of their actual value, which had the effect of making the transfers appear normal but effectively spread the county's loss among all participants in the commingled pool. (Platte, Wilgoren, and Lait 1995, p. A28)

According to Citron's attorney, Citron did nothing wrong since his philos-ophy was to hold securities to maturity when they could be redeemed for their face value. "At the time that they were transferred, there was no loss. There was no loss based in book value" (Platte et al. 1995, p. A1).

Although the county's Board of Supervisors was supposed to receive regu-lar reports about the activities of the treasurer's office and the investment pool, purportedly it was first alerted to problems with the fund on November 10, 1994. At that time, Ernie Schneider, the county's chief administrative officer, briefed the supervisors with the incredible understatement, "We've got a little liquidity problem with the fund." Citron quickly assured them that, "It's fixable" (Lynch 1994, p. 6).

Citron and his assistant, Raabe, desperate to avoid a run on the fund, tried to soften the news of the investment pool's financial difficulties. They provided the public and investors with as little information as possible (Mulvaney and Lanser 1995). Finally, on December 1, 1994, Citron was forced to disclose that the investment fund had suffered "paper loses" estimated at $1.6 billion. Precipitated by a call for payment under a repurchase agreement with CS First Boston that it could not meet, Orange County and its investment pool each filed for Chapter 9 bankruptcy protection on December 6, 1994.

Throughout this period, Citron, with the aide of others—Ernie Schneider, Ron Rubino, and Matthew Raabe—violated laws. Some of these violations were civil, others were criminal. The system of checks and balances was clearly ineffective.

Although Citron often pushed the limits of the law, few, outside of John Moorlach, seriously questioned the activities in his office. In fact, audits and investigations by the county auditor, the SEC, and Orange County's grand jury that criticized the organizational structure of the treasurer's office, the office's lack of clear policies and procedures, and the county's ineffective system of checks and balances, and raised questions about violations of government codes (GCs), fell on deaf ears. (10)

In his Treasurer Division Report for Audit Year Ending December 31, 1991 (Orange County 1993), Steven Lewis noted many of the same problems that were cited in his 1987 audit and reported an increase in violations of California's GCs. Most of these transgressions were violations of GC 53635—a code designed to protect local government investments. GC 53635 allows no more than 30 percent of surplus money to be invested in medium-term notes. Investments could be made in medium-term notes issued by corporations only if the corporations were owned and operated in the United States and only if they were rated "A" or better. Citron violated each of these conditions (Romney and Weber 1994, p. A30). (11) He then arrogantly informed the county auditor that these violations were conscious decisions made to maximize returns (Orange County 1993, p. 6).

Few changes occurred in the treasurer's office as a result of these audits and reports. Oversight from the Board of Supervisors remained lax. It functioned more as a rubber stamp than as a check against misconduct or as a protector of citizen's funds. In the very year that the supervisors gave Citron the power to use "an aggressive investment strategy that involved heavy borrowing," they permitted him to discontinue reading his annual reports out loud at its meetings (Kramer et al. 1994, Special Report 2). County officials, accustomed to Citron's investment successes, were more likely to seek him out on ways to increase revenues than to censor his activities. The supervisors were comfortable in their ignorance. Even when the county's investment practices were an issue during the 1994 election, the supervisors, who were reaping political benefits by not confronting the county's financial issues, chose not to ruin "a good thing." Former Supervisor Ralph Clark explained the lack of supervision by stating, "you felt a sense of security with him [Citron], and the figures always supported it. . . . There was always money coming in" (Kramer et al. 1994, Special Report 2). In this environment of little or no oversight and an absence of clear procedures, Citron was able to run the treasurer-tax collector's division in any manner that suited him. Maximization of returns for political benefit rather than the protection of public monies was the inevitable result.

Merrill Lynch's involvement with Orange County began in the early 1970s. Over time, it became the brokerage house that conducted the most business with the county. Between 1986 and 1992, sales by Merrill Lynch on behalf of Orange County equaled $1,317,325,000. Business derived from the county accounted for a large portion of the success of its medium-term notes division, as well as other divisions (Weike, Landsbaum, and Lichtblau 1995).

The multiple roles Merrill Lynch played provided a potential conflict of interest. It not only sold bonds for the county but also sold investment instruments to the county, lent the county at least $2 billion, and underwrote bond issues. Each transaction earned commissions for the brokerage house and generated a motive to sell whatever it could, regardless of suitability.

Merrill Lynch disavowed any responsibility for Orange County's bankruptcy, claiming it warned Citron on numerous occasions of potential problems with the portfolio. Time and time again, however, these warnings were followed with offers to sell the county more notes and a willingness to underwrite additional issues for increased fees. In fall 1993, Merrill Lynch warned Citron of the potential dangers with the portfolio, yet that fall it sold another $277 million in inverse floaters to the county (Brazil 1995, p. A1). Early in 1994, despite preparing a 29-page report that clearly cited potential risks with inverse investments, it sold the county another $855 million of the very derivatives that it had warned about. After a February 1994 meeting, at which Merrill Lynch shared its concern about rising interest rates, the brokerage firm underwrote another $125 million in inverse floaters. Each transaction meant more profits for the company (Brazil 1995). San Jose City Attorney Joan Gallo, drawing on her city's experience with Merrill Lynch and gambling on interest rates, explained that officials can get blinded by potential profits because they "don't understand that the brokers are acting in their own interest in pushing profitable products" (Henderson and Fromson 1994, p. 171).

Orange County acted like a gambling addict, while Merrill Lynch and the other brokerage houses behaved like dealers offering a revenue-starved community new chances to win. (12) Once the county was hooked on the "easy" source of revenue, brokerage firms could divert blame from themselves by providing written documentation that they warned of the dangers and tried to dissuade it from purchasing new issues. But how believable is their argument when they were far too willing to provide new issues that increased their corporate wealth while placing the county in greater peril? When asked why they continued to sell these risky investments to Orange County if their own analysis showed potential problems, a spokesman would only say, "Well, that's a legitimate question" (Brazil 1995, p. A23).

Many laws have been established to protect unsophisticated investors, including local governments, from unscrupulous brokers who are all too willing to sell complex and risky instruments. The lawsuit filed by Orange County against Merrill Lynch and other brokerage firms accused the firms of "wantonly and callously" selling high-risk investments in violation of state and federal laws (Jereski 1995). The county maintained that the Investment Company Act of 1940 directs dealers to trade in "suitable" investments. Furthermore, according to Arthur Levitt, chairman of the SEC,

> Broker-dealers that recommend the purchase or sale of a security, are subject both to sales practice standards arising from the anti-fraud provisions of the Federal Securities laws, and to the suitability and other fair dealing rules of the securities self-regulatory organizations. (FDCHT 1995, p. 18)

Merrill Lynch and other firms have settled or lost several suits that have challenged the suitability of the investments that they offered local governments, leading one to believe that the courts are sending a message that brokerage firms must use caution when selling investments for use with public funds (Knetch 1994). (13)

California courts have assumed that brokerage firms know state laws restricting investments and expect that they will not knowingly sell products that violate those laws. Article XVI, Section 18 of the California State Constitution forbids a county from incurring "any indebtedness or liability in any manner or for any purpose exceeding in any year the income and revenue provided for that year." Furthermore, "any county debts or liabilities incurred in violation of these Constitutional and statutory provisions are therefore void" ("Orange County Sues Merrill Lynch" 1995, p. 192). Between June 1993 and December 1994, Orange County had more than $13 billion in reverse repurchase obligations—several times the county's anticipated revenue for that period (Osborne 1995).

Merrill Lynch's legal problems with Orange County extended beyond the issue of suitability. At one point, the relationship between Citron and Stamenson, Merrill Lynch's primary salesman in Orange County, was so good that Citron did favors for Merrill Lynch. A county audit revealed that "Citron made questionable transactions totaling more than $50 million at the request of the (Wall Street) broker, Merrill Lynch, to help the broker meet financial statement ratios required by the SEC" (Romney and Weber 1994, p. A26). In addition to the $50 million changing hands between June and July 1991, the audit uncovered several other transactions in December 1990 and January 1991 that were made "solely to benefit Merrill Lynch, a favored brokerage" (Romney and Weber 1994, p. A26).

Orange County's District Attorney Michael Capizzi announced on June 19, 1997, that he agreed to drop the criminal prosecution against Merrill Lynch as it was willing to pay the county $30 million to avoid prosecution (Grad, Wagner, and Romney 1997, p. A1). This agreement does not prevent the county from continuing to pursue the brokerage through its civil lawsuit, nor does it prevent the SEC from continuing its investigation of Merrill Lynch.

RISKY BUSINESS OR WHITE-COLLAR CRIME?

It seems clear from the events that led up to the county's bankruptcy that multiple factors and persons contributed to the financial crisis. As in the case of the savings and loan debacle, the causes of the county's financial problems can be attributed to poor judgment and mismanagement, desperation gambling, and fraud (Calavita et al. 1997). While it is certainly possible that some individuals, through good intentions or errors in judgment, may have unintentionally caused part of the county's financial crisis, it is true that numerous individuals and groups deliberately engaged in illegal activities. As trial evidence and testimony has come to light, there has been evidence of massive cover-ups. (14) While fraud has played a role in the bankruptcy, the true extent of white-collar crime in the $2 billion debacle remains to be officially determined.

Organizational political white-collar crime should be rare in the United States for two reasons. First, diffuse power within government and governmental organizations would encourage a system of checks and balances and diminish the opportunity for an individual, or small group of individuals, to consolidate enough power to direct illegal activities. Second, political behavior, in contrast to corporate behavior, tends to be more visible, therefore subject to review and criticism (Geis and Meier 1977, p. 207). By not reviewing the treasurer's and auditor's reports during its regular public meetings, the Board of Supervisors precluded the public and the media from voicing their concerns.

For many reasons, the barriers against organizational white-collar crime crumbled in Orange County. The bankruptcy exposed structural conditions and motivations that permitted illegal activities to take place. As a result, Orange County's bankruptcy presents an opportunity to learn about this special type of organizational white-collar crime.

By pleading guilty to six felony counts, including the misappropriation of public funds and the making of false material statements in connection with the sale of securities, Robert Citron reluctantly accepted some responsibility for the debacle. But, he was not willing to shoulder all the blame, nor should he. Regardless of how much autonomy and control Citron had over the investment fund, he could not have caused Orange County's financial disaster by himself. (15)

A focus on Citron obscures the roles of related individuals and groups that enabled his actions, as well as the structural components that provided a criminogenic environment (Needleman and Needleman 1979) and facilitated events leading to the bankruptcy. The environment within Orange County and its government was ripe for insider fraud. Many of the factors present in Orange County correspond to what Black and Pontell (1995) have identified as manifest elements that make insider fraud attractive in financial institutions. (16)

First, given the voters' mandate to be fiscally conservative and to not raise taxes, minimal ethical barriers to insider fraud existed among government officials. County officials failed miserably in overseeing the use of county funds.

At best, they appeared content "not to know" how such high returns were possible. These high returns were used to provide services and helped ensure that the supervisors remained in political favor. Such an environment—where leaders are not fiscally responsible yet need to raise funds to provide services—contains minimal ethical barriers to insider fraud. Swindlers typically attempt to get something for nothing, and, in essence, this is the same mentality that permeated Orange County government. The fiscal conservatism demanded by the public, when coupled with the contradictory need to provide for services without raising taxes, produced exactly the opposite: gross fiscal mismanagement and wild speculation with public funds by elected officials. For years, Orange County officials spoke one way and acted another. County financial practices were anything but fiscally conservative.

Second, the government's laxity in oversight on numerous occasions, even after warnings from different sources including those within its own organizational structure, allowed for virtually complete insider domination by the treasurer. The system of controls in government had broken down to the point where one person had free reign in making investments and reporting on the status of funds. Related to this insider domination was the treasurer's ability to have the investment pool grow quickly. Legislation that expanded the type of investments the county could make allowed funds to increase dramatically over the six years prior to the bankruptcy. Such growth, along with temporary high returns without full disclosure of the high degree of risk, "implies financial success to most people, it leads to favorable media coverage, and the suggestion that the person is unusually gifted" (Black and Pontell 1995, p. 5). This allowed for the continued hiding of losses, the creation of phony income that could lure investors, and keeping those already in the pool from withdrawing their funds. The investment pool was in trouble for years, but by shifting investments and using complex financial instruments such as derivatives, Citron was able to hide the face value of the county's bonds and notes. This ability to dominate and grow also allowed the treasurer to deflect charges of incompetence and fraud and impede detection of his illegal activities, until finally his betting strategy could no longer be hidden; a massive loss in the financial markets exposed the house of cards he had built.

The code of silence, or "concerted ignorance" (Katz 1979), that permeated Orange County governmental offices facilitated unlawful behavior by providing an atmosphere that discouraged questions and criticisms. In this environment, the fiction that Citron's Midas touch would endlessly provide the gold of the realm easily developed and flourished. Since it did not serve their purpose, the Board of Supervisors, county staff and officials, and the public were as unlikely to challenge Citron's magic as the members of the kingdom were ready to tell the emperor that he was not wearing clothes. Clues reverberated throughout county government that set the tone, provided justifications and neutralizations, and gave permission to disregard laws to serve a designated higher good. A former Orange County budget manager testified that he was told, "This is the type of thing, if the grand jury ever asks, you don't want to know" (Maharaj 1996b, p. A1). When he asked if "'everything was all right with this stuff' [the windfall the county was to receive from its investments], his boss replied: 'If they're doing something, this is the thing we honestly don't want to know about'" (Maharaj 1996b, p. A12).

The Board of Supervisors did not have to be told not to ask questions. Its members understood that too much knowledge was dangerous to their political health. By not asking questions, by claiming ignorance of financial matters and the activities of other elected officials, they removed themselves from the uncomfortable position of making hard choices that may have threatened the revenue that Citron was able to garner, and freed themselves from having to make the unpopular move of raising taxes. As long as Citron "did whatever he did," they would not have to increase taxes and their elected positions would be guaranteed. They benefited too much from the interest rate scheme to be a threat. The supervisors realized that the hierarchical structure of the county offered them some protection. Although they were entrusted with oversight of the various county's offices, it suited them to claim ignorance and dependence on experts as a way to protect themselves from criticism. This notion was underscored when Supervisor Steiner testified before the grand jury that he never thought it was his responsibility to supervise the conduct of other elected officials. Furthermore, he ignored Citron's annual reports because, "I was not able to read the volume of material coming across the desk unless someone brought it to my attention" (Weber, Wagner, and Lait 1995, p. A14). The "someone" whom he relied on to bring things to his attention testified that he did not fully understand the ramifications of the paperwork. Once the scandal broke, the supervisors had hoped their demands for investigations and resignations would deflect responsibility and give the appearance that they were protecting the public's interest.

Citron's political opponent Moorlach, on the other hand, threatened the fiction and all elected and appointed members of the county government. He had no obligation to keep silent; rather, it behooved him to speak out. But it was easy to construct him and denounce him as a self-serving opponent. His charges were but enemy propaganda. Those who believed Moorlach but remained silent protected the status quo.

The role of the county auditor, Steven Lewis, provides an interesting variation to the notion of "concerted ignorance." As part of his job, Lewis wrote reports and sent memos to the Board of Supervisors apprising it of some of the problems with the way that the investment pool was run. Although the reports did contain some inflammatory information, the executive summaries—documents that the supervisors were most likely to read—were considerably toned down. In addition, Lewis chose not to push the issues with the supervisors. Ironically, these efforts did not protect Lewis from indictment. Charges were levied against him on the basis that he did not do enough to protect the public trust. At all levels, people learned not to rock the boat. Their concerted ignorance allowed power to be consolidated and checks on illegal behavior to disappear (Katz 1979).

Wheeler (1992), drawing on his work with Weisburd and other colleagues, provides insights that are useful in understanding the motivations of officials' actions in this case. He identifies three models of crime motivation for white-collar criminals: greed, risk seeking, and fear of falling. (17) Outside of campaign contributions from brokerage houses, none of the actors appeared to have profited economically from their role in the events leading up to the bankruptcy. (18) The fear of falling model describes someone who

> would be reasonably happy with the place they have achieved through conventional means if only they could keep that place. But the fate of organizational success and failure, or the changing nature of the economy in their line of work, may put them at least temporarily under great financial pressure, where they risk losing the lifestyle that they have achieved. They may perceive this situation as a short-term threat that can be met through short-term fraud—a temporary taking to be restored as soon as business fortunes turn around. The motivation for their crime is not selfish ego gratification, but rather the fear of falling—of losing what they have worked so hard to gain. (Weisburd, Wheeler, Waring, and Bode 1991, p. 224)

This model does not place stress on getting ahead but rather on avoiding falling back. It applies to those who fear losing status and prestige, as well as those who fear losing money. County officials responsible for the bankruptcy seem to clearly fit this motivational profile for white-collar crime. (19) Citron, who lacked a college degree, savored his reputation as a financial genius. The county's financial house of cards was built partly out of Citron's desire to construct and maintain a favorable reputation. When the house of cards started falling apart, Citron, with the assistance of others, gambled and became involved in an elaborate cover-up as part of their desperate attempts to hold their positions, power, and prestige intact.

Wheeler (1992) believes that the fear of falling model could be extended from a focus on individuals to groups to explain organizational deviance, such as the Watergate break-in. An interview with former Watergate coconspirator, Donald Segretti, lends support to this contention. Segretti, who bent the rules because of perceived pressure to win a presidential campaign, recognized a similar willingness on the behalf of Orange County officials in their quest to raise revenues without raising taxes (Kass 1995).

In sum, structural conditions present in the Orange County government both facilitated organizational deviance and crime and stifled criticism. This criminogenic environment contained an occupational subculture value system that emphasized both the goals of reelection and providing public services without raising taxes. These expectations created an environment conducive to illegal activities.

CONCLUSION

Financial frauds may represent the most complex form of white-collar crime. They can involve myriad financial transactions, vague laws and regulations, and immense paper trails, making the essence of crime—intent—extremely difficult to establish. Recent financial scandals show that many experts who study such matters are not inclined to see them as crimes at all. Instead, they are seen as business ventures gone sour or cases of excessive risk taking, incompetence, or irresponsibility. These characterizations, as Sutherland (1940) noted decades ago, are often questionable. Black, Calavita, and Pontell (1995) have recently demonstrated, for example, that economists' assertions regarding the minimal role of white-collar crime in the savings and loan debacle are refuted by both logic and empirical facts. Black and colleagues used deductive reasoning to distinguish between ordinary business transactions (which can involve risk taking) and white-collar crime, and showed that fraud provides a better explanation for the largest thrift failures than does the risk taking or managerial incompetence models.

As this case study demonstrates, organizational compliance models and policy must seriously consider fraud and malfeasance—not just from individuals within or outside the organization but from the organization itself. That is, regulations must provide for a system of checks and balances at different organizational levels, and laws cannot allow for the concentration of responsibility and power at any single point in the hierarchy. The Orange County bankruptcy demonstrates how the lack of oversight that was built into existing organizational relationships allowed fraud to take place, resulting in the largest municipal government failure in U.S. history. Effective regulation must recognize the potential for such criminogenic organizational environments if social policies are to prevent other debacles and protect public coffers in the future.

Susan Will: *Doctoral Candidate, School of Social Ecology, University of California, Irvine.*

Henry N. Pontell: *Professor of Social Ecology and Social Sciences, and Chair of the Department of Criminology, Law and Society, University of California, Irvine.*

Richard Cheung: *Graduate of the School of Social Ecology, University of California, Irvine, and a law student at the University of San Diego.*

NOTES

1. The Security and Exchange Commission (SEC) decided not to proceed against two of Merrill Lynch's managing directors, Richard M. Fuscone and Robert Simonson; however, it is continuing its investigation of the brokerage and its employee, Michael Stamenson (Mulligan 1997, p. D6).

2. So far, Budget Director Ronald Rubino, Assistant Treasurer Matthew Raabe, County Auditor Steven Lewis, and Supervisors Roger Stanton and William Steiner have been indicted. After the judge declared a mistrial, Rubino pled "no contest" to violating a public records law and was sentenced to two years probation and 100 hours of community service. Raabe was convicted of five felony counts of misappropriating funds, keeping false records, and lying to investigators. He was sentenced to three years in prison and ordered to pay a $10,000 fine. The county prosecutor was ordered by the court to show why Lewis, Stanton, and Steiner should be brought to trial since they were not running for

office and the penalty for the charge against the three—willful misconduct—is removal from office. Charges against Stanton and Steiner were dropped. It is unclear whether Lewis will be prosecuted for his involvement (Maharaj 1997, p. A30).

3. As part of his plea agreement, Citron agreed to cooperate with investigators and testify at Raabe's trial. Citron was ordered to pay a fine of $100,000 and was sentenced to one year in jail. Instead of serving time in jail, he entered a work release program that allows him to spend his nights at home (Maharaj 1997, p. A30). The felony counts to which Robert Citron pleaded guilty are the following: Count 1, using false and misleading statements to sell securities; Count 2, using false statements about the condition and earnings of the county pool to sell $1.39 billion worth of bonds and notes; Count 3, diverting to county accounts more that $80 million in interest earned by pool participants; Count 4, improperly transferring securities that were losing value from a county fund to one including other investors; Count 5, making a false entry or erasure in bookkeeping and accounts that caused false interest statements to be kept or mailed; and Count 6, failing to properly apportion investment interest to pool participants.

4. Since 1987, Merrill Lynch, through its Sacramento lobbyist—the law firm of Orrick, Herrington, & Sutcliff—has been a driving force in the California legislature behind five bills that increased counties' authority to invest in more exotic instruments. Orrick, Herrington, & Sutcliff's involvement extended beyond lobbying. They also served as a bond counsel on at least 15 Orange County bond deals (Morain and Bailey 1994, p. A1).

5. That Orange County's yield was so much higher than the state's became an issue in the election campaign for state treasurer. The Los Angeles Times questioned whether Citron's investment record lived up to his reputation. While Citron's supporters have suggested that "he probably earned an extra $2.02 billion for the county during his 22-year tenure—an amount that would equal the portfolio's spectacular loss— . . . an analysis of his tract record shows that he actually netted . . . at best about a third of that sum" (Brazil, Wilgoren, and Lait 1995, p. A1). A comparison of Orange County's high-risk investment strategy to that of Sacramento revealed that during the past 12 years, Sacramento's investment pool had yields higher than Orange County's half of the time. In addition, the city's 12-year average yield was 9.295 percent, compared to Orange County's slightly better 9.31 percent (Brazil et al. 1995, p. A14).

6. Floating interest rate securities or structured notes were "issued by federal government sponsored entities ("GSEs"), such as Fannie Maes and Sallie Maes. Some of these securities were 'structured' to provide a rate of return equal to a fixed rate less a multiple of a floating rate index, commonly called inverse floaters" (Federal Document Clearing House Congressional Testimony 1995). Reverse repurchase agreements—the sale of a security with an agreement that the security will be repurchased on or before a specific date for a specific amount—along with structured notes made the county's investment pool extremely sensitive to changes in interest rates.

7. These agencies included 28 cities within Orange County, 6 cities from outside the county, 32 school districts, 5 community college districts, 53 special district accounts, and 31 various agencies governed by the Orange County Board of Supervisors and funds sent to the county treasurer by the municipal and superior court systems throughout the county.

8. At this time, the county investment pool was earning 11.5 percent interest, while the more conservative state pool was earning 4 percent (Maharaj 1996b, p. A17). Which county officials were involved with the establishment of the "economic uncertainty fund" is a subject of controversy. A Los Angeles Times article stated that Ernie Schneider, the county's former chief administrative officer, and former Budget Director Ron Rubino helped create the fund (Wilgoren, Platte, and Vrana 1995, p. A1). However, at Rubino's trial, Citron testified that he never told Rubino of his plans to illegally divert funds that belonged to pool participants into the county treasury. In his grand jury testimony, Raabe claimed that Rubino was the developer of the diversion scheme, but Raabe refused to testify at Rubino's

trial on the ground that what he says may incriminate him (Maharaj 1996a, p. A12). It is also believed that Steven Lewis, in his capacity as county auditor, should have had to approve account transfers (Platte, Wilogren, and Lait 1995, p. A29).

9.   One set of books showed the actual amount of interest earned, and the other showed the amount credited to investing agencies (Maharaj 1996b, p. A1).

10.   The 1985 Orange County grand jury report raised concerns about Citron's unregulated power (Orange County Grand Jury 1985, p. 5). In 1987, Orange County's auditor-controller also expressed concern that "the county's investment strategy is designed and carried out by one person, the County Treasurer. At his sole discretion, the county purchases and sells securities, and enters into repurchase and reverse repurchase agreements" (Orange County 1986, p. 11). The audit also noted that items remained unresolved for periods ranging from 30 days to periods in excess of six months (Orange County 1986, p. 12). Particularly troubling, the audit reported that

> The treasurer charges for the cost of the entire Treasurer division and, therefore, not only recovers the cost associated with the investment program, but also charges for the costs of other treasurer operations. . . . Government Code section 27013 [only] allows the treasurer to recover the actual cost of the investment program from those entities for whom he invests. (Orange County 1986, p. 10)

11.   The following violations were cited: (1) The treasurer invested $125 million in Chrysler Corporation medium-term notes that were rated less than "A"; (2) the treasurer invested $80 million in two-year, medium-term notes rated less than "A" issued by GPA Holland, a corporation organized in the Netherlands; and (3) for 10 of 12 months, the percentage of surplus money invested in medium-term notes ranged from 31.5 to 44.6 percent.

12.   Merrill Lynch was but one of many firms eager to sell risky investments to Orange County. Two firms—Bear Steams and Goldman, Sachs & Company—did not participate in the county's high-risk investment strategy. A company policy against selling risky securities to public investment funds prevented Goldman, Sachs & Company from joining in the frenzy of buying, selling, and underwriting instruments for Orange County.

13.   In the City of San Jose v. Paine Webber, E.F. Hutton, Case No. C84-20601 RFP, Northern District of California (1990), the court ruled that the city did not have the authority to purchase reverse repurchase agreements, which were similar to those in the Orange County debacle (Bencivenga 1995). San Jose recovered $12 million from 13 brokerage firms, including Merrill Lynch. Merrill Lynch paid $750,000 to settle the dispute (Hirsch and Pulliam 1994, Special Report 3).

14.   Secrets, secret meetings, and cover-ups became a way of life for many of the county's highest ranking officials. County officials deliberately delayed fulfilling a request by the SEC for documents until after the election. The release of the documents prior to the election would have subjected them to too much scrutiny (Weber, Wagner, and Lait 1995, p. A12).

15.   Apparently, investigators concurred. In addition to charges against Citron's assistant Matthew Raabe, former Budget Director Ron Rubino, Auditor Steven Lewis, and Supervisors Stanton and Steiner, the SEC served Well's notices to several entities in October 1995 asking them to show reason why the SEC should not bring proceedings against them.

16.   Key among these are (1) high liquidity and minimal ethical barriers to insider fraud, (2) insider domination, (3) the ability to grow quickly, (4) the ability to hide losses and create phony income, and (5) the ability to impede detection of illegal activities (Black and Pontell 1995).

17.   Black and Pontell (1995) dichotomize motivation for white-collar crime as based on either "greed" or "need." The need category encompasses "the historically honest owner whose business is about to fail absent fraud" (p. 4). This category is similar to Wheeler's "fear of failing."

18. Brokerage houses and their sales personnel, primarily Merrill Lynch and Michael Stamenson, profited handsomely from their transactions with Orange County. Some individual school districts leveraged their investments with Orange County in the hopes of raking in huge profits. Their officials, like Orange County's, seemed to have been motivated by the prestige and profits generated for their districts rather than by personal financial gain.

19. The fear of falling model does not describe the majority of errant savings and loan operators.

REFERENCES

Archer, Jules. 1975. Watergate: America in Crisis. New York: Crowell.

Bencivenga, Dominic. 1995. "Derivatives Litigation: Suits Claim Higher Suitability Standards Apply." New York Law Journal 213(March 16): 5.

Bernstein, Carl and Bob Woodward. 1974. All the President's Men. New York: Simon and Schuster.

Bianco, Anthony. 1985. "The Casino Society." Business Week, September 16, pp. 78–90.

Black, William K., Kitty Calavita, and Henry N. Pontell. 1995. "The Savings and Loan Debacle of the 1980s: White-Collar Crime or Risky Business?" Law and Policy 17:23–55.

Black, William K. and Henry N. Pontell. 1995. "Regulatory and Economic Incentives for White Collar Crime: The U.S. Savings and Loan and Insurance Crises of the 1980s." University of California, Irvine. Unpublished manuscript.

Bradley, Ben Jr. 1988. Guts and Glory: The Rise and Fall of Oliver North. New York: Fine.

Braithwaite, John. 1984. Corporate Crime in the Pharmaceutical Industry. London: Routledge Kegan Paul.

Brazil, Jeff. 1995. "Broker Warned Citron, Kept Selling Him Bonds." Los Angeles Times, January 15, pp. A1, A22–23.

Brazil, Jeff, Jodi Wilgoren, and Matt Lait. 1995. "Study Casts Doubt on Citron's Fiscal Record." Los Angeles Times, January 8, pp. A1, A14.

Calavita, Kitty, Henry N. Pontell, and Robert Tillman. 1997. Big Money Crime: Fraud and Politics in the Savings and Loan Crisis. Berkeley: University of California Press.

California Legislature, Senate Special Committee on Local Government Investments. 1995. Hearing on the Orange County Bankruptcy. Sacramento, CA: Senate Publications, January 17.

Chambliss, William J. 1988. On the Take: From Petty Crook to Presidents. 2d ed. Bloomington: Indiana University Press.

———. 1993. "State Organized Crime." Pp. 290–314 in Making Law: The State, the Law, and Structural Contradictions, edited by W. J. Chambliss and M. Zatz. Bloomington: Indiana University Press.

Clinard, Marshall B. and Peter Yeager. 1980. Corporate Crime. New York: Free Press.

Cook, Fred J. 1981. The Crimes of Watergate. New York: Franklin Watts.

Cressey, Donald R. 1953. Other People's Money: A Study of the Social Psychology of Embezzlement. Glencoe, IL: Free Press.

Davis, Mike. 1995. "Bankruptcy on the Backs of the Poor: Rotten Orange County." Nation, January 30, p. 4.

Draper, Theodore. 1991. A Very Thin Line: The Iran-Contra Affairs. New York: Hill and Wang.

Ermann, David M. and Richard J. Lundman. 1978. Corporate and Governmental Deviance: Problems of Organizational Behavior in Contemporary Society. New York: Oxford University Press.

Federal Document Clearing House Congressional Testimony (FDCHT). 1995. Testimony of Arthur Levitt, Chairman United States Securities & Exchange Commission, House Municipal Finance. January 12.

Friedrichs, David O. 1996. Trusted Criminals: White Collar Crime in Contemporary Society. Belmont, CA: Wadsworth.

Geis, Gilbert. 1977. "The Heavy Electric Equipment Anti-Trust Case of 1961." Pp. 117–32 in White-Collar Crime, rev. ed., edited by G. Geis and R. F. Meier. New York: Free Press.

Geis, Gilbert and Robert F. Meier, eds. 1977. White-Collar Crime: Offenses in Business, Politics, and the Professions. Rev. ed. New York: Free Press.

Gottschalk, Earl C. Jr. 1994. "Derivatives Roil California Political Race." The Wall Street Journal, April 15, pp. C1, C22.

Grad, Shelby, Michael G. Wagner, and Lee Romney. 1997. "Reactions Mixed to Bankruptcy Accord in O. C." Los Angeles Times, June 20, pp. A1, A18.

Henderson, Nell and Brett D. Fromson. 1994. "Merrill Lynch: The Broker Behind Orange County; Wall Street Giant, Officials Did Billions in Business." The Washington Post, December 10, pp. F1, F7.

Hirsch, Jerry and Liz Pulliam. 1994. "Betting and Losing: Merrill Lynch, Stamenson Dealt Closely With Citron." The Orange County Register, December 8, Special Report p. 3.

Hofmeister, Sallie. 1995. "A Bankruptcy Peculiar to California." The New York Times, January 6, pp. D1, D16.

Jereski, Laura. 1995. "In House Battle: Merrill Lynch Officials Fought Over Curbing Orange County Fund." The Wall Street Journal, April 5, pp. A1, A8.

Jesilow, Paul, Henry N. Pontell, and Gilbert Geis. 1993. Prescription For Profit: How Doctors Defraud Medicaid. Berkeley: University of California Press.

Kass, Jeff. 1995. "In Person; Watergate Figure Sees Past Echoed in O.C. Chaos; Success at Any Cost? Don Segretti Knows Price of Such Policy." Los Angeles Times, September 11, p. B3.

Katz, Jack. 1979. "Concerted Ignorance: The Social Construction of Cover-Up." Urban Life 8: 295–316.

Knetch, G. Bruce. 1994. "Merrill Lynch's Role as Broker to Fund May Expose It to Liability, Lawyer Says." The Wall Street Journal, December 8, p, A13.

Kramer, Jeff, Susan Kelleher, and Kim Christensen. 1994. "Crisis of Confidence: A Gambler Was in Charge of Other People's Money. Citron Seen as Frugal, Took Risks." The Orange County Register, December 11, Special Report pp. 1–3.

Lynch, David J. 1994. "Orange County/How It Happened/How Golden Touch Turned to Crisis." USA Today, December 23, p. 1B.

Maharaj, Davan. 1996a. "Citron's Testimony Back's Rubino." Los Angeles Times, August 21, pp. A1, A12–A13.

———. 1996b. "Rubino Rebuffed Fund Questions, Ex-Aide Says." Los Angeles Times, August 22, pp. A1, A22.

———. 1997. "How They Fared." Los Angeles Times, October 4, p. A30.

Martinez, Gebe. 1995. "Citron, Not Derivatives, Takes Blame at Hearings." Los Angeles Times, January 6, p. A14.

Morain, Dan and Eric Bailey. 1994. "Brokerage Urged More Authority for County Treasurers." Los Angeles Times, December 10, pp. A1, A20.

Mulligan, Thomas S. 1997. "Merrill Ruling Removes Firm's Biggest Cloud." Los Angeles Times, June 20, pp. D1, D6.

Mulvaney, Jim and Jonathan Lanser. 1995. "Ex-Orange Treasurer Meant to Conceal Crisis, Tape Suggests." Sacramento Bee, January 8, p. A7.

Needleman, Martin L. and Carolyn Needleman. 1979. "Organizational Crime: Two Models of Criminogenesis." Sociological Quarterly 20:517–28.

Noonan, John. 1984. Bribes. New York: Macmillan.

O'Dell, John. 1987. "County Will Reap Profits From Arbitrage; Innovative Product Has Guaranteed Returns." Los Angeles Times, August 26, p. D3.

Orange County. 1987. Treasurer Division Report on Examination for Year End Dec. 31, 1986. Unpublished report.

———. 1991. Treasurer Division Report on Audit Year End Dec. 31, 1991. Unpublished report.

Orange County Grand Jury. 1985. Review of Orange County Treasurer/Tax Collector Investment Function. June 26. Unpublished report.

"Orange County Sues Merrill Lynch, Says Firm Breached Fiduciary Duty." 1995. BNA's Banking Report, 64:192.

Osborne, D. M. 1995. "Orange County v. Merrill Lynch: Changing Faces of Municipal Finance." The American Lawyer 17(May): 42.

Platte, Mark, Jodi Wilgoren, and Matt Lait. 1995. "County Shifts Losses Into Pool." Los Angeles Times, January 28, pp. A1, A28–A29.

Quinney, Richard. 1968. "Occupational Structure and Criminal Behavior: Prescription Violations by Retail Pharmacists." Pp. 189–96 in White-Collar Crime, rev. ed., edited by G. Geis. New York: Free Press.

Romney, Lee and Tracy Weber. 1994. "County Was Told in '93 of Treasurer's Risky Strategies." Los Angeles Times, December 9, pp. A1, A30.

Simon, David R. and D. Stanley Eitzen. 1982. Elite Deviance. Boston: Allyn and Bacon.

Sutherland, Edwin H. 1940. "White Collar Criminality." American Sociological Review 5:1.

Trillin, Calvin. 1989. "Zsa Zsa's Crowd Knows Why the Rich and Famous Deserve a Capital-Gains Cut." Los Angeles Times, October 4, p. B7.

Vaughan, Diane. 1983. Controlling Unlawful Organizational Behavior. Chicago: University of Chicago Press.

Weber, Traci, Michael G. Wagner, and Matt Lait. 1995. "How Deceit, Blunders Triggered O.C. Disaster." Los Angeles Times, December 31, pp. A1, A14–A15.

Weike, Dan, Mark Landsbaum, and Eric Lichtblau. 1995. "Donations to O.C. Supervisors Said to be Influential." Los Angeles Times, January 22, p. A1.

Weisburd, David, Stanton Wheeler, Elin Waring, and Nancy Bode. 1991. Crimes of the Middle Classes: White-Collar Offenders in Federal Courts. New Haven, CT: Yale University Press.

Wheeler, Stanton. 1992. "The Problem of White-Collar Crime Motivation," Pp. 108–23 in White-Collar Crime Reconsidered, edited by K. Schlegel and D. Weisburd. Boston: Northeastern University Press.

Wilgoren, Jodi, Mark L. Platte, and Debora Vrana. 1995. "Books May Have Been Falsified." Los Angeles Times, January 22, pp. A1, A17.

6

The Parliamentary Enquiry on Fraud in the Dutch Construction Industry Collusion as Concept Between Corruption and State-Corporate Crime

Grat Van Den Heuvel

In December 2002 the final report of the Royal Commission concerning Irregularities in the Dutch Construction Industry was published. The broadcasting of the public hearings in the months before was breaking news. It proved the whole sector participated in illegal practices, ranging from fraud, unjustified subsidies and license issuance to real bribery and money or favours to individual politicians or higher-ranking public servants; from under-cutting the market, monopolisation and forcing up prices, to selective control by partial inspectorates. In his article the author, an advisor to the Commission, summarises the mayor types of irregularities the report reveals with special interest in the network dimension they had in common. The Commission spoke about collusion as the key problem. Collusion can be described as secret agreement for a fraudulent or deceitful purpose, especially to defeat the course of law. Theoretically this concept can have many faces. In this parliamentary enquiry it was illustrated in three ways: as anti-trust illegalities, as a kind of governmental crime, and as kind of corruption. The report showed a long-lasting structural interrelation between these three types with a special role for the twining between collusion and corruption. Corruption research often mentions collusion as a cause, condition or explanation of corruption. But rarely is that argument illustrated in detail. This article seeks to do so. Especially when corruption is hard to grasp in modern society, a solution could be to take collusion as 'a network offence' more seriously. The collusion subsystems revealed here are relatively stable networks, invulnerable to individualised anti-corruption legislation. The author pleads for stricter rules governing state-corporate interrelationships, more severe control on network abuses, and the introduction of minimum standards for public contracting as proposed by Transparency International.

INTRODUCTION

Early in November 2001, in a television documentary entitled "Sjoemelen met miljoenen" ("Fiddling by the Millions"), a Dutch public broadcasting corporation paid attention to double-entry bookkeeping, slush funds, forced-up prices, illegal prior consultation, cartelisation, bribery and fraud in the construction industry. It was also alleged that corrupt contacts existed between public servants and contractors. Virtually at the same time, the news media reported that three large construction companies had entered into a transaction with the Public Prosecutor's Office to avert prosecution for fraud in connection with the Schiphol Train Tunnel Facility Project. In this transaction, companies had paid a fine of 1,000,000 Euros each. In addition, the three construction companies were to pay back to their client, Dutch Rail (NS), the amount of 5,000,000 Euros each. NS, in turn, was to pay back 25,000,000 Euros to the Dutch Ministry of Transport, Public Works and Water Management (V & W) because of subsidies it should not have received.

This concurrence of events produced such a disconcerting picture that the Lower House of the Dutch Parliament decided to conduct a parliamentary inquiry. The objective of the inquiry was to gain an insight into the nature and extent of the irregularities and the role of the authorities as both client and law enforcer. After preliminary investigations had been conducted, public hearings were held in August and September 2002, in which over 60 witnesses were questioned. These hearings and the Final Report, which came out on 12 December 2002, confirmed the shocking picture the media had presented in the beginning of that year, that the entire sector was in on the fraud and other illegal practices. Management knew about it and authorities helped to perpetuate the system.

In this article, I would like, in my role as co-investigator, to present a synopsis of the case, analyse the conduct of its protagonists and deal with the explicatory theory which the—Parliamentary Commission arrived at. It may be summed up as a 'concept theory' founded on secret deals and relationships; a collusion theory. The Commission distinguished three forms of collusion in the course of its investigations: collusion between contractors themselves, such as illegal price fixing; collusion between the authorities and the construction sector, such as favouring certain contractors; and collusion at the individual level as the pathway to or initial phase in the bribery of public servants, such as the wining and dining of public servants in positions of authority. In the case under discussion, it became evident that one form of collusion followed on from the other. Jointly, they formed a culture, in which those within the sector placed themselves above the law and were able to manipulate the authorities. Where they succeeded, the authorities were also in large part to blame. In this article, I intend to comment on this and make an endeavour to place the collusion theory within a criminological context.

THE SCHIPHOL TUNNEL

What illegal acts were committed by the three construction companies and their clients in building the Schiphol Tunnel? The companies had sent 189 forged invoices for the purpose of transferring the favourable business results of one of them, KSS, to the other two, Strukton and HBW. Through this practice and by sending additional invoices for general costs, transferring interest accrued on liquidity surpluses and directly benefiting the other two in acquisitions, the actual profit of 42,000,000 Euros was brought down to 13,000,000 Euros, a difference of close to 30,000,000 Euros. The decision to lower the profit and deposit it into a slush fund was taken by the Management of the co-operating three companies (PECB, 2003: 213). The decision was not put in writing. In addition to this, there was a second slush fund, which was fed with the proceeds from the sale of surplus materials and VAT returns, for instance when workers bought materials for private trading through the company. The Management of the three companies was aware of this slush fund as well. The auditing accountant had not noticed the irregularities. According to the Management, the motive behind the 30,000,000 Euros was to build up a (hidden) reserve. The Committee deemed it plausible that the idea behind it was to gain a better negotiating position, since fresh negotiations had to be held with NS for each subsequent piece of tunnel. This was the result of the Construction Team Agreement, in which the tender had been worked out. It is a form of tendering on the basis of a skeleton contract, in which the offering and the bidding party, on the basis of open accounts and fair market prices, renegotiate the project and settle the account phase-by-phase. In complex construction projects, this option may be chosen in order to get the work started quickly, although it is an expensive way of tendering; getting rid of the competition always leads to cost increases. Nevertheless, NS chose this course, which becomes understandable in view of the fact that Strukton was a wholly-owned subsidiary of NS and that KSS in turn was a combination of Strukton and HBW. Client and victim in name, NS had also a direct interest therefore in two of the three contractors.

Against the advice of its own construction office, the Ministry of V & W— the granter of the subsidy and the party which ultimately footed the bill for the project—had approved NS' wish, in any case for the first half of the project. Without the Ministry's approval, NS then continued the practice for the second half. When the Ministry found out, it had no other option, it testified, than to 'approve a fait accompli'. In a later stage, NS requested yet a third subsidy of 60,000,000 Euros. The Ministry's Financial and Economic Affairs Office refused to approve the subsidy. Some time later, the then Minister did approve the additional subsidy 'without allowing herself to be well-informed on the matter', according to the Committee. It described the procedure as messy with the Ministry 'being overtaken by events' (PECB, 2003: 280). That, in fact, was an understatement. The Ministry was, after all, familiar with the interconnections. Also for this reason, public servants had recommended a public tender and had advised against the extra money for NS. The Minister decided to go ahead anyway. She gladly granted the sector the overpriced construction work and could not surmise that her decision making would be exposed in such detail because of the contractors' deception.

THE "SHADOW ACCOUNTS"
OF WHISTLEBLOWER BOS

When investigating the Bos ledgers (and subsequently three more shadow accounts), the Commission learned that extraordinary alliances were no exception in the construction world. This case file formed the key to the answers in the Schiphol Tunnel case.

Ex-director Ad Bos of the Koop Tjuchem construction company kept handwritten records of the years 1988–1998, in which all kinds of setoffs with other companies had been entered. These setoffs related to market sharing, price fixing and mutual compensation. Project by project, it was recorded who participated, who was given the work, and how much other bidders were owed or would expect. Prior consultation was always prohibited in the case of public tenders, but until 1986 it was possible in the Netherlands to report cartels. From 1986 onwards, the prohibition was absolute. Practice proved to be different, however. In 1992, the co-operating contractors were fined by the European Commission on the grounds of cartel practices. In spite of this, the practice of cartelisation continued. In 1996, the new Dutch Competition Act (Mededingingswet) expressly affirmed the prohibition, as the Parliamentary

Commission stated, but many did not observe the rules. Virtually all major national contractors figured in the various shadow accounts. This was no clandestine conspiracy between incidental companies within a certain region; this was much bigger: a sector-wide practice, in fact. Cartelisation was known to be prohibited, but it was done anyway; (a) because virtually no control took place, whether by the market or the authorities and (b) it secured profit margins, lowered the risks, facilitated planning and optimally ensured continuity. Cases of failed tenders, a minority, show that Belgian construction companies often worked 30 per cent under the price quoted by Dutch companies and still made a profit.

In the many partial investigations the Commission conducted as a result of the shadow accounts, it uncovered a variety of underlying criminal offences, such as tax fraud and social insurance fraud. Many companies held undisclosed savings accounts. In only very few cases were the contractors not familiar with the standard figures employed by the administration. Public servants and the engineering and law firms advising the administration leaked like a sieve; however, accountability of individuals could not be established. In sum, these were networks of illegal practices in which both clients and contractors were involved. Even the Tender Arbitration Board proved to be far from impartial.

In addition to evidence of secret accounts, whistleblower Bos had detailed lists of money spent on bribes; these were entered into the Koop Tjuchem books as materials or acquisition costs. From his own experience Bos explained to the Committee that such expenditure was considered normal by the sector. His statement was subsequently corroborated by other witnesses. Several million Euros spent annually was seen as nothing out of the ordinary for the larger construction companies.

COLLUSION

Before going into the matter of bribes, it is prudent to first discuss the Committee's collusion approach more in general, and position the approach within a criminological context. According to the Committee:

> The notion of 'collusion' plays a key role in explaining the irregularities in the construction industry. Three meanings have been found in the investigations. The first refers to companies secretly engaging in conspiracy in order to prejudice clients. An example is the price increasing cartels investigated by the Committee.
>
> The second is an indication of a conflict of interests and responsibilities of companies and public services, as a result of which—in the interest of the two, but not necessarily aimed at personal gain—statutes and subordinate regulations are flouted. This form shows the dangers of too intimate a relation between public administrators and officers of public authorities and private enterprise. The Committee encountered many examples of this type of collusion, such as illegal preferential treatment of certain 'friendly' companies.

The third meaning of collusion does not have to do with organisations, but with the conduct of individuals, as the antechamber to corruption and fraud. As a result of the nature of the activities, the frequent contacts between individual public servants and contractors lead to an increased risk of breaches of integrity. (PECB, 2003: 270).

From a socio-scientific perspective, such differentiation as to meaning within a single phenomenon may be referred to as a 'concept theory', in which the sensitising concept is 'collusion', within the meaning of secret arrangements or understandings, and the independent variable the mutual relation between the three.

FORBIDDEN CARTELS

Collusion by proscribed cartels is a distinct criminal category. As early as 1967, Geis gave a very vivid description of the anti-trust cases relating to the heavy electric equipment industry in the US. He outlined the techniques applied and justifications put forward by the sector and painted a clear picture of the vice-president of General [Electric], who was responsible for his company's market behaviour (Geis & Meier, 1977). Subsequently, Clinard and Yeager (1980), Shapiro (1984) and Jamieson (1994) elaborated on this image in more comprehensive studies. According to these investigators, anti-trust law violations formed the most persistent, but also the most lucrative form of corporate crime. Criminal investigation and prosecution of these cases were seen to be fraught with difficulty. Jamieson (1994: 44) found that in the United States in three-quarters of the cases, competitors had instituted proceedings, whereas just one quarter had been uncovered by public agencies. Other results were the following: it was no coincidence that the most inveterate repeat offenders made the most profit and that politics coloured investigative policy at that time as well. Under the Reagan administration, there were 75 per cent fewer convictions than under his predecessor, Carter. Interpreting suspected collusion turned out to be a delicate activity, with possible political overtones (Jamieson, 1994: 88). This also held true for sanctions. In most cases, the damage remained limited to compensation and fines. However, in some cases, members of the management board were held personally responsible on the basis of strict liability, especially in notorious cases. They were sentenced to severe custodial sentences, fines and disqualification from practising their profession (Geis & Meier, 1977: 119/120; Jamieson, 1994: 70). Ian Ayers (1993: 295) conducted research into the internal dynamics of cartels. He pointed out in his research that only extremely severe sentences or extremely high civil claims could in effect keep entrepreneurs from engaging in cartel practices (read also: Posner & Easterbrook, 1981: 336).

This picture is substantiated by these Dutch cases. Although forbidden since 1992, until 1998 cartels were not subject to serious control in the

Netherlands. A small office at the Ministry of Economic Affairs with a handful of employees was charged with the supervision. This could be interpreted in only one way: prosecution of cartel offences had no priority in the Netherlands (Quaedvlieg, 2001: 11). Under pressure from the European Union, an independent supervisory body was established in 1998: the National Anti Trust Authority (NMa). However, until 2002 enforcement had been lax. During the parliamentary hearings, the NMa director admitted that controls were exercised in exceptional cases only. After publication of the Commission's Final Report matters changed. A new director was appointed and new powers were afforded, in part obtained through the courts and in part based on new statutes. From the end of 2003 onwards, all major investigations were reported in the media. In December 2003, some twenty companies that were listed in the Final Report, including major well-established Dutch construction companies, were charged and fines were imposed of over 100,000,000 Euro. In January 2004, all construction companies were encouraged to confess to the NMa before May 1, 2004 to all "cartel sins" committed in the past. If such sins were uncovered after that date, exclusion from future public construction projects would be a possibility. This approach was very successful: on May 3, the NMa announced that four hundred (!) shadow accounts, whose existence had not been known until that date, had been surrendered.

PUBLIC–PRIVATE NETWORK CRIMES

In addition to and ensuing from these cartel offences, there were two other forms of collusion, since these cartel offences were encouraged in part by authorities that were extremely accommodating to construction companies. Without necessity, the authorities would often eliminate competition by putting out projects to private tender only. They also had no objections to all types of unnecessary forms of co-operation between companies or groups of companies. All the above forced up prices. In some instances, public clients allowed themselves needlessly to be placed under pressure of time by contractors, which had a price-increasing effect, or fair distribution of the risk involved was lacking so that the client was disproportionately burdened with such risk. Furthermore, arbitration after a 'niet passend' declaration, by which a bid was rejected, could be described as biased, i.e. in favour of the contractors (PECB, 2003: 262).

The public authority, as the client, was often less than critical where the form of contract and the price were concerned. On the contrary, the authorities were very pliable when it came to the construction industry with its price protecting constructions. Here we encounter the second variant of collusion: institutional conspiracy between public services and the construction industry. Such conspiracy revealed itself, for instance, in the secret favouring of certain construction companies. A classic example was the awarding of work by private

tender exclusively to a group of 'friendly contractors', using the regional employment argument, for instance. It could also consist in a plain good turn done
to one or several contractors by an alderman or engineer of Rijkswaterstaat,
the Public Works Department of the Ministry of Transport, Public Works and
Water Management. The common denominator in all these cases was that free-
market forces were sacrificed and the resulting price increases were taken for
granted. This may be called institutional collusion, not committed, incidentally, at the local level alone. At the national level the double role played by NS
during the construction of the Schiphol Tunnel was also an example of this, as
was the role in that case played by the Minister of V & W.

STATE-CORPORATE CRIMES, COLLUSION AND CORRUPTION

Ronald C. Kramer referred to institutional collusion by public authorities as
state-corporate crimes (Kramer, 1992: 215), solicitation by authorities to commit such illegal acts being the principal form. His study of the space shuttle
Challenger disaster was an example of this. At a later stage, he distinguished,
together with Michalowski, between state-initiated corporate crimes and state-
facilitated corporate crimes (Kramer e.a., 2002: 272/3). From the perspective
of responsibility of superiors, the first category constituted a more serious
offence than the second. As regards the first category, it was the authority
which took the initiative and solicited illegal practices; the second type consisted of collusion patterns, in which the authorities 'merely' served as facilitators and therefore acted as accessories. In his theoretical state-corporate crimes
model, Kramer does not link collusion to corruption. I mention this, because
in much criminological research into corruption, the facilitating or condoning
attitude of the authorities is seen precisely as the core cause of corruption.
Were there two schools of thought on this? In studies of corruption, collusion
by public authorities is indeed referred to as the possible cause of corruption
(Shleifer & Vishny, 1993: 78; Doig, 1995: 55; Goudie & Stasavage, 1998:
153/157; Rose-Ackerman, 1999: 66/67; Vander Beken, 2002: 273; Eigen &
Eigen-Zucchi, 2003: 269); however, these authors seemed so focused on corruption that they offered no separate description of these forms of collusion as
distinct from corruption.

Nevertheless, this was exactly what the Dutch case has taught us:

Collusion involving the authorities formed a separate and complex problem. As stated earlier, it occurred both at institutional and individual level. At
the institutional level, it manifested itself, for instance, where a public authority secretly tolerated illegal practices by companies or where the authorities
gave preferential treatment to certain companies by accepting overpriced
construction bids. Conversely, it was observed that public servants were not
averse to gifts offered by companies. The Parliamentary Inquiry Commission

described this culture of 'grease and feasts' as widespread. Without calling it a bribe, the construction sector spent large sums of money on favours rendered to individual public servants and administrators. Formally, they were not involved in institutional collusion by public authorities, but jointly these acts could be seen as an endemic collusion pattern, in which, institutionally, the authorities 'gave' and 'gave away' too much and the individual public servant 'received' too much. This endemic form of collusion was labelled as such and described for many specific countries. Well known examples—outside the third world—are Japan (Upham, 1987; Mamiya, 1995; Van den Heuvel, 1992), Italy (Savona, 1995; Bufacci & Burgess, 2001; Jones, 2003), United Kingdom (Crowley, 2003), Australia (Dalgliesh, 1995; Royal Commission Cole, 2003, quoted in The Age, 27.3.2003, Building Industry lawless: inquiry), Eastern Europe (Varese, 2000, 2001; Wedel, 2001, 2003) or New York (Jacobs, 1999; Anechiarico & Jacobs, 1996). These were all, direct or indirect, construction related case studies with something 'special' (different culture, political transition, or controlled by the mob) and ending up with the focus on corruption. But here in Holland we got a close up in a typical Rhine-land state without anything 'special'. For years Transparency International has ranked Holland amongst the most non-corrupt states of the world. Its last Global Corruption Report 2005 put special focus on corruption in construction. Although Holland was not mentioned in the special part of this report, in the general corruption perception index, Holland dropped from place 7 in 2003, towards place 11 in 2005. The Dutch media interpreted this drop as mainly caused by the revelations of the inquiry commission.

The Dutch inquiry, preliminary investigations and the hearings revealed a picture of an all too accommodating public sector and a substantial number of high-ranking officials and politicians who enjoyed being showered with lavish gifts. Although only four hard cases of corruption (with traceable services rendered in return) were uncovered, the Commission did encounter a wide range of cases of 'winning over', which reeked of corruption. Air trips to Scotland (to play golf) or Switzerland (to watch ice-skating), the use of yachts with crew, visits to brothels, the use of vacation homes, being regaled with almost new cars, maintenance or doing-up of gardens, or the gratis paving of a driveway, these were things that could not really be seen as the traditional Christmas bonus being delivered in kind.

In Germany, the most comparative neighbour state in Dutch eyes, a series of construction scandals in the beginning of the nineties had led to a boom in prosecutions and publications (Sommermann, 1998; Mohrenschlager, 1996: 829/830; Claussen a.o., 1995; Ludwig, 1992; Pijl, 1988). There a direct link was made between the existence of construction cartels and local corruption. Italian anti-corruption and anti-Mafia legislation had served as an example in the German case. If a municipality had excluded market forces in tenders over a specific lower limit, this was seen as Kollusion, as a form of network offence (Schaupensteiner, 1990, 1993, 1996; Rugemer, 1996, 2003; on network offences in general: Nielsen, 2003). Subsequently, in order to get to the individuals involved as well, the definition of 'administrative corruption' was stretched to include being receptive to serious inducements, formulated, as only the Germans can, as sanktionierung Dankeschon-Bestechung politischer Mandatstrager, which also included public servants with negotiating powers. (The term Bestechung renders any special gift made to a public servant an offence.)

In order to deal also with the individual gift givers much work was done to introduce anti-corruption registers of suspect companies (Schnorr & Wissing, 2002; Notzel, 2002: 53). With the introduction of this new 'black-listing' legislation and penalising network offences, Germany seems to have taken serious steps towards getting a better grip on collusion between public authorities and the business world, both at the institutional and the individual level. Bannenberg and Schaupensteiner, leading experts in this field, are still unsatisfied and predict that in a few years new cases will come out ahead. They plea for more strict regulations with severe sanctions (Bannenberg & Schaupensteiner, 2003).

The Netherlands has not yet progressed to this point and the question is whether such development will happen there in the short term. To prove corruption of a public servant in the Netherlands there must be evidence of a gift or favour on the part of one party, and a demonstrable act in return at individual level on the part of the other. Such clear evidence is found in extreme cases only. Annually five public servants are convicted for bribe or other corruption related crimes (Huberts and Nelen, 2005). Labour law, not criminal law, is the dominant language for most corruption suspects in the Netherlands. Even without hard proof troublesome civil servants can be relieved of office. As in many other countries administrations in the Netherlands avoid the 'hard way' of an official criminal investigation (Kilchling, 2001; Nelen & Nieuwendijk, 2003). In part for these reasons, the Commission called their inquiry an investigation into 'irregularities'. She organised its investigative activities and public hearings in a way which made it possible to map out all the various secret dealings and co-operation patterns, in the full knowledge that it would be very difficult to distinguish provable corruption from all other patterns of abuse and illegal intent.

It was that open space fore collusion rather than hard corruption that played a key part in all this. Institutional and individual collusion were committed frequently, but it was often difficult to separate even these two. Take the civil servant (authorised to put projects out tender) who learns to play golf so that he can negotiate better and who attends golf tournaments organised by contractors in the boss's time. He is not only on a rather slippery slope as a representative of his service, but also as an individual public servant, irrespective of the fact of whether during such a tournament a deal is closed or not.

Cases of collusion were not only uncovered between companies themselves and between public authorities and companies; all kinds of providers of services to both parties were also involved in these collusion patterns, as were tender consultancies, consulting accountants, law firms, architects and project developers. In this national construction scandal, the practice of collusion was, in effect, a case of 'networking above the law'. In the shadow of the collusion, all kinds of illegal practices flourished, ranging from fraud, unjustified subsidies and licence issuance to money or favours to individual politicians or higher-ranking public servants; from undercutting the market, monopolisation and forcing up prices to selective supervision by partial inspectorates.

CONTROL AGENCIES

To control agencies, collusion forms a classic risk. This phenomenon is known among economists as capturing: the encapsulation of the monitoring organisations by the companies under their supervision (Ayers & Braithwaite, 1992). If we look at the investigation into the construction fraud, we find several examples of such capturing at various levels and in various degrees.

I have already referred to the NMa, the authority that monitors competition and anti-trust regulation in the Netherlands. During the hearings, the (now former) director of the organisation, Kist, confessed that, since its establishment, the staff had been kept busy handling all kinds of applications for exemptions and for mergers and forms of co-operation. Hardly any time had been left to monitor competition (PECB, 2003; Verhoren: 1147). Subsequently, this policy underwent a thorough revision under the new board of directors and after new powers had been granted. Since 2003 the Netherlands has a more serious cartel police but 'blacklisting' companies that operate illegally is a bridge to far even for this renewed authority.

The Committee was increasingly surprised by the knowledge accountants possessed in their capacity of auditors about the irregularities in the construction industry. Much was known, but there had been no willingness to attach consequences to this knowledge. Taking action, let alone acting to remedy matters was the exception rather than the rule, even where this was prescribed by statute or called for by their professional code of conduct. They turned a blind eye to structural fraud. The Commission was astonished by the disdain with which some accountants referred during the hearings to the—in their eyes insignificant—amounts that were involved in the illegal set offs, costs of preparatory work and acquisition. The fact that accountants both audited and advised the same company had already been openly criticised, even in the Netherlands (Van Wijk e.a., 2002: 207). These hearings illustrated the consequences of this quasi control.

The Tax Authorities had also contributed to the perpetuation of the competition fraud and the 'grease and feast' culture, a case in point being the deductibility of acquisition costs. However, this public agency could not be seen as colluding, as far as could be detected. It was mainly a case of 'institutional autism'. The Tax Authorities were accused of being too much focused on their own fiscal interest in controlling the books. Where it knew about fraud, it failed to report it. Neither did it report to the Public Prosecutor's Office that palms had been greased. Had the Public Prosecutor's Office been informed of these facts sooner, many irregularities in the construction industry could have been dealt with at an earlier stage. However, even today, the Tax Authorities prefer to keep their role as stool pigeon as limited as possible. Although the Lower House had asked for legal regulation during the parliamentary debates on the Final Report, the Minister of Finance refused to propose such a regulation, arguing that it would curtail the freedom of agency of tax inspectors too much.

Corporate control bodies—compliance offices and works councils—are not discussed here. They do exist, but the inquiry revealed that, where the top management backed certain illegal practices, internal offices were hardly able to counteract it. Individual whistleblowers revealed the irregularities behind the Schiphol Tunnel case and exposed the first shadow accounts. One of the effects of the parliamentary inquiry is that whistleblowers are now protected by a statute modelled on the British Public Interest Disclosure Act 1998 (Tweede Kamer, 2003, nr. 28.990: 12).

The Prosecutor's Office as monitor of corporate crime must be seen as a rarity in general. Its role in this area is limited, although it is vested with appropriate powers. It mainly serves as repressive ultimum remedium if administrative control fails (Ayres and Braithwaite, 1992). The word 'fails' sounds more negative than is intended here. In some instances, the 'big stick' of the criminal law may be used after administrative control has failed, since, unlike administrative inspections, the Public Prosecutor's Office may request the court to impose custodial sentences on those actually in control of the illegal acts. They are able to proceed at a more individual and personal level than would co-operation based control. Deployment of these heavy instruments is intended in particular for the more serious cases, which also serve as a major general deterrent. The organisation of the Dutch Public Prosecutor's Office was not really geared towards this type of criminality, as these cases proved. According to the Commission, the Public Prosecutor's Office had failed in the construction fraud cases. Two years (!) had needlessly been allowed to pass before it had lent an ear to whistleblower Bos. The transaction in the Schiphol Tunnel case was called 'a succession of miscommunications' by the Commission. The joint Procureurs-Generaal (top of the Public Prosecutor's Office) had not provided guidance and communication either to the rank and file involved in these cases, or to the Minister of Justice. Shortly before publication of the final report the Minister withdrew; however, his only mistake was 'not knowing' (PECB, 2003: 157).

Also in this respect, things changed after the publication of the Final Report. Expertise was substantively enlarged at the Functioneeel Parket (the 'White Collar Crime Division' of the Public Prosecution Department). In December 2003, sixteen companies and twelve managing directors were charged in connection with this parliamentary investigation. These cases will not be brought in court before fall 2004/spring 2005.

SELF-JUSTIFICATIONS AND NEUTRALISATIONS, DAMAGE AND VICTIMS

After this tour through the processes and agencies involved, a brief comment on the perpetrators, the damage and the victims is in order. A number of entrepreneurs justified their illegal and fraudulent conduct by claiming that the idea had mainly been to strengthen their own company and make it financially sounder and that such a healthy company was good for the economy: the 'slush funds' were really contingency funds. There had been no extreme self-enrichment and there were no physical victims, so why the fuss? Some even questioned out loud whether holding secret prior consultations was indeed a criminal offence. Such self-justification or neutralisation attempts are well known in criminology (Sykes and Matza, 1957). Responsibility is denied, and so are the unlawful character and the damage inflicted. The illegal practice was inevitable; it was beyond one's control and there had been no intent or evil purpose (Minor, 1981; Benson, 1985; Reichman, 1993). In fact, the arguments strongly resembled those recorded by Geis some forty years earlier (Clinard and Quinney, 1967: 122).

What was observed, however, was the shift that occurred in the neutralisation efforts during and after the inquiry. Initially, the secret arrangements were denied and made little of ('it was not real money; they were jelly beans, just candy'). In a later stage, when the hearings produced more and more evidence of structural and substantial fraudulent practices, in which the entire sector had participated, the persons under investigation began to justify their conduct by referring to history ('in the past, it was allowed, and more recently it had still been somewhat permissible') or the authorities ('I thought they still allowed it') or colleagues ('you had to join in, or you were not a player'). Only after publication of the Final Report did one odd ex-director concede that, although wrong in essence, it also had been very tempting, and that such temptation had caused it to be so pervasive and to continue for such a long time. As far as I know, words of regret were never uttered. What was requested by the chairman of the whole construction sector some time after the Report came out, was the possibility of collectively and conclusively settling all damage incurred by a collective fine. This request was denied by the Public Prosecution Department and the NMa. And rightly so, since even a considerable time afterwards companies voluntarily reported to the NMa, confessing their past 'cartel sins'.

The other side of the justification coin was the actual 'quantifiable' damage: the Commission calculated that the secret prior consultations had resulted in an average price increase of 8.8 per cent. Investigation conducted by the Netherlands Court of Audit showed that construction of government offices had turned out 14 per cent more expensive on average than those in the private sector. The OECD (2002) operated a norm of 'between 15 and 20 per cent' increase in costs due to cartelisation, compared with open markets; sufficient indices, therefore, to refer to the damage as considerable. This is, after all, a sector which turns over many billions of Euros annually, so that 10 per cent or more represents a lot of money. This is without considering the indirect costs of the effects of market undercutting. Most of the damage was inflicted on public authorities. By the end of the year 2003, these had instituted test cases to explore their chances of recovering the money. Smaller municipalities got together and joined their claims, whereas the City of Amsterdam and the Ministries acted separately. In March 2004 BAM, the largest construction company in the Netherlands, disclosed that its profit over the preceding year had been 30 millions Euros less, which could be solely attributed to the fines imposed on it by the NMa as a result of the investigation into fraud committed by the construction industry. It was not prepared or could not say anything about the impact of future civil claims for damages (Volkskrant, 26.3.04). Apart from material damage, there was 'moral' damage. The sector had really showed itself to be dishonest and unreliable. Although damage to reputation is seen as an important guiding tool to call dishonest organisations to order (Fisse & Braithwaite, 1984), I dare to call into question whether this also holds true for the construction fraud case. Perhaps, when the individual criminal cases are heard, these effects will become relevant. In its inquiry, however, the Commission's criticism was particularly aimed at the construction industry as a sector; a sector which had strayed collectively across the board. The investigation and its aftermath pointed at a sector problem, not at persons or separate companies.

CONCLUSION

Only some of the principal elements from the inquiry are explained in this article, which focuses on analysis on the basis of a collusion concept theory. To the Commission, 'collusion' was a relatively novel and vague concept. During the inquiry, it gained definition. It was not a factor, in any case, in the Preparatory Committee formulating the terms of reference. However, gradually and quite naturally, the collusion concept emerged. The Commission distinguished three forms. All three forms were found in rather large numbers. It also turned out that there was a rather strong correlation between the three variants: the cartel practices showed a historically arrogant attitude towards rules and public authority. Collusion between public authorities and business reinforced a convention that seamlessly matched that arrogance. This existed at both the institutional and individual level. Public servants and administrators allowed themselves, whenever convenient, to be personally wined and dined. The fact that this has not led to more criminal cases of corruption prosecution teaches us two things. The standard of proof concerning corruption is even after new legislation in 2001 still high in the Netherlands, whereas 'collusion' is a criminological phenomenon, which may be seen as being separate from corruption.

These two (new) lessons do not detract from the (old) fact that where corruption is established, it may be in part explained by practices of collusion.

In the parliamentary inquiry, a distinction was made between 'corruption' and 'collusion'. In the criminological literature this distinction was often vague. Collusion was too readily seen as synonymous with institutional corruption, whereby institutional corruption in turn was considered a graver offence than individual corruption. With the Report on the parliamentary inquiry into fraud in the construction industry, a new chapter has been added. In the Netherlands, collusion (outside the context of severe threatening crimes like terrorism) is considered less serious than corruption. The word 'corruption' in itself, maybe as part of our protestant heritage, is extremely loaded in any case.

The Committee and its investigators did not set out to compare the Netherlands with Nigeria, Indonesia or even Italy, for that matter. They just wanted to take a thorough look at what went on in the construction industry with the evidence they had been given. They discovered that a lot was wrong in that world, but frequent incidences of provable corruption they did not find. The conclusion that the Netherlands is a country of collusion rather than corruption, can be seen as significant: 'collusion' has connotations of 'not transparent', 'eschewing control', 'selective condoning', 'furtiveness', 'conducive to economic conspiracy and favouritism'. In sum, a rather porous legal order, which calls for much tighter organisation with stricter rules governing business and the authorities. The Commission spoke about the need for a 'new businesslike approach' in dealings between public administrators and the business world (PECB, 2003: 296). This could be translated as: collusion practices must be subjected to more severe administrative regulation and control with clearer links to the criminal law. Preventive ex post control remains insufficient without threatening severe (more German like) ex ante control in the background. And, to begin with, the Transparency International Minimum Standards for Public Contracting have to be taken seriously. They provide a framework for preventing and reducing corruption based on clear rules, transparency and effective control and auditing procedures throughout the contracting process (T.I. Global Corruption Report, 2005).

Indeed, the German approach may serve as an example here. It is unfortunate that the Dutch administration did not wish to adopt it, in addition to all the good measures it had taken as a result of the Report. The government refused to regulate contacts between the authorities and the business world more strictly and to introduce more serious sanctions. In the memorandum Toekomstperspectief Bouwsector (the future of the construction industry) by the three Ministries (Economic Affairs; Spatial Planning, Housing and the Environment; and Transport, Public Works and Water Management, 2003), even less regulation was expressly advocated, as if excessive regulation was to blame for the illegal escapades of these gentlemen. The inquiry did have the effect that certain control agencies (NMa, the accountancy profession and the Public Prosecution Department) tightened their policies (ex post). The parties involved, public authorities and construction companies, have been encouraged to set up a

more fair and honest and a more transparent tender and control practice, and
to discontinue the 'grease and feast' practice. However, without ironclad nor-
malisation and control instruments (ex ante), this remains a risky operation,
especially in the collusion paradise of the Netherlands.

ACKNOWLEDGMENTS

I would like to thank Duncan and Rhonda Chappell, Wies Rayar and the
journal's reviewers for their comments and suggestions.

Grat Van Den Heuvel Faculty of Law, University of Maastricht, P.O. Box 616,
6200 MD Maastricht, The Netherlands

REFERENCES

Anechiarico, F. and J. Jacobs, The Pursuit of Absolute Integrity; How Corruption Control
    Makes Government Ineffective (Chicago: University of Chicago Press, 1996).

Ayres, I., "How Cartels Punish: A Structural Theory of Self-enforcing Collusion," Columbia
    Law Review, 1993 (87: 217), 295–323.

Ayres, I. and J. Braithwaite, Responsive Regulation; Transcending the Deregulation Debate
    (New York: Oxford University Press, 1992).

Bannenberg, B. and W. Schaupensteiner, Korruption in Deutschland. Portrait einer
    Wachstum-branche (Munchen: Beck, 2004).

Benson, M.L., "Denying the Guilty Mind," Criminology, 1985(25), 583–607.

Bufacchi, V. and S. Burgess, Italy Since 1989. Events and Interpretations (London: Palgrave
    MacMillan, 2001).

Claussen, H.R. u.a. (eds), Korruption im offentlichen Dienst (Berlin: Heymann, 1995).

Clinnard, M. and R. Quinney (eds), Criminal Behavior Systems (New York: Holt,
    Rinehart & Winston, 1967).

Clinnard, M. and P. Yaeger, Corporate Crime (New York: Free Press, 1980).

Crowley, T., Construction and Fraud [available via: www.maxima-group.com/a-0509.shtml],
    2003.

Dalgliesh, R., Construction Industry Perspective (Canberra: Australian Institute of Crimi-
    nology, 1995).

Doig, A., "A Fragmented Organizational Approach to Fraud in a European Context:
    The Case of the United Kingdom Public Sector," European Journal on Criminal
    Policy and Research, 1995 (3: 2), 48–64.

Eigen, P. and Chr. Eigen-Zucchi, "Korruption und globale offentliche," Guter PROKLA
    2003 (33: 2), 257–281.

Fisse, B. and J. Braithwaite, The Impact of Publicity on Corporate Offenders (Albany: State
    University of New York Press, 1983).

Geis, G., "The Heavy Electrical Equipment Antitrust Cases of 1961," in G. Geis and R.F.
    Meier (eds), White Collar Crime, Offenses in Business, Politics and the Professions
    (New York: Free Press, 1977), 117–132.

Goudie, A. and D. Stasavage, "A Framework for Analysis of Corruption," Crime, Law & Social Change, 1998 (29), 113–159.

Huberts, L.W. and J.M. Nelen, Corruptie in het Nederlandse openbaar bestuur; Omvang, aard en afdoening (Den Haag: Lemma, 2005).

Jacobs, J. with C. Friel and R. Radick, Gotham Unbound, How New York City was Liberated from the Grip of Organized Crime (New York: New York University Press, 1999).

Jamieson, K., The Organization of Corporate Crime: Dynamics of Anti Trust Violation (London: Sage, 1994).

Jones, T., The Dark Heart of Italy (London: Faber and Faber, 2003).

Kilchling, M., "Tracing, Seizing and Confiscating Proceeds from Corruption (and other Illigal Conduct) Within or Outside the Criminal Justice System," European Journal of Crime, Criminal Law and Criminal Justice, 2001 (9/4), 264–280.

Kramer, R., The Space Shuttle Challenger Explosion; A Case Study of State-Corporate Crime, in K. Schlegel and D. Weisburd (eds), White Collar Crime Reconsided (Boston: Northeastern University Press, 1992), 214–243.

Kramer, R., R. Michalowski and D. Kauzlarich, "The Origins and Development of the Concept and Theory of State-Corporate Crime," Crime & Delinquency, 2002 (48: 2), 263–282.

Ludwig, J., Wirtschaftskriminalitat; Schleichewege zum grossen geld Frankfurt a/M: Fisher., 1992.

Mamiya, J., Government and Contractors Prove: It Takes Two to 'Dango' Tokyo Business Today July 1995, 28–31.

Minor, W.W., "Techniques of Neutralization: A Reconceptualization and Empirical Examination," Journal of Research in Crime and Delinquency, 1981 (18), 295–318.

Mohrenschlager, M., "Strafrechtliche Vorhaben zur Bekampfung der Korruption auf nationaler und internationaler," Ebene Juristen Zeitung, 1996, 822–831.

Nelen, H. and A. Nieuwendijk, Geen ABC, Analyse van rijksrechercheonderzoeken naar ambtelijke en bestuurlijke corruptie (Den Haag: BOOM, 2003).

Nielsen, R.P., "Corruption Networks and Implications for Ethical Corruption Reform," Journal of Business Ethics, 2003 (42), 125–149.

Notzel, M., Investigation Strategies and Tactics in the Prosecution of Corruption Offences: Experiences from Germany, in C. Fijnaut and L. Huberts (eds.), Corruption, Integrety and Law Enforcement (The Hague: Kluwer, 2002) 49–58.

OESO, Competiton Committee on Effective Action Against Hard Core Cartels—Second Report (Paris: Oeso ed., 2002).

PECB (Parlementaire Enquete Commissie Bouwnijverheid), De Bouw uit de Schaduw (Eindrapport, Den Haag: SDU, 2003).

PECB (Parlementaire Enquete Commissie Bouwnijverheid), De Bouw uit de Schaduw; deel 2 (Verhoren, Den Haag: SDU, 2003).

Pijl, D., "Corruptiebestrijding dient serieus genomen te worden," in W. Valkenburg en A. de Weert (red) Corruptie, verschijningsvormen, opsporing, bestrijding en voorkoming (Lelystad: Vermande, 1998) 59–74.

Posner, R. and F. Easterbrook, Antitrust, Cases, Economics, Notes and Other Materials (New York: Columbia University Press, 1981).

Quaedvlieg, H., Ondernemende autoriteiten? Een onderzoek naar de handhaving van het Nederlandse en communautaire kartelrecht (Deventer: Kluwer, 2001).

Reichman, N., Insider Trading, in M. Tonry and A.J. Reiss Jr (eds.), Beyond the Law (Chicago: University of Chicago Press, 1993), 55–96.

Rose-Ackerman, S., Corruption and Government; Causes, Consequences and Reform (Cambridge: Cambridge University Press, 1999).

Rugemer, W., "La Justice Allemande et la," Corruption Deviance et Societe, 1996 (20: 3), 275–290.

Rugemer, W., "Global Corruption," PROKLA 2003 (33: 2), 235–256.

Savona, E.U., "Beyond Criminal Law in Devising Anticorruption Policies; Lessons from the Italian Experience," European Journal on Criminal Policy and Research, 1995 (3: 2), 20–37.

Schaupensteiner, W., Korruptions—Kartelle Kriminalsitik, 1990, 509–515.

Schaupensteiner, W., "Submissionsabsprachen und Korruption im offentlichen," Bauwesen Zeitschrift fur Rechtspolitik, hft 1993 (7), 250–162.

Schaupensteiner, W., "Gezamtconzept zur Eindammung der Korruption," Neue Zeitschrift fur Strafrecht, 1996, 409–416.

Schnorr, S. and V. Wissing, "Korruptionsbekampfung," Zeitschrift fur Rechtspolitik, heft 2002 (6), 279–280.

Shapiro, S., The Wayward Capitalists (New Haven: Yale University Press, 1984).

Shleifer, A. and R. Vishny, "Corruption," Quaterly Journal of Economics, 1993 (108: 3), 599–617.

Sommermann, K.P., "Brauchen wir eine Ethik des offentlichren Dienstes?," Verwaltungs Archiv, 1998, 290–305.

Sykes, G.M. and D. Matza, "Techniques of Neutralization: A Theory of Delinquency," American Sociological Review, 1957 (22), 664–670.

Transparency International, Global Corruption Report, Corruption in the construction and post-conflict reconstruction (London: Pluto Press, 2005).

Upham, F.K., Law and Social Change in Post-War Japan (Harvard: Harvard University Press, 1987).

Van den Heuvel, G., Corporate Crime in East and West: in Search of Collusion, in H. Strang and J. Vernon (eds), International Trends in Crime: East Meets West (Canberra: AIC, 1992), 212–137.

Vander Beken, T., "A Multidisciplinary Approach for Detection and Investigation of Corruption," in C. Fijnaut and L. Huberts (eds), Corruption, Integrity and Law Enforcement (The Hague: Kluwer Law International, 2002), 269–282.

Van Wijk, J. e.a., Opdeugdelijke grondslag; een explorerende studie naar de private forensische accountancy (Zeist: Kerckebosch, 2002).

Varese, F., Pervasive Corruption, Economic Crime in Russia (The Hague: Kluwer Law International, 2000) in A. Ledeneva, M. Kurkchiyan 99–112.

Varese, F., The Russian Maffia. Private Protection in a New Market Economy (Oxford: Oxford University Press, 2001).

Wedel, J.R., Collision and Collusion: The Strange Case of Western Aid to Eastern Europe (New York: Palgrave, 2001).

Wedel, J.R., "Corruption and Organized Crime in Post-Communist States: New Ways of Manifesting Old Patterns," Trends in Organized Crime, 2003 (7: 1), 3–61.

7

Globalization and the Federal Prosecution of White Collar Crime (Twelfth Survey of White Collar Crime)

Ellen S. Podgor

Congress needs to incorporate international provisions into the federal white collar crime laws it drafts to provide the courts with clear guidance when prosecutors attempt to enforce the law beyond US borders. Federal criminal law is expanding within the US, and US criminal law is being increasingly applied to persons outside the US. Generic extraterritoriality clauses in statutes fail to provide courts and the world guidance on whether the particular statute can and will be enforced outside the US. Economic globalization dictates that white collar crime laws address these issues.

I. INTRODUCTION

Legal literature on the federalization of criminal law has grown significantly in the last two years. (1) Noteworthy in this discussion are references to increases in the number of federal crimes, (2) the number of federal prosecutors, (3) and

"Globalization and the Federal Prosecution of White Collar Crime" by Ellen S. Podgor from *American Criminal Law Review,* Vol. 32, No. 2, pp. 325–346. Reprinted with permission of the publisher, American Criminal Law Review © 1997.

the number of criminal actions in federal courts. (4) This scholarship often reflects upon federal prosecution of what were traditionally considered state and local offenses. (5) Although United States v. Lopez (6) provides a landmark case for the halting of federal criminal jurisdiction's extension into the province of local criminal activities, (7) the federal prosecution of state and local activities remains a matter of concern. (8)

There is, however, another aspect to the increase in federal criminal jurisdiction that is omitted from most of the recent discussions on federalization. This is the increase (9) and anticipated growth (10) in federal investigations and prosecutions involving international activities. (11) Unlike the expansion of federal power into areas traditionally considered state and local activities, the government's entry into the realm of international activity does not present overlapping jurisdictional concerns within the United States.

This Essay focuses on the "international flavor" (12) that is developing in the prosecution of white collar crime. (13) The discussion is limited to prosecutions by the United States, as opposed to white collar offenses that may be prosecuted by foreign entities. (14)

This Essay considers two approaches that allow for an expansion of federal white collar prosecutions involving international activities. (15) First, one finds legislative language that provides a clear indication that extraterritoriality is intended to be covered by the statute. In this regard, one sees the enactment of specific statutes with a direct international focus, (16) and statutes that are not directly addressing international criminality, but instead incorporate extraterritoriality provisions within the statute. (17) Although this first approach is premised upon legislative action that expressly provides for extraterritoriality, judicial interpretation may be necessary to ascertain the scope of the extraterritoriality provision.

In the second approach, one finds judicial interpretation of criminal statutes permitting an international component. (18) In this second grouping, the statute does not directly address extraterritoriality, which leaves courts to discern whether the silence was intended as a prohibition of external application.

In addition to congressional and judicial acceptance of these prosecutions, procedural expediency also impacts the increase in ability to prosecute white collar crimes that have an international perspective. (19) Equally influential is the executive role in these prosecutions. The prosecutorial prerogative can, of course, be impacted by legislation and court precedent.

Whether the statute provides for extraterritoriality or is silent on the subject, in allowing an external application, it is also necessary that the conduct fall within the legitimate scope of U.S. jurisdiction. (20) Although there are five bases for jurisdiction accepted in international law, the United States has been more limited in its acceptance of principles of international jurisdiction. (21) Where Congress has formally addressed extraterritoriality in the statute or focused the entire statute on international activities, courts will often bypass an examination of the jurisdiction's legitimacy under principles of international law. Questions relating to the propriety of U.S. jurisdiction under international principles are most often seen in cases where courts are attempting to discern whether the congressional intent was to provide for an extraterritorial application. (22)

An array of issues accompanies the prosecution of white collar crime with an "international flavor." (23) This Essay considers a sampling of the jurisdictional questions that have arisen as a result of white collar criminal activity exceeding the borders of the United States. (24) Ambiguity in statutes as well as insignificant case law often provide little guidance in resolving these issues.

Congressional consideration of the international implications to federal criminal statutes is needed. (25) Substantive issues that arise as a result of alleged criminal activity transcending the borders of the United States must be resolved. This is particularly true with respect to white collar crime because the global economy facilitates both criminal activity and its prosecution. (26) Equally important is the necessity to place restraints on the type of white collar international activities that will be subject to U.S. federal prosecution.

II. INCORPORATING EXTRATERRITORIALITY INTO WHITE COLLAR OFFENSES BY DIRECT LEGISLATIVE ACTION

A. Statutes Directly Focused on International Activities

Where Congress explicitly enacts a statute with the intent to control conduct occurring outside its borders, the decision to focus on international activity is clear. In the white collar area, several criminal statutes fall within this realm. (27) Perhaps the most noteworthy is the Foreign Corrupt Practices Act. (28)

The Foreign Corrupt Practices Act, enacted in 1977, prohibits certain foreign trade practices by issuers (29) and domestic concerns. (30) The Act contains both accounting and anti-bribery provisions. (31) Watergate's exposure of major corporations bribing of foreign officials served as the impetus for the passage of the Act. (32) The Foreign Corrupt Practices Act was intended to curtail these huge payments being made by U.S. companies to foreign officials. (33) The Act has been criticized on occasion by the business community, which argues that the Act places U.S. businesses at a competitive disadvantage in the international business market. (34) The United States is the "only major economy that has laws barring companies from paying bribes abroad." (35) Although such bribery may be technically illegal in a foreign jurisdiction, in some countries it is accepted as a common practice. (36)

The Act was amended in 1988, resolving certain ambiguities in the statute and in some instances limiting the conduct that the statute could reach. (37) Payments made as part of "routine governmental action" (38) now focus on the "purpose or nature of the payment" as opposed to the "status of recipient." (39)

The amendments offer an affirmative defense when the payment is lawful under the laws of the foreign official's country and when the payments are "bona fide expenditures." (40) The amendments also eliminate a "has reason to know" standard in the statute, requiring that the acts be committed "knowingly." (41) Willful blindness, however, will not serve as an excuse. (42)

In United States v. Castle, (43) the Fifth Circuit Court of Appeals stated that Congress deliberately excluded foreign officials who accept bribes from the Act's imposition of criminality. (44) Although international law permits this extension, Congress was "equally aware of, and actively considered, the 'inherent jurisdictional, enforcement, and diplomatic difficulties' raised by the application of the bill to non-citizens of the United States." (45) In Castle, the court held that prosecutors could not circumvent Congress' omission of foreign officials from the statute, by charging foreign officials under the general conspiracy statute (46) with conspiring to violate the Foreign Corrupt Practices Act. (47)

When Congress drafts a statute specifically focused on international activities, it is likely that there has been congressional reflection on the international ramifications of the criminal application. The enactment of the Foreign Corrupt Practices Act demonstrates a clear intent on the part of Congress to transcend the borders of the United States with regard to specific conduct. Congress has, however, tailored the statute to encompass limited conduct and individuals. In Castle, the court noted that "[m]ost likely Congress made this choice because U.S. businesses were perceived to be the aggressors, and the efforts expended in resolving the diplomatic, jurisdictional, and enforcement difficulties that would arise upon the prosecution of foreign officials was not worth the minimal deterrent value of such prosecutions." (48)

B. Extraterritoriality Provisions

Statutes with specific provisions of extraterritoriality also leave no doubt of Congress' intent to reach outside the borders of the United States. (49) Because the statute itself is focused on activities both within and outside of the United States, the conduct and individuals to whom the statute applies usually remain constant. Unlike a statute specifically focused on international activities, such as the Foreign Corrupt Practices Act, a statute with an extraterritoriality provision is seldom specifically tailored to address the concern of unchecked prosecutorial discretion in the international sphere. (50) Prosecutors are left to apply the generic provisions of the statute without examination of the international implications of the prosecution. (51)

In the context of white collar crime, there exists an array of statutes with extraterritorial provisions. (52) These statutes encompass a spectrum from specific to broad provisions that permit extraterritoriality. Extraterritorial provisions can also be found in procedural statutes. (53)

A statute may include extraterritoriality with respect to a specific aspect of the statute. For example, the central perjury statute (54) provides that "[t]his section is applicable whether the statement or subscription is made within or without the United States." (55) A statute may specifically limit the scope of criminality by delineating individuals that can serve as a basis for extraterritoriality. For example, the "Prohibitions With Respect to Biological Weapons" statute provides that "[t]here is extraterritorial Federal jurisdiction over an offense under this section committed by or against a national of the United States." (56) In a money laundering statute, Congress permitted extraterritoriality if, "(1) the conduct is by a United States citizen or, in the case of a non-United States citizen, the conduct occurs in part in the United States; and (2) the transaction or series of related transactions involves funds or monetary instruments of a value exceeding $10,000." (57)

Other statutes include general words of extraterritoriality, allowing the entire statute to be applied to conduct outside the United States. (58) For example, the false declarations statute provides that "[t]his section is applicable whether the conduct occurred within or without the United States." (59) General words of extraterritoriality are seen in statutes such as the witness tampering statute, which provides that "[t]here is extraterritorial Federal jurisdiction over an offense under this section." (60)

Some criminal statutes use the term "foreign commerce," (61) offering a jurisdictional hook when the conduct transcends the borders of the United States. One finds this term in several white collar offenses. (62) In United States v. Braverman, (63) a case involving transportation in foreign commerce of counterfeit money orders, (64) the Second Circuit Court of Appeals noted that, "[t]here would seem to be no logical reason for holding that Congress intended to punish those who cause the violation of a law regulating and protecting foreign commerce only when they act within the borders of the United States. . . ." (65)

Congressional intent is also clearly indicated when Congress explicitly places a territorial limitation in the statute. For example, the "Assaults Within Maritime and Territorial Jurisdiction" statute requires that the conduct occur "within the special maritime and territorial jurisdiction of the United States." (66) Express limitations within a statute can preclude extraterritorial application. (67)

Although explicit reference in a statute to extraterritoriality provides some guidance in answering the initial question of whether Congress intended an extraterritorial application, it often does not clarify the extent to which extraterritoriality will be permitted. With the exception of statutes such as money laundering, (68) there are few extraterritorial provisions that specifically reflect a recognition that U.S. citizens should be examined differently than non-citizens. One does not find explicit statutory language considering distinctions between citizens being either the perpetrator or the victim of the criminal acts. Generic expressions of extraterritoriality do not for the most part offer consideration of the political and foreign relations ramifications.

III. INCORPORATING EXTRATERRITORIALITY INTO WHITE COLLAR DEFENSES BY JUDICIAL INTERPRETATION

The haziest area involves instances where Congress does not specifically focus on international criminal activities in enacting legislation (69) and where the statute omits any reference to extraterritoriality. The failure of Congress to directly address the application of extraterritoriality can result in the presentation of this issue to a court when a prosecutor uses the statute to prosecute activities that transcend the borders of the United States. In some instances, courts will not be determining the international application of the entire statute, but rather a specific element of the offense.

The general rule is that, absent an express intent on the part of Congress to regulate conduct abroad, federal law does not apply extraterritorially. (70) As with hearsay, however, the exceptions and qualifiers consume the rule itself. (71) Offenses posing a threat to national security, such as those involving espionage, are interpreted to allow for extraterritoriality, despite the fact that Congress did not expressly state an extraterritorial application in the statute. (72) A merchant vessel provides jurisdiction to the sovereignty under whose flag it flies for acts occurring on the vessel, despite its presence in the navigable waters of another sovereignty. (73) Frauds against the government are assumed to "include by implication acts committed in foreign countries." (74) Thus, conspiracies prosecuted under the "conspiracy to defraud" section of 18 U.S.C. [sections] 371 are given extraterritorial effect. (75) If the effect of limiting a statute to acts within the United States would greatly curtail the usefulness of the statute, intent to legislate extraterritorially is inferred. (76)

In United States v. Bowman, (77) the Supreme Court provided a two-part analysis for determining extraterritoriality when a statute is silent on the issue. The Court stated that "[t]he necessary locus, when not specifically defined, depends upon the purpose of Congress as evinced by the description and nature of the crime (78) and upon the territorial limitations upon the power and jurisdiction of a government to punish crime under the law of nations." (79) In a later case applying Bowman, the Fourth Circuit stated that "crimes against the peace and good order of the community apply only to acts committed within the territorial jurisdiction of the United States unless Congress directs otherwise; in contrast laws punishing fraud against the government include by implication acts committed in foreign countries." (80) The Court in Bowman permitted an extraterritorial application against U.S. citizens, finding "no offense to the dignity or right of sovereignty of Brazil to hold them for this crime against the government to which they owe allegiance." (81)

The holding in Bowman is particularly applicable to white collar cases involving international frauds against the United States. It is cited in support of extraterritoriality for crimes involving theft of government property and conspiracy. (82) Bowman also served as the basis for a court finding jurisdiction in a bankruptcy concealment prosecution. The court in Stegeman v. United States (83) noted that 18 U.S.C. [sections] 152 "was enacted to serve important interests of government, not merely to protect individuals who might be harmed by the prohibited conduct." (84) The court noted that the section was not premised upon locality and that "[t]o exclude concealments by debtors outside the United States from the statute's coverage would frustrate the statute's purpose by creating an obvious and readily available means of evasion." (85)

Bowman has been distinguished when the acts are committed by people other than U.S. citizens. (86) This distinction, however, does not always preclude an extraterritorial application. When there is a clear indication that Congress intended that the statute apply extraterritorially, a court will allow its external application despite the fact that foreign citizens are being subject to prosecution. For example, a foreign citizen making a false statement in a visa application to an American consular in a foreign country is not immune from prosecution. (87) It has been found that since visa applications are routinely made outside the United States, Congress "contemplated" that a statute prohibiting this conduct would be applied extraterritorially. (88)

Recently, in United States v. Boots, (89) the First Circuit Court of Appeals refused to apply the wire fraud statute (90) to a scheme to deprive a foreign government of its taxes. (91) Distinguishing between schemes involving domestic tax fraud and frauds against private foreign businesses and individuals, the court noted the ramifications of applying the wire fraud statute to a scheme relating to foreign revenue laws. (92) The court stated that "[o]f particular concern is the principle of noninterference by the federal courts in the legislative and executive branches' exercise of their foreign policymaking powers." (93) In the context of white collar crime, issues have also been raised concerning whether specific provisions in a statute can be applied extraterritorially. In United States v. Parness, (94) the Second Circuit Court of Appeals examined whether the "enterprise" element of the Racketeer Influenced and Corrupt Organization Act (RICO) (95) was limited to domestic enterprises. (96) Although the definition of "enterprise" (97) does not specify whether the term applies only to domestic enterprises, the court found that the legislative history called for a broad reading of the statute. (98) The court in Parness found that this legislative history "leaves no doubt that Congress intended to deal generally with the influences of organized crime on the American economy and not merely with its infiltration into domestic enterprises." (99) In permitting an extraterritorial application of the "enterprise" element of RICO, (100) the court noted that a contrary construction would "permit those whose actions ravage the American economy to escape prosecution simply by investing the proceeds of their ill-gotten gains in a foreign enterprise." (101) The court also commented that this application "cannot conceivably endanger American foreign relations." (102)

Whether a foreign entity is subject to U.S. jurisdiction also was an issue in one court's analysis of an element of the bank fraud statute. (103) In United

States v. Lewis, (104) the Ninth Circuit Court of Appeals confronted the issue of whether the bank fraud statute applied to a foreign bank's branch that was chartered by a state. In a case of "first impression," (105) the court found that merely because a bank is "subject to regulation, examination and supervision by the Federal Government," (106) does not mean the bank is "federally chartered." In reversing a bank fraud conviction, the court in Lewis found that a bank operating under an Oregon state charter was neither federally insured nor federally chartered, thus not operating "under the laws of the United States within the meaning of [sections] 1 344(b)(5)" for purposes of the bank fraud statute. (107)

When a statute is silent as to its external application, courts bear the ultimate responsibility of determining the congressional intent. (108) Since Congress has often failed to focus on extraterritoriality in drafting statutes, courts are frequently left to consider the international ramifications of an extraterritorial application. (109) Once a determination has been made that Congress intended for extraterritorial application of a statute, the jury is left to decide whether the government has proven the jurisdictional elements contained within the statute and the existence of a sufficient nexus between the alleged criminal conduct and the United States. (110)

IV. JURISDICTIONAL BASES FOR UNITED STATES PROSECUTION OF EXTRATERRITORIAL WHITE COLLAR CRIME

On occasion, international principles are also examined by the courts to ascertain whether the conduct and individuals involved in the alleged criminality should be the subject of an extraterritorial application. (111) The RESTATEMENT (THIRD) OF THE FOREIGN RELATIONS LAW OF THE UNITED STATES (112) provides that "[u]nder international law, a state is subject to limitations on (a) jurisdiction to prescribe . . . (b) jurisdiction to adjudicate . . . [and] (c) jurisdiction to enforce." (113) As a limitation on the "jurisdiction to prescribe," courts consider whether the extraterritorial application is "unreasonable." (114) There is, however, no direct constitutional prohibition against extraterritoriality. (115)

Whether it is proper to determine congressional intent for extraterritoriality prior to ascertaining the international law basis for jurisdiction is unclear. Some courts focus on the congressional intent before examining the jurisdictional bases, (116) while other courts claim that there needs to be a jurisdictional source before Congress can act. (117) Some courts only examine the congressional intent and finding an express allocation for extraterritoriality never reflect upon its propriety under international principles of jurisdiction.

There are five generally recognized bases of "jurisdiction to prescribe" under international law. (118) These are the territorial, nationality, protective, universality, and passive personality principles. (119) In some cases courts premise jurisdiction on more than one principle. (120)

The primary principle applied by U.S. courts is the territorial principle. (121) The territorial principle has in recent years been termed the "objective territorial principle." (122) The principle, as defined by Justice Holmes in the case of Strassheim v. Daily, (123) states that "[a]cts done outside a jurisdiction, but intended to produce and producing detrimental effects within it, justify a state in punishing the cause of the harm as if he had been present at the effect, if the state should succeed in getting him within its power." (124)

The protective principle is premised upon a national interest or national security being threatened or injured by the conduct. (125) It is distinguishable from the objective territorial principle, in noting that with the protective principle, "all the elements of the crime occur in the foreign country and jurisdiction exists because these actions have a 'potentially adverse effect' upon security or governmental functions, and there need not be any actual effect in the country as would be required under the objective territorial principle." (126)

In the context of white collar crime, an extraterritorial application premised on "protective jurisdiction" was found in United States v. Birch, (127) a case involving extraterritorial forgery or false use of government documents. (128) Despite the fact that the conduct occurred in Germany, the court in Birch held that "the national interest is injured by falsification of its official documents." (129) The court found that "protective jurisdiction" was proper even where the indictment alleged that the defendants "intended to use the forgeries to deceive foreign officials and airline employees." (130) Likewise, when proceeding against an individual on a charge of a false statement under oath in a visa application, (131) the Second Circuit Court of Appeals found that the protective principle permitted prosecutions against aliens who commit the perjury in a foreign country. (132) Both the territorial and protective principles have been used in enforcing some of the income tax laws in the United States. (133)

The nationality principle permits a country to assert jurisdiction over the conduct of its nationals anywhere. (134) This principle was recognized in a white collar case premised upon the false statement statute. (135) The court in United States v. Walczak (136) noted that false statements on customs forms, although made outside the United States, were within the literal language of the statute. (137) The court stated that the nationality principle applied because "American authority over [U.S. citizens] could be based upon the allegiance they owe this country and its laws if the statute concerned . . . evinces a legislative intent to control actions within and without the United States." (138) The passive personality principle allows "jurisdiction on the basis of the nationality of the victim." (139) It is utilized for conduct that harms a citizen outside of his or her country. (140) The universality principle authorizes jurisdiction for crimes against humanity irrespective of the location of the offense. (141)

In addition to the bases of jurisdiction, international law also provides limitations that can assist courts in deciding whether extraterritoriality is proper. (142) Legislators need to be cognizant of these principles in drafting extraterritoriality provisions. For example, consideration needs to be given to respecting the sovereignty of other countries. Likewise, issues of human rights should not be overlooked. (143)

V. CONCLUSION

The globalization of the world necessitates that Congress consider international implications when drafting statutes. (144) A myriad of questions need to be resolved. (145) For example, should the United States be at the forefront of criminalizing activities, as in the Foreign Corrupt Practices Act? Should deference be given to laws of other countries? (146) Should both citizens and non-citizens be subject to criminality under a statute? Will non-citizens be afforded the constitutional rights given to citizens? (147) What are the political and foreign relations ramifications of imposing criminality on conduct occurring outside the borders of the United States? (148)

As prosecutors increase criminal prosecutions that include international activity, (149) a growing need arises to ascertain the limits of U.S. jurisdiction. Explicit congressional reflection can assist all parties and the courts in resolving these issues. (150) Placing generic provisions of extraterritoriality in a criminal statute fails to consider which individuals will be subject to prosecution. Generic provisions also do not offer legislative guidance on the international implications in prosecuting specific conduct. The complexity of international relations necessitates an examination in the context of each statute to determine whether an external application is warranted and necessary.

In the context of white collar crime, it is particularly important to provide explicit legislative guidance for prosecuting international activities. White collar crime is complex by nature. (151) The line between what will be considered civil and what will be subject to criminal prosecution is often "blurred." (152) Business practices are increasingly scrutinized as criminal violations. (153) The rules in white collar crime are often not easily discernable, with issues of statutory interpretation commonly a question. (154) It is in the white collar crime context that two recent Supreme Court cases have recognized that ignorance of the law may excuse. (155) Before proceeding into the international arena with white collar prosecutions, there needs to be a clear understanding of what is considered criminal conduct subject to U.S. prosecution and what is not encompassed within our jurisdiction.

Decisions regarding the applicability of a statute to foreign activities should not be left to prosecutorial discretion. (156) Prosecutors, although part of the executive branch of government that participates in foreign policymaking, do not serve as the decisionmakers or facilitators in determining the role of the

United States in international affairs. (157) Yet, absent clear legislative guidance, prosecutors are left to influence international relations by their decisions to prosecute activity outside the United States. (158) This expanding federal jurisdiction needs to be monitored, not only with respect to the inclusion of state and local activities, but also with respect to activities with an "international flavor." (159)

Ellen S. Podgor, Professor of Law, Georgia State University College of Law; 3 B.S. 1973, Syracuse University; J.D. 1976, Indiana University School of Law at Indianapolis; M.B.A. 1987, University of Chicago; L.L.M. 1989, Temple University School of Law. The author wishes to thank Georgia State University College of Law for its support during the drafting of this Essay. Thanks also go to the 1996 Temple-Tel Aviv Summer Program, including co-directors Burt Caine and Omri Yadlin, and to the students who participated in the class "White Collar Crime from a Global Perspective." Special thanks go to Dean Eli Lederman of Tel Aviv University Buchmann Faculty of Law for his thoughtful comments during the initial drafting stages of this Essay. Thanks also go to Professors Natsu Jenga, Ray Lanier, and Charles Marvin of Georgia State University College of Law for their helpful comments on a later draft.

NOTES

1. See, e.g., Symposium: Federalism and the Criminal Justice System, 98 W. Va. L. Rev. 757 (1996); The Federal Role in Criminal Law, 543 Annals Am. Acad. Pol. & Soc. Sci. 9 (ed. J. Strazzella Jan. 1996); Symposium-Federalization of Crime: The Roles of the Federal and State Governments in the Criminal Justice System, 46 Hastings L.J. 965 (1995); Peter J. Henning, Forward: Statutory Interpretation and the Federalization of Criminal Law, 86 J. Crim. L. & Crimilogogy 1167 (1996).

2. Sara Sun Beale, Federalizing Crime: Assessing the Impact on the Federal Courts, 543 Annals Am. Acad. Pol. & Soc. Sci. 39, 42–44 (1996) ("[b]y the mid-1990s, there were more than 3000 federal crimes").

3. Id. at 45 (noting that the number of federal prosecutors in United States Attorney's Offices increased from approximately 3000 in the mid-1970's to over 8000 by the middle of the 1990's).

4. Id. at 45–46; cf. Rory K. Little, Myths and Principles of Federalization, 46 Hastings L.J. 1029 (1995) (discussing arguments for and against federalization of crimes, and advocating federalization in instances of "demonstrated state failure").

5. See, e.g., Kathleen F. Brickey, Criminal Mischief: The Federalization of American Criminal Law, 46 Hastings L.J. 1135 (1995).

6. 115 S.Ct. 1624 (1995).

7. The Court held that the Gun-Free School Zones Act exceeded Congress' Commerce Clause authority.

8. See, e.g., Kathleen F. Brickey, Crime Control and the Commerce Clause: Life After Lopez, 46 Case W. Res. L. Rev. 801 (1996) (discussion of cases after Lopez).

9. In addition to the increase in prosecutions, it has also been argued that courts have "expanded the traditional bases of jurisdiction over extraterritorial crimes. The major

impetus behind that expansion is the burgeoning problem of extraterritorial conspiracies to import narcotics into the United States." Christopher L. Blakesley, A Conceptual Framework for Extradition and Jurisdiction Over Extraterritorial Crimes, 1984 Utah L. Rev. 685 (1984).

10.   The globalization of certain human activities in the world is apparent. One sees an increase in communication, international trade, and international travel. It is only natural to assume that there will be an increase in both international criminal activities and in the prosecution thereof. Professor Ethan A. Nadelmann notes that, "[l]aw enforcement, traditionally a domestic function of government, has become more internationalized. Police and prosecutors who rarely dealt with their foreign counterparts now do so with increasing frequency." Ethan A. Nadelmann, The Role of the United States in the International Enforcement of Criminal Law, 31 Harv. Int'l L.J. 37 (1990); see also David Johnston, Strength Is Seen in a U.S. Export: Law Enforcement, N.Y. Times, Apr. 17, 1995, at A1, A8 ("American law enforcement agencies are rapidly expanding oversees, deploying agents to dozens of countries in scores of joint investigations."); R. Jeffrey Smith & Thomas W. Lippman, FBI Plans to Expand Overseas, Wash. Post, Aug. 20, 1996, at A1 ("Domestic law enforcement specialists at the Federal Bureau of Investigation are planning to nearly double their presence overseas during the next four years, opening offices in 23 foreign cities to cope with what they say is a dramatic expansion of international terrorism, organized crime and narcotics trafficking that affects U.S. citizens.").

11.   Businesses in the United States are subject to an "increased exposure to criminal liability." Bruce Zagaris, Avoiding Criminal Liability in the Conduct of International Business, 21 Wm. Mitchell L. Rev. 749, 752 (1996) ("Export control and economic sanctions present another clear example of the globalization impact of criminal liability."). "Increasingly, modern crime is international crime." Report of the ABA Task Force on Teaching International Criminal Law, 5 Crim. L. F. 91, 91 (1994). Recent international white collar crime cases also demonstrate the government's entry into new areas. See Ronald Smothers, U.S. Gets a Break in Curbing Nigeria Business Fraud Schemes, N.Y. Times, Mar. 24, 1996, at A34 ("A Nigerian man was sentenced to two and half years in prison, to be followed by deportation, on Friday in what Federal investigators say is the first arrest and conviction related to international business fraud schemes emanating from the African nation."); Florida Executive Is Convicted of Overseas Securities Fraud, N.Y. Times, May 9, 1996, at D8 ("A Florida executive has been convicted of securities fraud in what the Securities and Exchange Commission said today was the first criminal case involving a scheme to avoid registering securities under a regulation governing sales to foreigners.").

12.   Professor Lea Brilmayer also uses the term "international flavor" in her article. Lea Brilmayer, The Extraterritorial Application of American Law: A Methodological and Constitutional Appraisal, 50 Law & Contemp. Probs. 11, 12 (1987).

13.   For purposes of this Essay, the term white collar crime is defined using an offense-based approach, as opposed to focusing on the status of the offender. A November, 1986 Bureau of Justice Statistics Special Report defines the term as:

> [N]onviolent crime for financial gain committed by means of deception by persons whose occupational status is entrepreneurial, professional or semi-professional and utilizing their special occupational skills and opportunities; also, nonviolent crime for financial gain utilizing deception and committed by anyone having special technical and professional knowledge of business and government, irrespective of the person's occupation.

Donald A. Manson, Bureau of Justice Statistics Special Report, Tracking Offenders: White-Collar Crime 2 (1986). The term white collar crime was originally coined by Edwin Sutherland in a speech given to the American Sociological Society in 1939. Reprinted in Edwin H. Sutherland, White-Collar Criminality, 5 Am. Soc. Rev. 1 (1940). In a later book, he stated that it "may be defined approximately as a crime committed by a person of respectability and high social status in the course of his occupation." Edwin H. Sutherland, White Collar Crime: The Uncut Version 7 (1983). Since Sutherland's use of the term, an array of definitions have been given to describe white collar crime. See generally David T. Johnson & Richard A. Leo, The Yale White-Collar Crime Project: A Review and Critique, 18 Law and Soc. Inquiry 63 (1993) (reviewing various definitions of white collar crime); Jerold H. Israel, Ellen S. Podgor, & Paul D. Borman, White Collar Crime: Law and Practice 1–11 (1996) (same).

14.   This Essay also does not reflect upon issues of venue once jurisdiction has been permitted. See 18 U.S.C. [sections] 3238 (1994) (outlining venue rules for offenders whose alleged crimes are committed abroad).

15.   In her article, Professor Lea Brilmayer describes the "relevant considerations" as "legislative intent," "presumptions," "international law," "judicial discretionary doctrines," and the "Constitution." Lea Brilmayer, supra note 12, at 14–16.

16.   See infra notes 27–48 and accompanying text.

17.   See infra notes 49–68 and accompanying text.

18.   See infra notes 69–110 and accompanying text.

19.   This Essay is not focused on procedural aspects of prosecuting white collar crime. Clearly the globalization of organized activities in the world and increased cooperation between countries has facilitated the ability to prosecute white collar international activities. See generally, Robert L. Pisani & Robert Fogelnest, The United States Treaties on Mutual Assistance in Criminal Matters, in International Criminal Law: A Guide to United States Practice and Procedure (V.P. Nanda & M.C. Bassiouni eds., 1987) (explaining the mutual assistance treaties granting the United States government access to evidence abroad); It's a Small World for Foreign Depositions, 10 BNA Crim. Prac. Manual 194 (1996) (discussing the ability of the United States government to depose witnesses abroad); Bradley O. Field, Comment, Improving International Evidence-Gathering Methods: Piercing Bank Secrecy Laws from Switzerland to the Caribbean and Beyond, 15 Loy. L.A. Int'l. & Comp. L.J. 691 (1993) (examining the means by which the United States obtains evidence from foreign banks under mutual assistance treaties).

20.   One author notes that an exercise of extraterritorial jurisdiction requires three elements, that being:

> It must first be established that Congress has the authority to create penal legislation having extraterritorial effect. Second, the government must show that Congress intended a particular statute to have effect beyond the borders of this country. Finally, it must be determined that such an extension into the sovereign bounds of another nation is permissible under one of the jurisdictional theories of international law.

Mark Peterson, Note, The Extraterritorial Effect of Federal Criminal Statutes: Offenses Directed at Members of Congress, 6 Hastings Int'l & Comp. L. Rev. 773, 776–77 (1983) (emphasis in original) (citation omitted).

21.   See infra notes 111–143 and accompanying text.

22.   See infra notes 127–138 and accompanying text; see also 1 Farhad Malekian, International Criminal Law: The Legal and Critical Analysis of International Crimes (1991) (general background).

23.   Brilmayer, supra note 12, at 12. In addition to substantive issues of law, procedural issues also arise in the prosecution of international white collar crime. For example, conflict of laws issues can arise when a foreign jurisdiction orders documents not to be released, while the United States orders the release of the same documents. See United

States v. Chase Manhattan Bank, 590 F. Supp. 1160, 1160 (S.D.N.Y. 1984) ("[O]rder of Hong Kong courts not to produce summoned documents did not preclude holding the bank in civil contempt."). But see United States v. First Nat'l Bank of Chicago, 699 F.2d 341 (7th Cir. 1981) (court should use a balancing test to determine if person should be required to produce information where person will be subjected to criminal sanctions in a foreign jurisdiction for the production). There are an array of issues raised when the government attempts to secure documents in a foreign jurisdiction. See United States v. Barona, 56 F.3d 1087 (9th Cir. 1995) (whether foreign wiretaps should be subject to the Fourth Amendment); In re Sealed Cases, 832 F.2d 1268 (D.C. Cir. 1987) (production of foreign company records); United States v. Davis, 767 F.2d 1025 (2d Cir. 1985) (confrontation clause issues related to records).

24. See infra notes 139–141 and accompanying text.

25. See infra notes 144–150 and accompanying text.

26. Other areas of criminality are also significantly impacted by globalization. "American law enforcement is being exported in response to the surge of international terrorism, narcotics trafficking, links between terrorists and drug dealers, illegal immigrant smuggling, financial fraud, corruption, arms smuggling, money laundering and the potential theft and sale of nuclear material and chemically and biologically hazardous substances." Johnston, supra note 10, at A1; see also R. Robin McDonald, International Securities Fraud Probe Targets Marietta Woman, Atl. Const., May 27, 1996, at D1 (describing the international securities fraud investigation of an American couple suspected of planning to sell firearms to South Africa).

27. See, e.g., Foreign Corrupt Practices Act (key provisions can be found at 15 U.S.C. [subsections] 78dd-1, 78dd-2, 78ff (1994)); Export Administration Act (50 U.S.C. [subsections] 2401–2420 (1994)); Arms Export Control Act (22 U.S.C. [subsections] 2751–2799aa-2 (1994)). There are also specific statutes pertaining to issues of foreign affairs. For example, statutes exist regarding Espionage and Censorship, 18 U.S.C. [subsections] 792–799 (1994), and Foreign Relations, 18 U.S.C. [subsections] 951–970 (1994). Not all of these statutes expressly provide for extraterritoriality. See United States v. Zehe, 601 E Supp. 196 (1985) (Espionage Act could be applied extraterritorially although no provision of the act explicitly so states).

28. Key provisions can be found at 15 U.S.C. [subsections] 78dd-1, 78dd-2, 78ff.

29. 15 U.S.C. [sections] 78dd-1(a) (1994) ("It shall be unlawful for any issuer which has a class of securities registered pursuant to section 781 of this title or which is required to file reports under section 780(d) of this tide, or for any officer, director, employee, or agent of such issuer or any stockholder thereof acting on behalf of such issuer. . . .").

30. 15 U.S.C. [sections] 78dd-2.

31. Donald R. Cruver notes:

The "foreign corrupt practices" prohibited by the Act have five separate elements:

1. the use of an instrumentality of interstate commerce (such as the telephone, telex, telecopies, air transportation, or the mail) in furtherance of

2. a payment of, or even an offer to pay, "anything of value," directly or indirectly

3. to any foreign official, foreign political party, or foreign political candidate

4. if purpose of the payment is the "corrupt" one of getting the recipient to act (or to refrain from acting)

5. in such a way as to assist the company in obtaining or retaining business or in directing business to any particular person.

Donald R. Cruver, Complying with the Foreign Corrupt Practices Act 15 (1994).

32. Id. at 1.

33. Id. at 1–2.

34. See Marlise Simons, U.S. Enlists Other Rich Countries in a Move to End Business Bribes to Foreign Officials, N.Y. Times, Apr. 12, 1996, at A7 ("Large American companies, including General Electric and Boeing, have openly complained that they have difficulty competing for contracts with European rivals who are free to use bribes."). "Several United States corporations seeking modifications to the strictures of the Act have complained that the FCPA constitutes an export disincentive and places them at a competitive disadvantage with respect to foreign corporations conducting international operations." Roben James Gareis & William Joseph Linkletter, The Foreign Corrupt Practices Act: A Pragmatic Analysis, in International Trade-Avoiding Criminal Risks [subsections] 13-9 to -10 (W.M. Hannay ed., 1991).

35. Id. Recently the twenty-six members of the Organization for Economic Cooperation and Development (OECD) agreed to rewrite their tax laws to disallow deductions for payoffs and kickbacks as foreign business expenses. Id.; see also Beverley Earle, The United States' Foreign Corrupt Practices Act and the OECD Anti-Bribery Recommendation: When Moral Suasion Won't Work Try the Money Argument, 14 Dick. J. Int'l L. 207 (1996) (discussing FCPA as the lone voice of reform in the international arena of business transactions). The American Bar Association recently passed a resolution that "supports efforts by the international community, by national governments, and by non-governmental organizations to encourage the adoption and implementation of effective legal measures and mechanisms to deter corrupt practices in the conduct of international business." Jay M. Vogelson, Corrupt Practices in the Conduct of International Business, Section Recommendations and Reports-American Bar Association Section of International Law and Practice Reports to the House of Delegates, 30 Int'l L. 193 (1996) (these recommendations were adopted by the ABA House of Delegates in February of 1995).

36. The Foreign Corrupt Practices Act can result in United States businesspeople being criminally liable under United States law for what may, in some instances, be considered "ordinary course of business" in that country.

37. See Cruver, supra note 31, at 15–18.

38. The exception for "routine governmental action" provides that, "Subsection (a) of this section shall not apply to any facilitating or expediting payment to a foreign official, political party, or party official the purpose of which is to expedite or to secure the performance of a routine governmental action by a foreign official, political party, of party official." 15 U.S.C. [sections] 78dd-1(b) (1994). This same provision appears in the statute regarding prohibited foreign trade practices by domestic concerns. 15 U.S.C. [sections] 78dd-2(b) (1994).

39. See Cruver, supra note 31, at 16.

40. The Act provides for the following affirmative defenses:

It shall be an affirmative defense to actions under subsection (a) of this section that—

1. the payment, gift, offer, or promise of anything of value that was made, was lawful under the written laws and regulations of the foreign official's, political party's, party official's, or candidate's country; or

2. the payment, gift, offer, or promise of anything of value that was made, was a reasonable and bona fide expenditure, such as travel and lodging expenses, incurred by or on behalf of a foreign official, party, party official, or candidate and was directly related to—

   (A) the promotion, demonstration, or explanation of products or services; or

   (B) the execution or performance of a contract with a foreign government or agency thereof.

15 U.S.C. [subsections] 78dd-1(c) (1994). This same provision appears in the statute regarding prohibited foreign trade practices by domestic concerns. 15 U.S.C. [subsections] 78dd-2(c) (1994).

41. In defining "knowing" the Act provides:

> (A) A person's state of mind is "knowing" with respect to conduct, a circumstance, or a result if—
>
>> (i) such person is aware that such person is engaging in such conduct, that such circumstances exists, or that such result is substantially certain to occur; or
>>
>> (ii) such person has a firm belief that such circumstance exists or that such result is substantially certain to occur.
>
> (B) When knowledge of the existence of a particular circumstance is required for an offense, such knowledge is established if a person is aware of a high probability of the existence of such circumstance, unless the person actually believes that such circumstance does not exist.

15 U.S.C. [sections] 78dd-1(f) (1994). This same provision appears in the statute regarding prohibited foreign trade practices by domestic concerns. See 15 U.S.C. [subsections] 78dd-2(h) (1994).

42. See generally Amarjeet S. Bhachu, Note, Foreign Corrupt Practices Act, 32 Am. Crim. L. Rev. 445, 450 (1995) (discussing the intent standard of the Act).

43. 925 F.2d 831 (5th Cir. 1991).

44. Id. at 834–36. "Given that Congress included virtually every possible person connected to the payments except foreign officials, it is only logical to conclude that Congress affirmatively chose to exempt this small class of persons from prosecution." Id. at 835.

45. Id. In speaking of "non-citizens" the court was only referring to Congress' exemption of "foreign officials" from prosecution under this statute.

46. 18 U.S.C. [sections] 371 (1994).

47. See Castle, 925 F.2d at 836 (5th Cir. 1991). Conspiracy charges can be used in prosecuting United States companies. Lockheed Corp. recently pled "guilty to federal conspiracy charges in connection with a bribe paid to an Egyptian legislator for assisting the company in obtaining a $79 million contract for the sale of three transport planes to the Egyptian government." Foreign Corrupt Practices, 2 Bus. Crimes Bull. Compliance & Litig. 8 (Mar. 1995). The Acts of Terrorism Transcending National Boundaries statute specifically states that, "[t]here is extraterritorial Federal jurisdiction—(1) over any offense under subsection (a), including any threat, attempt, or conspiracy to commit each offense; and. . . ." 18 U.S.C. [sections] 2332(e) (1994).

48. Castle, 925 F.2d at 835. The court also noted that "foreign nations could and should prosecute their own officials for accepting bribes." Id. at 836. In Israel Aircraft Industries, Ltd, v. Sanwa Business Credit, 16 F.3d 198 (9th Cir. 1994), the court held that a provision of the Export Administration Act did not provide a private right of action for those claiming to be victims of foreign boycotts.

49. See, e.g., 18 U.S.C. [subsections] 2331-39A (1994) (Terrorism).

50. The Final Report of the National Commission on Reform of Federal Criminal Laws proposed a Federal Criminal Code that contained an express provision on extraterritorial jurisdiction:

> [sections] 208. Extraterritorial Jurisdiction. Except as otherwise expressly provided by statute or treaty, extraterritorial jurisdiction over an offense exists when:
>
> (a) one of the following is a victim or intended victim of a crime or violence: the President of the United States, the President-elect, the Vice-President, or, if there is no Vice-President, the officer next in the order of succession to the office of President of the United States, the Vice-President-elect, or any individual who is acting as President under the Constitution and laws of the United States, a candidate for

President or Vice-President or any member or member designate of the President's cabinet, or a member of Congress, or a federal judge;

(b) the offense is treason, or is espionage or sabotage by a national of the United States;

(c) the offense consists of a forgery or counterfeiting, or an uttering of forged copies or counterfeits, of the seals, Currency, instruments of credit, stamps, passports, or public documents issued by the United States; or perjury or a false statement in an official proceeding of the United States; or a false statement in a matter within the jurisdiction of the government of the United States; or other fraud against the United States, or a theft of property in which the United States has an interest, or, if committed by a national or resident of the United States, any other obstruction of or interference with United States government function;

(d) the accused participates outside the United States in a federal offense committed in whole or in part within the United States, or the offense constitutes an attempt, solicitation, or conspiracy to commit a federal offense within the United States;

(e) the offense is a federal offense involving entry of persons or property into the United States;

(f) the offense is committed by a federal public servant who is outside the territory of the United States because of his official duties or by a member of his household residing abroad or by a person accompanying the military forces of the United States;

(g) such jurisdiction is provided by treaty; or

(h) the offense is committed by or against a national of the United States outside the jurisdiction of any nation.

Foreign Report of the National Commission on Reform of Federal Criminal Law [sections] 208 (1971); see also I Working Papers of the National Commission on Reform of Federal Criminal Laws 69–76 (1970) (discussing the drafting of proposed section [sections] 208 on extraterritorial jurisdiction); Kenneth R. Feinberg, Extraterritorial Jurisdiction and the Proposed Federal Criminal Code, 72 J. Crim. L. & Criminology 385 (1981) (discussing, ten years later, the consideration by Congress of a proposed codification of extraterritorial jurisdiction as part of overall efforts to reform the federal criminal code).

51.   Department of Justice Guidelines state that "express authorization" is required before an action is brought under the Foreign Corrupt Practices Act. U.S. Dep't of Justice, United States Attorneys Manual 9-2.135 (1993). Consultation with the Criminal Division's Office of International Affairs is requested in matters related to extradition and obtaining evidence. In some instances, approval is required. For example, "[b]efore issuing any subpoena to obtain records located in a foreign country, and before seeking the enforcement of any such subpoena, approval must be obtained from the Office of International Affairs." Id. at 9-2.151. Guidelines exist regarding national security matters. Id. at 9-2.132. Guidelines also exist requiring criminal division approval before charging certain offenses. See, e.g., id. at 9-110.101 (prior approval from the Criminal Division required before instituting a RICO action). Department of Justice guidelines, however, merely provide internal guidance and have been held unenforceable as law. See, e.g., United States v. Gusher, 817 F.2d 1409, 1411 (9th Cir. 1987) (relying on statement in the guidelines themselves that they did not create any rights enforceable at law).

52.   Many of the statutes with extraterritorial application are limited in scope. Major Susan S. Gibson, Lack of Extraterritorial Jurisdiction Over Civilians: A New Look at an Old Problem, 148 ML. L. REV. 114, 136 n.140 (1995).

53.   See, e.g., 18 U.S.C. [sections] 3042 (1994) (extraterritorial jurisdiction applied for [sections] 3041 power of courts and magistrates); 18 U.S.C. [sections] 3183 (1994) (fugitives from States, Territory, or Possession into extraterritorial jurisdiction of United States).

54. 18 U.S.C. [sections] 1621 (1994). There are other perjury statutes throughout the United States Code that do not specifically include an extraterritoriality provision. See, e.g., 26 U.S.C. [sections] 7206 (1994) (filing of a perjurious tax return). Under the Federal Sentencing Guidelines, sentencing under key tax statutes may be subject to an increase for failure to report certain income from "criminal activity." "Criminal activity" is defined as "any conduct constituting a criminal offense under federal, state, local, or foreign law." U.S. Sentencing Guidelines Manual [sections] 2T1.1 commentary at 3 (1995).

55. 18 U.S.C. [sections] 1621. A limitation on conduct covered by extraterritoriality can also be seen in a drug statute which provides in pertinent part that, "[t]his section is intended to reach acts of manufacture or distribution committed outside the territorial jurisdiction of the United States." 21 U.S.C. [sections] 959(c) (1994).

56. 18 U.S.C. [sections] 175(a) (1994).

57. 18 U.S.C. [sections] 1956(f) (1994).

58. See, e.g., 18 U.S.C. [sections] 351(i) (1994) (provision regarding the assassination, kidnapping, or assault of a member of Congress, the Cabinet, or the Supreme Court provides that "[t]here is extraterritorial jurisdiction over the conduct prohibited by this section."), 18 U.S.C. [sections] 1751(k) (1994) (providing extraterritorial jurisdiction over similar behavior aimed at the President, Vice-President, or a member of their staffs).

59. 18 U.S.C. [sections] 1623(b) (1994).

60. 18 U.S.C. [sections] 1512(g) (1994). This same provision is also found in the "Retaliating Against a Witness, Victim, or an Informant" statute. 18 U.S.C. [sections] 1513(c) (1994).

61. Foreign commerce "includes commerce with a foreign country." 18 U.S.C. [sections] 10 (1994).

62. See, e.g., 18 U.S.C. [sections] 1343 (1994) (wire fraud); 18 U.S.C. [sections] 1962 (1994) (RICO). In United States v. Robertson, 514 U.S. 669 (1995), the Court, in response to a lower court ruling that certain activities did not affect interstate commerce, expressed a view that sufficient jurisdiction can in fact be obtained either by being "engaged in, or the activities of which affect, interstate or foreign commerce." Id. at 669–70 (emphasis added).

63. 376 F.2d 249 (2d Cir. 1967).

64. 18 U.S.C. [sections] 2314 (1994) ("Whoever transports, transmits, or transfers in interstate or foreign commerce any goods, wares, merchandise, securities or money, of the value of $5,000 or more, knowing the same to have been stolen, converted or taken by fraud . . . ."). In the Braverman case the defendant raised the issue of whether Congress "intended the combination of 18 U.S.C. [subsections] 2 and 2314 to apply to acts . . . committed solely in a foreign country but intended to have an effect in the United States." Braverman, 376 F. 2d at 250.

65. Braverman, 376 F.2d at 251. The court continued, "or that Congress is powerless to protect foreign commerce and those who engage in foreign commerce from intentionally injurious acts, simply because those acts occur outside our borders." Id.; see also United States v. Goldman, 830 F.2d 459, 463–64 (3d Cir. 1987) (finding that justification exists for the exercise by the United States of jurisdiction over the [sections] 2314 violation where intentional effect upon foreign commerce was shown at trial). In United States v. Gilboe, 684 F.2d 235 (2d Cir. 1982), the court found that 18 U.S.C. [sections] 2314 covered the electronic transfer of funds.

66. 18 U.S.C. [sections] 113 (1994).

67. See United States v. Velasquez-Mercado, 697 F. Supp. 292, 294 (S.D. Texas 1988) (holding that criminal statutes are given extraterritorial application only if "the nature of the law permits and Congress intends it," end that Congress had "explicitly placed a territorial limitation on the applicability of the statutes in question"), aff'd on other grounds, 872 F.2d 632 (5th Cir. 1989).

68.   See supra note 57 and accompanying text.

69.   In discussing the Arms Export Control Act, a court noted that, "[t]he Reporters' Notes to the Seventh Tentative Draft of the Restatement on Foreign Relations Law provides that 'it is more plausible to interpret a statute of the United States as having reach beyond the nation's territory when it is international in focus . . . them when it has a primarily domestic focus. . . .'" United States v. Evans, 667 F. Supp. 974, 981 (S.D.N.Y. 1987), aff'd on other grounds, 844 F.2d 36 (2d Cir. 1988).

70.   Gary B. Born, A Reappraisal of the Extraterritorial Reach of U.S. Law, 24 LAW & Pol'y Int'l Bus. 1 (1992). In a civil action, the Second Circuit reasoned that a presumption against the extraterritorial application of legislation "'protect[s] against unintended clashes between our laws and those of other nations which could result in international discord.'" Kollias v. D & G Marine Maintenance, 29 F.3d 67, 70 (2d Cir. 1994) (citing EEOC v. Arabian Am. Oil Co., 499 U.S. 244, 248 (1991)). In EEOC v. Arabian American Oil Co., the Court stated that, "[i]t is a longstanding principle of American law 'that legislation of Congress, unless a contrary intent appears, is meant to apply only within the territorial jurisdiction of the United States.'" 499 U.S. at 248 (quoting Foley Bros., Inc. v. Filardo, 336 U.S. 281, 285 (1949)); see also Smith v. United States, 507 U.S. 197, 204 (1993) (Federal Tort Claims Act's waiver of sovereign immunity not given extraterritorial application).

71.   See Born, supra note 70, at 1 (arguing "that the rationale for the territoriality presumption has become obsolete and that the presumption should be abandoned").

72.   United States v. Zehe, 601 F.Supp. 196 (D. Mass. 1985). There is no presumption against an extraterritorial application for the offense of treason. Chandler v. United States, 171 F.2d 921 (1st Cir. 1948); Gillars v. United States, 182 F.2d 962 (D.C. Cir. 1950).

73.   United States v. Flores, 289 U.S. 137, 155–56 (1933). Jurisdiction, under 18 U.S.C. [sections] 7(3) (1994), was provided for acts occurring in an "embassy in a foreign country acquired for the use of the United States and under its concurrent jurisdiction." United States v. Erdos, 474 R2d 157, 160 (4th Cir. 1973).

74.   United States v. Birch, 470 F.2d 808, 811 (4th Cir. 1972) (citing United States v. Bowman, 260 U.S. 94, 97–98 (1922)).

75.   United States v. Cotten, 471 F.2d 744, 750 (9th Cir. 1973). The conspiracy statute found in 18 U.S.C. [sections] 371 (1994) can be divided into two distinct types of conspiracies; namely, conspiracies to defraud and conspiracies to commit a specific offense. In United States v. Castle, 925 F.2d 831 (5th Cir. 1991), the court did not allow extraterritoriality with respect to a conspiracy charge under [sections] 371. This case is distinguishable from Cotter, in that the conspiracy charged in Castle was not a conspiracy to defraud the government, but rather a conspiracy to commit a specific offense, namely to violate the Foreign Corrupt Practices Act. Further, the Foreign Corrupt Practices Act did not cover the individuals attempted to be charged with the conspiracy in Castle. Id. at 831; see also supra notes 2942 and accompanying text (discussing the Foreign Corrupt Practices Act).

76.   United States v. Perez-Herrera, 610 F.2d 289, 290 (5th Cir. 1980) (citing United States v. Bowman, 260 U.S. 94, 98 (1922)).

77.   260 U.S. 94 (1922).

78.   Courts refer to this as the "intent of Congress/nature of the offense test." See United States v. Larsen, 952 F.2d 1099, 1100 (9th Cir. 1991) (applying intent of Congress/nature of offense test to 28 U.S.C. [sections] 841(a)(1) (1994)).

79.   Bowman, 260 U.S. at 97–98. The Court continued:

> Crimes against private individuals or their property, like assaults, murder, burglary, larceny, robbery, arson, embezzlement and frauds of all kinds, which affect the peace and good order of the community must, of course, be committed within the territorial jurisdiction of the government where it may properly exercise it. If

> punishment of them is to be extended to include those committed outside of the strict territorial jurisdiction, it is natural for Congress to say so in the statute, and failure to do so will negative the purpose of Congress in this regard. . . .

But the same rule of interpretation should not be applied to criminal statutes which are, as a class, not logically dependent on their locality for the Government's jurisdiction, but are enacted because of the right of the Government to defend itself against obstruction, or fraud wherever perpetrated, especially if committed by its own citizens, officers or agents. Some such offenses can only be committed within the territorial jurisdiction of the government because of the local acts required to constitute them. Others are such that to limit their locus to the strictly territorial jurisdiction would be greatly to curtail the scope and usefulness of the statute and leave open a large immunity for frauds as easily committed by citizens on the high seas and in foreign countries as at home.

Bowman, 260 U.S. at 98.

80. United States v. Birch, 470 F.2d 808, 811 (4th Cir. 1972).

81. Bowman, 260 U.S. at 102. Bowman involved conspiracies and false claims against the United States. Id. at 96.

82. See, e.g., United States v. Cotten, 471 F.2d 744 (9th Cir. 1973) (applying extraterritoriality to conspiracy statute and theft of government property statute).

83. 425 F.2d 984 (9th Cir. 1970).

84. Id. at 986.

85. Id. In United States v. Layton, 855 F.2d 1388 (9th Cir. 1988), the court held that, "it would be a 'perversion of logic' to infer extraterritorial jurisdiction under statutes governing theft of government property or concealment of assets in bankruptcy yet decline to infer such jurisdiction under a statute prohibiting the killing of a member of Congress." Id. at 1395.

86. United States v. Pizzarusso, 388 F.2d 8, 9 n.2 (2d Cir. 1968).

87. Id. at 9. The court in Pizzarusso appears to be allowing for extraterritoriality on the same basis as Bowman with respect to offenses against the government. The court in Pizzarusso stated: The utterance by an alien of a 'false statement with respect to a material fact' in a visa application constitutes an affront to the very sovereignty of the United States. These false statements must be said to have a deleterious influence on valid governmental interests. Therefore, 18 U.S.C. Section 1546, as applied to an alien's perjurious statements before a United States consular officer in a foreign country, represents a law which is 'necessary and proper for carrying into Execution,' U.S. Const. Art. 1, Section 8, the Congressional power over the conduct of foreign relations. Id. at 9–10.

88. Id.; see also 18 U.S.C. [sections] 1546 (1994) (fraud and misuse of visas, permits, and other entry documents); United States v. Aguilar, 756 F.2d 1418 (9th Cir.1985) (impersonating government official implicates authority of nation).

89. 80 F.3d 580 (1st Cir. 1996).

90. 18 U.S.C. [sections] 1343 (1994).

91. The court noted that "[t]he government's evidence supports a reasonable inference that the calls were made between Maine and New York." Boots, 80 F.3d at 585.

92. Id. at 587–88.

93. Id. "National policy judgments made pursuant to that authority could be undermined if federal courts were to give general effect to wire fraud prosecutions for schemes of this type aimed at violating the revenue laws of any country." Id. at 588.

94. 503 F.2d 430 (2d Cir. 1974).

95. 18 U.S.C. [subsections] 1961–1968 (1994).

96.   This issue was also examined in Alfadda v. Fenn, 935 F.2d 475 (2d Cir. 1991), where the court held that "[t]he mere fact that the corporate defendants are foreign entities does not immunize them from the reach of RICO." Id. at 479.

97.   "'[E]nterprise' includes any individual, partnership, corporation, association, or other legal entity, and any union or group of individuals associated in fact although not a legal entity." 18 U.S.C. [sections] 1961 (4) (1994).

98.   Parness, 503 F.2d at 439 (discussing the legislative history of [sections] 1962(b)).

99.   Id.

100.   Criminal RICO has been applied extraterritorially. See United States v. Noriega, 746 F. Supp. 1506, 1512 (S.D. Fla. 1990) (court determined that United States had "power to reach the conduct in question under traditional principles of international law" and that the statutes involved intended to have extraterritorial effect). In contrast, the courts have split on whether civil RICO should be applied to conduct outside the United States. See Jose. M/V Fir Grove, 801 F. Supp. 349 (D. Or. 1991) (civil RICO does not apply extraterritorially). But see Biofeedtrac, Inc. v. Kolinar Optical Enterprise & Consultants S.R.L., 817 F. Supp. 326, 332 (E.D.N.Y. 1993) (defendant may be charged in RICO action if served within the United States or if defendant "satisfies both federal due process requirements and the forum state's jurisdictional requirements").

101.   Id.

102.   Id. at 440.

103.   18 U.S.C. [sections] 1344 (1994).

104.   67 F.3d 225 (9th Cir. 1995).

105.   Id. at 226.

106.   Id. at 232.

107.   Id. at 228. The court noted that "[a]lthough the legislative history does not answer the ultimate question whether a non-federally insured, state chartered branch of a foreign bank is 'federally controlled' for purposes of the bank fraud statute, the jurisdictional distinction between the mail and wire fraud statutes on the one hand and [sections] 1344 on the other suggests that the latter's reach is more limited than that of its sister statutes." Id. at 230.

108.   Despite the fact that computer usage extends beyond the United States, Congress failed to directly address extraterritoriality in the Computer Fraud and Abuse Act of 1986. See Robert J. Sciglimpaglia, Jr., Comment, Computer [lacking: A Global Offense, 3 Pace Y.B. Int'l L. 199, 233 (1991)]; Steve Shackelford, Note, Computer-Related Crime: An International Problem in Need of an International Solution, 27 Tex. Int'l L.J. 479, 503 (1992).

109.   Professor Lea Brilmayer notes that

[i]t seems sensible to interpret the statute in line with the court's own view of how far statutes ought to reach. In certain respects, this gives the court the best of both worlds. The court decides according to its own ideas of justice, usually shaped by principles and traditions of international law, but it need not assume explicit responsibility for having done so. The result is then couched in the language of deference to Congress.

Brilmayer, supra note 12, at 17.

110.   See United States v. Medjuck, 48 F.3d 1107 (9th Cir. 1995) (reversing conviction under the Maritime Drug Law Enforcement Act where court did not submit the jurisdiction question for jury determination). In United States v. Londono-Villa, 930 F.2d 994 (2d Cir. 1991), the court reversed drug related convictions finding that "in order to establish the offenses defined in [21 U.S.C.] [subsections] 952, 960, and 963, the government is required to prove that the defendant knew or intended that the destination of the narcotics would be the United States." Id. at 998.

111. See generally Louts Henkin et al., International Law: Cases & Materials, 1046–1111 (3d ed. 1993) (general overview of various bases of jurisdiction). Limitations can also result from an inability to procure information or individuals from foreign countries. In some cases consideration is necessary to determine whether a conflict with foreign law will preclude the release of documents. See, e.g., United States v. First Nat'l Bank of Chicago, 699 F.2d 341 (7th Cir. 1983) (applying a balancing test to determine if production of documents is required where person will be subject to criminal sanctions in foreign jurisdiction).

112. Restatement (Third) of the Foreign Relations Law of the United States [sections] 401 (1986).

113. "The Restatement (Third) of the Foreign Relations Law of the United States [sections] 401, Categories of Jurisdiction," states:

Under international law, a state is subject to limitations on

(a) jurisdiction to prescribe, i.e., to make its law applicable to the activities, relations, or status of persons, or the interests of persons in things, whether by legislation, by executive act or order, by administrative rule or regulation, or by determination of a court;

(b) jurisdiction to adjudicate, i.e., to subject persons or things to the process of its courts or administrative tribunals, whether in civil or in criminal proceedings, whether or not the state is a party to the proceedings;

(c) jurisdiction to enforce, i.e., to induce or compel compliance or to punish non-compliance with its laws or regulations, whether through the courts or by use of executive, administrative, police, or other nonjudicial action.

114. See, e.g., United States v. Felix-Gutierrez, 940 F.2d 1200, 1204–06 (9th Cir. 1991) (holding that no constitutional bar existed to application of U.S. penal law and that an assessment of jurisdiction should involve examining congressional intent of relevant statute and "reasonableness" under international law principles). The Restatement (Third) of the Foreign Relations Law of the United States states that "[e]ven when one of the bases for jurisdiction under [sections] 402 is present, a state may not exercise jurisdiction to prescribe law with respect to a person or activity having connections with another state when the exercise of such jurisdiction is unreasonable." Restatement (Third) of the Foreign Relations Law of the United States [sections] 403(1) (1986) ([sections] 403(2) provides relevant factors that may be considered in determining whether the exercise of jurisdiction over persons and activities are unreasonable).

115. In Chandler v. United States, the First Circuit stated that

[t]he Sixth Amendment providing that in all criminal prosecutions, the accused shall enjoy the right to a speedy and public trial by an impartial jury of the State and district wherein the crime shall have been committed, which district shall have been previously ascertained by law, has no present relevance, for "that amendment has reference only to offenses against the United States committed within a State."

Chandler v. United States, 111 F.2d 921, 931 n.3 (1st Cir. 1948) (citing Cook v. United States, 138 U.S. 157 (1891)); see also Brilmayer, supra note 12, at 24 ("In the international context . . . the Constitution plays virtually no role al all."). Professor Brilmayer calls for use of the Due Process Clause to "promote greater flexibility and deference to the interests of other nations." Friedrich K. Juenger, Constitutional Control of Extraterritoriality? A Comment on Professor Brilmayer's Appraisal, 50 Law & Contemp. Probs. 39, 40 (1987).

116. In United States v. Velasquez-Mercado, the Southern District of Texas stated that "before exploring whether any theory of international law supports a congressional effort

to apply our criminal laws extraterritorially, the initial question is whether the Congress even intended such an application." 697 F. Supp. 292, 294 (1988) (citing United States v. Baker, 609 F.2d 134 (5th Cir. 1980), affirmed 872 F.2d 632 (5th Cir. 1989)).

117.   In United States v. Felix-Gutierrez, the Ninth Circuit Court of Appeals stated that "prior to giving extraterritorial effect to any penal statute we must consider whether extraterritorial application would violate international law." Id. at 1205. In United States v. Noriega, Judge Hoeveler stated that

> [w]here a court is faced with the issue of extraterritorial jurisdiction, the analysis to be applied is
>
> 1) whether the United States has the power to reach the conduct in question under traditional principles of international law; and
>
> 2) whether the statutes under which the defendant is charged are intended to have extraterritorial effect.

746 F.Supp. 1506, 1512 (S.D. Fla.1990). Finally, in United States v. Cotten, 471 F.2d 744, 749–50 (9th Cir. 1973), the court first found that the extraterritorial application was permissible constitutionally and internationally, and then determined the congressional intent for an extraterritorial application.

118.   Some commentators list six aspects of jurisdiction. In this instance the "territoriality" principle and "effect" theory are designated separately. See, e.g., David A. Koplow, Long Arms and Chemical Arms: Extraterritoriality and the Draft Chemical Weapons Convention, 15 Yale J. Int'l L. 1, 36–41 (1990). Some delineate these further, recognizing seven principles. See United States v.Vasquez-Velasco, 15 F.3d 833, 840 n.5 (9th Cir.1994) (citing Restatement (Third) of the Foreign Relations Law of the United States [sections] 402 cmt. a (1986)).

119.   Harvard Research in International Law, Jurisdiction With Respect to Crime, 29 Am. J. Int'l, L. 437 (Supp. 1935). Jurisdiction principles are often used to find extraterritoriality in cases involving drugs. "Our circuit has repeatedly approved extraterritorial application of statutes that prohibit the importation and distribution of controlled substances in the United States because these activities implicate national security interests and create a detrimental effect in the United States." Vasquez-Velasco, 15 F.3d at 841 (applying extraterritoriality to 18 U.S.C. [sections] 1959).

120.   See, e.g., United States v. Benitez, 741 F.2d 1312 (11th Cir. 1984) (using the protective and passive personality principles).

121.   Christopher L. Blakesley, A Conceptual Framework for Extradition and Jurisdiction Over Extraterritorial Crimes, 1984 Utah L. Rev. 685, 688 (1984).

122.   See United States v. Pizzarusso, 388 F.2d 8 (2d Cir. 1968) (holding that U.S. District Court had jurisdiction to indict and convict a foreign citizen of crime of knowingly falsifying information in a visa application taken by American Consular located in foreign country).

123.   221 U.S. 280 (1911).

124.   Id. at 285.

125.   Nadelmann, supra note 10, at 41.

126.   United States v. Pizzarusso, 388 F.2d 8, 10–11 (2d Cir. 1968) (citation omitted).

127.   470 F.2d 808 (4th Cir. 1972).

128.   The court in Birch found that 18 U.S.C. [sections] 499 was intended by Congress "to apply to persons who commit its proscribed acts abroad." Id. at 812.

129.   Id.

130.   The court in Birch stated

> [t]he gravamen of the offenses is the assault on the integrity of the United States and its official documents. The United States has a legitimate interest in assuring foreign governments that its military passes are valid and that counterfeits of its official documents cannot be used with impunity to deceive the citizens and officials of foreign countries.

131.   18 U.S.C. [sections] 1546 (1994).

132.   United States v. Pizzarusso, 388 F.2d 8, 10 (2d Cir. 1968).

133.   See Marc Rich & Co. v. United States, 707 F.2d 663, 666 (2d Cir. 1983) (since there is jurisdiction to punish, there is likewise jurisdiction to investigate the alleged criminal action).

134.   See Geoffrey R. Watson, Offenders Abroad: The Case for Nationality-Based Criminal Jurisdiction, 17 Yale J. Int'l L. 41 (1992). "The United States approach is somewhat conservative when compared to the position taken by many civil law countries which generally consider their domestic law to be binding almost in its entirety on citizens abroad." John Patrick Collins, Traffic in the Traffickers: Extradition and the Controlled Substances Import and Export Act of 1970, 83 Yale L.J. 706, 719 (1974).

135.   18 U.S.C. [sections] 1001 (1994). Under a nationality principle, it has been found permissible for Congress to punish citizens who violate the Protection of Children Against Sexual Exploitation Act. See United States v. Harvey, 2 F.3d 1318, 1328–29 (3d Cir. 1993).

136.   783 F.2d 852 (9th Cir. 1986).

137.   Id. at 854.

138.   Id. at 854 (quoting United States v. King, 552 F.2d 833, 851 (9th Cir. 1976)).

139.   United States v. Felix-Gutierrez, 940 F.2d 1200, 1206 (9th Cir. 1991). In Felix-Gutierrez, the court noted that three international principles applied, namely, the territorial, protective, and passive personality principles. The court applied the principles cumulatively finding that one who helps another who has kidnapped and murdered a DEA agent in a foreign nation to avoid apprehension, trial, or prosecution for such crimes may be prosecuted for that offense in a court of the United States, even though all of his criminal conduct occurred beyond the territorial limits of this country.

140.   Nadelmann, supra note 10, at 41.

141.   Id. The universality and passive personality principles provided jurisdiction in a case of alleged terrorism. Abraham Abramovsky, Extraterritorial Jurisdiction: The United States Unwarranted Attempt to Alter International Law in United States v. Yunis, 15 Yale J. Int'l L. 121, 136 (1990); see also M. Cherif Bassiouni, Human Rights in the Context of Criminal Justice: Identifying International Procedural Protections and Equivalent Protections in National Constitutions, 3 Duke J. Comp. & Int'l L. 235 (1993) (discussing protections and limitations on the potential abusive exercise of power by states).

142.   Violations of international law may not necessarily result in a dismissal of the prosecution. See United States v. Alvarez-Machain, 112 S.Ct. 2188, 2196–97 (1992) (holding that the forcible abduction of the defendant was not in violation of extradition treaty and didn't prohibit trying defendant in U.S. courts for violation of U.S. criminal laws).

143.   See Christopher L. Blakesley & Otto Lagodny, Finding Harmony Amidst Disagreement Over Extradition, Jurisdiction, the Role of Human Rights, and Issues of Extraterritoriality Under International Criminal Law, 24 Vand. J. Transnat'l L. I (1991) (focusing on the relationship between jurisdiction and extradition in the context of human rights law).

144.   In United States v. Boots, the First Circuit Court of Appeals noted that the long-standing rule instructs the courts to leave this area alone, so that the legislative and

executive branches may exercise their authority and bargaining power to deal with such issues, and also so that a foreign government's revenue laws are not subjected to intrusive scrutiny by the courts of this country. 80 F.3d 580, 588 (1st Cir. 1996).

145.　In addition to substantive questions, procedural issues also provide significant issues. See supra note 23 (discussing procedural issues); see also Raymond Banoun & Christopher F. Robertson, Challenging Subpoenas for Foreign Business Records, 1995 ABA White Collar Crime H-11; Paul L. Perito, E. Lawrence Barcella, Jr., & Timothy J. Wellman, The Pervasive Reach of Long Arms—Confronting Jurisdiction When Representing Foreign Companies in United States Grand Jury Investigations, 1995 ABA White Collar Crime H-1.

146.　See, e.g., In re Grand Jury Proceedings (Bank of Nova Scotia), 691 F.2d 1384 (11th Cir. 1982) (compelled production of bank records where compliance would have allegedly violated Bahamian laws).

147.　Professor Lea Brilmayer considers the argument of whether "nonresident aliens may have fewer constitutional rights than American citizens." Brilmayer, supra note 12, at 31.

148.　Procedural issues, in obtaining evidence for prosecution of international white collar crime, can have foreign relations ramifications. See C. Todd Jones, Compulsion Over Comity: The United States Assault on Foreign Bank Secrecy, 12 NW. J. Int'l L. & Bus. 454 (1992); John Tagliabue, Breaking the Swiss Banking Silence—A Prosecutor's Fight Against Dirty Money Ruffles the Industry, N.Y. Times, June 4, 1996, at C1, C3.

149.　See, e.g., United States v. Boots, 80 F.3d 580 (1st Cir. 1996) (mail and wire fraud case involving international scheme to defraud).

150.　Professor Lea Brilmayer aptly states that "[l]egislatures are better situated than courts to lay out a code in advance." Brilmayer, supra note 12, at 19. She also notes that "if Congress addressed the problem in the first instance, there is some hope that Congress will take it up again when readjustment is needed." Id.

151.　See generally Ellen S. Podgor, Corporate and White Collar Crime: Simplifying the Ambiguous, 31 Am. Crim. L. Rev. 391 (1994).

152.　See generally John C. Coffee, Jr., Paradigms Lost: The Blurring of the Criminal and Civil Law Models—And What Can Be Done About It, 101 Yale L.J. 1875 (1992); Kenneth Mann, Punitive Civil Sanctions: The Middleground Between Criminal and Civil Law, 101 Yale L.J. 1795 (1992).

153.　See generally John C. Coffee, Jr., Does "Unlawful" Mean "Criminal"? Reflections on the Disappearing Tort/Crime Distinction in American Law, 71 B.U. L. Rev. 193 (1993).

154.　See generally Kenneth Mann, Defending White-Collar Crime: A Portrait of Attorneys at Work 114–15 (1985).

155.　See Ratzlaf v. United States, 510 U.S. 135 (1994) (to establish violation of a specific anti-restructuring law, the government must prove a defendant knew that his conduct was unlawful); Cheek v. United States, 498 U.S. 192 (1991) (case involving a specific tax statute where the court held that a good faith misunderstanding of the law can negate willfulness). In Ratzlaf, the Court stated

> [w]e do not dishonor the venerable principle that ignorance of the law generally is no defense to a criminal charge. In particular contexts, however, Congress may decree otherwise. That, we hold, is what Congress has done with respect to 31 U.S.C. [sections] 5322(a) and the provisions it controls. To convict Ratzlaf of the crime with which he was charged, violation of 31 U.S.C. [sections] [sections] 5322(a) and 5324(3), the jury had to find he knew the structuring in which he engaged was unlawful.

510 U.S. at 149 (citations omitted).

156. "Prosecutors, who operate within the executive branch, might of course be expected not to pursue wire fraud prosecutions based on smuggling schemes aimed at blatantly hostile countries, but whether conduct is criminal cannot be a determination left solely to prosecutorial discretion." United States v. Boots, 80 F.3d 580, 588 (1st Cir. 1996).

157. The extent that the legislature should defer to the executive in drafting extraterritorial provisions is left for a future discussion.

158. A summary of a recent ABA panel, entitled "Law Enforcement and Intelligence Gathering: The Legal Dilemma," reported on comments of Paul Schott Stevens, "formerly the National Security Council's executive secretary and legal advisor," stating that

> [t]he problem with looking at law enforcement intelligence from the DOJ's point of view is that the DOJ 'has only one small piece of the larger policy picture,' he said. The way is open for the DOJ to become a foreign policy agency in a way that it has never been before. This has led to an increase in the number of U.S. law enforcement agents abroad, and also to the development of jurisdictional theories far broader than those of other countries. Stevens complained that these theories have sometimes been employed without the involvement or even awareness of the president's foreign policy advisors.

ABA Panel Ponders Overlap of Criminal Enforcement, Foreign Intelligence Gathering, 57 Crim. L. Rptr. 1546, 1548 (1995).

159. Brilmayer, supra note 12, at 12.

Enterprise Crime, Contrepreneurial Crime, and Technocrime

8

Protect Yourself Against Identity Theft: Here's How to Guard Against the Nation's Fastest-Growing White-Collar Crime

Marcy Tolkoff

Internist Paul Phillips of Johnson City, TN, was in the middle of hospital rounds when he got a call from the FBI. "They said they needed to meet with me right away," Phillips (not his real name) recalls. The agents were investigating a man who had duped a few local doctors by taking out loans in their names to buy a 45-foot, $249,000 powerboat and to lease two cars, one of which was a $60,000 SUV leased in Phillips' name.

"I received a number of calls from the car company until it was cleared up," says Phillips, "and I had to go over my credit report to make sure there weren't other fraudulent loans or accounts." The theft was traced to an incident around three years earlier, when Dr. Phillips had applied for disability insurance. The insurer contracted with a lab to obtain blood and urine samples. Apparently, the lab technicians, who went to the doctor's house to do the tests, obtained—and later misused—some of the personal data on his application forms.

Tucson ED physician Keith R. Kaback was "more careful than the average guy" when it came to giving out his personal information. Even so, a thief opened a Sears card in Kaback's name and charged $3,300 for a diamond ring and a camera. Luckily, Sears' fraud unit called to verify the charges, and the doctor wasn't held responsible.

These doctors' experiences are far from unique. Between 1998 and 2003, more than 27 million Americans fell victim to some form of identity theft, according to the Federal Trade Commission. Called the "Crime of the New Millennium" in a report by the US Department of Justice, identity theft refers to the co-opting and criminal use of personal data such as names, Social Security numbers, birth dates, and credit card or financial account numbers.

An identity thief typically applies for loans and new credit cards in another's name, and also makes purchases using the real cardholder's existing cards. Often, the victim doesn't find out about the theft until he applies for and is denied credit. The price of having one's identity stolen is tallied in more than dollars, phone calls, and letters to amend erroneous credit records, though; there's also considerable mental anguish, which only increases if the matter becomes public.

PHYSICIANS ARE PARTICULARLY AT RISK

Exactly how do these identity thieves succeed? One of the most common methods is by gaining information from stolen or lost wallets, according to the FTC Identity Theft Clearinghouse. Others include stealing mail, such as pre-approved credit card offers, new checks, bills, and the like, and "dumpster diving," the descriptive term for rummaging through trash to retrieve financial paperwork.

Then there's computer-aided theft. Someone with legitimate access to an organization's computer network may steal personal information that's stored on it (called database compromise). Or the thief may hack into the system, uncovering passwords and breaking into electronic files where private information is available. This can allow him to steal thousands of records. For instance, the admission records of nearly 5,000 heart patients were downloaded by a man who hacked into the computer network of the University of Washington Medical Center in Seattle; similarly, crooks broke into a computer at the Center for Sleep Disorders laboratory at the Indiana University School of Medicine in Indianapolis and accessed the personal information of 7,000 patients.

"Doctors are more susceptible to identity theft for a variety of reasons," explains California-based attorney Mari Frank, former identity theft victim and founder of Identity Theft: Prevention and Survival (www.identitytheft.org). "They have high incomes as well as good credit, which makes them appealing targets, plus their personal information is readily obtainable in the records of hospitals and insurers, where many instances of identity theft take place."

Another reason doctors are often victims is their tendency to delegate financial matters to others. Diane Terry, senior director of credit-reporting firm TransUnion's Fraud Victim Assistance Department, points out, "Physicians tend to have their personal bills paid by bookkeepers, accountants, or others who may not know if, for example, that pair of airline tickets is a legitimate charge."

GUARD YOUR PERSONAL INFORMATION

You're far from powerless in this name game, however. Here are some of the key ways to be proactive in protecting your identity, your credit, and your good name:

- Don't release personal information—including DEA registration and employer and Medicare ID numbers—except to those who must know, and never give it out over the phone unless you've initiated the call. Also, keep prescription pads in a secure place.

- Be aware of your surroundings and people who may be lurking when using ATM machines and calling cards at public phones.

- Shred all documents from your home and business. A cross-cut shredder that dices paper into tiny pieces is better than one that just cuts strips that are easy to tape back together. You can buy one in any office supply store for around $30.

- Put a lock on your mailbox. Thieves can steal your mail or merely "borrow" it long enough to swipe your personal information. "Sometimes, criminals open envelopes, copy what they need, and re-seal them, leaving a person with no clue that someone has rifled through his private papers," says Transunion's Terry.

- Don't carry personal numbers in your wallet. There's no need to have your Social Security number with you or to have it printed on your checks. If your state usually prints this number on drivers' licenses, or your insurer uses it as an account number on insurance cards, ask for a different number.

- Change passwords often and never check the box that asks you to "Remember my password." Install a firewall and antivirus software, and use an Internet browser that "encrypts" or scrambles your personal data into a secret code.

Get copies of your credit report from each of the three major credit bureaus at least once a year and check for bogus accounts and errors. The three bureaus are Equifax (888-685-1111; www.equifax.com), Experian (888-397-3742; www.experian.com), and TransUnion (800-888-4213; www.transunion.com).

IF YOU'RE A VICTIM

If your identity is stolen, ask one of the major credit bureaus to have a fraud alert placed on your name; a call to one bureau will result in alerting all three. Once there's a fraud alert, a bureau will request that creditors contact you before opening any new accounts in your name, so that you can verify whether you—and not someone else—requested them.

Next, inform all of your creditors that you're a victim of identity theft. Be sure to follow up phone calls with letters to document all details and have a record that you've informed the pertinent parties; send them by certified mail, return receipt requested, for proof of delivery.

Contact the authorities, too, starting with the local police. Having the facts on file will help you erase black marks on your credit record even if the crooks are never caught.

Finally, notify the FTC, the national clearinghouse for ID theft complaints. It'll provide you with an "ID Theft Affidavit," a form that will help in your efforts to close unauthorized accounts and have fraudulent charges removed.

RESOURCES

Federal Trade Commission
(877-IDTHEFT; www.consumer.gov/idtheft)

Identity Theft: Prevention and Survival
(800-725-0807; www.identitytheft.org)

Identity Theft Resource Center
(858-693-7935; www.idtheftcenter.org)

Privacy Rights Clearinghouse
(619-298-3396; www.privacyrights.org)

Explaining White Collar Crime: Theories and Accounts

9

Control Fraud as an Explanation for White-Collar Crime Waves: The Case of the Savings and Loan Debacle

W. Black

INTRODUCTION: CONTROL FRAUDS AND THE S & L DEBACLE

Economists and white-collar criminologists tend to come from opposite ends of the political spectrum, so it should not be a surprise that their views on the relative importance of white-collar crime in general and the role of white-collar crime in the savings and loan debacle of the 1980s should be polar. Economists tend to view fraud as being of marginal importance in general, and "distracts" policy makers trying to prevent future crises. (1)

One scholar who specializes in law and economics, Professor Daniel Fischel of the University of Chicago's School of Law, has written articles and books that reflect the conventional wisdom of many economists about these subjects. The title of his 1995 book, Payback: The Conspiracy to Destroy

"Control fraud as an explanation for white-collar crime waves: The case of the savings and loan debacle," by W. Black from *Crime, Law and Social Change,* 43(1): 1 (2005). Reprinted by permission of Springer Science + Business Media.

Michael Milken and His Financial Revolution, conveys both the thesis and the polemical style of the argument. While Payback deals primarily with Milken and the investment banking firm he became synonymous with, Drexel, Burnham & Lambert, it also discusses the S & L debacle at some length and argues that, as with Milken, the government sought to grossly exaggerate the role of fraud in the debacle.

In the course of Payback, Fischel asks the question that this article is intended to answer:

> Why was there a sudden simultaneous explosion of fraud and criminality at savings and loans across the country? Did a new generation of morally depraved thrift operators just coincidentally appear at the same time? (2)

Professor Fischel intended these questions to be rhetorical and sarcastic, he believed they exposed the fact that: "The government's simple fraud and insider-abuse explanation for the thrift crisis defied common sense (Id)."

This article answers Professor Fischel's questions. There was a sudden explosion of criminality because a series of factors came together to create a new S & L environment that was nearly optimal for fraud by controlling persons ("control fraud"). The entry of a substantial number of new controlling persons into the S & L industry who were seeking opportunities to commit control fraud was not coincidental, but the product of this optimal environment. Key elements of the new environment were regulatory and economic changes that made entry into the S & L industry far easier, and made S & Ls chartered by states that had undergone radical deregulation nearly ideal vehicles for ponzi schemes. Most S & Ls, however, were not ideal fraud vehicles, and the vast majority of traditional S & Ls that did not engage in changes of control did not engage in fraud. This explains why the explosion of fraud did not occur "across the country." Instead, fraud was concentrated in the states in which deregulation and lax supervision combined to make S & Ls more attractive vehicles for control fraud.

And, yes, the new entrants that acquired S & Ls in order to loot them were "morally depraved." I term such entrants "opportunistic" control frauds. Another variety of control fraud helped produce the debacle, those who reacted to the imminent failure of their S & Ls by engaging in fraud. I use the term "reactive" to distinguish such frauds. The wave of control fraud in the S & L debacle occurred, as do "rogue" waves in the ocean, when the crest of these two waves came together and amplified into a financial tsunami.

I do not defend "the government's . . . simple fraud . . . explanation" because that is a strawman characterization. There is no single "government" explanation of the S & L debacle. Indeed, the early conventional wisdom, defined most starkly by economists (including many who were in the government), was that fraud made a trivial contribution to the overall crisis. (3) I am one of several scholars to challenge that conventional wisdom.

I demonstrate here that economic theory's core assumptions of rationality, constrained optimization, and self-interest are fully consistent with my theory of control fraud and predict periodic waves of white-collar crime. Indeed, I show that Fischel's efforts to rehabilitate those who engaged in control fraud force him into repeated inconsistencies with the very economic theories he purports to champion. The central irony to Fischel's question is that the facts he presents answer his own question. Fischel is blind to the implications of these facts because they do not support his ideological beliefs and the case he wishes to present of a rapacious and mendacious government engaged in a witch hunt against S & L owners.

This article has four parts. First, I explain why opportunistic and reactive control frauds can be rational. Second, I show why some environments can be vastly more attractive for opportunistic or control fraud. Third, I show why the environment can become attractive simultaneously for both variants of control fraud—which can produce a wave of control fraud. I also show that policy makers, including economists, were absolutely blind to these incentives contemporaneously. Fourth, I demonstrate that Fischel's claims that control fraud was a minor contributor to the debacle rest on internally inconsistent views, repeated factual errors, and a failure to appreciate the implications of even the facts that he gets right.

THE RATIONALITY OF CONTROL FRAUD

Control frauds using firms as both a weapon and victim of fraud are common and rational (as that term is used by economists), but many economists seem to resist this conclusion. Control frauds are rational at failed or failing firms. The fundamental dynamic that makes control frauds rational combines four key elements. First, the absence of a good, legal option. A firm that is insolvent and losing money often cannot be saved, so the probable alternative to control fraud is the imminent failure of the firm. The failure of the firm can often cause financial and social ruin to the controlling shareholder/CEO.

Second, control fraud is most attractive where the CEO/owner can over-state asset values and hide losses. This allows the firm to claim false profits and hide real losses. This permits the CEO/owner to both delay the firm's failure and loot the firm in the interim. Further, it permits the owner to do so in ways that make prosecution most difficult. For example, a firm becomes a more attractive vehicle for control fraud if it deals in assets that have no readily ascertainable market value, e.g., large, unique real estate projects. This makes it far easier to overstate values, which is the key to hiding losses and inflating "profits." If a "Big Five" audit firm can be induced to "bless" the financials, the firm can then declare a seemingly legitimate dividend—which converts firm assets to assets of the controlling shareholder. If the firm can grow rapidly, which is the essence of any ponzi scheme, the payoff to control fraud expands.

Of course, control fraud will eventually kill the firm, but only after a period of (false) profitability. Moreover, the firm was already dead and because of limited liability and bankruptcy law priority principles, the dominant share-holder will not lose any more money if the firm is insolvent by $1 billion than if it were insolvent by $100. So, reactive control fraud can delay failure, allow a very substantial looting of firm assets that would otherwise go to creditors, and create a record of purported success that makes it easier for the CEO to minimize reputational damage by claiming that the firm was doing great until the regulators fouled things up, or the economy turned bad.

Similarly, opportunistic control fraud can be rational and attractive for those who do rate the description "morally depraved." They seek out opportunities to acquire a failed firm cheaply and then create phony profits that allow them to loot the firm before its demise. The purchase price of an insolvent, unprofitable firm (at least outside the "dot.com" world!) should be minimal. Those engaged in opportunistic control fraud can often reduce that price to zero through the means used by Don Dixon to acquire Vernon Savings, e.g., the existing share-holders will loan the money to the acquirer to purchase their shares (or, worse, cause the S & L to loan the money to the acquirer), or get a friendly felon to front the money in return for illegitimate return favors after the acquisition.

Nevertheless, control frauds by CEOs/owners strike most people upon first hearing as nuts. Why would the owner of a firm cause it to fail? One author whose book focused on the second most notorious S & L felon, Don Dixon, the CEO/owner of Vernon Savings in Texas (known to the regulators as "Vermin Savings"), concluded:

> To a man, Dixon and his fellow entrepreneurs probably didn't set out to de-stroy and plunder the savings and loans they had acquired. That wouldn't have made any sense. Keeping the thrifts alive was the only way they could keep their pockets full. They were simply agents of avarice who operated on the financial margin and got carried away. (4)

The same conclusion that control fraud is irrational has been reached by econ-omists in the case of "bust outs."

> It is sometimes reported that the underworld becomes involved in legitimate businesses by foreclosing on them when they are unable to pay off debts to usurers. These businesses sometimes go bankrupt. This is not surprising, for the advantage of owning a business which was forced to borrow at 200 percent interest from a loan shark is not immediately obvious. (5)

These conclusions appear to be the epitome of common sense. The econo-mist, Dr. Rubin, does admit that there are reported sightings, akin to UFOs, of control frauds by the mob, but the tone is snidely academic: the poor fools, too stupid to realize that their "foreclosures" on legitimate businesses will lead to failure.

Three things combined to make control fraud appear nonsensical to these authors. First, there was no recognized economic theory of fraud or crimino-logical theory of control fraud extant and, as I will develop, an existing eco-nomic theory of the firm seemed to suggest that a CEO who was also the dominant shareholder should have every incentive to avoid looting a firm.

Second, there was a complete absence of understanding of how the CEO/ dominant shareholder could profit by looting the firm—honest people often have only the faintest understanding of how a scam works. Third, in the case of the journalist O'Shea, there was an (inaccurate) implicit assumption that Dixon and his ilk had an honest option that would cause their firms to prosper.

Academic economists who write about the problems of firms tend to view the control of a firm by a single dominant owner not as a problem, but as a solution, for their focus is on the problems posed by the separation of ownership and control. As Berle & Means made famous among economists, the typical large firm is owned by thousands of shareholders, none of whom owns a controlling interest. (6) As a result, large firms tend to be controlled by their senior officers, who commonly select the outside members of the board of directors. The resultant problem that economists have concentrated on is that of the unfaithful agent. "Agency cost" theory analyzes the means, and costs, by which the diffuse owners of large firms seek to prevent their agents from being unfaithful. One way agents can be unfaithful is to defraud the firm, but economists have assumed that this problem lies primarily with older, unsuccessful managers. Economists' primary concern is that agents will be unfaithful by failing to cause the firm to take enough risks. From this agency cost perspective, the problem is lack of control by the firm's owners and the ideal structure is the CEO who owns 100% of the firm, which should minimize agency problems. (7)

What O'Shea and Rubin missed is that world becomes upside down for a failing or insolvent firm. The incentives of a CEO/owner of a healthy firm, as Easterbrook & Fischel urge, should be to maximize the value of that firm, not loot it. Easterbrook & Fischel, however, recognize that the controlling shareholder's interests become sharply perverse when the firm is insolvent:

> When the firm is in distress, the shareholders' residual claim goes under water, and they lose the appropriate incentives to maximize on the margin. (p. 69)

They also recognize that when the controlling shareholder's interests become perverse, the firm's creditors will become the target for abuse.

> The interests of shareholders may conflict with the interests of creditors. Shareholders have an incentive to adopt various strategies with the effect of transferring wealth to themselves, such as choosing risky investment projects and withdrawing assets from the firm. (p. 68)

"Withdrawing assets" is a law and economics euphemism for fraud. Easterbrook & Fischel are correct in these later points, but they understate the problem. The shareholders' incentive to engage in control fraud can arise well before the firm becomes insolvent (which is the point at which "the shareholers' residual claim goes under water"). The controlling shareholders' financial incentives become perverse as soon as his expected "take" from control fraud exceeds the expected gains to him from running a firm that may well fail. (8) Akerlof & Romer make this point:

> Bankruptcy for profit will occur if poor accounting, lax regulation, or low penalties for abuse give owners an incentive to pay themselves more than their firms are worth and then default on their debt obligations. (p. 2)

Thus, in terms of conventional economic definitions and theories, it can be a rational (albeit criminal and unethical) act for the controlling shareholder/CEO to loot his failing or failed firm. Indeed, the logical implications of the economic theory of moral hazard include a prediction that controlling shareholders/CEOs will have strong economic incentives to engage in control fraud. (9)

Dr. Rubin is correct that the advantages of controlling an insolvent, money-losing firm are "not immediately obvious." He is incorrect in two related points: the mob does not "foreclose" on usurious loans and the bust outs do not "sometimes" end up in bankruptcy, they virtually always do so (the exception is when the mob wants a longer term "front" business). Usurious loans were unenforceable at law, so foreclosure was never an option. Instead, the owner of the failed legitimate business was extorted into signing over the ownership of the business to the mob or its associates.

Dr. Rubin assumes, seemingly logically, that the eventual bankruptcy of the firm represents a loss to the mob. This assumption doubtless comes from Dr. Rubin's failure to understand how an insolvent and unprofitable firm can be looted by a control fraud. As Easterbrook & Fischel recognize, an insolvent firm is used in a control fraud primarily as a weapon to loot the creditors. The classic "bust out" vehicle is probably the bar. The mob loots two types of creditors in such a bust out. Trade creditors supply booze on credit. The mob resells it, perhaps to another bar whose owner is already using the mob's loan sharking facilities. The mob also makes sure the bar is over-insured. Then it burns down the bar, collects and diverts the insurance proceeds, and declares bankruptcy.

O'Shea makes a faulty, implicit assumption in reaching his conclusion that it wouldn't make "any sense" for S & L CEOs/owners to loot their thrifts because: "Keeping the thrifts alive was the only way they could keep their pockets full (O'Shea, 1991: 279)." O'Shea missed the implications of four facts that he reports in his book. First, Dixon knowingly acquired a deeply insolvent and unprofitable S & L without any financial assistance from the government. I have explained why that provides a strong financial incentive to engage in control fraud. Pause to consider the question of rationality from the opposite perspective. What rational reason is there for an individual (who has recently emerged from personal bankruptcy and has minimal assets) to pay millions of dollars to acquire what he knew to be a deeply insolvent and unprofitable firm (i.e., a net liability)? In simple economic terms, Dixon was paying millions of dollars to acquire not an asset but a liability. Another way of viewing it is that Dixon was agreeing to buy assets for a price well above their market value. If you assume that Dixon did not intend to loot Vernon Savings, then his actions are irrational.

O'Shea implicitly assumes that Dixon had an honest option to "keep [his] thrift alive." But Dixon had no such option. Owning a deeply insolvent, unprofitable, old technology sector business is not a route to honest riches. To compound the problem, Dixon had no skills as an honest manager. Dixon had only three choices: manage Vernon Savings as well as he could and report to the regulators that it had failed, which would have meant financial ruin for Dixon; find a greater fool to sell it to; or engage in control fraud.

Second, O'Shea shows that Dixon began to engage in behavior immediately after acquiring Vernon Savings that Dixon had to know ensured that Vernon Savings could never recover (Id. 50–51). Third, O'Shea reports accurately that Dixon's purchase of Vernon Savings was financed in large part by the already notorious (and soon to be two-time felon), Herman Beebe, who routinely financed control frauds in the Southwest and received illegal loans in return from the S & Ls and banks acquired. Beebe's loans produced huge losses to dozens of S & Ls and banks, including Vernon Savings (Id. 10). Similarly, Dixon promptly began employing prostitutes to service Vernon Saving's board of directors and Texas' top S & L regulator (Id. 103–04; 116). These are associations that only make sense for a control fraud. Fourth, O'Shea reports in detail how Dixon caused Vernon Savings to falsely inflate its earnings and hide its real losses so Dixon could retain control and loot Vernon Savings (Id. passim).

O'Shea illustrates a key advantage of control fraud; even those who know enough to conclude that it walks, talks, and quacks like a control fraud often cannot bring themselves to conclude that it is a control fraud because the entire concept seems irrational to them. It can be very difficult for regulators and prosecutors to overcome such skepticism by finders of fact.

OPTIMAL ENVIRONMENTS FOR CONTROL FRAUDS

Control frauds are more likely to arise in some environments than others, and the S & L industry in the period 1981–1984 provided a close to ideal environment for encouraging and at least initially masking such frauds. Understanding why is critical to recognizing that fraud is an integral part of the explanation of the S & L crisis, and that the fraud that occurred is not just the product of the moral failings of a small number of random S & L operatives.

The two forms of control fraud (reactive and opportunistic) are not mutually exclusive. The CEO/owner of a failing firm in one industry may react to the imminent failure by choosing to engage in fraud but may decide to enter an industry that offers superior opportunities for control fraud. Such a CEO is engaging in both reactive and opportunistic control fraud. Nevertheless, it is useful to think of both varieties in analyzing which environments are most likely to maximize control fraud. Reactive control frauds will be far more common in industries that are in systemic crisis. For example, essentially every

S & L in America was insolvent on a market value basis by mid-1982 as a result of record interest rates and the systemic exposure of the industry to interest rate risk.

Failing industries also provide superior environments for opportunistic control fraud. The first requisite of opportunistic control fraud is the ability to acquire the firm. That is often extremely difficult for those who wish to engage in opportunistic control fraud. The really rich usually have too much to lose from such frauds—they become attractive "deep pockets" for civil suits—and would bear severe opportunity costs were they to engage in control fraud because their reputation and wealth give them many avenues of legitimate profit. Mass industry insolvency is perfect for allowing those other than the super rich to acquire firms because it reduces the cost of acquisition, offers many takeover targets in multiple jurisdictions, makes the sellers eager to offer incentives to facilitate the acquisitions (e.g., loans from the S & L to the acquirer), and puts immense pressure on the regulators to cut red tape and approve deals. The acquirer who agrees to buy a failing S & L without governmental financial assistance started out as a hero to the regulators. The regulators may also aid deals by means that have no (immediate) cost to the government, e.g., flaky accounting standards that hide the firm's insolvency and create phony profits.

As I described above, the key need in any control fraud is to claim false profits and hide real losses. This allows looting with minimal risk of prosecution and staves off the inevitable failure of the firm. Several environmental factors are critical in this regard. First, you need an industry with substantial assets that have no readily ascertainable market value. This means that asset values may be set largely not on the basis of arm's length market transactions but on the somewhat subjective opinion of experts, particularly appraisers and accountants. Because the CEO/owner has the power to determine which professionals will be hired by the firm to provide these opinions, a control fraud can "shop" for accommodating auditors and appraisers. In the S & L context, the top audit firms in the nation and prestigious appraisers routinely provided absurdly inflated values for real estate assets. S & Ls that were deeply insolvent obtained "clean" audit opinions for financial statements that bore no resemblance to reality (or GAAP).

Second, control frauds prefer industries with weak regulation. Regulators often have a strong incentive to cover up a systemic industry crisis. For example, in the S & L context, neither the President, the Congress, nor the regulators initially wanted to recognize the extent of the crisis because the U.S. Treasury was on the hook (through deposit insurance) for essentially the entire insolvency of the industry (which was roughly $150 billion by 1982). The means to avoid recognizing this contingent liability of the federal government (which would have deepened the reported budget deficit by $150 billion) was to keep the industry from recognizing its insolvency.

Regulators may also face what I term "regulatory hazard." Rather than accepting the reputational price of acknowledging a massive industry failure on their watch, they may gamble by encouraging the industry to take high risk investments and grow rapidly. If these gambles fail, the ultimate cost to the Treasury may grow massively.

A further complication can occur in a federal system. Those interested in opportunistic control fraud may be able to select among over 50 competing jurisdictions eager to attract new entrants. Worse, the regulators may engage in a "competition in laxity." In the S & L context, this clearly happened, with California and Texas "winning" the competition. By far the worst S & L losses occurred in California and Texas-chartered S & Ls.

Economists have even darker views about regulation. The "economic theory of regulation" asserts that "regulatory capture" by the industry is common. Economists have claimed that the S & L industry is a classic example of such capture. (10)

Third, control frauds thrive in industries with limited private market discipline by creditors. While control frauds use firms as both a victim and weapon of fraud, the latter use is far more important because control fraud only becomes economically rational when the firm is failing. Creditors, however, normally have the incentive, and frequently have the ability, to protect themselves from such frauds by insisting on more rigorous financial information even if the regulators are captured. Creditors have a great advantage over the regulators—the due process clause does not apply to them. They can decide not to loan money to a firm for virtually any reason (other than discrimination based on race, etc.), including rumor or a bad feeling.

In some circumstances, however, creditors may have little incentive to exercise such discipline. The classic example is deposit insurance. Depositors are the overwhelmingly dominant creditors of S & Ls and banks, and the vast bulk of depositors are fully insured against loss. Their financial incentive is simply to loan their funds to the bank paying the highest rate of interest.

The fourth key environmental factor is the ability to grow rapidly. This allows the fraud to operate as a ponzi, which extends its life and the amount of assets that can be looted. The S & L industry, given its almost non-existent capital requirements, deposit insurance, and the absence of any direct regulatory limitations on growth approached perfection in this regard. It was common for control frauds to grow by over 50% per year.

The final key to constructing an environment receptive to control fraud is minimal risk of criminal prosecution, conviction, and severe sentences. Many of the factors I have just discussed help explain why control frauds that rely on overstated asset values blessed by top, purportedly independent professionals, and lead to facially regular dividends present cases that [are] most unlikely to be successfully prosecuted.

Two other factors may be less obvious, but are critical in this regard. Control frauds may produce no identifiable, sympathetic, and individual victim. Our political institutions and juries are moved far more by the testimony of such individuals than by "paper cases" involving billions of dollars. Deposit insurance means that virtually no depositor, and absolutely zero non-wealthy depositor, loses any money. It took Charles Keating of Lincoln Savings, who took the tactically brilliant but strategically disastrous step of deliberately targeting non-wealthy widows to scam using uninsured junk bonds to put a human face on the S & L debacle and (in conjunction with his recruitment of the five U.S. Senators that came to be known as the "Keating Five") turn it into a political scandal.

The other factor is prosecutorial priorities. In part because of the reasons stated immediately above, but also because the Attorney General took a number of white-collar federal prosecutors and assigned them to an anti-pornography crusade (of which, in one of life's great ironies, Charles Keating was a top leader), virtually no S & L CEO was prosecuted for a serious white-collar crime during the early 1980s when the wave of opportunistic control frauds entered the S & L industry. The Charles Keatings and Don Dixons of the world had no reason to believe when they entered the industry and began their control frauds that they faced any non-trivial risk of prosecution.

These control frauds fell into a classical fallacy of composition: a strategy that can work for a few will often fail if many adopt the same strategy. Because hundreds of control frauds produced scores of billions of dollars of losses, and defrauded elderly widows, and suborned top public officials the result was a political scandal that caused the new Bush Administration to make prosecution of top S & L control frauds a high priority. The result was over 1000 convictions of senior S & L officers and their associates.

The above exposition helps to show why the attractiveness of firms as vehicles for control fraud in different industries, or even in the same industry at different times, can vary greatly. Thus, two industries that seem very similar, e.g., savings and loans and banks, can offer vastly different opportunities for control fraud. Because banks were rarely exposed to serious interest rate risk, the sharp rise in interest rates that began in 1979 did not lead to serious problems for banks.

Even mutual savings banks (MSBs), which were very similar to S & Ls, and experienced mass insolvency in the 1979–1982 interest rate crisis proved to be far less favorable control fraud vehicles than S & Ls because they were regulated and insured by a different entity, the Federal Deposit Insurance Corporation (FDIC). The FDIC followed a somewhat analogous policy of covering up the scope and depth of the MSB crisis, but it never permitted the easy entry of new acquirers with clear conflicts of interest, did not engage in dramatic deregulation, and did not desupervise the industry. Unlike its federal S & L regulatory counterparts, the FDIC fund remained strong because MSBs were tiny relative to the broader, healthier banking industry. As a result, the MSB industry suffered material losses, but nowhere near the scope of the S & L industry losses. The MSBs were far less attractive vehicles for fraud and control fraud was far less common among MSBs than among S & Ls.

Even short periods of time can lead to dramatic changes in the relative attractiveness of an industry for control fraud. For example, the arrival of a new regulatory head can produce sudden changes. The S & L case demonstrates this point—the industry was the clearly superior environment for control fraud for roughly 5 years, 1981–1985. By 1986, the new chief regulator's "reregulation" of the industry and personnel changes had combined to make the industry decidedly inhospitable to control frauds. Federal Home Loan Bank Board (Bank Board) Chairman Gray succeeded Chairman Pratt (an academic finance expert and the principal author of federal deregulation and desupervision) in 1983 and identified control frauds as a central concern. Gray's reregulation and resupervision of the industry began late in 1983 and continued during his term, which ended on June 30, 1987. While Gray's successor, Danny Wall, opposed most of Gray's initiatives, he was largely unable to reverse the changes.

CREATING A WAVE OF CONTROL FRAUD: THE S & L DEBACLE

This section argues that a special dynamic can exist when a single industry provides a clearly superior environment for control fraud, and that this dynamic produces periodic waves of control frauds such as occurred in the S & L debacle. Moreover, while beyond the scope of this article, widespread control fraud is likely to generate other white-collar crimes for myriad reasons. (11) I have explained why the mass insolvency of an industry will greatly increase the incentives to engage in reactive control fraud. Further, such systemic crises make acquisition of failed firms much cheaper and fairly common regulatory responses to such industry crises can lead to regulatory coverups and risk taking that can increase the incentives for opportunistic control fraud by new entrants to the failing industry. Mass insolvency, then, can generate large waves of both forms of control fraud.

In most circumstances, those who would wish to engage in control fraud are both constrained and dispersed. The first constraint is their limited access to capital. As I explained, substantial capital is ordinarily necessary to gain control of a legitimate firm, and those with such capital have plentiful opportunities for lawful gain and too much to lose from causing firms they own to fail. Absent mass industry insolvency, the marginal white-collar types inclined to commit control fraud find it too difficult to gain control for a wave of either opportunistic or reactive control fraud to occur in a particular industry.

A second constraint is provided by creditors and regulators. The marginal white-collar entrants who acquired S & Ls in 1981–1983 and engaged in control fraud did so during a period in which the change of control regulations were a farce. Few of them would have been remotely attractive to regulators absent the desperation that they felt to deal with a massively insolvent industry with no resources (because the federal insurance fund for S & Ls was itself massively insolvent). Most of them were real estate developers with obvious potential conflicts of interest. With rare exceptions, the opportunistic control frauds that entered the S & L industry in 1981–1983 would not have been permitted to acquire banks.

Dispersal of those who would like to engage in opportunistic control frauds is also probably the norm. While it is certainly possible that there are industries with weak ethical norms (at one time, for example, it was routine for used car dealers to roll back odometers), there are doubtless good and bad managers in every line of work. They are presumably dispersed by random processes, e.g., Fred would like to engage in a large control fraud, but Fred is an assistant manager at a department store because that was where Fred's dad worked. But concentration in a particular industry of those who wish to engage in opportunistic control fraud could easily occur if entry into that industry were extremely easy (a circumstance that mass industry insolvency and extremely weak regulation would produce) and the risk: reward tradeoff for control fraud in a particular industry was much better than all alternatives. When the opportunistic entrants are added to the reactive frauds, the result is a tsunami of control fraud.

There is agreement that all of these factors were true of the S & L industry in 1981–1983. There is also agreement that a wave of new acquirers entered the S & L industry in 1981–1983, that the entrants disproportionately chose to obtain California and Texas charters, that these two states provided the best environment for control fraud of any jurisdiction, that S & Ls chartered in these states and acquired by the new entrants in 1981–1983 produced grossly disproportionate losses, and that large numbers of the new entrants were subsequently convicted of fraud. In sum, the entrants acted in an economically rational but illegal and immoral manner. Together with the reactive control frauds (which fortunately represented a very small percentage of CEOs/owners) they caused a material share of the debacle's losses.

Fischel argues in vehement terms that all of these things took place in response to the 1979–1982 interest rate crisis in the S & L industry and that new, criminal entrants took control of many failed S & Ls in response to the incentives for abuse (Id.: 211–13). Fischel's own logic answers his question as to why a wave of control fraud occurred at S & Ls, but he shrinks from the implications of his logic. (12)

FISCHEL FACES REPEATED INTERNAL INCONSISTENCIES IN HIS EFFORT TO TRANSMUTE CONTROL FRAUDS INTO VICTIMS

Fischel comes out of a law and economics tradition that frequently sees firms and those who control them in starkly unfavorable terms. They are assumed to be "rent seekers" in their dealings with government and striving to achieve, or more likely, retain, their "capture" of regulatory bodies. If, despite such capture, they still cross over the line and commit crimes, there are two logical reactions Fischel could take. Fischel could argue as he does on behalf of Milken that the regulator has been captured by other (evil) industry members who use the government to suppress competition from (righteous) Milken and Drexel. Fischel portrays Drexel's private sector opponents as lazy, inept, envious, and anti-Semitic. Otherwise, Fischel should condemn control frauds as particularly pernicious criminals. Fischel chooses neither alternative, which causes him to flounder in repeated logical dilemmas.

Fischel is in a bind on the S & L front. None of the arguments he uses to defend Milken and Drexel make any sense in the S & L context. His problem is threefold. The rest of the S & L industry cannot be made to look evil, the S & L control frauds cannot be made to look righteous, and most troubling for Fischel, the attack he wants to make on the government cannot be made internally consistent.

Fischel has several major problems in attacking the "traditional" S & Ls that dominated the industry. He cannot claim anti-Semitism, and the inescapable facts are that the traditional S & Ls rarely engaged in reactive fraud and were the great survivors of the debacle while every non-traditional S & L that became what was known as a "high flier" failed. So, it's hard to make the traditional S & L managers come off as the morons (particulary relative to the high fliers' CEOs). Moreover, the traditional thrifts were rarely direct competitors of the control frauds because they specialized in separate business lines (even their competition for depositors was limited given the high fliers' reliance on "hot money"). While it is certainly true that traditional S & Ls generally detested the control frauds, the traditional S & Ls were largely supportive of Pratt's deregulatory policies and generally opponents of Gray's efforts to reregulate the industry. Thus, it cannot be claimed that regulatory capture led to Gray's crackdown on the high fliers. Indeed, Gray was detested by the industry and its powerful trade association, the U.S. League of Savings Institutions (the League).

Fischel's problems mount in attempting to defend the control frauds. Even Fischel finds the CEOs/owners repulsive (Id: 211):

> a new breed of owners, many with existing vast fortunes and lavish lifestyles, entered the industry. . . . Jurors were bound to be unsympathetic to multi-millionaire S & L tycoons who used their thrifts as private piggy banks but then left taxpayers holding the bag when institutions failed.

Fischel is inaccurate in one important area, none of the new breed who entered the S & L industry and committed control fraud had a "vast fortune" prior to entry. Their fortunes were invariably made by looting the S & Ls they controlled. Take the case of Charles Keating, which Fischel discusses at some length. Fischel's take on Keating is that he is a rich, highly successful real estate developer who acquires an S & L in order to expand his booming real estate business (Id: 215). In fact, Keating was recruited to the S & L industry by Michael Milken, who desired another "captive" issuer/purchaser of junk bonds through Drexel. Keating's real estate business (ACC) was not highly successful, indeed, ACC had been steadily withdrawing from its markets because of problems with its building quality and marketing. The purported profits shown on ACC's financial statements are, given Keating's track record in massively overstating asset values (i.e., by over $3 billion in the case of Lincoln Savings), absurd for Fischel to rely on.

Keating had no vast personal fortune before acquiring Lincoln Savings, and he could not have acquired it without Milken's aid. In fact, Keating did not put up any of his own money, or even ACC's own funds, to acquire Lincoln Savings—Drexel provided the entire purchase price of $51 million. Drexel, as was its normal practice, overfunded the acquisition by causing ACC to issue junk bonds through Drexel greatly in excess of the purchase price. The overfunding achieved two of Milken's key objectives: it made ACC precariously over leveraged and wholly dependent on Drexel for survival, which meant that Keating and Lincoln Savings would be utterly compliant captives of Drexel, and it maximized Drexel's underwriting fees.

In later years, this captive role would cause large problems for Lincoln Savings and the taxpayers. Lincoln Savings had a $1 billion portfolio of junk bonds, purchased overwhelmingly from Drexel, and it did no underwriting prior to purchasing junk bonds from Drexel because Lincoln Saving did not make decisions on junk bond sales and purchases—Drexel did. Lincoln Savings officers only learned at the end of the day what junk bonds the S & L now owned. Unsurprisingly, Drexel churned the account to produce additional fees and as Lincoln Savings sank into massive insolvency and a government takeover loomed, Drexel stuffed ever junkier junk bonds in Lincoln Savings' portfolio, which led to substantial losses to the taxpayers. These facts are not presented by Fischel.

Instead, Fischel states that Keating acquired Lincoln Savings in order to increase his "capital" (Fischel, 1995: 215). This is a curious claim given the fact that Lincoln Savings was insolvent, on a market value basis, by approximately $100 million at the time of its acquisition. This, of course, exceeded ACC's entire purported capital of $80 million (Fischel, 1995: 215), so the acquisition, in real economic terms (assuming for this purpose only the $80 million net worth of ACC was real) eliminated Keating's and ACC's capital. It made no logical sense, assuming that Keating was honest, for him to agree to pay $51 million to buy a $100 billion net liability.

Similarly, the other notorious S & L felons that Dixon discusses at length, Don Dixon of Vernon Savings, and David Paul of CenTrust Savings had no vast fortunes prior to acquiring S & Ls. Dixon had emerged recently from bankruptcy and lacked the cash even to acquire an insolvent Texas S & L. He did not spend a penny of his own funds to acquire Vernon Savings; his acquisition was financed as I explained earlier by the existing S & L owner and a soon-to-be-convicted felon (Id: 247). Paul was another Drexel captive, who, prior to the acquisition, ran a failing real estate company. (Indeed, Keating, Dixon, and Paul all ran failing real estate companies prior to acquiring, and looting, S & Ls. As such, they represent both reactive and opportunistic control frauds.) Paul bought an S & L that was insolvent by over $500 million (Id: 263).

Fischel's description of David Paul illustrates the logical inconsistencies Fischel must rely upon to avoid the conclusion that Paul was engaged in opportunistic control fraud. Fischel appears to acknowledge that Paul was a failing real estate developer who scammed the Bank Board into approving his purchase of CenTrust by greatly overstating the value of real estate (Id). Fischel also concedes that: "Paul, in short, was a liar, a con man who had spent lavishly on himself and defrauded taxpayers in the process (Id: 266)." Fischel also understands that it makes no sense to pay money to acquire a net liability of over $500 million. Nevertheless, Fischel assumes that Paul must not have intended originally to engage in control fraud.

> The rational course for anyone in Paul's position, the course encouraged by the government's regulatory policies, was to adopt a high-risk, rapid-growth investment strategy. If the strategy was successful, Paul, as CenTrust's largest shareholder, would be the biggest winner. And if the strategy flopped, taxpayers would be the losers. (Id: 264)

But Fischel's concept of "the rational course" makes no sense as a matter of logic, morality, or economics. Put morality aside for a moment, in that event economics is clear that rational behavior involves optimization. In the context of David Paul, that would mean optimizing his utility by maximizing his wealth and prestige. But Paul plainly would not have maximized his utility had he followed "the rational course" that Fischel ascribes to him, i.e., a purely legal strategy eschewing fraud and relying solely on making extremely risky investments. Indeed, I will show that the strategy Fischel claims that Paul followed was about as bad a strategy as one can imagine.

Note that Fischel has implicitly limited Paul's options to acting in a legal fashion, though Fischel emphasizes Paul's moral depravity. Fraud offered a sure thing. (13) An S & L that engaged in control fraud and grew extremely rapidly was certain to report record profits. Lincoln Savings, Vernon Savings, and CenTrust each claimed to be among the five most profitable S & Ls in America—and each was massively insolvent at the time it issued these fraudulent financial statements. Dixon, Paul, and Keating were all able to retain prominent audit firms to bless these false financial statements. Absent moral constraints, control fraud was the optimal strategy for Paul to follow because it was certain to succeed. Fischel's failure to consider control fraud as an available strategy for Paul to follow is unexplained and inexplicable.

The second logical inconsistency in Fischel's analysis of Paul's optimal strategy stems from the inappropriate starting point Fischel chooses in evaluating Paul's options. Fischel starts the analysis at the point where Paul has already acquired CenTrust. The flaw in this choice of starting points is that Paul had many other choices than to acquire CenTrust. Paul could have acquired existing S & Ls that were dramatically less insolvent than CenTrust or he could have started a new, solvent S & L. In either event he could have followed a high risk, high growth strategy. Why, under Fischel's logic, was it a rational strategy for Paul to acquire CenTrust?

Remember that Fischel's logic implicitly assumes that Paul is committed to following a legal strategy of high risk investments and high growth to overcome CenTrust's more than $500 million insolvency and still make Paul rich. Assume that this is true, and ask first what it would take for such a strategy to succeed. A shareholder only has equity in a solvent firm, so Paul would be starting out with greater than a $500 million "hole" he would have to fill with spectacular earnings before he would be entitled to any gain from owning shares in CenTrust. The primary beneficiary of the first $500 million in profits would not be Paul, but CenTrust's insurer, the Federal Savings and Loan Insurance Corporation (FSLIC).

It is almost impossible in the real world to take an S & L of CenTrust's size and with over $500 million more in interest bearing liabilities than interest earning assets and make any profit, much less $500 million in profit. By definition, the ultra high risk investments that would have to be made would be extremely likely to fail, even if the CEO had great investment expertise. Thus, the almost certain result of buying CenTrust and following the strategy Fischel ascribes to Paul would be Paul's financial ruin through the loss of his entire investment in CenTrust.

Acquiring a firm that is insolvent by over $500 million for the purpose of engaging in a legal strategy of high risk, high growth investments is analogous to a jockey entering a race and voluntarily adding 500 pounds of lead to his saddle. It is profoundly irrational. Paul could have acquired S & Ls that were only slightly insolvent or started a new, solvent S & L if his goal was to engage in a legal (albeit immoral) gamble. No rational, honest acquirer would have purchased CenTrust. That fact escaped the regulators who approved the CenTrust deal at a time when there were "no Cassandras"—but it should not escape any scholar writing after the debacle. In sum, it is hard to conceive of a more irrational strategy than that ascribed by Fischel to Paul.

Fischel's logic becomes even more vulnerable once considerations of morality are introduced. Fischel's use of "the" instead of "a" before "rational course" implies that Paul would have been irrational had he not engaged in risky investments likely to cause massive losses to the taxpayers. As the very name of the applicable economic theory ("moral hazard") conveys, however, this issue is inherently ethical. It is abusive behavior for an insolvent firm to engage in extremely risky investments that are likely to fail and cause far greater losses to the creditors. A CEO/owner could decline to engage in such abusive behavior without being irrational, she would instead be ethical. The vast majority of CEOs of insolvent S & Ls did not engage in high risk, high growth strategies or reactive fraud even though they faced moral hazard— which is the key reason the debacle did not become a national economic disaster.

Fischel asserts that Paul was eager to acquire CenTrust in a situation in which his only rational strategy was an abusive one that was highly likely to fail and greatly expand the taxpayers' losses. Fischel concedes that Paul was an inveterate liar and fraud. There is no logical reason for Fischel to discount

Paul's willingness to engage in opportunistic control fraud, which was certain to succeed in creating record (albeit false) profits in league with his fellow-felon Milken. Yet, Fischel fails to even consider that possibility—though it was the optimal strategy for someone with the morality that Fischel ascribes to Paul.

Fischel's third problem with his attempt to defend the S & L control frauds is that the behavior of the government frequently contradicts the case he wants to present. This forces him into a series of internally inconsistent arguments. His description of government behavior begins accurately enough with the coverup of the scope of the crisis that was implemented by Bank Board Chairman Pratt (Id: 190–197). The coverup required the adoption of phony regulatory accounting standards and the desupervision of the industry (e.g., "forbearance"). Pratt also (moderately) deregulated federally chartered S & Ls' asset powers, which led to a "competition in laxity" in which California and Texas "won" the race to the bottom by effectively eliminating meaningful regulation. Fischel is also correct in describing all this as a "recipe for disaster." Fischel states that this recipe was used because of "intense lobbying by the politically powerful U.S. League of Savings and Loans" (Id: 193). The correct course, Fischel argues, was to close insolvent S & Ls.

Given Fischel's analysis, there are two villains to the piece: the insolvent S & L who made their regulators captives and the government officials who caved in to the industry. Fischel, however, has three problems in identifying his villains. First, he should reserve a special circle of hell for the government chefs who created the recipe for disaster. Those chefs, however, are kindred ideological spirits to Fischel, consisting of President Reagan, Bank Board Chairman Pratt, and all the top officials in Reagan's Treasury Department.

While Fischel is correct that the League lobbied in favor of the Administration's deregulation bill (which was known popularly as the "Pratt Bill"), the League was preaching to the choir. Fischel's preferred strategy, closing all insolvent S & Ls, would have cost the government approximately $150 billion (in 1982 dollars)—and the cash required to liquidate a roughly $800 billion industry (virtually every S & L was insolvent) would have been several times that large. The FSLIC insurance fund had $6 billion, so following Fischel's recipe would have required some combination of large tax increases, steep budget cuts in other areas, or a material increase in the deficit. All three choices were anathema to the Reagan Administration (and Congress) so the League's lobbying made no contribution to the recipe for disaster. Indeed, the Administration was so insistent on a coverup that it forbade FSLIC from drawing on a $750 million line of credit from the Treasury (provided by statute) that would have been used to resolve several failed S & Ls and a senior Treasury official testified against the Bank Board in the case of an admittedly insolvent S & L closed by Pratt's predecessor. The Treasury official expressly testified that it was not important whether an S & L was insolvent.

But the Administration bill, and Pratt's regulatory "reforms" did not simply cook the books to ensure a coverup. In addition, they deregulated and desupervised a massively insolvent industry. Fischel argues that this is a recipe for disaster, but he exempts the cooks from any culpability. Indeed, he cites Pratt, the head chef, as his sole support for the remarkable proposition that the deregulation ingredient in the recipe for disaster was no problem (Id: 196–197). Fischel bases this remarkable proposition on the fact that "the industry was already insolvent before any [de]regulatory intervention (Id: 196)." That is a true statement, but the conclusion he draws is illogical. Plainly, an industry can become more insolvent. Indeed, that is just what Fischel meant by the phrase "recipe for disaster." He was arguing, accurately, that the steps the government took in 1981–1983, at a time when the industry was already insolvent, made the problem much worse. Deregulation was an important ingredient in producing the disaster. Everyone agrees that the worst losses the taxpayers ultimately had to pay for were caused by S & L investments in non-traditional assets made possible by deregulation. (14)

In sum, Fischel's analysis requires him to see Ronald Reagan, Pratt, insolvent S & Ls who influence politicians to prevent their closure, and deregulation as the prime villains of the S & L debacle. For ideological reasons, he cannot bring himself to follow the dictates of his own logic. So, without discussion, the chefs who created the recipe for disaster get a complete pass from Fischel.

Having excused the chefs, Fischel has to come up with a substitute villain. His choice forces him into additional logical inconsistencies. Recall that the problem, as identified by Fischel, is as follows:

1. phony accounting has been adopted to cover up the scope of the industry's insolvency,

2. this coverup and regulatory forbearance have permitted hundreds of insolvent S & Ls to remain open,

3. the combination of mass insolvency and deposit insurance has created widespread "moral hazard,"

4. induced "a new breed" of despicable CEOs/owners to enter the industry, and

5. the new breed is engaged in abusive practices that are greatly increasing the eventual losses to the taxpayers.

Fischel, in his role as food critic, has also come up with the proper recipe: close insolvent S & Ls.

Given Fischel's logic about the nature of the problem and solution, it is easy to see what a new top regulator should do if he inherits an agency where the books are cooked and discovers that his predecessor has left a stew that is a recipe for disaster. He should order an end to cooking both S & Ls' and FSLICs' books. He should start to close insolvent S & Ls. Because the FSLIC fund does not have remotely enough money to permit this, he should raise the insurance premia charged the industry to the maximum permitted by law and go to Congress and inform them that the resources are grossly inadequate and must be increased. He should seek to minimize moral hazard by increasing capital requirements, cleaning up the accounting to ensure that the capital is real, and restricting the asset powers of weak S & Ls. He should tighten up entry requirements to prevent the "new breed" of S & L owners from expanding. He should restrict the abuses of existing S & Ls by minimizing moral hazard, restricting growth, reregulating, resupervising, and tightening examination and supervision by greatly increasing the number and quality of the regulators. He should improve his information systems and operate under triage principles that focus on closing fraudulent S & Ls.

Fischel's logic (he is a proponent of the economic theory of regulation and public choice theory) would also predict the reaction of fraudulent and abusive S & Ls to a new chef who so abruptly tossed the recipe for disaster on the coals. The rent seeking S & Ls would attack such a regulator using their essentially unlimited access to depositors to suborn politicians through generous political contributions and special access to business opportunities. Other fraudulent S & Ls might seek to buy him off by offering him a position with their S & L at a far higher salary. The Administration, eager to continue the coverup would seek to get him to resign. If he persisted, he would not be reappointed and his job prospects would be ruined. After he left office he would be sued for hundreds of millions of dollars by the fraudulent S & Ls.

The above paragraphs summarize what the new Bank Board Chairman Gray did after succeeding Pratt in 1983, and what happened to Gray when he persisted in closing insolvent S & Ls. Logically, Gray should be Fischel's hero. At worst, Fischel should complain that Gray did not adopt these reforms quickly enough or stringently enough. Again, the villains of the piece should be the new breed of S & L owners, their political allies in the Reagan Administration and Congress, and their professional allies (much of the flak Gray took came from "Triple A"—accountants, attorneys, and appraisers).

But Fischel is not bound by his own logic or the economic theories he normally espouses. Gray is the villain and the politicians who tried to keep Gray from closing insolvent S & Ls are "a model of how democracy is supposed to work (Id: 245)." In order to reach these unusual conclusions Fischel plays fast and loose with the facts throughout the portions of the book dealing with the S & L crisis. I provide two illustrative examples dealing with Vernon Savings and the Keating Five (Fischel's model of democracy in action).

Fischel's discussion of Vernon Savings is naive, illogical, and inaccurate throughout. Consider the following passage:

> Developers flocked to Vernon Savings because it was willing to finance risky deals and developers would still receive a 2 to 4 percent up-front developer's fee out of the loan proceeds even if the deal subsequently fell through. Vernon Savings also profited handsomely from these deals by charging interest rates and loan-origination and renewal fees that were often twice as high as the rest of the industry charged. All of this was completely legal and disclosed to the regulators. (Id: 248)

Fischel is primarily a consultant who testifies on financial and economic topics, and he has to know better. The first two sentences are contradictory. Interest rates and total fees for these kind of acquisition, development, and construction (ADC) loans that Fischel is attempting to describe would have been roughly 15–20% at other Texas S & Ls involved in control frauds similar to Vernon Savings. Assume that Fischel is correct that Vernon Savings "often" charged rates twice as high for the same kind of ADC loans (which also included up-front developer's "profits" at similar S & Ls). Why would honest developers "flock" to pay twice as much for the same kind of loan? Even if you assume (inaccurately, as Fischel does) that only Vernon Savings offered an up-front developer's profit payment of 2 to 4%, why would they "flock" to pay 15–20% more in costs in order to receive this relative pittance?

The paragraph contains a more subtle blunder, but one that would be plain to anyone who had studied economics and finance, particularly the concept of "adverse selection." Assume that Fischel is correct that developer's flocked to Vernon so they could pay twice as much for their loans. Fischel assumes, and asserts, that this would mean that Vernon Savings would "profit . . . handsomely." That may seem logical, but it is 180 degrees off. The only honest borrower that agrees to pay twice as much as competitors would charge for a loan is a borrower that could not get the loan approved by a competitor. In the context of the U.S. economy, there are only two reasons that Vernon Savings' borrowers could not have borrowed from its competitors—discrimination, e.g., based on race, or the fact that the borrowers were not creditworthy. No one claims that Vernon Savings' borrowers came to it because of discrimination by other lenders. What is well known is that Vernon Savings' borrowers were almost universally uncreditworthy. This explains why virtually all of Vernon Savings' ADC loans not simply defaulted, but defaulted without the borrower ever putting a single penny of his cash into repayment. Adverse selection is an economic concept that describes precisely this process, one selects for the worst possible customers.

Fischel ends the paragraph with the assertion that this "was completely legal." Given the fact that many of Vernon Savings' officers and ADC borrowers were convicted of frauds, this assertion would seem to require at least some supporting analysis. There are two logical reasons why Vernon Savings could have ended up with nearly universal defaults on its ADC loans.

The Texas real estate reason is not one of these reasons. Vernon Savings' default rate on its Texas ADC loans was far worse than other Texas ADC lenders and virtually all of its ADC loans outside Texas in robust real estate markets defaulted. Another explanation that is illogical is that Dixon was knowingly engaging in high risk, legal investments. Under that strategy Dixon would only gain if the high risk loans were repaid. Dixon would therefore have a strong incentive to avoid adverse selection and underwrite the ADC loans fully. In fact, Vernon Savings routinely failed to engage in even the most rudimentary underwriting (e.g., doing credit checks on the borrowers and requiring an independent appraisal of the value of the collateral). Moreover, Vernon

Savings persisted in these practices despite repeated criticisms by state and federal regulators. So, none of Dixon's actions are logically consistent with a theory that he was engaged in a legal, high risk strategy.

One logical possibility is that Don Dixon was the dumbest banker in history. But Fischel makes no such claim and consider how dumb someone must be, despite repeated criticism, to fail to even get a credit check or appraisal before making a multi-million dollar ADC loan.

The other logical possibility is that Don Dixon was using Vernon Savings as a vehicle for control fraud. In the upside down world of S & L control fraud, consciously making a bad ADC loan was a superb means of booking record (albeit phony) profits. This is because it was possible to find a "Big Eight" accounting firm to give a clean opinion allowing the S & L to book as income the upfront fees and interest expense—even though the borrower had not paid one cent of those fees and interest "payments." Instead, the S & L self-funded the payments, it literally paid itself. As long as the S & L grew extremely rapidly, put the bulk of its investments in ADC loans, and found an audit firm that would approve its income recognition, it was mathematically guaranteed to report that it was one of the most profitable S & Ls in the U.S. Further, because the loans were interest-only until they matured, and the interest payments were self-funded by the S & L, the ADC loans could not default! What a superb means of hiding real losses and booking false gains. Even when the loan matured, the fraud could be extended by scams ranging from simply refinancing the loan (and self-funding more fees that were booked as income!) to funding straw purchasers who would buy the collateral backing the ADC loan that was about to default a price well above the loan value. This, with the aid of the outside auditor/alchemist would transmute a real loss into a Potemkin profit. Vernon Savings routinely used such scams.

These scams also explain why control frauds wanted to deal with borrowers that would default on their ADC loans. The key attraction of such borrowers was that they had nothing to lose. They had no financial risk because the S & L financed 100% of the expenses and required no personal guarantee (or made secret, illegal side-deals agreeing not to enforce the purported guarantee). They had no reputational risk to being associated with a failed development because they were not reputable real estate developers.

Vernon Savings' ADC borrowers did, however, have much to gain. The upfront developer's profit was the obvious carrot, but they could gain far more if the S & L (in order to avert a default) arranged a scam purchase of their property at a "gain." They also controlled millions of dollars of poorly monitored construction funds—allowing many opportunities for kickbacks from subcontractors, diversion of construction funds to their personal benefit, and substituting inferior materials and pocketing the savings.

The combination of having nothing to lose and much to gain meant that Dixon had tremendous leverage over Vernon Savings' ADC borrowers. They had no reason to resist "paying" higher fees and interest rates because they were neither paying nor liable for these expenses. And while Fischel is wrong in claiming that Vernon Savings charged twice the rate of other Texas S & Ls engaged in control fraud, it is true that Vernon Savings was able to charge (but never collect) very high fees and interest rates on its ADC loans. The other virtue of this leverage is that Dixon could easily arrange for one of the ADC borrowers to serve as a straw purchaser of a real estate project securing a different ADC loan. In short, the ADC loans were not "completely legal" but the essence of a sophisticated financial fraud—one that was not disclosed to Vernon Savings' regulators.

Fischel then adds to his logical inconsistencies by claiming:

> In truth, Dixon and the regulators were playing the same game. Both were betting on a turnaround in the Texas economy, which would in turn lead to higher real estate values. (Id: 250–251)
>
> Eventually, Dixon resigned under pressure from Vernon's board of directors in the summer of 1985. In September 1986, the state regulators seized control and made a bad situation worse. Rather than closing the thrift, the regulators kept it open under government control. Loans started lapsing into default rapidly as borrowers encountered due dates and could not get their loans extended by the state authorities in charge. Vernon's income from loans fell off dramatically. By late 1986, federal regulators were pushing for a complete federal takeover of the S & L. Dixon attempted to get Speaker of the House Jim Wright to exert pressure on Edwin Gray . . . to give Dixon time to find new investors to inject capital into Vernon Savings. Rather than shut down the S & L, take over its assets, and pay off depositors, the [Bank Board] . . . voted to allow Vernon to remain open. . . . The Bank Board even [agreed] to advance funds to Vernon in order to cover its mounting cash needs, thereby throwing good money after bad. (Id: 250)
>
> The irony here was obvious. The regulators condemned Dixon and many others for their reckless and irresponsible banking practices, including financing aggressive growth strategies in a declining market by paying above-market rates of interest to attract deposits. But when the regulators seized control, they did exactly the same thing. (Id: 251)

In his eagerness to rehabilitate Dixon, who even Fischel has to admit is unredeemable, Fischel decides to switch the focus and portray the Bank Board and Dixon as parallel actors. The portrayal, however, is false and deceptive. First, Fischel argues that the Bank Board did not shut down Vernon Savings, or similar S & Ls in 1986 because "In truth" it was "playing the same game" as Dixon, delaying in hopes of a turnaround in the Texas economy. But adding "in truth" doesn't make it so. In 1985 and 1986, the Bank Board took the following principal actions with regard to Texas S & L control frauds:

1. Gray personally recruited Joe Selby, a senior banking regulator with a reputation for toughness to become the top supervisor for Texas.

2. Gray created the Southwest Task Force, which brought hundreds of examiners and supervisors from other regions to help the Federal Home Loan Bank of Dallas cope with the wave of control frauds that had overwhelmed their resources.

3. The Bank Board requested authority to borrow $15 billion to be used to recapitalize the FSLIC fund and permit closure of scores of control frauds, primarily in Texas and California.

4. The Bank Board adopted rules restricting ADC loans of the kind made by Vernon Savings and allowing examiners to classify problem assets and write off asset values.

Neither the Bank Board nor Dixon were playing the game Fischel ascribes to them. Dixon was running a control fraud that was based on an ADC ponzi scheme. This required him to finance even more office buildings in a grotesquely overbuilt Dallas market. Far from being a victim of a bad Texas economy, he was one of the important contributors to causing the recession to become so severe. The Bank Board was not engaged in waiting for a turn-around in Texas. Quite the opposite, the Bank Board had declared war on the Texas control frauds, and had virtually emptied the FSLIC fund in closing control frauds. The Attorney General of Texas announced that he was conducting an investigation of the Bank Board, claiming that it was discriminating against Texas S & Ls and failing to provide forbearance. So, the Bank Board was acting in the opposite manner that Fischel claims.

Having gotten exactly wrong the Bank Board's strategy in Texas, Fischel departs even further from reality in his next paragraph, first claiming that Dixon resigned as CEO under pressure from Vernon's board of directors. In fact, Dixon resigned because the regulators demanded he be removed.

Fischel then claims that the state of Texas "made a bad situation worse" by taking control of Vernon Savings but not shutting it down. But Vernon Savings could not be "shut down" because it would have taken roughly $1.5 billion to do so, and FSLIC did not have the money. FSLIC did not have that much cash for two reasons. First, the Bank Board had been aggressively closing control frauds, which had depleted the fund. By Spring 1987, FSLIC had only $500 million—to insure a massively insolvent industry with well over $1 trillion in liabilities. Second, the control frauds (including, but not limited to, Charles Keating and Don Dixon) had induced Senator Cranston and Speaker-elect Jim Wright to block the 1986 FSLIC recapitalization bill. To blame the regulators for not closing Vernon Savings, rather than blaming Dixon et al., is like the old joke about the definition of chutzpah being the child who murders his parents and then demands sympathy as an orphan.

But Fischel compounds his error by saying the state regulators made matters worse by—get this!—requiring Vernon's borrowers to repay their loans when they came due. What exactly does Fischel think the state should have done when the borrowers "encountered due dates" and wouldn't pay their debts—not a penny of them? Since he explicitly criticizes "throwing good money after bad" only a few paragraphs later, he surely cannot be claiming that the state should have refinanced hundreds of bad ADC loans to uncreditworthy borrowers. That would have made a bad situation worse. What the state did was the opposite.

Fischel compounds this error with a revealing slip. He writes that after the state takeover: "Vernon's income from loans fell off dramatically." Fischel doesn't get it even years later. Vernon never had "income from loans" made by Dixon. Virtually all of Vernon's ADC loans defaulted, normally with zero interest paid. Vernon's reported "income from loans" under Dixon was false. Virtually all such "income" was self-funded by Vernon. Thus, Vernon's real "income" from loans made by Dixon was negative—massively negative. Of course, as the state regulators refused to make new bad loans Vernon's reported income fell, but that was a good thing because the reports were false.

Having gotten the effect of the state of Texas' regulatory takeover completely wrong, Fischel turns to whitewashing Speaker Wright's actions on behalf of several S & L control frauds, including Dixon. Wright supposedly acts solely to give Dixon time to arrange to a purchase of Vernon Savings by an unidentified third party. Fischel has to avoid discussing Wright's repeated efforts to prevent the Bank Board from closing failed Texas S & Ls, e.g., by preventing passage of FSLIC recapitalization and trying to get Joe Selby fired, because such a discussion would make Dixon a villain and Gray a hero.

Fischel then turns to blame the Bank Board, again, for not shutting down Vernon Savings when it took it over in March 1987. Again, the Bank Board did not have remotely enough cash to shut down Vernon Savings. If it had liquidated Vernon Savings it would have had to immediately make a payment of well over $1 billion to Vernon's depositors, which was impossible precisely because of the losses caused to FSLIC by the control frauds and the political power of the these frauds that had prevented the recapitalization of FSLIC.

At this juncture Fischel adds what he apparently feels is a new criticism of the Bank Board's management of the failed Vernon Savings. He purports to be outraged that the receiver, faced with deposit withdrawals that could not be funded, raised deposit interest rates to stem the withdrawals. Fischel claims this is "throwing good money after bad." But this argument is financially naive. Depositors, even with deposit insurance, are reluctant to keep their deposits in a deeply insolvent, failed S & L. They are even more reluctant to do so when they know the federal insurance fund is deeply insolvent and that Congress is refusing to recapitalize the fund.

So, Vernon Saving's receiver had only two choices. It could keep its deposit interest rates relatively low, which would lead to continued deposit withdrawals. The receiver could not fund substantial withdrawals because the vast majority of Vernon's assets were in the form of loans that were in default—not cash. Once the receiver ran out of cash to fund the deposit withdrawals, which could occur in a few days or even hours, he risked sparking a run on the S & L that could sink not only Vernon but FSLIC as well (which could have precipitated a national run on S & Ls). All of this is to say that the first choice was no choice at all.

The second alternative was to pay a high enough interest rate to maintain nervous depositors' accounts at Vernon Savings. The Bank Board, of course, knew that closing hopelessly insolvent S & Ls like Vernon Savings was the superior alternative. Indeed, I explicitly cited to Congress the dilemma we faced in setting deposit interest rates at receiverships like Vernon as one of the reasons that it was essential that FSLIC be recapitalized promptly so that we would have enough funds to close S & Ls like Vernon.

In his eagerness to defend Dixon and attack "the regulators" Fischel offers a purported "irony" that is simply baseless. He claims that after Vernon Savings' takeover, the regulators followed the same policies that Dixon had. Specifically, the receiver supposedly followed Dixon's policy of "aggressive growth strategies in a declining market." The receiver did the opposite of what Fischel claims. Instead, the receiver reduced Vernon's investment in the declining Dallas real estate market and sought to shrink the institution.

CONCLUSION

Waves of control frauds are a critical part of the explanation of the S & L crisis. Yet, in the absence of a well developed, recognized, and understood theory of control fraud, the leading commentators on the debacle completely failed to recognize the phenomenon, even while commenting (and typically mischaracterizing) its component parts. Their mispresentation of the facts, and misdiagnosis of the problem stands in the way of using the S & L crisis to better understand and predict the potential for other financial crises.

W. Black, Lyndon B. Johnson School of Public Affairs, University of Texas, Austin

NOTES

1.   Lawrence J. White, The S & L Debacle: Public Policy Lessons for Bank and Thrift Regulation 117 (New York: Oxford Press, 1991).

2.   Daniel Fischel, Payback: The Conspiracy to Destroy Michael Milken and His Financial Revolution 210 (1995).

3.   See, e.g., James R. Barth, The Great Savings and Loan Debacle (Washington, D.C.: AEI Press, 1991); R. Dan. Brumbaugh, Jr., Thrifts under Siege (New York: Ballinger Publishing, 1988); White, supra note 1. All three authors were economists who served in senior positions with the Bank Board. Professor White was a Bank Board member, Professor Barth was Chief Economist, and Brumbaugh was Deputy Chief Economist. Each of them believes that excessive risks by the CEOs of insolvent S & Ls, not fraud, caused the vast bulk of all losses.

4.   James O'Shea, Daisy Chain 279 (emphasis added) (New York: Pocket Books, 1991).

5.   Rubin 1973: 161 (emphasis added, footnote omitted).

6.   Adolf A. Berle & Gardiner C. Means, The Modern Corporation and Private Property (Rev. ed. 1982).

7.   Frank H. Easterbrook & Daniel R. Fischel, The Economic Structure of Corporate Law 10, 70, 72, 91, 112, 112–113, 133 (Cambridge, MA: Harvard University Press, 1991).

8.   More precisely, the expected gains from control fraud v. running an honest, but in danger of failing, firm would be discounted by risk premia. The expected gain from running an honest firm, theoretically, should be the market valuation of the shareholders' residual claim on the firm (i.e., the market capitalization of a publicly traded firm's stock—which should already reflect the discount for risk). Of course, once a successful control fraud begins, the market capitalization of the firm will no longer reflect the firm's true value.

9.   White, supra note 1, at 41.

10.   Brumbaugh, supra note 3.

11.   For example, control frauds require the suppression of internal controls that constrain other insider abuses, the CEO/owner engaged in control fraud is likely to hire people of weak and malleable ethics, the ethical tone set by the CEO will encourage other officers and employees to engage in abuses, and control frauds operate by selecting corrupt (or corrupting) individuals and firms, such as independent professionals and real estate developers to aid the control fraud. As a result, control frauds act like infectious agents that spread crime and degrade ethical and moral constraints that serve as the primary constraint against white-collar crime.

12.   Ultimately, Fischel's disagreement with the existence of a wave of control fraud in the S & L debacle is neither empirical nor logical, but ethical. He believes it is outrageously unfair for "the government" to condemn private behavior that is induced in part by incentives created by government policies. In essence, though he does not phrase his argument this way, Fischel proposes a radical expansion of the entrapment principle. Fischel condemns any prosecution of white-collar crime, no matter how predisposed the defendants may have been to commit the crime, if the government has at any time created a financial incentive for the perpetrator to engage in fraud. This is quite a remarkable proposition, and under Fischel's own logic it would virtually end the prosecution of white-collar crimes for several reasons. First, Fischel is a strong adherent to the economic theory of regulation which predicts regulatory capture by the industry, particularly if the industry is suffering from a systemic crisis. So, Fischel would predict that the government, at the behest of the regulated industry, would commonly engage in coverups of industry crises and that such coverups would create a financial incentive to engage in control fraud. Fischel's logic would seem to require him to condemn such industries, but he does not do so. Instead, any industry successful in achieving such regulatory capture would be immunized from prosecution.

Even if a change in regulatory leadership subsequently led to an end to regulatory capture and the coverup and even if the rules that the control fraud was prosecuted for violating were adopted subsequent to the coverup, the immunity from prosecutions for control fraud would continue forever. Fischel assumes that the sole motive subsequent regulators could have for escaping regulatory capture is to find scapegoats. Adopting Fischel's quasi-entrapment policies, of course, would vastly increase the payoffs to succeeding in regulatory capture and create a far stronger incentive for an industry to achieve capture.

Second, even without regulatory capture it is often impossible for the government to act in a fashion that does not create an economic incentive for fraud. For example, a rule requiring the safe disposal of toxic substances creates an economic incentive to violate the rule if unsafe dumping is cheaper to the chemical manufacturer. Virtually any tax creates an economic incentive to engage in tax fraud.

Third, regulators often fail to understand the incentives they are creating to engage in control fraud. One of the best known quotations about the S & L debacle is former Bank Board member Larry White's comment that there were "no Cassandras" warning that Bank Board Chairman Pratt's deregulation and desupervision of the industry would lead to disaster. This failure is startling given the fact that it was known that deregulating and desupervising the industry at a time of mass insolvency was an insane policy under conventional economic and finance theory (particulary "moral hazard"), that it was clear in retrospect that it created a nearly optimal environment for control fraud, and that Pratt, who had been an academic finance expert should have been the perfect person to recognize that his plan would produce a disaster. Economists, who largely shaped S & L regulatory policy, saw no nexus between such policies and white-collar crime. Their training and experience offer them no basis for seeing such a nexus.

Fischel's implicit ethical argument: the government should not be able to sanction fraudulent behavior if the government creates any economic incentive to engage in such behavior, is supported only by the assertion that such sanctions would be unfair. Victims, however, frequently provide criminals with an incentive to engage in crime against them. Computers are stolen constantly on college campuses from students who leave their computers unattended in the library. People who drink too much are targets for robberies. Fancy cars increase incentives for car theft. We normally do not think the perpetrators are less culpable because they had an economic incentive to engage in crime. Indeed, we assume that blue-collar property crimes occur precisely because the thief had an economic incentive to steal.

Similarly, the cops may be inept or corrupt in a particular city or precinct. Criminals may gravitate to that precinct in response. No one has suggested that they should receive any immunity from prosecution because the government increased the incentive to engage in crime.

13.   George A. Akerlof & Paul M., "Looting: The Economic Underworld of Bankruptcy for Profit," Brookings Papers on Economic Activity 1993 (2), 1–73; Black (1993a).

14.   White, supra note 1; NCFIRRE (1993) 1.

Policing and Regulating
White Collar Crime

10

Investigative Planning: Creating a Strong Foundation for White-Collar Crime Cases

Arthur L. Bowker

Investigating white-collar crimes requires a comprehensive, documented plan because such crimes are growing increasingly complex. The investigative plan should include four basic elements. The first is predication, which should include the allegation, its source, and the date it was received. The second is the elements to prove or elements necessary to warrant for an investigation. The third is the preliminary steps or methods that the investigator will use to obtain the necessary information. The last is the investigative steps.

Few individuals would feel comfortable constructing a building without blueprints or plans. This holds particularly true when the structure is complex, will take years to construct, and will be expected to stand the test of time. Construction experts know that without thorough planning, they may miss or unnecessarily repeat important steps.

Ironically, many law enforcement officers have no qualms about hastily building cases with little or no planning, expecting their investigations to weather attacks by defense counsels and survive years of appellate review. And, given their complexity, white-collar crime cases especially require thorough, documented investigative plans.

"Investigative planning: Creating a strong foundation for white-collar crime cases,"
by Arthur L. Bowker from *The FBI Law Enforcement Bulletin*, 68(6): 22 (1999).
Reprinted by permission.

THE NEED FOR AN INVESTIGATIVE PLAN

Consider the following scenarios:

A detective receives an embezzlement allegation from a company's officers. He promptly submits suspected checks for analysis. Over the next 2 years, he directs his efforts only at getting the suspect to take a polygraph and interviewing the suspect's boyfriend, who is rumored to have received money from the suspect. The statute of limitations finally tolls on the crime.

Another detective has spent 6 months investigating an insurance fraud case. She has interviewed hundreds of victims of an unscrupulous insurance agent. She has written up many of the interviews, while others remain in dictation, and still others only exist as her rough notes. Unexpectedly, she dies, and the case gets assigned to another detective. Before proceeding, the new detective first must determine what records still need to be examined and who needs to be interviewed. The investigation is delayed several months during this transition period.

A third detective investigates a kickback case. For 3 months, he interviews witnesses and examines financial records. He writes a final report and refers the matter for prosecution. He subsequently receives a call from the prosecuting attorney, who notes that witness interviews and financial records examined do not fully substantiate the major offense cited in the report. The detective must reinterview all witnesses regarding the unsubstantiated issues.

Had these fictional detectives devised written investigative plans, many of these problems could have been minimized, if not eliminated entirely. Documented plans provide a frame of reference for the investigation to ensure that all aspects of the crime are covered in a timely manner. Specifically, a properly formulated plan

- focuses the investigative process to ensure that all offense elements are addressed;
- limits unnecessary procedures and step duplication;
- coordinates the investigative activities of numerous personnel on large cases;
- provides stability to the investigation if staff changes occur;
- enhances communication with prosecuting officials by providing an outline of the investigation and identifying strengths and weaknesses in the case;
- provides a framework for the final report; and
- becomes a training aid for inexperienced staff members.

It takes no special skill to create and follow an investigative plan; rather, investigators must have a working knowledge of the statutory elements of the crimes under their agency's purview; any special penalty enhancements for certain offenders, offenses, or victimizations; and basic investigative techniques.

Investigators must keep the plan objective and not reflect that they already have established the suspect's guilt.

COMPONENTS OF AN INVESTIGATIVE PLAN

A written investigative plan contains four basic components. These are the predication, elements to prove, preliminary steps, and investigative steps.

Predication

An investigative plan must include a predication, or brief statement justifying why the case initially was opened. Predications have three features: the basic allegation, the source of the allegation, and the date the allegation was received. For example, after receiving an embezzlement allegation, the investigator might write this predication: "On June 1, 1998, received information from ABC Union Auditor Jane Smith that she discovered that former bookkeeper Tom Roberts had written $20,000 in unauthorized checks to himself during 1997."

In short, predications clearly identify what particular offense(s) may have been committed. This initial step gives investigators a foothold for the elements they must prove in order to establish that a criminal act has occurred.

Elements to Prove

The plan must reflect all of the elements that the investigator needs to prove for the case to be prosecuted successfully. This component must clearly reflect what is needed to establish a criminal violation, thus focusing the investigation and providing a framework for the steps that follow. At a minimum, this component should contain all of the statutory elements and any special jurisdictional issues, such as venue and statutes of limitations. Special penalty enhancements represent another area that this component might include, particularly for federal offenses. (1)

The following example illustrates the possible elements to prove for a federal investigation of union embezzlement. (2)

1. The victim was a labor organization as defined by the Labor Management Reporting and Disclosure Act of 1959 (as amended).
2. The suspects were officers or employees of the labor organization.
3. The suspects unlawfully took funds or assets belonging to the victim.
4. The suspects converted the assets or funds taken to their own, or someone else's, personal use.
5. The violation was willful.
6. The violation occurred within the last 5 years.

The plan must clearly reflect the issues that must be proven but remain fluid enough to change if the investigation leads in another direction. Thus, any modification to the initial plan should not be a major overhaul but merely should represent a refinement as the investigation develops.

For cases involving multiple violations, investigators should outline only the most serious offenses and refer to the others as violations that also may be considered during the investigation. In any case, delineating the elements to prove and other important issues, such as sentencing enhancements, helps investigators identify the steps they need to take to complete the investigation. These steps encompass two types: preliminary and investigative.

Preliminary Steps

Preliminary steps represent the methods the investigator will employ to obtain basic background information on the victim, the complainant, and the suspects. These include such procedures as reviewing files on prior allegations or investigations; conducting an in-depth interview of the complainant; obtaining and reviewing public records, such as incorporation papers or financial reports filed with government agencies; and conducting a criminal background check of pertinent parties. Typically, step completion under this component does not require a great expenditure of time or personnel.

Investigative Steps

The investigative plan also must include the steps necessary to resolve the issues and complete the investigation. These investigative steps lay out the general parameters needed to establish that a crime has occurred and include who will be interviewed and what records will be obtained and examined. Investigative steps should parallel the elements that need to be proven. For example, in an embezzlement case, the investigator would need to examine bank records and interview bank tellers to prove that the suspect converted agency funds to personal use. For other investigations, a partial list of applicable steps includes interviewing victims; serving subpoenas; obtaining and serving search warrants; gaining access to financial records; examining records; identifying and interviewing key witnesses; obtaining exemplars; forwarding questionable documents for analysis; identifying and interviewing suspects; briefing prosecuting officials; and preparing a final report.

In large cases involving multiple investigators, individual steps could be assigned to specific individuals, who become responsible for their completion. In addition, when investigators need to interview numerous witnesses, they can compile an itemized list, keep it separate from the investigative plan, and merely refer to the list in the plan. Specifically, the investigative step would read "identify and interview key witnesses (see list)." As a general rule, the plan lists the steps to be completed in generic terms without including such specifics as names. However, the investigator could modify the plan later to incorporate such information.

HELPFUL HINTS

Investigators should seriously consider keeping copies of investigative plans on computer. Once they develop a plan for a particular case, they can continue to use it as a model, or boilerplate, for similar cases. Good boilerplate plans greatly reduce the initial time needed to develop new plans for offenses investigated frequently. Storing the plan on computer also allows investigators to easily note when they complete or modify steps or procedures.

Still, a hard copy of the plan should remain in the case file. By consulting the plan on a periodic basis, the case officer keeps the investigation on the right track. As important, anyone reviewing the file can determine the status of the investigation.

CONCLUSION

The word "routine" is fast disappearing from the law enforcement lexicon. Even investigations that once seemed simple are growing increasingly complex, especially in the area of white-collar crime.

Without a frame of reference, investigators may find themselves becoming overwhelmed by these often-complicated investigations. Documented plans focus an investigation from the start while providing a blueprint for investigators to follow. Using written plans, law enforcement officers provide a firm foundation for the investigation and prosecution of white-collar offenders.

An Investigative Plan—

- focuses the investigative process to ensure that all offense elements are addressed;
- limits unnecessary procedures and step duplication;
- coordinates the investigative activities of numerous personnel on large cases;
- provides stability to the investigation if staff changes occur;
- enhances communication with prosecuting officials by providing an outline of the investigation and identifying strengths and weaknesses in the case;
- provides a framework for the final report; and
- becomes a training aid for inexperienced staff members.

Arthur L. Bowker is a U.S. probation officer for the Northern District of Ohio in Cleveland.

NOTES

1. Felony sentencing in the federal system is governed to a large extent by the U.S. Sentencing Guidelines. Each offense has a base offense level assigned to it, with points being added or subtracted for aggravating or mitigating circumstances present in the offense conduct. For example, pursuant to section 3B1.3, two points are added to the base offense level for offenders who violate a position of trust during the commission of their crimes. The higher the offense level, the more severe the penalty the individual faces. The second part of the equation factors in criminal history. Also, the more points assigned for criminal history, the harsher the penalty.

2. Union embezzlement violates 29 U.S.C. [section] 501(c).

11

Firm Self-Regulation Through International Certifiable Standards: Determinants of Symbolic versus Substantive Implementation

Petra Christmann and Glen Taylor

International certifiable management standards that have been advocated as a governance mechanism for firm self-regulation of corporate social responsibility issues are effective only if certified firms comply with the requirements of the standards. Our empirical analysis shows that ISO-certified firms in China strategically select their level of compliance depending on customer preferences, customer monitoring, and expected sanctions by customers. Our findings have implications for the effectiveness of a global system of self-regulation based on certifiable standards, research on certifiable standards, and for practicing managers who require suppliers to obtain standard certifications.

INTRODUCTION

Globalization raises concerns that firms will exploit differences in national regulations of environmental conduct and working conditions. Falling barriers to trade and foreign direct investment allow firms to shift unsavory production activities to suppliers or subsidiaries in countries with lax regulations (Korten, 1995; Vernon, 1998). These concerns have prompted demands for firm self-regulation of corporate social responsibility (CSR) (Christmann, 2004; Rappaport and Flaherty, 1992; United Nations, 1993). Firm self-regulation refers to a firm's commitment to control its own conduct beyond what is required by the law. International certifiable standards provide a potential governance mechanism for firm self-regulation of CSR in the global economy (Christmann and Taylor, 2001; Rugman and Verbeke, 2001; Cashore, 2002; Boiral, 2003a; Potoski and Prakash, 2004), because the adoption of international standards restricts opportunities for firms to take advantage of cross-country differences in government regulations. However, the effectiveness of self-regulation based on international certifiable standards has received little empirical attention (O'Rourke, 2003). This paper aims to contribute to a better understanding of the conditions under which international certifiable standards are effective governance mechanisms, by empirically examining the determinants of firm compliance with these standards.

International certifiable standards that improve CSR have been proposed as a global governance mechanism for corporate behavior in areas where firms are likely to take advantage of cross-country differences of national government regulations. CSR refers to 'actions that appear to further some social good, beyond the interests of the firm and that which is required by law' (McWilliams and Siegel, 2001, 117). International standards such as the ISO 14000 environmental management system standard and the SA 8000 social accountability standard advance CSR because they require certified firms to implement specific management processes that are intended to improve environmental conduct or working conditions. These standards are developed by global non-governmental organizations such as the International Organization for Standardization (ISO), and specify requirements that go beyond government regulations. Firms seeking certification are monitored by independent third-party auditors, who certify firms' compliance with standard requirements. This governance mechanism relies on the assumption that firms voluntarily adopt these standards because customers prefer to purchase products from certified suppliers (Cashore, 2002; Christmann and Taylor, 2002).

International certifiable standards facilitate international trade by reducing the cost of managing global supply chains in two ways. First, establishing harmonized international requirements avoids a proliferation of country-, industry- and customer-specific requirements, which would increase the costs of international sourcing. Second, using third-party auditors to certify suppliers' compliance with international standards lowers monitoring costs for customers in global supply chains. Therefore, international certifiable standards are often adopted in response to pressures from foreign customers, and have become de facto requirements for many firms engaged in international business (Christmann and Taylor, 2001; Cashore, 2002). Because their adoption is driven primarily by foreign customers, export-oriented firms are likely to come under pressure to adopt higher standards for CSR than firms producing for the domestic market. This suggests that globalization may actually lead to improvements of CSR of firms in emerging economies characterized by lax environmental regulations (Christmann and Taylor, 2001).

For a certifiable standard to be an effective governance mechanism for firm self-regulation, certified firms need to comply with the standard's requirements. Most empirical research on standards treats certification as a binary variable that measures the adoption of the specified practices (e.g., Corbett and Kirsch, 2001; Delmas, 2002; Guler et al., 2002). This assumes that certification is a reliable indicator of the actual implementation of the specified practices. However, questions about auditor qualification, auditor independence, and the periodic nature of audits raise concerns about the effectiveness of third-party certifications (Van der Wiele and Brown, 1997; Stenzel, 2000; Swift et al., 2000; O'Rourke, 2002; Boiral, 2003b, 2005; Yeung and Mok, 2005). Recent research has shown that many firms do in fact pass periodic audits for continued certification without complying with a standard's requirements on an ongoing basis (Boiral, 2003b, 2005; Yeung and Mok, 2005), which raises concerns about the effectiveness of certifiable standards as a governance mechanism.

The conditions that determine whether certified firms comply with a standard's requirements have not been adequately researched. To address this issue we examine the determinants of the quality of standard implementation among firms that are certified to an international management standard. We suggest that the quality of standard implementation ranges from symbolic, where firms fail to use the practices prescribed by a certified standard in daily operations, to substantive, where firms consistently use the certified standard's practices.

We propose that firms approach implementation of certifiable standards strategically by choosing a quality of implementation that matches their perceived costs and benefits. Assuming that substantive implementation is more costly for firms than symbolic implementation, firms will choose symbolic implementation unless they anticipate benefits beyond the symbolic value of certification. Because customer requirements have been identified as a primary determinant of firms' adoption of certifiable standards (Christmann and Taylor, 2001; Corbett and Kirsch, 2001; Guler et al., 2002; Potoski and Prakash, 2004), we examine whether customer characteristics and the characteristics of the exchange relationship between suppliers and their customers influence the quality of standard implementation by suppliers.

We use the ISO 9000 quality management system standard as the empirical setting for our study. Because ISO 9000, ISO 14000 and SA 8000 have similar implementation requirements and auditing procedures, we expect firms to exhibit the same pattern of strategic behavior with respect to their quality of standard implementation regardless of the issue addressed by the standard. Using survey data from 172 randomly selected ISO 9000 certified suppliers in China, our results confirm that suppliers strategically choose their quality of implementation. Our results highlight the importance of external monitoring and expected sanctions as key drivers of implementation quality. We discuss implications for the design of systems for global self-regulation based on certifiable CSR standards, for future research on international certifiable CSR standards, and for practicing managers.

INTERNATIONAL CERTIFIABLE STANDARDS: THEORY AND EMPIRICAL EVIDENCE

At the 1992 United Nations Rio Conference on Environment and Development many participants agreed that business self-regulation is essential to sustainable development, and called for the development of a global system of self-regulation of firm environmental conduct. In response, the International Organization for Standardization launched ISO 14000, an environmental management system standard, in 1996 (Delmas, 2002). This standard, which is based on the popular ISO 9000 quality management system standard, is now the most widely diffused CSR standard, with more than 60,000 certifications by 2003 (ISO, 2004). Social Accountability International (SAI), a human rights organization focused on workplace conditions, introduced its Social Accountability 8000 management standard (SA 8000) in 1998, and by 2005 710 certifications had been awarded. SA 8000 uses a management system approach modeled on the ISO standards, in addition to setting standards for key labor rights. ISO is currently developing a standard (ISO 26000) to establish a comprehensive, harmonized global approach to CSR that provides 'practical guidance related to operationalizing social responsibility, identifying and engaging with stakeholders and enhancing credibility of reports and claims made about social responsibility' (ISO, 2005).

All of these standards are management system standards that specify internal organizational processes and management practices that firms implement to obtain certification without imposing specific performance targets. The management system by which a product or service is produced plays a critical role in identifying internal problems and in building capacity for implementing needed changes.

DRIVERS OF FIRM SELF-REGULATION THROUGH CERTIFIABLE MANAGEMENT STANDARDS

Customer demands for CSR are a key driver for firm self-regulation, but customer pressures are effective only if suppliers' CSR characteristics can be discerned (McWilliams and Siegel, 2001). Potential customers might not know whether suppliers have effective environmental or social management systems. Certification overcomes these information asymmetries by informing customers which suppliers have implemented a management system conforming to specific standards. Without certifiable standards, customers would need to incur higher costs of collecting and verifying information about all suppliers. Consequently, management system certifications are signals of supplier characteristics that lower search and monitoring costs in supply chains (Christmann and Taylor, 2002; King et al., 2005; Terlaak and King, 2006), and enable customers to consider environmental and social responsibility in purchasing decisions. Research confirms that pressures from actual and potential customers are an important external driver of standard certification (Christmann and Taylor, 2001; Corbett and Kirsch, 2001; Guler et al., 2002; Potoski and Prakash, 2004).

SYMBOLIC AND SUBSTANTIVE IMPLEMENTATION OF STANDARDS

Certifiable standards are effective only if certification improves firm performance with respect to the certified issue. However, empirical research on the relationship between certification and firm performance with respect to the issue addressed by the standard is inconclusive. Whereas some studies found that ISO 14000 certification improves environmental performance (Potoski and Prakash, 2005), others found no such effect (Andrews et al., 2003). To the contrary, King et al. (2005) found that firms with lower environmental performance were more likely to obtain certification, perhaps using certification to increase their legitimacy. One possible reason for these findings is that certified firms may not fully comply with the standard's requirements.

Research has shown that firms often adopt policies or codes of conduct for symbolic purposes without necessarily applying them in practice (Westphal and Zajac, 1994, 2001; Stevens et al., 2005). Stevens et al. (2005) found that financial executives in many firms do not use their companies' ethics codes in their decision-making. Thus the act of policy adoption can be decoupled from actual implementation (Meyer and Rowan, 1977).

Third-party monitoring of standards reduces the risk that certification is decoupled from the implementation of certified practices (King et al., 2005).

Third-party monitoring of international CSR standards is performed by independent, external auditors, who assess an organization's management system and issue a standard certificate if the system conforms to the standard's requirements. To ensure that standards are audited consistently throughout the world, standard-setting bodies develop systems for accrediting auditors.

Despite these efforts, concerns about auditing quality suggest that certification may not ensure a firm's ongoing compliance with a standard's requirements. First, some auditors lack sufficient business knowledge (Swift et al., 2000) or technical knowledge of specific industries (Seddon, 1997; Van der Wiele and Brown, 1997; O'Rourke, 2002; Boiral, 2003b; Yeung and Mok, 2005). These problems are exacerbated by the fact that management system standards specify process requirements, making verification of implementation difficult. Because certified firms play a vital role in the auditing process by providing documentation to external auditors, less qualified auditors may uncritically accept the internal report prepared by the firm (Yeung and Mok, 2005). As a result one auditor might certify a firm whereas another auditor would fail the same firm (Boiral, 2003b; Yeung and Mok, 2005). Second, auditor independence is essential to ensure unbiased certification, but auditors are selected and paid by the firm seeking certification. Firms may be inclined to select lenient auditors (Swift et al., 2000). Thus auditors face a potential conflict of interest, and may certify undeserving companies to avoid losing clients (Seddon, 1997). Third, the ongoing nature of complying with a standard diverges from the periodic nature of certification. Compliance with management system standards requires ongoing active utilization of the management system. Certification and recertification audits are scheduled periodically at pre-announced dates. ISO 14000 is recertified every 3 years and supplemented by less extensive pre-announced biannual or annual surveillance audits. Critics contend that infrequent factory visits do not allow the evaluation of normal day-to-day operations, and that the audits themselves are too short to identify more than the most obvious problems, missing many important issues (O'Rourke, 2002, 2003; Boiral, 2003b).

Research from China, Canada and Italy finds that firms that do not meet the requirements of ISO standards are able to obtain certification (Boiral, 2003b; Biazzo, 2005; Yeung and Mok, 2005). In addition, customers do not believe that the system of third-party certification works effectively. For quality management standards where certification requirements are similar to ISO 14000 and SA 8000, most customers directly monitor their certified suppliers' quality management practices in addition to requiring certification (Swift et al., 2000). Furthermore, many customers require their Chinese suppliers to obtain certification from specific foreign auditors (Yeung and Mok, 2005), indicating that customers are concerned about variations in auditor quality.

Because standard certification can be decoupled from implementation, the quality of standard implementation differs across certified firms. Firms that pursue symbolic implementation do not use the certified management system in their daily operations, and make last-minute efforts to prepare for certification audits. For these firms the standard serves a symbolic purpose (Meyer and

Rowan, 1977). They obtain certification to satisfy customer requirements and maintain greater legitimacy (DiMaggio and Powell, 1991), without substantive implementation of standard requirements. In contrast, firms that pursue substantive implementation embed standard requirements in their daily routines. For these firms the standard serves a substantive purpose. They do not just obtain certification for the purpose of appearance.

HYPOTHESES DEVELOPMENT

We suggest that firms choose a level of quality of implementation of certified standards that matches their perceived costs and benefits. We assume that substantive standard implementation is more costly for firms than symbolic implementation, because the ongoing costs of maintaining management systems are substantial (Delmas, 2002). The high costs of complying with the continual improvement principle of management system standards are a main reason why ISO-certified firms in China did not fully implement the standards (Yeung and Mok, 2005). Thus, firms will invest in substantive implementation only to the extent that their perceived benefits exceed costs.

Response to customer pressures is a primary determinant of standard certification. So far, research on certifiable standards has treated customers as a homogeneous group. We provide a differentiated approach to customer pressures by explicitly incorporating differences in customer preferences and activities as well as characteristics of the exchange relationship with customers in our hypotheses about the determinants of suppliers' quality of implementation.

In developing our hypotheses about the role of customers we draw on transaction cost economics (TCE). A central assumption of TCE is that firms behave opportunistically. Opportunism is defined as the seeking of self-interest with guile (Williamson, 1985). Using a TCE framework, symbolic implementation of certifiable management standards can be interpreted as opportunistic supplier behavior. Symbolic implementation of a standard means suppliers are 'making ... false or empty, that is self-disbelieved ... promises' (Williamson, 1975), because they use certification as a signal without fully complying with the standard's requirements.

Some customers may be concerned only about their suppliers' standard certification and not their quality of standard implementation. A supplier's symbolic implementation would meet these customers' expectations. We explore this possibility in Hypothesis 1. TCE suggests that monitoring and the threat of sanctions are important instruments for ensuring compliance with the terms of an agreement (Williamson, 1996). In Hypotheses 2–4 we explore the role of customer monitoring, and in Hypotheses 4 and 5 we explore the role of sanctions.

Suppliers need incentives to justify incurring the higher costs of substantive implementation. The importance that customers place on the issue addressed by a standard affects suppliers' incentives for substantive implementation. Some customers require their suppliers to obtain standard certification for symbolic reasons, to respond to legitimacy concerns by demonstrating that they are taking steps to control the conduct of firms in their supply chains. These customers are likely to be satisfied that their suppliers have obtained certification without concern for their quality of implementation. If suppliers perceive that the issue is not of high importance to their customers, they have no incentive to invest more in standard implementation beyond what is minimally required to achieve certification. Thus we expect these suppliers to choose symbolic implementation. Other customers have valuable brand-name reputations to lose if their suppliers do not act in a socially responsible manner, or see high supplier CSR as a way to differentiate their products. These customers are more substantively concerned about the issue addressed by a standard and about suppliers' performance regarding the issue. Therefore they are likely to be interested in substantive standard implementation by suppliers, and may reward suppliers for substantive implementation and/or punish suppliers for symbolic implementation. This provides incentives to suppliers to choose substantive implementation.

> H1: The more important a supplier perceives the issue that is addressed by a certifiable management system standard to be for its customers, the more likely the supplier is to choose substantive implementation of the standard.

Our next three hypotheses address how the probability that customers will detect their suppliers' quality of standard implementation affects suppliers' choice of symbolic versus substantive implementation. Without direct monitoring, customers are unlikely to have sufficient information to determine their suppliers' quality of implementation. Transaction cost theory suggests that limited information about partners' behavior in exchange relationships is an important determinant of opportunistic behavior (Alchian and Demsetz, 1972). When performance is difficult to measure, parties have incentives to limit their efforts toward fulfilling the agreement. Consequently, we suggest that suppliers who believe that their customers will not detect their quality of standard implementation will be more likely to choose symbolic implementation, whereas suppliers who believe that their customers will be able to detect their quality of standard implementation will be more likely to choose substantive implementation.

TCE suggests that monitoring reduces information asymmetries between customers and suppliers (Balakrishnan and Koza, 1993), and that monitoring is a principal mechanism to reduce the likelihood of opportunistic behavior of exchange partners, because deviations can result in sanctions such as penalties or termination of the contract (Lal, 1990). Because of the high cost of direct monitoring many customers may prefer to rely on third-party monitoring and certification. However, despite the added costs, direct customer monitoring of certified suppliers is quite common (Swift et al., 2000), perhaps because of concerns about the effectiveness of third-party monitoring. Monitoring suppliers directly allows customers to discern the quality of implementation of a certified management system. The probability that customers will detect symbolic standard implementation can be expected to be related to the frequency of customers' direct monitoring.

H2: The more frequently customers monitor a supplier's performance on the issue that is addressed by a certifiable management system standard, the more likely it is that the supplier will choose substantive implementation of the standard.

The frequency of customer monitoring can be expected to have a larger effect on suppliers' quality of standard implementation if customers' quality of monitoring is high. Firms in emerging economies such as China are likely to have lower capabilities to monitor firms in their supply chains than customers from developed countries (Dunning, 1995). Therefore we expect that for suppliers in emerging economies the frequency of customer monitoring will have a larger effect on quality of implementation for firms that sell a larger proportion of their output to foreign customers than for firms that produce primarily for the domestic market.

H3: In emerging economies the effect of frequency of customer monitoring on quality of standard implementation is stronger for suppliers that sell more of their output to foreign customers.

Some customers rely on supplier certification programs to develop a list of approved suppliers from which they choose (Stump and Heide, 1996). These programs specify and measure criteria for supplier selection and retention such as quality performance, manufacturing capabilities, capabilities for environmental management, working conditions, and financial strength. Suppliers that do not meet the specified criteria will be eliminated from consideration. To avoid monitoring costs these programs rely on criteria that can be measured at low cost, such as third-party supplier certification. Because these programs tend to rely on third-party certification rather than on direct monitoring the probability that customers who rely heavily on such programs will detect suppliers' quality of implementation is relatively low. Thus we expect that suppliers will choose symbolic implementation of standards if their customers rely on supplier certification programs.

H4: The higher customers' reliance is on supplier certification programs, the less likely it is that the supplier will choose substantive implementation of certifiable management system standards.

Our next two hypotheses explore how sanctions affect the quality of standard implementation. TCE suggests that sanctions for opportunistic behavior reduce the likelihood that an exchange partner will act opportunistically (Williamson, 1996). Suppliers' perceptions of the likelihood that customers will impose sanctions such as contract termination if symbolic implementation is detected will affect suppliers' quality of standard implementation. The likelihood of a supplier being terminated for symbolic implementation depends on two joint conditions: (1) customers' cost of switching to another supplier, and (2) the importance of suppliers' quality of standard implementation to customers. First, customer switching costs arise from the difficulties involved in replacing current suppliers (Heide and John, 1988). Customers with high switching costs are less likely to terminate suppliers for opportunistic behavior. Instead they may impose lesser sanctions, or work with suppliers on correcting the situation. Thus suppliers who perceive their customers' switching costs to be high may believe that they are less likely to be terminated for symbolic standard implementation. Second, customers are likely to impose sanctions for symbolic implementation only if the issue addressed by the standard is important to them. Both conditions—low switching costs and high issue importance for customers—need to be satisfied simultaneously.

> H5: The likelihood that a supplier will choose substantive implementation of a certifiable management system standard is higher when the supplier perceives that customers place a high importance on the issue certified by the standard and that customers have low costs of switching suppliers.

The costliness of sanctions to suppliers also affects the likelihood of opportunistic behavior by suppliers (Becker, 1968). A supplier's cost of being terminated by a customer depends on the extent to which the supplier has made relationship-specific investments (Klein et al., 1978; Williamson, 1979). Relationship-specific investments include investments of time and effort required to establish working relationships with customers as well as investments in specialized assets such as customer-specific equipment. Relationship-specific investments are worth less if the customer terminates the relationship. Consequently, high levels of relationship-specific investments make suppliers more committed to the relationship (Parkhe, 1993) and more likely to take efforts not to lose the customer. If suppliers make relationship-specific investments with customers that place a high importance on an issue addressed by a standard, their efforts to retain customers are likely to include substantive implementation of the standard. Thus the effect of a supplier's level of relationship-specific investments on the supplier's quality of standard implementation is moderated by the importance of the issue to its customers.

> H6: The likelihood that a supplier will choose substantive implementation of a certifiable management system standard is higher when the supplier perceives that customers place high importance on the issue addressed by the standard, and when the supplier has made investments that are specific to the relationship with particular customers.

DATA AND METHOD

Research Setting

To test our hypotheses we need a research setting in which many customers require their suppliers to obtain standard certification and in which some customers consider their suppliers' quality of standard implementation to be very important and invest in directly monitoring their certified suppliers. The ISO 9000 quality management system standard meets these criteria.

ISO 9000 is the most widely adopted management system standard in the world, with more than 500,000 certifications in 2003 (ISO, 2004). For most customers, incentives to directly monitor their suppliers' environmental conduct and working conditions in addition to requiring ISO 14000 or SA 8000 certification are low. Only a few customers are singled out by special interest groups or the media to face close scrutiny of their suppliers' environmental or labor practices. In contrast, for certifiable quality management standards, incentives to invest in directly monitoring certified suppliers are high because the quality of products purchased from suppliers is of concern to many customers. The Institute of Quality Assurance found that 63% of customers directly monitor the quality management of ISO 9000 certified suppliers (Swift et al., 2000).

Although the ISO 9000 standard addresses a different issue than ISO 14000 and SA 8000, broader interpretations of CSR suggest that total quality management is linked to CSR because the core elements of quality management 'establish norms of behavior for the firm which extend beyond self-interest' (Wicks and Freeman, 1998). In addition, the KLD database, which is widely used in academic research to operationalize CSR (Berman et al., 1999), includes product quality as one dimension of CSR. Thus adoption of the ISO 9000 quality management standard may foster CSR. In addition, there are three parallels between ISO 9000 and standards that explicitly address CSR that suggest that the determinants of the quality of standard implementation tested in this study will not differ between these standards. First, all of these standards are part of an integrated set of management system standards that impose identical types of requirements (implementation and documentation of a management system) on firms. The management system approach of ISO 14000 and SA 8000 is modeled after ISO 9000, and firms can implement ISO 14000 and ISO 9000 as an integrated management system. Second, the auditing process and concerns about auditing are similar for the all management standards. The auditing processes are so similar that ISO has developed a joint auditing standard for ISO 9000 and ISO 14000. The time between re-certification audits is three years for both ISO 14000 and ISO 9000, and most auditors are accredited to perform both certifications. ISO 9000 faces the same criticisms as ISO 14000 about audit quality and the resulting concerns about the quality of standard implementation (Boiral, 2003b; Yeung and Mok, 2005). Third, just as in the case of standards explicitly addressing CSR, firms obtain ISO 9000 certification primarily because of customer pressures (Waller and Ahire, 1996). Given these similarities we expect that firms will exhibit the same strategic behavior with respect to their choice of quality of implementation, and that our independent variables will have the same effects on the quality of implementation regardless of the issue addressed by the management system standard. Therefore we believe that our findings can be generalized to any international management system standard. We shall discuss potential biases from using ISO 9000 rather than environmental or social standards in our conclusions.

China provides an ideal research setting for testing our hypotheses because its export orientation and high export growth (about 30% annually), combined with concerns about the stringency and enforcement of Chinese environmental and labor regulations, give rise to concerns that it is becoming a global production and export platform for goods produced under substandard environmental and working conditions. China is home to six of the ten most polluted cites in the world (Balfour, 2005), and working conditions in China have been described as leading the world in abusive practices (Sethi, 2003). This suggests that international certifiable standards for CSR have the potential to play an important role in reducing the negative effects of globalization in China. Demands from foreign customers have led to a tremendous growth in the number of ISO 9000 certifications in China—from 507 in 1995 to almost 97,000 in 2003 (Christmann and Taylor, 2001; ISO, 2004; Yeung and Mok, 2005), resulting in China having the highest number of ISO 9000 certifications of any country (ISO, 2004).

Sample, Survey Design, and Data Collection

Given that data on the variables included in our study are not available from public sources, and that our hypotheses suggest that suppliers' perceptions of customer characteristics determine their quality of standard implementation, we needed to collect survey data to test our hypotheses. We were able to secure the cooperation of the China Quality Certification Center (CQC), the largest standards auditor in China, to support the data collection for our study. CQC has issued ISO 9000 certificates to more than 5,000 facilities in China, which constituted our study population. We mailed surveys to a sample of 550 firms that were randomly selected from their database. This mailing sample was large enough to obtain sufficient responses for our data analysis but small enough to perform intensive follow-up with non-respondents to ensure a high response rate.

We designed our survey in several steps. We first designed a preliminary version, which we discussed with managers and auditors from CQC during a visit to China in 2001. We revised the survey based on their comments, and discussed the new version again with CQC auditors as well as with Chinese quality managers. We created a final version of the survey incorporating their feedback, which was professionally translated into Chinese and back-translated into English in order to ensure accuracy of the translation.

The target respondent for the survey was the person in charge of ISO 9000 certification, whose name was included in the CQC database. In almost all cases this individual was the quality manager of the firm. Although this methodology restricted us to using only one respondent per firm, we identified the most knowledgeable and appropriate person to complete the questionnaire, the principal methodological solution to using single respondents (Campbell, 1955; John and Reve, 1982).

The survey was mailed in 2003. The mailing of the survey included a cover letter from CQC explaining the purpose of the survey, and guaranteeing respondents that CQC would not have access to data for individual companies. To ensure a high response rate and to obtain truthful answers, respondents were not asked to identify themselves or their company on the survey. The surveys simply had a control number to keep track of respondents versus non-respondents. Firms that did not return the survey received a follow-up phone call by CQC staff. In addition, non-respondents received a follow-up mailing of the survey three months after the initial mailing. We obtained 206 completed responses, resulting in a response rate of 37%, a very high response rate for a mail survey. Some responses needed to be eliminated from our analysis because of missing data, leaving us with a sample of 172 for this study. The median firm size for respondents was between 101 and 500 employees, and about 23% were wholly or partially foreign owned.

In order to evaluate whether respondents are representative of the mailing sample it would be desirable to compare respondents with non-respondents along known characteristics. Unfortunately, we did not have access to information about non-respondents that would allow us to perform this analysis. We were, however, able to use wave analysis, which measures non-response bias by comparing respondents who respond readily to the survey with those who respond after the follow-up steps are taken. This procedure is based on the observation that, in mail surveys, late respondents tend to be more similar to non-respondents than early respondents (Fowler, 1993). Comparisons of means and correlations for surveys that were received after the first mailing and after the second mailing show that the two groups do not differ significantly in the level of or the relationships between variables. Thus a non-response bias is unlikely to exist.

Measures

Unless otherwise noted, the survey items were measured on a five-point Likert scale. For our multi-item measures we assessed the psychometric measurement properties by performing a confirmatory factor analysis, and achieved acceptable results. Fit indices, correlations between the residual variance and any pair of measurement items, and modification indices for theta-delta (Anderson and Gerbing, 1988) provide strong evidence that our measures are unidimensional. Tests for reliability indicate acceptable values: average variances extracted all exceed 0.5, and composite reliabilities all exceed 0.6 (Bagozzi and Yi, 1988). (1) In addition, all Cronbach alpha coefficients are greater than the threshold value of 0.7, indicating good internal consistency of the survey items (Nunnally and Bernstein, 1994).

Dependent Variable

The dependent variable quality of management system standard implementation was measured as the average of three survey items that had previously been used by Naveh and Marcus (2004):

1. 'To what extent are the documents created for the purpose of ISO 9000 used in daily practice?'

2. 'To what extent has the ISO 9000 system become part of your regular routine?'

3. 'To what extent are preparations for external audits made at the last minute?' (reverse scored).

(1 = not at all, 5 = to a very large extent). A low score indicates symbolic implementation and a high score indicates substantive implementation.

Independent Variables

The independent variable importance of issue to customers was measured by the average of two survey items: 'How important are the following criteria for your major customers in their selection of supplier? (1) quality of products, (2) on-time delivery' (1 = not important, 5 = most important). The independent variable frequency of direct customer monitoring was measured by the average of two survey items: (1) 'Our major customers assess our quality performance through formal evaluations,' and (2) 'Our major customers provide us with feedback about the results of their evaluations' (1 = never, 5 = very frequently).

The independent variable supplier certification program was measured by the survey item 'Our major customers use a supplier certification program to certify suppliers' quality' (1 = never, 5 = very frequently).

Perceived customer switching costs were measured by the survey item 'It is easy for our major customers to find alternative suppliers for the products we are providing' (1 = strongly disagree, 5 = strongly agree). Note that for this variable a high score means low customer switching costs.

Relationship-specific investments by suppliers are measured by the survey item 'Establishing a working relationship with new customers is a time-consuming process' (1 = strongly disagree, 5 = strongly agree).

Sales to foreign customers is measured as the sum of the percentage of total sales exported and the percentage of total sales sold to foreign customers in China as reported in the survey.

Control Variables

Because the ISO 9000 standards are considered less well adapted to small organizations, and small firms often lack the resources to implement management systems, substantive implementation may be easier for larger firms. We control for firm size using the number of employees in China (measured on a seven-point scale from $1 =$ less than 50 to $7 =$ more than 10,000). Foreign MNEs may be able to transfer superior implementation capabilities and financial resources from their operations abroad to their Chinese subsidiaries. To control for this effect we include the percentage of foreign ownership as a control variable. ISO 9000 standards are better adapted to the manufacturing sector than to the service sector, resulting in service firms being more likely to pursue symbolic implementation (Boiral, 2003b). We control for industrial sector by including a dummy variable that takes the value 1 for service firms and 0 for manufacturing firms. Finally, it is likely to be easier for firms to achieve a substantive implementation if the technology used in the firm's production processes is stable and does not change over time. To control for this effect we include a survey item that asks respondents to rate their process technology on a five-point scale from 'evolving' to 'mature'.

TABLE 1   Descriptive Statistics and Correlation Matrix

	Mean	s.d.	1
1. Issue importance to customers	4.63	0.50	1.00
2. Frequency of customer monitoring	4.10	0.82	0.32 ★★★
3. Supplier certification program	3.14	1.09	0.09
4. Sales to foreign customers	0.30	0.38	0.03
5. Low switching costs for customers	3.10	1.15	0.12
6. Supplier's relationship-specific investments (a)	3.65	1.03	0.19 ★★
7. Frequency of customer monitoring $\times$ Sales to foreign customers (a)	0.12	0.96	0.09
8. Issue importance to customers $\times$ Low switching costs for customers (a)	0.18	0.96	-0.39 ★★★
9. Issue importance to customers $\times$ Supplier's relationship-specific investments	0.17	0.86	-0.18 ★★
10. Number of employees	2.98	1.16	0.03
11. Percentage of foreign ownership	0.16	0.33	0.01
12. Service industry	0.06	0.24	0.05
13. Mature process technology	3.84	1.00	0.14 [†]
14. Quality of ISO 9000 implementation	4.22	0.65	0.30 ★★★

Continued

TABLE 1 *Continued*

	2	3
1. Issue importance to customers		
2. Frequency of customer monitoring	1.00	
3. Supplier certification program	0.20 ★★	1.00
4. Sales to foreign customers	0.18 ★	0.18 ★
5. Low switching costs for customers	0.06	−0.11
6. Supplier's relationship-specific investments (a)	0.16 ★	−0.01
7. Frequency of customer monitoring × Sales to foreign customers (a)	−0.09	0.15 (†)
8. Issue importance to customers × Low switching costs for customers (a)	−0.16 ★	0.04
9. Issue importance to customers × Supplier's relationship-specific investments	−0.07	0.08
10. Number of employees	0.10	−0.03
11. Percentage of foreign ownership	0.08	0.02
12. Service industry	0.16 ★	0.10
13. Mature process technology	0.02	0.16 ★
14. Quality of ISO 9000 implementation	0.21 ★★	−0.09

	4	5
1. Issue importance to customers		
2. Frequency of customer monitoring		
3. Supplier certification program		
4. Sales to foreign customers	1.00	
5. Low switching costs for customers	−0.16 ★	1.00
6. Supplier's relationship-specific investments (a)	−0.05	0.11
7. Frequency of customer monitoring × Sales to foreign customers (a)	0.25 ★★★	−0.11

TABLE 1 *Continued*

	4	5	
8. Issue importance to customers × Low switching costs for customers (a)	−0.15 [†]	0.04	
9. Issue importance to customers × Supplier's relationship-specific investments	−0.14 [†]	0.00	
10. Number of employees	0.24 ★★	0.09	
11. Percentage of foreign ownership	0.42 ★★★	−0.16 ★	
12. Service industry	−0.09	0.14 [†]	
13. Mature process technology	0.11	−0.02	
14. Quality of ISO 9000 implementation	−0.06	0.09	

	6	7	8
1. Issue importance to customers			
2. Frequency of customer monitoring			
3. Supplier certification program			
4. Sales to foreign customers			
5. Low switching costs for customers			
6. Supplier's relationship-specific investments (a)	1.00		
7. Frequency of customer monitoring × Sales to foreign customers (a)	−0.05	1.00	
8. Issue importance to customers × Low switching costs for customers (a)	−0.01	−0.01	1.00
9. Issue importance to customers × Supplier's relationship-specific investments	0.09	0.02	0.23 ★★
10. Number of employees	−0.04	0.15 [†]	−0.11
11. Percentage of foreign ownership	0.01	0.07	−0.11
12. Service industry	0.02	−0.14 [†]	0.00
13. Mature process technology	−0.11	0.08	−0.07
14. Quality of ISO 9000 implementation	0.08	0.10	0.03

Continued

TABLE 1 *Continued*

	9	10	11
1. Issue importance to customers			
2. Frequency of customer monitoring			
3. Supplier certification program			
4. Sales to foreign customers			
5. Low switching costs for customers			
6. Supplier's relationship-specific investments (a)			
7. Frequency of customer monitoring × Sales to foreign customers (a)			
8. Issue importance to customers × Low switching costs for customers (a)			
9. Issue importance to customers × Supplier's relationship-specific investments	1.00		
10. Number of employees	−0.17 ★	1.00	
11. Percentage of foreign ownership	0.00	0.08	1.00
12. Service industry	0.01	−0.14 (†)	−0.05
13. Mature process technology	0.00	0.12	0.06
14. Quality of ISO 9000 implementation	0.10	−0.03	−0.07

	12	13	14
1. Issue importance to customers			
2. Frequency of customer monitoring			
3. Supplier certification program			
4. Sales to foreign customers			
5. Low switching costs for customers			
6. Supplier's relationship-specific investments (a)			
7. Frequency of customer monitoring × Sales to foreign customers (a)			
8. Issue importance to customers × Low switching costs for customers (a)			

TABLE 1 *Continued*

	12	13	14
9. Issue importance to customers $\times$ Supplier's relationship-specific investments			
10. Number of employees			
11. Percentage of foreign ownership			
12. Service industry	1.00		
13. Mature process technology	-0.03	1.00	
14. Quality of ISO 9000 implementation	0.02	0.20 $\star\star$	1.00

(†) $P < 0.10$; $\star$ $P < 0.05$; $\star\star$ $P < 0.01$; $\star\star\star$ $P < 0.001$.
(a) Interaction terms are calculated using standardized scores.

PRELIMINARY DATA ANALYSIS AND METHOD

Descriptive statistics and correlations for all variables are presented in Table 1. The relatively high mean value (4.2) for the dependent variable quality of standard implementation warrants attention. Such a high value is to be expected, given that all the firms in our sample were ISO 9000 certified, which requires that they have implemented the certified practices to some extent. Values for this variable range from 2.67 to 5, and its distribution is non-normal. If the dependent variable and, thus, the error term is not normally distributed, ordinary least square (OLS) is not the most efficient method of estimating the slope parameters of a multiple regression model (Judge et al., 1988). Robust regression, an iterative estimation technique in which smaller weights are assigned to outlying data points to minimize their impact on the estimation process, yields more efficient estimates in this situation (Rousseeuw and Leroy, 1987). When the assumptions of OLS are met, robust regression produces estimates identical to OLS (Western, 1995). To assess the extent to which the non-normal distribution of the dependent variable affects our results we report results of robust regression analysis using Andrews et al. (1972) weight function as well as OLS regression results. (2)

To test Hypothesis 3 we constructed an interaction term between the variables frequency of customer monitoring and sales to foreign customers. To test Hypotheses 4 and 5 we constructed interaction terms between the variables issue importance for customers and customer switching cost and relationship-specific investments respectively. To reduce multicollinearity between the main and the interaction effects, we computed all interaction terms as the product of standardized construct scores (Aiken and West, 1991).

Before testing the hypotheses we explored the likely extent of multi-collinearity in the data by analyzing the correlations between the independent variables. Most of the correlations are below 0.3, indicating no problems of multicollinearity (see Table 1). We also evaluated the presence of multivariate multicollinearity in our OLS regression using several diagnostic tests suggested by Belsley et al. (1980). Examinations of variance inflation factors and condition indexes revealed that no multicollinearity was present in the data.

Common method bias can pose problems for survey research that relies on self-reported data (Campbell and Fiske, 1959) by artificially inflating observed relationships between variables. To diminish if not avoid the effects of consistency artifacts we placed the dependent variables after the independent variables in the survey (Salancik and Pfeffer, 1977). In addition, a post hoc analysis using Harman's single-factor test (Podsakoff and Organ, 1986) showed no evidence of common method variance.

RESULTS

Our regression results for both robust and OLS regression can be seen in Table 2. Model 1 shows control variables only, model 2 adds main effects, and model 3 shows the complete model, including interaction effects. The coefficient estimates of the OLS regression and the robust regression are substantively similar, indicating that the non-normality of the error term does not affect this study's findings. Therefore we describe only our robust regression results in this section. Comparing models 2 and 3 indicates that adding interaction effects does not change our findings regarding the main effect hypotheses.

Hypothesis 1 states that the importance that customers place on the issue addressed by a standard contributes to substantive standard implementation by suppliers. This hypothesis is supported by the data. The coefficient for the variable issue importance to customers is positive and significant ($P < 0.001$).

Hypothesis 2 states that the frequency of direct customer monitoring contributes to substantive standard implementation by suppliers. This hypothesis is supported by the data. The coefficient for the variable frequency of customer monitoring is positive and significant ($P < 0.01$).

Hypothesis 3 states that the effect of frequency of customer monitoring on quality of standard implementation is moderated by sales to foreign customers. This hypothesis is supported by the data. The coefficient for the interaction term between frequency of customer monitoring and sales to foreign customers is positive and significant ($P < 0.1$).

Hypothesis 4 states that supplier certification programs contribute to symbolic standard implementation by suppliers. This hypothesis is supported by

TABLE 2 Regression Results

Dependent Variable: Quality of ISO 9000 Implementation

	Robust Regression		
	(1) Control Variables Only	(2) Main Effects Only	(3) Full Model
Intercept	3.98 ★★★	4.53 ★★★	4.54 ★★★
	(0.19)	(0.20)	(0.18)
Explanatory variables			
Issue importance to customers (a)		0.22 ★★★	0.24 ★★★
		(0.04)	(0.04)
Frequency of customer monitoring (a)		0.07	0.10 ★★
		(0.04)	(0.04)
Supplier certification program		−0.13 ★★★	−0.10 ★★
		(0.04)	(0.03)
Sales to foreign customers (a)		0.04	0.06
		(0.04)	(0.04)
Low switching costs for customers (a)		0.03	0.02
		(0.04)	(0.04)
Supplier's relationship-specific investments (a)		0.04	−0.02
		(0.04)	(0.04)
Frequency of customer monitoring × Sales to foreign customers			0.08 (†)
			(0.04)
Issue importance to customers × Low switching costs for customers			0.16 ★★★
			(0.04)
Issue importance to customers × Supplier's relationship-specific investments			0.09 ★
			(0.03)
Control variables			
Number of employees	−0.08 ★	−0.06 (†)	−0.04
	(0.04)	(0.03)	(0.03)
Percentage of foreign ownership	−0.20	−0.10	−0.07
	(0.12)	(0.12)	(0.10)
Service industry	−0.03	−0.07	−0.12
	(0.17)	(0.15)	(0.13)
Mature process technology	0.16 ★★★	0.10 ★	0.09 ★
	(0.04)	(0.04)	(0.04)
R^2	0.11	0.33	0.42
Adjusted R^2	(0.09)	(0.28)	(0.37)

Continued

TABLE 2 *Continued*

	OLS Regression		
	(1) Control Variables Only	**(2) Main Effects Only**	**(3) Full Model**
Intercept	3.79 ★★★	4.14 ★★★	4.18 ★★★
	(0.22)	(0.26)	(0.32)
Explanatory variables			
Issue importance to customers (a)		0.15 ★★	0.19 ★★★
		(0.05)	(0.05)
Frequency of customer monitoring (a)		0.13 ★	0.15 ★★
		(0.06)	(0.05)
Supplier certification program		−0.10 ★	−0.13 ★★
		(0.05)	(0.04)
Sales to foreign customers (a)		−0.02	−0.02
		(0.05)	(0.05)
Low switching costs for customers (a)		0.02	0.01
		(0.05)	(0.05)
Supplier's relationship-specific investments (a)		0.02	0.00
		(0.05)	(0.05)
Frequency of customer monitoring × Sales to foreign customers			0.10 [†]
			(0.06)
Issue importance to customers × Low switching costs for customers			0.11 ★
			(0.05)
Issue importance to customers × Supplier's relationship-specific investments			0.09 [†]
			(0.05)
Control variables			
Number of employees	−0.02	−0.04	−0.03
	(0.04)	(0.04)	(0.04)
Percentage of foreign ownership	−0.15	−0.14	−0.13
	(0.15)	(0.16)	(0.14)
Service industry	0.05	−0.05	0.00
	(0.20)	(0.20)	(0.19)
Mature process technology	0.14 ★★	0.13 ★★	0.13 ★★
	(0.05)	(0.05)	(0.05)
R^2	0.05	0.18	0.24
Adjusted R^2	(0.03)	(0.12)	(0.17)

Standard errors are in parentheses.
[†] $P < 0.10$; ★ $P < 0.05$; ★★ $P < 0.01$; ★★★ $P < 0.001$.
(a) Standardized scores.

the data. The coefficient for the supplier certification program variable is negative and significant ($P < 0.01$).

Hypothesis 5 suggests that suppliers are more likely to choose substantive implementation when their customers place a high importance on the issue addressed by the standard and have low costs of switching suppliers. This hypothesis is supported by the data. The coefficient for the interaction term between issue importance to customers and low customer switching costs is positive and significant ($P < 0.001$).

Hypothesis 6 states that suppliers are more likely to choose substantive implementation when customers place high importance on the issue addressed by the standard and suppliers have made high levels of relationship-specific investments. This hypothesis is supported by the data. The coefficient for the interaction term between issue importance to customers and suppliers' relationship-specific investment is positive and significant ($P < 0.01$).

CONCLUSIONS

The effectiveness of international certifiable management standards as a governance mechanism for self-regulation of CSR in the global economy has not yet been established. Self-regulation can be effective only if firms embrace the intent and substance of certifiable standards and pursue substantive implementation by continuously applying their management processes rather than merely acquiring formal external recognition through certification. Weak third-party monitoring allows firms to obtain certification without continuously complying with standard requirements. We suggest that if symbolic implementation is enough to satisfy customers, or if monitoring is so weak or sanctions so slight that firms see no economic justification to do more than the minimum, then firms will choose symbolic implementation, which gives them a public relations benefit without making real progress toward CSR. Our findings indicate that suppliers are more likely to choose substantive implementation if customers place high importance on an issue, monitor their suppliers directly, possess monitoring capabilities, and do not rely on third-party certification in selecting their suppliers. We also find that the likelihood and cost of sanctions contribute to substantive standard implementation by suppliers. Our findings have important implications for the prospect of firm self-regulation of environmental and social responsibility through certifiable management system standards, for future research on certifiable standards, and for management practice.

DISCUSSION

For suppliers in emerging economies such as China the primary pressure for self-regulation stems from customers in industrialized countries requiring adoption of certifiable standards by their suppliers (Christmann and Taylor, 2001; Corbett and Kirsch, 2001; Guler et al., 2002). Our results suggest that the role of customers in promoting effective international self-regulation goes beyond requiring their suppliers to obtain standard certification. Customers directly affect their suppliers' quality of standard implementation through their preferences and actions. Our results show that suppliers do not perceive customer pressures for standard certification as a homogeneous requirement. Variations in the frequency and quality of customer monitoring and in the perceived costs and likelihood of customer sanctions affect supplier's compliance with standards' requirements. When customers rely too heavily on standard certification without maintaining some of their own direct monitoring effort, and when costly sanctions for poor standard implementation are not expected by suppliers, suppliers are likely to act opportunistically. Suppliers circumvent the intent of certifiable standards by doing the minimum necessary to maintain certification, knowing either that their customers will not notice this failure or that sanctions are not likely or not costly.

IMPLICATIONS FOR DEVELOPMENT OF INTERNATIONAL CERTIFIABLE STANDARDS

Our findings have important implications for the future development of international certifiable standards for CSR. Customers are less likely to directly monitor their suppliers' environmental and social responsibility conduct than their quality performance, which suggests that suppliers should be even more inclined toward symbolic implementation when it comes to CSR standards. Thus the credibility of international certifiable CSR standards is more suspect than the credibility of quality standards.

Given the similarities in the requirements and auditing procedures for international management system standards, we believe that our findings have implications for any such standard, not just CSR standards. Periodic third-party audits are not sufficient to ensure effective implementation of international certifiable management system standards. Additional monitoring and sanctions are required for substantive implementation of such standards. This suggests either that customers need to play a more active role in monitoring their suppliers' conduct or that third-party auditing needs to be made more effective. Although our study highlights the important contribution of direct customer monitoring, monitoring suppliers' conduct is costly for customers.

Certification is a cost-effective mechanism to reduce information asymmetries in global supply chains because information about unobservable supplier characteristics is collected and verified only once. Thus symbolic implementation can be cost-effectively deterred by improving third-party monitoring practices, increasing audit transparency, and increasing the accountability of auditors (Stenzel, 2000; O'Rourke, 2002). International standard-setting bodies such as ISO, which provides a forum in which experts and diverse stakeholders can identify and discuss issues that impact on the effectiveness of international standards, must design monitoring mechanisms that address the risk that achievement of a standard's goals will be jeopardized by standards adopted for symbolic purposes. This will increase the credibility of international certifiable standards as signals of unobservable supplier attributes and thus the effectiveness of such standards as a governance mechanism for firm self-regulation in the global economy.

IMPLICATIONS FOR RESEARCH

Researchers interested in environmental and CSR standards need to pay attention to how firms actually implement standards, and not only to certification. Our study suggests that the quality of standard implementation varies among certified firms as they exploit auditing systems that allow them to strategically select the extent to which they comply with the standard's requirements. In addition, previous research has shown that some firms implement management systems but do not obtain certification (Terlaak and King, 2006), and that some certified firms go beyond standards' requirements (Naveh and Marcus, 2004). All of these findings suggest that it may not be appropriate to use certification as a measure of the adoption of CSR management practices. Researchers need to acknowledge the limitation of certification as a measure, and need to evaluate how variations in the quality of standard implementation may affect their results. Symbolic implementation may explain why many studies (e.g., Andrews et al., 2003; King et al., 2005) found that certification did not improve firms' performance with respect to the issue addressed by the standard.

Research on certifiable standards has so far conceptualized customer pressures for self-regulation as a unified variable, which assumes that customers are a homogeneous group. Our results show that suppliers' responses vary depending on customer preferences and activities, which suggests that customer pressures need to be analyzed in a more differentiated way. Thus future research should go beyond treating customers as a homogeneous group by including the types of requirements and preferences that different customers impose on suppliers. This may be done by distinguishing between different types of customers that exhibit different preferences and behaviors. For example, business customers can be expected to be more likely than end consumers to directly monitor their suppliers.

IMPLICATIONS FOR PRACTICING MANAGERS

Our findings also have implications for practicing managers in firms that use certifiable management standards to select their suppliers. Customers cannot rely on certifiable standards to assure their suppliers' conduct. Customers seeking to avoid symbolic implementation need to tell their suppliers that the actual implementation of the standard's requirements is important, and invest in direct monitoring. Suppliers with high investments in relationship-specific assets may be less likely to pursue symbolic implementation, which suggests that customers do not have to monitor these suppliers as frequently.

LIMITATIONS AND SUGGESTIONS FOR FUTURE RESEARCH

Because our study included only certified firms, we cannot address differences between certified and non-certified firms. It is possible that certified firms pursuing symbolic implementation have better management systems than non-certified firms. All we can say is that we observed a variance in the implementation of standards among certified firms, which seems to be caused by deliberate strategic choices.

Using data from firms that have been certified by a single auditing firm (CQC) allowed us to hold auditor quality constant, but precluded us from examining whether there is an 'auditor effect' on the quality of standard implementation. An interesting extension of this study would be to include firms that have been certified by different auditors. Research has shown that the adoption and implementation of management standards are affected by domestic cultural, political, and institutional environments (Casper and Hancke, 1999; Delmas, 2002; Potoski and Prakash, 2004). Testing our hypotheses in the context of a single country allowed us to hold the environment constant, but weakens the generalizability of our findings. China is in transition from a centrally planned economy to a market-based economy. Thus the concepts of self-regulation and 'voluntary' initiatives are still relatively new, and businesses may still act with a 'compliance' mentality even with respect to 'voluntary' standards as a legacy of the pervasive role of government regulations under the centrally planned system. This may result in firms doing the minimum required to achieve certification. Thus firms in China may be more likely to pursue symbolic implementation than firms in other countries. Cross-country studies could explore how cultural, political, and institutional environments affect the quality of standard implementation.

Despite these limitations, we believe our main findings concerning the role of customer monitoring and sanctions hold true for international certifiable standards across a wide range of countries. Although cultural differences may lead to differences in the magnitude of firm responses to monitoring and sanctions across countries, we expect the basic relationships between monitoring and sanctions on the one hand and quality of international certifiable standard implementation on the other hand to hold across countries.

Our study provides important insights into the conditions that affect substantive implementation of standards, which is necessary for the functioning of a global governance system for firm self-regulation based on certifiable standards. The lack of effectiveness of certifiable CSR standards as tools for firm self-regulation is not limited to China and other transition economies, but also exists in industrialized countries. Our findings about the importance of monitoring and sanctions provide some guidance on how to alleviate the problem of symbolic adoption of global CSR standards in a global context.

ACKNOWLEDGEMENTS

We gratefully acknowledge the financial support for completing the research leading up to this paper received from the Asia Pacific Economic Cooperation (APEC), the Darden Foundation, the Batten Institute of the Darden School of Business Administration, University of Virginia, and a Faculty Research Grant from Rutgers Business School—Newark and New Brunswick. We would like to thank the China Quality Certification Center (CQC) for their help with the data collection for this study. We would like to thank Margaret Cording and Jim Wade, the guest editor Donald Siegel, two anonymous reviewers and participants at the JIBS Three Lenses Workshop in Phoenix, AZ, for insightful comments on earlier drafts of this paper. All errors and omissions remain our responsibility.

Received: 10 September 2005

Revised: 28 February 2006

Accepted: 20 April 2006

Online publication date: 7 September 2006

Accepted by Lorraine Eden, Amy Hillman, Peter Rodriguez and Donald Siegel, Guest Editors, 20 April 2006. This paper has been with the author for two revisions.

Petra Christmann (1) and Glen Taylor (2)

(1) Rutgers Business School—Newark & New Brunswick, Rutgers University, Newark, NJ, USA;

(2) Sykes College of Business, University of Tampa, Tampa, FL, USA

Petra Christmann (PhD, UCLA) is an Assistant Professor of Management and Global Business at Rutgers Business School—Newark and New Brunswick. Her research focuses on firm self-regulation and environmental strategies, especially in an international context. Her work has been published in leading journals including the Academy of Management Journal, the Academy of Management Executive, and the Journal of International Business Studies.

Glen Taylor (PhD, York University) is an Associate Professor of Management and Director of the Center for Innovation and Knowledge Management at the University of Tampa, Sykes College of Business. His research focuses on firm innovation and firm self-regulation in an international context. His work has been published in Management International Review, International Journal of Technology Management, Academy of Management Executive, and the Journal of International Business Studies.

Correspondence: P Christmann, Rutgers Business School—Newark & New Brunswick, Rutgers University, 111 Washington Street, Newark, NJ 07102, USA.

NOTES

1. Factor analysis results and more information about the reliability of individual measures are available from the authors upon request.

2. Our dependent variable was constructed based on survey items on a five-point Likert scale. This scale has ordinal values, but distances between adjacent categories are unknown. To test the sensitivity of our results to potential differences in the distances between categories we also performed an ordered logit regression analysis (Long, 1997). Results showed that it is appropriate to treat differences between adjacent categories as identical, so that the use of linear regression models such as robust regression and OLS is appropriate. Results with respect to our hypotheses were identical between the ordered logit and the two linear models. Detailed results are available from the authors upon request.

REFERENCES

Aiken, L. S. and West, S. G. (1991) Multiple Regression: Testing and Interpreting Interactions, Sage: Newbury Park, CA.

Alchian, A. A. and Demsetz, H. (1972) 'Production, information and economic organization', American Economic Review 62(5): 777–795.

Anderson, J. C. and Gerbing, D. W. (1988) 'Structural equation modeling in practice: a review and recommended two-step approach', Psychological Bulletin 103(3): 411–423.

Andrews, D. F., Tukey, J. W. and Bickel, P. J. (1972) Robust Estimates of Location: Survey and Advances, Princeton University Press: Princeton, NJ.

Andrews, R. N. L., Amaral, D., Darnall, D., Gallagher, D. R., Edwards, D., Hutson, A., D'Amore, C., Sun, L. and Zhang, Y. (2003) Environmental Management Systems: Do They Improve Performance?, The University of North Carolina: Chapel Hill, NC.

Bagozzi, R. P. and Yi, Y. (1988) 'On the evaluation of structural equation models', Journal of the Academy of Marketing Science 16(Spring): 74–94.

Balakrishnan, S. and Koza, M. P. (1993) 'Information asymmetry, adverse selection and joint ventures: theory and evidence', Journal of Economic Behavior and Organization 20(1): 99–117.

Balfour, F. (2005) 'A big, dirty growth engine', Business Week 3948(22 August): 122.

Becker, G. (1968) 'Crime and punishment: an economic approach', Journal of Political Economy 76(2): 169–217.

Belsley, D., Kuh, E. and Welsch, R. (1980) Regression Diagnostics: Identifying Influential Data and Sources of Collinearity, John Wiley & Sons: New York.

Berman, S. L., Wicks, A. C., Kotha, S. and Jones, T. (1999) 'Does stakeholder orientation matter? The relationship between stakeholder management models and firm financial performance', Academy of Management Journal 42(5): 488–506.

Biazzo, S. (2005) 'The new ISO 9001 and the problem of ceremonial conformity: how have audit methods evolved?', Total Quality Management and Business Excellence 16(3): 381–400.

Boiral, O. (2003a) 'The certification of corporate conduct: issues and prospects', International Labor Review 142(3): 317–340.

Boiral, O. (2003b) 'ISO 9000: outside the iron cage', Organization Science 14(6): 720–737.

Boiral, O. (2005) 'ISO 14001: A Rational Myth?', Paper presented at the Academy of Management Conference, Honolulu, HI.

Campbell, D. T. (1955) 'The informant in quantitative research', American Journal of Sociology 60(4): 339–342.

Campbell, D. T. and Fiske, D. W. (1959) 'Convergent and discriminant validation by the multitrait-multimethod matrix', Psychological Bulletin 56(2): 81–105.

Cashore, B. (2002) 'Legitimacy and the privatization of environmental governance: how non-state market-driven (NSMD) governance systems gain rule making authority', Governance 15(4): 503–529.

Casper, S. and Hancke, B. (1999) 'Global quality norms within national production regimes: ISO 9000 standards in the French and German car industries', Organization Studies 20(6): 961–985.

Christmann, P. (2004) 'Multinational companies and the natural environment: determinants of global environmental policy standardization', Academy of Management Journal 47(5): 747–760.

Christmann, P. and Taylor, G. (2001) 'Globalization and the environment: determinants of firm self-regulation in China', Journal of International Business Studies 32(3): 438–458.

Christmann, P. and Taylor, G. (2002) 'Globalization and the environment: strategies for international voluntary initiatives', Academy of Management Executive 16(3): 121–135.

Corbett, C. J. and Kirsch, D. A. (2001) 'International diffusion of ISO 14000 certification', Production and Operations Management 10(3): 327–342.

Delmas, M. A. (2002) 'The diffusion of environmental management standards in Europe and in the United States: an institutional perspective', Policy Sciences 35(1): 91–119.

DiMaggio, P. and Powell, W. (1991) The New Institutionalism in Organization Analysis, University of Chicago Press: Chicago, IL.

Dunning, J. H. (1995) 'Reappraising the eclectic paradigm in an age of alliance capitalism', Journal of International Business Studies 26(3): 461–491.

Fowler Jr, F. J. (1993) Survey Research Methods, Sage: Newbury Park, CA.

Guler, I., Guillen, M. F. and MacPherson, J. M. (2002) 'Global competition, institutions, and the diffusion of organizational practices: the international spread of ISO 9000 quality certificates', Administrative Science Quarterly 47(2): 207–232.

Heide, J. B. and John, G. (1988) 'The role of dependence balancing in safeguarding transaction-specific assets in conventional channels', Journal of Marketing 52(1): 20–35.

ISO (2004) The ISO Survey of ISO 9001:2000 and ISO 14001 Certificates—2003, ISO Central Secretariat: Geneva.

ISO (2005) 'Comments received on WG SR N 31, Proposal for Design Specification', ISO/TMB/WG SR 2005/09/06, ISO, Geneva, p: 38.

John, G. and Reve, T. (1982) 'The reliability and validity of key informant data from dyadic relationships in marketing channels', Journal of Marketing Research 19(4): 517–525.

Judge, G. G., Griffiths, W. E., Hill, R. C., Lutkepohl, H. and Lee, T.-C. (1988) The Theory and Practice of Econometrics, Wiley: New York.

King, A. A., Lenox, M. J. and Terlaak, A. (2005) 'The strategic use of decentralized institutions: exploring certification with the ISO 14001 management standards', Academy of Management Journal 48(6): 1091–1106.

Klein, B., Crawford, R. G. and Alchian, A. A. (1978) 'Vertical integration, appropriable rents, and the competitive contracting process', Journal of Law and Business 21 (2): 297–326.

Korten, D. C. (1995) When Corporations Rule the World, Berrett-Koehler Publishers: San Francisco.

Lal, R. (1990) 'Improving channel coordination through franchising', Marketing Science 9(4): 299–318.

Long, J.S. (1997) Regression Models for Categorical and Limited Dependent Variables, Sage: Thousand Oaks, CA.

McWilliams, A. and Siegel, D. (2001) 'Corporate social responsibility: a theory of the firm perspective', Academy of Management Review 26(1): 117–127.

Meyer, J. W. and Rowan, B. (1977) 'Institutionalized organizations: formal structure as myth and ceremony', American Journal of Sociology 83(2): 340–363.

Naveh, E. and Marcus, A. A. (2004) 'When does the ISO 9000 quality assurance standard lead to performance improvement? Assimilation and going beyond', IEEE Transactions on Engineering Management 51(3): 352–363.

Nunnally, J. C. and Bernstein, I. H. (1994) Psychometric Theory, 3rd edn, McGraw-Hill: New York.

O'Rourke, D. (2002) 'Monitoring the Monitors: a Critique of Corporate Third-Party Labor Monitoring', in R. Jenkins, R. Pearson and G. Seyfang (eds.) Corporate Responsibility and Ethical Trade: Codes of Conduct in the Global Economy, Earthscan: London, pp: 196–208.

O'Rourke, D. (2003) 'Outsourcing regulation: analyzing nongovernmental systems of labor standards and monitoring', Policy Studies Journal 31(1): 1–29.

Parkhe, A. (1993) 'Strategic alliance structuring: a game theoretic and transaction cost examination of interfirm cooperation', Academy of Management Journal 36(4): 794–829.

Podsakoff, P. M. and Organ, D. W. (1986) 'Self-reports in organizational research: problems and prospects', Journal of Management 12(4): 531–544.

Potoski, M. and Prakash, A. (2004) 'Regulatory convergence in nongovernmental regimes: cross-national adoption of ISO 14001 certification', Journal of Politics 66(3): 885–905.

Potoski, M. and Prakash, A. (2005) 'Green clubs and voluntary governance: ISO 14001 and firms' regulatory compliance', American Journal of Political Science 49(2): 235–248.

Rappaport, A. and Flaherty, M. F. (1992) Corporate Response to Environmental Challenges, Quorum Books: New York.

Rousseeuw, P. J. and Leroy, A. M. (1987) Robust Regression and Outlier Detection, Wiley: New York.

Rugman, A. M. and Verbeke, A. (2001) 'Environmental Policy and International Business', in A. M. Rugman and T. L. Brewer (eds.) Oxford Handbook of International Business, Oxford University Press: Oxford, pp: 537–557.

Salancik, G. R. and Pfeffer, J. (1977) 'An examination of need-satisfaction models of job attitudes', Administrative Science Quarterly 22(3): 427–456.

Seddon, J. (1997) In Pursuit of Quality: The Case against ISO 9000, Colour Books: Dublin.

Sethi, P. (2003) Setting Global Standards: Guidelines for Creating Codes of Conduct in Multinational Corporation, Wiley: Hoboken, NJ.

Stenzel, P. L. (2000) 'Can the ISO 14000 series environmental management standards provide a viable alternative to government regulations?', American Business Law Journal 37(2): 237–298.

Stevens, J. M., Steensma, H. K., Harrison, D. A. and Cochran, P. L. (2005) 'Symbolic or substantive document? The influence of ethics codes on financial executives' decisions', Strategic Management Journal 26(2): 181–195.

Stump, R. L. and Heide, J. B. (1996) 'Controlling supplier opportunism in industrial relationships', Journal of Marketing Research 33(4): 431–441.

Swift, T. A., Humphrey, C. and Gor, V. (2000) 'Great expectations?: the dubious financial legacy of quality audits', British Journal of Management 11(1): 31–45.

Terlaak, A. and King, A. A. (2006) 'The effect of certification with the ISO 9000 quality management standard: a signaling approach', Journal of Economic Behavior and Organization 60(4): 579–602.

United Nations (1993) Environmental Management in Transnational Corporations: Report on the Benchmark Corporate Environmental Survey, United Nations: New York.

Van der Wiele, T. and Brown, A. (1997) 'ISO 9000 series experiences in small and medium-sized enterprises', Total Quality Management 8(3): S300–S304.

Vernon, R. (1998) In the Hurricane's Eye: The Troubled Prospects of Multinational Enterprises, Harvard University Press: Cambridge, MA.

Waller, M. A. and Ahire, S. (1996) 'Management perception of the link between product quality and customer's view of product quality', International Journal of Operations and Production Management 16(9): 23–33.

Western, B. (1995) 'Concepts and suggestions for robust regression analysis', American Journal of Political Science 39(3): 786–817.

Westphal, J. D. and Zajac, E. J. (1994) 'Substance and symbolism in CEOs' long-term incentive plans', Administrative Science Quarterly 39(3): 367–390.

Westphal, J. D. and Zajac, E. J. (2001) 'Decoupling policy from practice: the case of stock repurchase programs', Administrative Science Quarterly 46(2): 202–228.

Wicks, A. C. and Freeman, R. E. (1998) 'Organization studies and the new pragmatism: positivism, anti-positivism, and the search for ethics', Organization Science 9(2): 123–140.

Williamson, O. E. (1975) Markets and Hierarchies, Free Press: New York.

Williamson, O. E. (1979) 'Transaction-cost economics: the governance of contractual relations', Journal of Law and Economics 22(2): 3–61.

Williamson, O. E. (1985) The Economic Institutions of Capitalism, Free Press: New York.

Williamson, O. E. (1996) The Mechanisms of Governance, Oxford University Press: New York/Oxford.

Yeung, G. and Mok, V. (2005) 'What are the impacts of implementing ISOs on the competitiveness of manufacturing industry in China?', Journal of World Business 40(2): 139–157.

Prosecuting, Defending, and Adjudicating White Collar Crime

12

In Enron's Wake: Corporate Executives on Trial (The Changing Face of White-Collar Crime)

Kathleen F. Brickey

There may never have been a worse time to be a corporate criminal. (1)

I wish we had never heard of Bernie Ebbers. (2)

I. INTRODUCTION

It was December 2001—a few months after Enron CEO Ken Lay was warned of an "elaborate accounting hoax" (3) that had disguised fraud on a magnificent scale, and not long after Enron had publicly disclosed record fourth quarter shortfalls. Notwithstanding these dire financial straits, Enron executives behaved like pigs at the trough, doling out more than $100 million in bonuses to themselves and delivering the checks by plane on the eve of the largest corporate bankruptcy filing in United States history. (4) It soon became evident

"In Enron's wake: Corporate executives on Trial," by Kathleen F. Brickey from *Journal of Criminal Law and Criminology*, 96(2): 37 (Winter 2006). Reprinted by special permission of Northwestern University School of Law, The Journal of Criminal Law and Criminology.

that Enron's collapse was only the first in a wave of accounting fraud scandals that would inflict huge financial losses and erode public confidence in the nation's financial markets.

Fast forward to December 2005. Ken Lay and two other top Enron executives, former President and CEO Jeff Skilling and Chief Accounting Officer Richard Causey, were then under indictment and only a month away from their criminal trial. (5) But here, the customary pretrial courtroom maneuvers were embellished by Lay's strategic effort to regain public relations momentum.

Speaking before a group of 500 Houston business and academic leaders, Lay blamed Enron's downfall on a handful of bad apples (6) and—perhaps borrowing a leaf from Mark Twain's album (7)—claimed that most of what had been said about Enron's demise was either "grossly exaggerated" or just plain wrong. (8) Moreover, he charged, the Enron Task Force, which spearheads Enron-related investigations and prosecutions, had unleashed a "wave of terror" through the relentless pursuit of innocent businessmen, the bullying of witnesses, and a host of other prosecutorial excesses. (9)

Following closely on the heels of Lay's highly charged speech, co-defendant Rick Causey rearranged the legal landscape for the trial by striking a deal with the prosecutors and agreeing to cooperate. (10) Former Enron Treasurer Andy Fastow, who was widely credited with engineering much of the Enron fraud, had already pled guilty and been cooperating for more than a year. (11) Causey's last minute defection, while not widely anticipated, was not without precedent. Surprise plea agreements reached on the eve of the Rite Aid trial, for example, left Rite Aid's Chief Legal Officer holding the bag. (12)

It is axiomatic that most criminal cases are resolved through guilty pleas, and the recent corporate fraud prosecutions are no exception. And, like Fastow and Causey, most corporate executives who have pled guilty have also become cooperating witnesses, agreeing to help the government build criminal cases against their former colleagues and friends.

I have written elsewhere about this building block technique and how it facilitates charging higher-ups like Skilling and Lay. (13) But this article turns to that rarer phenomenon of post-Enron prosecutions—cases that have actually gone to trial.

We know relatively little about the corporate fraud trials because executives on trial have been relatively few and far between. It has taken roughly three years for these prosecutions to reach the trial stage and yield enough trial-related data to report and analyze. (14) Thus, until now, our knowledge about these trials has been largely anecdotal. But after a brief hiatus following Arthur Andersen's obstruction of justice conviction in 2002, (15) high profile executives began to find themselves in the dock—beginning with Adelphia CEO John Rigas (guilty), WorldCom CEO Bernie Ebbers (guilty), Health-South CEO Richard Scrushy (not guilty), (16) and Enron CEOs Jeff Skilling and Ken Lay (currently on trial).

Now that we are deeply enough into the prosecution cycle that major cases have been tried, jury verdicts returned, and sentences imposed, this seems an opportune time to take a closer look at these prosecutions through the prism of newly compiled data on the trials. Although the number of cases is relatively small, the data set provides the most comprehensive picture of executives on trial available to date.

Part II of this article addresses a range of questions about corporate fraud trials and verdicts. Which and how many cases have gone to trial, who has been tried, and what is a typical outcome? Does the government enjoy a high degree of success at trial, or are high-profile executives more likely to win juries over to their side? Part II addresses these and other core trial-related questions.

Part III then turns to the flip side of the coin—cases that have ended in mistrials—and considers whether mistrials have been major government setbacks. How often have mistrials been declared? What factors come into play when a trial ends without a verdict? Were cases that ended in mistrials flawed from the outset? Are prosecutors' decisions about whether to retry a defendant a reliable gauge of the relative strength of the case? Are decisions to retry accompanied by discernable shifts in trial strategy? Part III provides a framework for taking a preliminary look at this intriguing set of issues.

II. CORPORATE FRAUD TRIALS AND VERDICTS

A. Trial Data

The data set used in this article covers the period March 2002 through January 2006 and is derived from my ongoing study of major corporate fraud prosecutions. (17) Although the full data base is far more comprehensive, this article extrapolates data relating to fraud cases that had gone to trial as of January 31, 2006, (18) and tracks trials relating to scandals at seventeen major companies and firms (Table 1). As of the end of January 2006, forty-six defendants had gone to trial in twenty-three separate prosecutions.

As a general rule, prosecutors typically charge multiple defendants in corporate fraud cases, (19) and this charging pattern is apparent in the cases that have gone to trial. More than two-thirds of the trials included in Table 1 had multiple defendants. Although four or more defendants were jointly tried in a handful of cases, (20) in most instances, no more than two defendants went to trial.

Table 1 does not, however, convey the full scope of the government's charging practices because it does not include co-defendants who bargained with prosecutors and did not go to trial. When those who entered guilty pleas are added to the mix, prosecutors charged three or more defendants in a third of the cases they tried. And when we include co-defendants who pled guilty while their colleagues went to trial, the total number of individuals charged in these cases will increase to sixty.

TABLE 1   Trials

Company	Number of Cases Tried (21)	Number of Defendants Tried
Adelphia	1	4
Cendant	1	2
CSFB	1	1
Duke Energy	1	2
Dynegy	1	1
Enron (22)	4	14
HealthSouth	3	4
ImClone (23)	2	3
Impath	1	1
McKesson HBOC	1	1
NewCom	1	1
Ogilvy & Mather	1	2
Qwest	1	4
Rite Aid	1	1
Tyco (24)	1	2
Westar Energy	1	2
WorldCom	1	1

Guilty pleas are critical to the government's successful pursuit of corporate fraud cases in two important respects. First, they are numerically significant. In a baseline study of prosecutions completed between March 2002 and July 2004, for example, charges against eighty-seven defendants were resolved. (25) But while more than ninety percent of the outcomes were convictions, only about ten percent of the convictions were products of jury verdicts. Simply put, these cases were overwhelmingly resolved through guilty pleas (Table 2).

Second, guilty pleas are strategically significant. Virtually all of the defendants who pled guilty during that two-year period became cooperating witnesses (26) who assisted the government in developing cases against their peers. (27)

In the current study, while guilty pleas were less prevalent in the twenty-three cases that went to trial, one or more co-defendants entered guilty pleas in nearly a third of those cases. With only a few exceptions, (28) the defendants who pled guilty became cooperating witnesses.

TABLE 2   Disposition of Charges in Federal Corporate Fraud Prosecutions (29)
March 2002–July 2004

Guilty Plea	Conviction	Acquittal	Hung Jury	Dismissal	Awaiting Trial
73	8	4	2	2	43

TABLE 3 Cases Tried with Guilty Pleas by Co-Defendants

Company	Guilty Verdicts	Not Guilty Verdicts	Mistrials (30)	Guilty Pleas by Co-Defendants
Adelphia	2	1	1	1
Duke Energy	0	1	1	1
Dynegy	1	0	0	2
Enron (31)	0	0	5	3
Impath	1	0	0	1
NewCom	2	1	0	2
Rite Aid	1	0	0	3

This does not, however, portray the full importance of cooperating witnesses in these trials. There are numerous separate but related cases in which defendants pled guilty and agreed to help prosecutors develop cases against, among others, defendants who ultimately went to trial (Table 4).

TABLE 4 Cooperating Witnesses in Separate but Related Prosecutions

Company	Related Cases with Cooperating Witnesses	Cooperating Witnesses
Adelphia	1	1
Cendant	3	3
CSFB	0	0
Duke Energy	0	0
Dynegy	1	4
Enron		
Case 1 (32)	1	1
Case 2 (33)	2	2
Case 3 (34)	1	1
HealthSouth		
Case 1 (35)	12	15
Case 2 (36)	2	2
Case 3 (37)	4	4
ImClone		
Case 1 (38)	1	1
Case 2 (39)	0	0
McKesson HBOC	2	2
NewCom	1	1
Ogilvy & Mather	0	0
Qwest	1	1
Rite Aid	2	2
Tyco	0	0
Westar Energy	0	0
WorldCom	4	5

Given the prevalence of guilty pleas and their pivotal role in these investigations, the question then becomes who actually goes to trial? Prosecutors have been chided for not aiming high enough and being content to charge mid-level managers whose guilt is easier to prove. But is it true that those in the middle are relegated to the role of scapegoat while the higher-ups enjoy a free pass? If the trial data are a reliable indicator, quite the opposite is true. Most of the defendants on trial have been high-level executives who held positions of responsibility and authority within their respective organizations. (40)

Of the forty-six defendants who have gone to trial, twelve held the title of Chief Executive Officer, Chief Operating Officer, President, Chairman of the Board or, in the case of a partnership, Senior Partner. (41) Defendants on trial also included five Chief Financial Officers (42) and an assortment of other financial and accounting executives. (43) There were also seven Executive or Senior Vice presidents, five Investment Advisors, a Chief Legal Officer, and a Vice President for Legal Affairs. (44) Only one entity, Arthur Andersen, has gone to trial to date. (45)

B. Verdicts

The trials tracked in this study have produced surprisingly mixed results. Juries have convicted eighteen defendants, acquitted eleven, and deadlocked on charges against fifteen others. Thus, at first blush, the government's trial record does not reflect overwhelming success and appears to validate—or at least provide support for—the criticism that prosecutors have overreached by trying to find crimes where none really exist. (46)

Introduction of another variable—how juries function when defendants are jointly tried—may help to flesh out the picture and provide a baseline for assessing the strength of cases the government takes to trial. Do juries tend to accept or reject the government's case in its entirety when defendants are jointly tried? That is, do they tend to convict or acquit all of the defendants on trial? If so, that signals that the prosecution's case, in total, was relatively strong or weak. Or, in the alternative, do juries tend to hand down split verdicts (i.e., some combination of guilty, not guilty, or deadlocked) when multiple defendants are on trial? If so, do the split verdicts shed light on the overall merits of the case? Table 5 sets the stage for analyzing these points.

As seen in Table 5, juries arrived at split verdicts in half of the cases in which multiple defendants were tried. As an initial matter, the verdicts in the Qwest and Duke Energy trials suggest that the cases were relatively weak. The juries in both trials split down the middle, acquitting half of the defendants and deadlocking on the rest. But the picture is incomplete until we know the ultimate disposition of the charges on which the juries hung. In the Qwest case, for example, rather than going through the rigors of a second trial, the two remaining defendants pled guilty and became cooperating witnesses. Thus, when all was said and done, the government ultimately prevailed against all four Qwest defendants. Duke Energy, in contrast, went the opposite way when the prosecutor decided to drop the remaining charges rather than retry the case.

TABLE 5 Verdicts (47)

Company	Convictions	Acquittals	Mistrials
Adelphia	2	1	1
Cendant	1	0	1
CSFB	0	0	1
Duke Energy	0	1	1
Dynegy	1	0	0
Enron			
Case 1 (48)	1	0	0
Case 2 (49)	5	1	0
Case 3 (50)	0	0	5
HealthSouth			
Case 1 (51)	0	1	0
Case 2 (52)	0	2	0
Case 3 (53)	1	0	0
ImClone			
Case 1 (54)	2	0	0
Case 2 (55)	0	1	0
Impath	1	0	0
McKesson HBOC	0	1	0
NewCom	0	1	0
Ogilvy & Mather	2	0	0
Qwest	0	2	2
Rite Aid	1	0	0
Tyco			
Case 1 (56)	0	0	2
Case 2 (57)	0	1	0
Westar Energy	0	0	2
WorldCom	1	0	0

In two other split verdict cases, Adelphia and Cendant, the juries convicted half of the defendants and either acquitted or deadlocked on the others. And in Enron Case 2, five of the six defendants were found guilty while only one was acquitted. In two of the multiple defendant trials that did not end with split verdicts, ImClone Case 1 and Ogilvy & Mather, the juries convicted all of the defendants. In the three remaining non-split verdict trials, hung juries resulted in mistrials for all of the defendants on trial. (58)

The government's record was equally mixed in cases in which only one defendant went to trial. Juries in those cases convicted six defendants, acquitted five, and deadlocked on one.

What explains this mixed trial record? As is true in other contexts, issues of complexity, witness credibility, juror sophistication, and myriad unquantifiable factors—including luck—can influence the outcome of a trial. (59) To illustrate just what can go wrong and how, let's consider what is perhaps the government's biggest loss to date.

In what once appeared to be one of the strongest fraud cases against a high-level corporate executive, (60) the prosecution of HealthSouth CEO Richard Scrushy totally collapsed. While other factors undoubtedly contributed to the jury's verdict of acquittal, one that clearly stands out is the indictment itself. Sweeping in its breadth, the more than eighty-count indictment (later pared down to thirty-six) included multiple charges of conspiracy, mail and wire fraud, securities fraud (under two different statutes), false statements, certification of false financial statements (including attempt), money laundering, obstruction of justice, and perjury. (61) After five months of sometimes mind-numbing testimony during a leisurely-paced trial, and after weeks of equally leisurely deliberations, the jury acquitted Scrushy on all counts.

Beyond the issues of complexity and juror boredom in the Scrushy case lurked the government's heavy reliance on the testimony of former executives who had pled guilty. (62) Once thought to be a plus because all five former CFOs were among the cooperating witnesses, (63) reliance on witnesses who had pled guilty proved to be a liability at trial. In addition to doubting those witnesses, who had something to gain because of their plea deals with the prosecutors, jurors further questioned the credibility of one who was a tax cheat, (64) of another who took antidepressants, and of yet another who cheated on his wife. (65) Prosecutors were also disadvantaged by the lack of a paper trail directly linking Scrushy to the fraud, (66) an unfortunate choice of venue, (67) Scrushy's waging of an effective public relations campaign before and during the trial, (68) and—believe it or not—the lack of fingerprint evidence. (69)

The Scrushy trial exemplified the adage that if something can go wrong, it will. But the combination of factors that contributed to Scrushy's acquittal cannot, standing alone, explain why the government has won so few cases at trial.

III. MISTRIALS

Prosecutors want—and often rightly expect—to win cases, and it goes without saying that convictions are wins and acquittals are not. But what about mistrials? When a jury is deadlocked and cannot decide whether to convict or acquit, should this be counted as a serious loss for the prosecution? Or is it merely a draw?

According to conventional wisdom, mistrials are defeats for the government, particularly in high-profile prosecutions. When the jury deadlocked in the obstruction of justice case against former CSFB star banker Frank Quattrone, for example, observers called the mistrial "a serious setback" for the prosecution team. (70) Similarly, the hung jury in the Enron Broadband trial was termed a "big zero" for the government that would provide "a major confidence boost" to defense lawyers in coming high profile trials, including that of Enron's Jeff Skilling and Ken Lay. (71) Others called the Broadband mistrial a setback and a "second blow" for the Enron prosecutors, (72) coming as it did on the heels of the Supreme Court's reversal of Arthur Andersen's obstruction of justice conviction. (73)

Thus we turn to the question of how many and which of the government's cases ended in mistrials and what the mistrials signify. Let's begin with a thumbnail sketch of the eight prosecutions that resulted in a mistrial on at least some of the charges.

- Adelphia: Adelphia founder John Rigas, his sons Timothy and Michael, and Michael Mulcahey—all Adelphia executives—were charged with looting the company of more than $100 million. (74) The jury found John and Timothy guilty, Mulcahey not guilty, and deadlocked on the charges against Michael Rigas.

- Cendant: Cendant Chairman of the Board Walter Forbes and Executive Vice President and Vice Chairman Kirk Shelton were accused of inflating revenue at CUC International (75) by $500 million. The jury convicted Shelton but could not reach a verdict on the charges against Forbes.

- CSFB: Frank Quattrone, Head of CSFB's Global Technologies Group, was tried on three counts of obstruction of justice for ordering the destruction of files. A hung jury resulted in a mistrial.

- Duke Energy: Three Duke Energy trading executives were charged with manipulating the company's gas and power trades and falsifying its books to increase reported profits. One defendant, who pled guilty and became a cooperating witness, did not go to trial. Of the two who were tried, the jury acquitted one on all charges, but returned a partial verdict for the other, acquitting him on some charges but deadlocking on others. The judge declared a mistrial on the unresolved charges.

- Enron: The government charged seven executives of Enron Broadband Services with misrepresenting the value and business capabilities of the internet venture. Two of the seven pled guilty and became cooperating witnesses, while the other five went to trial. The jury returned partial verdicts of acquittal for three of the defendants, but could not reach a verdict on the remaining charges against them. The jury also deadlocked on all of the charges against the remaining two defendants.

- Qwest: Four executives of Qwest Communications were accused of inflating the company's revenue by more than $100 million. The jury acquitted two of the executives but deadlocked on charges against the other two.

- Tyco: The six-month trial of Tyco CEO Dennis Kozlowski and CFO Mark Swartz for looting the company of $600 million ended in a mistrial.

- Westar Energy: The jury could not reach a verdict in the trial of Westar's CEO and its Executive Vice President for looting the utility company.

Conventional wisdom holds that cases ending in mistrials are marginal to begin with. (76) But how do prosecutors view them? On the one hand, it seems safe to assume that prosecutors would think twice before devoting scarce resources to retrying cases they thought they would lose. On the other hand, if these cases are not necessarily weak to begin with, how can we explain why more than a third have ended in mistrials?

To put this question in context, let's look first at the circumstances surrounding the inconclusive results in the Tyco, Enron Broadband, and CSFB trials.

Juror Publicity: Technically speaking, Tyco ended in a mistrial because of publicity surrounding a courtroom incident in which a juror reportedly gave an "O.K." sign to the defense table. (77) I say "technically" because the atmosphere during jury deliberations had become "poisonous," (78) and it appeared that the juror would be a holdout in any event. (79) But the contentious deliberations were partly a byproduct of a failed prosecution strategy that allowed the six-month trial to be dominated at times by lavish lifestyle evidence that had little to do with proving the charges against Kozlowski and Swartz, (80) and at other times to become bogged down in complexity. (81) In what must have been a mind-numbing experience, the jury heard testimony from forty-eight witnesses and considered some seven hundred exhibits.

Truncated Deliberations: The Enron Broadband trial ended in a mistrial when the jury declared itself deadlocked after only four days of deliberations. (82) Over those four days, the jury had reached not guilty verdicts on twenty-four counts of the indictment, but declared itself deadlocked on the remaining 168 charges. To some observers, declaring a mistrial so early in deliberations that followed a lengthy, complex case with nearly two hundred charges against five defendants seemed a bit "quick on the trigger." (83) Indeed, the judge's abrupt halt to the deliberations prompted one defense lawyer to complain that "[t]here was no logic to this at all." (84)

Witness Credibility: In the CSFB trial, although three jurors steadfastly held out for an acquittal, others vacillated on the question of guilt. (85) After the mistrial was declared, one juror posited that the only reason Frank Quattrone had not been acquitted was his decision to take the stand. The credibility of his testimony was seriously compromised during cross-examination, when the government produced e-mails that contradicted his testimony in chief. (86) "He did a bad job going up there.... I heard a lot of jurors say if he hadn't been a witness, it would have been 'not guilty' the first day." (87) Thus, in contrast with the Tyco trial, in which the prosecutors' trial strategy may have backfired with the jury, the defense decision to put Quattrone on the stand appears to have been a pivotal strategic mishap in the jury's eyes. (88)

Complexity: As mentioned before, prosecutors in the Tyco trial allowed the case to become bogged down in complexity, and that undoubtedly contributed to the jury's inability to reach a verdict for or against either Kozlowski or Swartz.

Perhaps demonstrating that mistrials can be a blessing for whoever per-formed the worst at trial, (89) the Tyco prosecutors learned from their mis-takes. On retrial, they trimmed the number of witnesses by half and scrapped much of the lifestyle and spending evidence. Although the second trial still consumed about four months and jury deliberations continued for eleven days, the prosecutors were vindicated in the end. Handing the prosecutors a major win, the jury convicted both Kozlowski and Swartz.

Federal prosecutors have been similarly plagued by charging practices that often make trials overly complex. The trial of four Qwest executives on a forty-four count indictment for conspiracy, securities fraud, false statements, and wire fraud ended in disappointment for prosecutors when the jury acquitted two of the defendants and deadlocked on charges against the other two. Afterward, jurors expressed annoyance that the government seemingly "threw everything" at the defendants and "hoped something would stick" (90) and said the overall case was hard to understand. (91)

Not long after the end of that trial, the ongoing fraud investigation culmi-nated in the December 2005 indictment of Qwest CEO Joseph Nacchio. But this time, the charges were surprisingly focused. While similar in one respect to the earlier Qwest indictment—Nacchio was charged with forty-three counts—it was different in that all of the charges were insider trading allega-tions. Although the charges are ultimately tied to what Nacchio knew about Qwest's financial outlook, which he publicly painted as rosy while he privately knew it was grim, the indictment does not try to link him to the underlying accounting fraud. And by focusing on just one crime, the government increases its chances of proving a pattern of illegal activity—repeatedly selling stock on the basis of inside information—which in theory should make it easier to con-vict. Simply put, this change in charging strategy simplifies the case for the jury. (92) Indeed, one securities lawyer commented that the government may well be using the strategy it successfully employed in several previous prosecu-tions. "If you look at Bernie Ebbers, Adelphia, and Martha Stewart, the gov-ernment has done an exceptional job when they keep it simple so juries understand." (93)

These glimpses at the dynamics of several high-profile trials provide possible, perhaps plausible, explanations for the outcomes. But at the end of the day, we can only speculate on the myriad reasons why these cases resulted in mistrials and partial acquittals. That said, we do have data that facilitate a relatively informed analysis of whether the mistrials signaled failed criminal prosecutions.

What happened after the mistrials were declared? Did the government give up because it thought the cases were losers? Or did the prosecutors persevere? The data in Table 6 [TABULAR DATA FOR TABLE 6 OMITTED] tell a compelling story.

In seven of the eight cases that ended in mistrials, prosecutors signaled their intention to retry the defendants. (94) The government's decision to retry most, if not all, of the defendants indicates that prosecutors have a greater degree of confidence in the merits of the cases than one might otherwise expect. That logically raises the question whether their confidence is warranted. What outcomes flow from the decision to retry?

The answer is fairly straightforward. To date, prosecutors have enjoyed considerable success after mistrials were declared. As seen in Table 6, defendants in two cases pled guilty to avoid the perils of a retrial, and in three of the four retrials, the juries convicted all the remaining defendants. (95) None of the retried defendants has been acquitted.

After the Cendant retrial ended with a second hung jury, one might reasonably have expected the prosecutor to throw in the towel. But it seems that a majority of the jury had favored conviction and that the prosecutor would gear up for another new trial, so the judge set a tentative date for a second retrial. (96)

Simply put, the results in three of the retrials are wins for the prosecution, and the fourth is a draw. Thus, prosecutors must surely—and perhaps, justifiably—view their success rate following mistrials as a vindication of the initial decision to prosecute.

IV. CONCLUSION

The corporate fraud prosecution cycle following Enron's collapse has produced an unparalleled number of criminal trials of senior corporate executives in just three years. While guilty pleas and cooperation agreements are strategically significant in developing these cases, the number of CEOs, CFOs, and other senior managers who have been charged and tried belies critics' assertions that mid-level managers who plead guilty become scapegoats, while their superiors go scot free.

Although at first glance the results of the corporate fraud trials seem surprisingly mixed, we have seen that the government enjoys a respectable, if not spectacular, conviction rate; that prosecutors, ever confident of the underlying merits of cases that end in mistrials, are far from reluctant to retry them; and that prosecutors' willingness and ability to shift strategies to secure convictions has paid off handsomely to date. The corporate fraud trials have also provided a unique opportunity to gain insights into prosecutorial charging practices in high profile white collar cases, to observe and evaluate trial strategies and dynamics, and to tentatively assess what seems to work (or not) and why.

The showcase trial of Enron's Skilling and Lay will not be the end of the road. Dozens of executives charged in similar fraud prosecutions are now awaiting trial, and additional fraud investigations are clearly underway. As these cases wend their way through the system, they will further enhance our understanding of the utility (or futility, as the case may be) of relying on individual criminal prosecutions to address systemic corporate fraud.

APPENDIX 1   Corporate Fraud Trials, March 2002–January 2006*

ADELPHIA

Prosecution	Defendant	Charges
United States v. Rigas	Adelphia President and Chairman of the Board	Conspiracy; Securities Fraud; Wire Fraud; Bank Fraud
Co-Defendants		
T. Rigas	Adelphia Executive Vice President, CFO, CAO, Treasurer, and Chairman of Board's Audit Committee	Same
M. Rigas	Adelphia Executive Vice President for Operations and Secretary	Same
J. Brown	Adelphia Vice President of Finance	Same
M. Mulcahey	Adelphia Director of Internal Reporting	Same

CENDANT

Prosecution	Defendant	Charges
United States v. Forbes	Cendant Chairman of the Board; CUC International CEO and Chairman of the Board	Conspiracy; Mail Fraud; Wire Fraud; Falsifying Books and Records; Securities Fraud; Insider Trading
Co-Defendant		
E. Shelton	Cendant Executive Vice President and Vice Chairman; CUC International President and COO	Conspiracy; Mail Fraud; Wire Fraud; Falsifying Books and Records; Securties Fraud

CREDIT SUISSE FIRST BOSTON (CSFB)

Prosecution	Defendant	Charges
United States v. Quattrone	CSFB Head of Global Technologies Group	Obstruction of Justice; Obstruction of Agency Proceedings; Witness Tampering

DUKE ENERGY NORTH AMERICA (DENA)

Prosecution	Defendant	Charges
United States v. Kramer	DENA Vice President for Eastern Trading Operations	Racketeering; Wire Fraud; Falsification of Books and Records; Money Laundering; Conspiracy; Circumventing Internal Company Controls

Continued

APPENDIX 1 *Continued*

Prosecution	Defendant	Charges
Co-Defendants		
T. Reid	DENA Senior Vice President of Managers and Supervisors	Racketeering; Wire Fraud; Falsification of Books and Records; Money Laundering; Conspiracy; Circumventing Internal Company Controls
B. Lavielle	DENA Director of Southeastern Trading Group	Racketeering; Wire Fraud; Falsification of Books and Records

DYNEGY

Prosecution	Defendant	Charges
United States v. Olis	Dynegy Senior Director of Tax Planning/International Tax and Vice President of Finance	Conspiracy; Securities Fraud; Mail Fraud; Wire Fraud
Co-Defendants		
G. Foster	Dynegy Vice President of Tax	Same
H. Sharkey	Member of Dynegy Risk Control and Deal Structure Group	Same

ENRON

Prosecution	Defendant	Charges
United States v. Arthur Andersen, LLP	Partnership	Obstruction of Justice

Prosecution	Defendant	Charges
United States v. Bayly	Merrill Lynch Head of Global Investment Banking Division	Conspiracy; Wire Fraud
Co-Defendants		
J. Brown	Merrill Lynch Head of Strategic Asset Lease and Finance Group	Conspiracy; Perjury; Obstruction of Justice; Wire Fraud
R. Furst	Merrill Lynch Enron Relationship Manager, Investment Banking Division	Conspiracy; Wire Fraud
S. Kahanek	Enron Accountant and Senior Director in APACHI Division	Conspiracy

APPENDIX 1 *Continued*

Prosecution	Defendant	Charges
W. Furst	Merrill Lynch Vice President	Conspiracy; False Statements; Obstruction of Justice; Wire Fraud
D. Boyle	Enron Vice President in Global Finance	Conspiracy; Wire Fraud

Prosecution	Defendant	Charges
United States v. Causey	Enron Chief Accounting Officer	Conspiracy; Securities Fraud; Wire Fraud; Making False Statements to Auditors; Insider Trading
Co-Defendants		
J. Skilling	Enron President and CEO	Same
K. Lay	Enron CEO and Chairman	Conspiracy; Securities Fraud; Wire Fraud; Bank Fraud
S. Kahanek	Enron Accountant and Senior Director in APACHI Division	Conspiracy

Prosecution	Defendant	Charges
United States v. Rice	Enron Broadband Services Chairman and CEO	Conspiracy; Securities Fraud; Wire Fraud; Insider Trading; Money Laundering
Co-Defendants		
J. Hirko	Enron Broadband Services President and CEO	Same
K. Hannon	Enron Broadband Services COO	Same
R. Shelby	Enron Broadband Services Senior Vice President of Engineering Operations	Same
S. Yaeger	Enron Broadband Services Senior Vice President of Strategic Development	Same
K. Howard	Enron Broadband Services President of Finance	Conspiracy; Securities Fraud; Wire Fraud; False Statements
M. Krautz	Enron Broadband Services Senior Director of Transactional Accounting	Same

Continued

APPENDIX 1 *Continued*

HEALTHSOUTH

Prosecution	Defendant	Charges
United States v. Scrushy	HealthSouth Co-Founder, CEO, and Chairman of Board of Directors	Conspiracy; Mail Fraud; Wire Fraud; Securities Fraud (Sarbanes-Oxley and Title 15 Charges); False Statements; Certifying False Financial Statement (Sarbanes-Oxley Charge); Attempt to Cause Certification of False Financial Statement (Sarbanes-Oxley Charge); Money Laundering; Obstruction of Justice; Perjury
United States v. Thomson	HealthSouth President and Chief Operating Officer	Conspiracy; False Books and Records; Travel Act Violation
Co-Defendant		
J. Reilly	HealthSouth Vice President for Legal Services	Same
United States v. Crumpler	HealthSouth Controller	Wire Fraud; Mail Fraud; Securities Fraud

IMCLONE

Prosecution	Defendant	Charges
United States v. Stewart (Martha)	Chairman of the Board and CEO of Marth Stewart Living Omnimedia	Conspiracy; False Statements; Obstruction of Justice; Securities Fraud
Co-Defendant		
P. Bacanovic	Merrill Lynch Financial Advisor	Conspiracy; False Statements; Making and Using False Documents; Perjury; Obstruction of Justice
United States v. Stewart (Larry F.)	Director of U.S. Secret Service Forensics Lab	Perjury

IMPATH

Prosecution	Defendant	Charges
United States v. Adelson	Impath President and COO	Conspiracy; Securities Fraud; Making False Filings with the SEC
Co-Defendant		
A. Saad	Impath Board Chairman and CEO	Same

APPENDIX 1 *Continued*

MCKESSON HBOC

Prosecution	Defendant	Charges
United States v. Hawkins	McKesson CFO	Conspiracy; Securities Fraud; False Statements

NEWCOM

Prosecution	Defendant	Charges
United States v. Khan	NewCom President, CEO, and Chairman of the Board	Conspiracy; Mail Fraud; Filing False Statements; Securities Fraud; Circumventing Internal Accounting Controls; Money Laundering
Co-Defendants		
A. Khan	NewCom Executive Vice President and Board Member	Conspiracy; Mail Fraud; Filing False Statements; Securities Fraud; Falsifying Required Books and Records; Circumventing Internal Accounting Controls; Money Laundering
S. Veen	NewCom CFO and Board Member and Aura Systems CFO	Filing False Statements

OGILVY & MATHER

Prosecution	Defendant	Charges
United States v. Early	Ogilvy & Mather Chief Financial Officer	Conspiracy; False Claims
Co-Defendant		
S. Seifert	Ogilvy & Mather Senior Partner and Executive Group Director	Same

QWEST

Prosecution	Defendant	Charges
United States v. Graham	Qwest Global Business Unit CFO	Conspiracy; Securities Fraud; False Statements; Wire Fraud
Co-Defendants		
T. Hall	Qwest Global Business Unit Senior Vice President	Same

Continued

APPENDIX 1 *Continued*

Prosecution	Defendant	Charges
J. Walker	Qwest Global Business Unit Vice President	Same
B. Treadway	Qwest Assistant Controller	Same

RITE AID

Prosecution	Defendant	Charges
United States v. Grass	Rite Aid Chairman and CEO	Securities Fraud; Conspiracy; Lying to the SEC
Co-Defendants		
F. Brown	Rite Aid Chief Legal Officer	Same
F. Bergonzi	Rite Aid Executive Vice President and CFO	Same
E. Sorkin	Rite Aid Executive Vice President	Conspiracy; Lying to Grand Jury

TYCO

Prosecution	Defendant	Charges
State v. Kozlowski	Tyco CEO	Conspiracy; Obstruction of Justice; Enterprise Corruption (State Charges)
Co-Defendant		
M. Swartz	Tyco CFO	Same
State v. Belnick	Tyco General Counsel	Falsifying Business Records; Grand Larceny; Securities Fraud (State Charges)

WESTAR ENERGY, INC.

Prosecution	Defendant	Charges
United States v. Wittig	Westar CEO	Conspiracy; Circumventing Internal Accounting Controls; Falsifying Books and Records; Wire Fraud; False Statements; Money Laundering
Co-Defendant		
D. Lake	Westar Executive Vice President	Same

WORLDCOM

Prosecution	Defendant	Charges
United States v. Ebbers	WorldCom CEO	Conspiracy; Securities Fraud; Making False Filings with the SEC

APPENDIX 1 *Continued*

ADELPHIA

Prosecution	Disposition	Status
United States v. Rigas	Convicted by Jury	Sentenced to 15 Years in Prison
Co-Defendants		
T. Rigas	Convicted by Jury	Sentenced to 20 Years in Prison
M. Rigas	After Hung Jury Resulted in Mistrial, Guilty Plea Entered	Awaiting Sentencing
J. Brown	Guilty Plea and Cooperation Agreement	Awaiting Sentencing
M. Mulcahey	Acquitted by Jury	—

CENDANT

Prosecution	Disposition	Status
United States v. Forbes	Hung Jury Resulted in Mistrial; Retrial Resulted in Second Mistrial	Awaiting Second Retrial
Co-Defendant		
E. Shelton	Convicted by Jury	Sentenced to 10 Years in Prison; $3.275 Billion Restitution

CREDIT SUISSE FIRST BOSTON (CSFB)

Prosecution	Disposition	Status
United States v. Quattrone	Hung Jury Resulted in Mistrial; Convicted by Jury on Retrial	Sentenced to 18 Months in Prison; 2 Years' Probation; $90,000 Fine

DUKE ENERGY NORTH AMERICA (DENA)

Prosecution	Disposition	Status
United States v. Kramer	Hung Jury Resulted in Mistrial	Prosecutor's Decision on Retrial Pending
Co-Defendants		
T. Reid	Acquitted by Jury	—
B. Lavielle	Guilty Plea and Cooperation Agreement	Awaiting Sentencing

DYNEGY

Prosecution	Disposition	Status
United States v. Olis	Convicted by Jury	Sentenced to 24 Years, 3 Months in Prison; $25,000 Fine; Sentence Overturned on Appeal and Case Remanded for Resentencing; Awaiting Resentencing

Continued

APPENDIX 1 *Continued*

DYNEGY

Prosecution	Disposition	Status
Co-Defendants		
G. Foster	Guilty Plea and Cooperation Agreement	Sentenced to 15 Months in Prison; 3 Years' Probation; $1,000 Fine
H. Sharkey	Guilty Plea and Cooperation Agreement	Sentenced to 30 Days in Prison

ENRON

Prosecution	Disposition	Status
United States v. Arthur Andersen, LLP	Convicted by Jury	Conviction Overturned by Supreme Court

Prosecution	Disposition	Status
United States v. Bayly	Convicted by Jury	Sentenced to 30 Months in Prison; $250,000 Fine; $295,000 Restitution
Co-Defendants		
J. Brown	Convicted by Jury	Sentenced to 46 Months in Prison; $250,000 Fine; $295,000 Restitution
R. Furst	Convicted by Jury	Sentenced to 37 Months in Prison; $665,000 Fine and Restitution
S. Kahanek	Acquitted by Jury	—
W. Furst	Convicted by Jury	Sentenced to 37 Months in Prison; $665,000 Fine and Restitution
D. Boyle	Convicted by Jury	Sentenced to 46 Months in Prison; $320,000 Fine and Restitution

Prosecution	Disposition	Status
United States v. Causey	Guilty Plea and Cooperation Agreement	Awaiting Sentencing
Co-Defendants		
J. Skilling	—	Trial in Progress
K. Lay	—	Trial in Progress
S. Kahanek	Acquitted by Jury	—

APPENDIX 1 *Continued*

Prosecution	Disposition	Status
United States v. Rice	Guilty Plea and Coopera-tion Agreement	Awaiting Sentencing
Co-Defendants		
J. Hirko	Hung Jury Resulted in Mistrial	Awaiting Retrial
K. Hannon	Guilty Plea and Cooperat-ing Agreement	Awaiting Sentencing
R. Shelby	Hung Jury Resulted in Mistrial	Awaiting Retrial
S. Yaeger	Hung Jury Resulted in Mistrial	Awaiting Retrial
K. Howard	Hung Jury Resulted in Mistrial	Awaiting Retrial
M. Krautz	Hung Jury Resulted in Mistrial	Awaiting Retrial

HEALTHSOUTH

Prosecution	Disposition	Status
United States v. Scrushy	Acquitted by Jury	—
United States v. Thomson	Acquitted by Jury	—
Co-Defendant		
J. Reilly	Acquitted by Jury	—
United States v. Crumpler	Convicted by Jury	Awaiting Sentencing

IMCLONE

Prosecution	Disposition	Status
United States v. Stewart (Martha)	Convicted by Jury	Sentenced to 5 Months in Prison; 5 Months' Home Detention; $30,000 Fine
Co-Defendant		
P. Bacanovic	Convicted by Jury	Sentenced to 5 Months in Prison; 5 Months' Home Detention; $4,000 Fine
United States v. Stewart (Larry F.)	Acquitted by Jury	—

IMPATH

Prosecution	Disposition	Status
United States v. Adelson	Convicted by Jury	Awaiting Sentencing
Co-Defendant		
A. Saad	Guilty Plea	Sentenced to 3 Months in Prison

Continued

APPENDIX 1 *Continued*

MCKESSON HBOC

Prosecution	Disposition	Status
United States v. Hawkins	Acquitted by Jury	

NEWCOM

Prosecution	Disposition	Status
United States v. Khan	Guilty Plea	Sentenced to 24 Months in Prison; $15,000 Fine
Co-Defendants		
A. Khan	Guilty Plea	Sentenced to 24 Months in Prison; $15,000 Fine
S. Veen	Acquitted by Jury	—

OGILVY & MATHER

Prosecution	Disposition	Status
United States v. Early	Convicted by Jury	Sentenced to 14 Months in Prison; 2 Years' Probation; $10,000 Fine
Co-Defendant		
S. Seifert	Convicted by Jury	Sentenced to 18 Months in Prison; 2 Years' Probation; $125,000 Fine

QWEST

Prosecution	Disposition	Status
United States v. Graham	After Hung Jury Resulted in Mistrial, Guilty Plea and Cooperation Agreement	Sentenced to 1 Year's Probation; $5,000 Fine
Co-Defendants		
T. Hall	Same	Same
J. Walker	Acquitted by Jury	—
B. Treadway	Acquitted by Jury	—

RITE AID

Prosecution	Disposition	Status
United States v. Grass	Guilty Plea and Cooperation Agreement	Sentenced to 7 Years in Prison; 3 Years' Probation; $500,000 Fine
Co-Defendants		
F. Brown	Convicted by Jury	Sentenced to 10 Years in Prison; 2 Years' Probation; $21,000 Fine

APPENDIX 1   *Continued*

RITE AID

Prosecution	Disposition	Status
F. Bergonzi	Guilty Plea and Coopera-tion Agreement	Sentenced to 28 Months in Prison
E. Sorkin	Guilty Plea and Coopera-tion Agreement	Sentenced to 5 Years in Prison

TYCO

Prosecution	Disposition	Status
State v. Kozlowski	Juror Controversy Resulted in Mistrial; Convicted by Jury on Retrial	Sentenced to 8 1/3–25 Years in Prison; $70 Million Fine; $97 Million Restitution
Co-Defendant M. Swartz	Same	Sentenced to 8 1/3–25 Years in Prison; $35 Million Fine; $38 Million Restitution
State v. Belnick	Acquitted	—

WESTAR ENERGY, INC.

Prosecution	Disposition	Status
United States v. Wittig	Hung Jury Resulted in Mistrial; Convicted by Jury on Retrial	Awaiting Sentencing
Co-Defendant D. Lake	Hung Jury Resulted in Mistrial; Convicted by Jury on Retrial	Awaiting Sentencing

WORLDCOM

Prosecution	Disposition	Status
United States v. Ebbers	Convicted by Jury	Sentenced to 25 Years in Prison

KATHLEEN F. BRICKEY, James Carr Professor of Criminal Jurisprudence, Washington University School of Law. I am grateful to Jim Brickey for his inspiration and unflagging support, and to Darren Grady and Barry Wormser for their able research assistance.

NOTES

1.   Shawn Young & Peter Grant, More Pinstripes to Get Prison Stripes, WALL ST. J., June 20, 2005, at C1.

2.   Suzanne Craig, Citigroup Quells Investor Claim over Research: Panel Rejects Charge That Analyst Misled Client on WorldCom Stock; Victory Highlights Trend on Street, WALL ST. J., Dec. 8, 2005, at C1 (quoting Citigroup CEO Charles Prince).

3. Anonymous Memorandum from Sherron Watkins, Vice President of Corporate Development, Enron, to Kenneth Lay, Chairman, Enron (Aug. 15, 2001) [hereinafter Anonymous Watkins Memorandum] (on file with author).

4. Official Employment-Related Issues Comm. of Enron Corp. v. Arnold (In re Enron Corp.), No. 01-16034, at 20 (Bankr. S.D. Tex. Dec. 9, 2005) (Mem.) (on file with author). The bankruptcy court later determined that many of these transfers were fraudulent and ordered the money returned. Id. at 98.

5. The charges against Lay were far more limited than those against his co-defendants and former colleagues Jeff Skilling (former Enron President and CEO) and Rick Causey (former Enron Chief Accounting Officer). See Indictment, United States v. Causey, CRH-04-25 (S.D. Tex. Jan. 21, 2004) (on file with author).

6. But for "the illegal conduct of less than a handful of employees," he charged, Enron would not have needed to seek protection in bankruptcy. Kenneth L. Lay, Speech, "Guilty, Until Proven Innocent" (Dec. 13, 2005) [hereinafter Lay Speech] (on file with author).

7. After the American press mistakenly published his obituary, Twain sent a cable from London declaring that "reports of my death are greatly exaggerated." THE NEW DICTIONARY OF CULTURAL LITERACY 137 (E.D. Hirsch, Jr. et al. eds., 2002).

8. "Most of what was and is still being said…is either grossly exaggerated, distorted, or just flat out false." Lay Speech, supra note 6.

9. Id. In taking this stance, he joined a chorus of other Justice Department critics who had been caught up in the prosecutorial net. See, e.g., Jonathan D. Glater, Indictment Broadens in Shelters at KPMG, N.Y. TIMES, Oct. 18, 2005, at C1 (quoting defense lawyers representing two of seventeen defendants in the KPMG tax shelter prosecution, who charged that prosecutors are taking "a misguided, overly aggressive, unprecedented view of a complicated legal area" and are "seriously overreaching" in bringing the charges); Health-South: Scrushy Enters Not Guilty Plea to Charges He Bribed Governor, CHI. TRIB., Oct. 29, 2005, at C2 (reporting that Richard Scrushy's lawyer claimed that Scrushy's indictment for political bribery was a product of overzealous prosecutors); Gretchen Ruethling, Four Additional Charges for Black in Hollinger Case, N.Y. TIMES, Dec. 16, 2005, at C4 (quoting Conrad Black's lawyer, who characterized new charges against his client as "unfounded" and "a blatant example of overreaching by the prosecutor"); Press Release, Arthur Andersen, LLP, Statement by Arthur Andersen, LLP (Mar. 14, 2002) (asserting that prosecution of the accounting firm would be unjust and "an extraordinary abuse of prosecutorial discretion") [hereinafter Andersen Mar. 14 Press Release] (on file with author).

10. John R. Emshwiller & John M. Biers, Enron Prosecutors Gain New Ally: Causey Plea May Offer Look into Top Officers' Actions Before Company's Collapse, WALL ST. J., Dec. 29, 2005, at A3.

11. Lay publicly placed most of the blame for Enron's woes at Fastow's feet. Lay Speech, supra note 6. Since Fastow had been accused of reaping enormous profits from the fraud and Causey had not, the addition of Causey to the prosecution's team was a strategic government home run. In addition, there was some suggestion that the defense lawyers would try to smear Fastow in the jury's eyes by introducing evidence of pornography habits "so extensive that when his computer files were seized they were submitted to the FBI for criminal investigation." Carrie Johnson, Lawyers Take Aim at Enron Witnesses, WASH. POST, Jan. 10, 2006, at D3 (quoting unspecified court filings submitted by the defense).

12. See infra Appendix 1, at Rite Aid; see also Ex-Chief Pleads Guilty in Rite Aid Case, N.Y. TIMES, June 18, 2003, at C10; 2 Defendants in Rite Aid Case Expected to Plead Guilty Today, N.Y. TIMES, June 26, 2003, at C6; Former Rite Aid Office Pleads Guilty, N.Y. TIMES, June 6, 2003, at C4; Mark Maremont, Rite Aid's Former Vice Chairman Doesn't Plead Guilty as Expected, WALL ST. J., June 27, 2003, at A8; Mark Maremont,

Rite Aid's Ex-CEO Pleads Guilty: Grass Is First Executive Held Criminally Liable in Major Accounting Fraud, WALL ST. J., June 18, 2003, at A3; cf. Ex-Lawyer for Rite Aid Is Found Guilty, N.Y. TIMES, Oct. 18, 2003, at C2; Rite Aid Ex-Counsel Is Convicted: Guilty Verdict Marks First by a Jury in Current Crop of Corporate Scandals, WALL ST. J., Oct. 20, 2003, at C8.

13.   Kathleen F. Brickey, Enron's Legacy, 8 BUFF. CRIM. L. REV. 221, 263–75 (2004) [hereinafter Brickey, Enron's Legacy]; Kathleen F. Brickey, From Enron to WorldCom and Beyond: Life and Crime After Sarbanes-Oxley, 81 WASH. U. L.Q. 357, 370–75 (2003) [hereinafter Brickey, Enron to WorldCom and Beyond].

14.   In Brickey, Enron's Legacy, supra note 13, at 275, I examined the criminal enforcement environment and explored some of the principal characteristics of major corporate fraud prosecutions, including parallel civil and criminal enforcement activity, charging practices in criminal cases, and disposition of criminal charges. As few cases had yet gone to trial at that time, the dispositions consisted primarily of guilty pleas, with a smattering of verdicts, mistrials, and dismissals.

15.   After a month-long trial, Andersen was convicted on the single count indictment charging the firm with violating 18 U.S.C. [section] 1512(b)(2) (2000). United States v. Arthur Andersen, LLP, 374 F.3d 281, 284 (6th Cir. 2004), rev'd, 125 S. Ct. 2129 (2005); see Kathleen F. Brickey, Andersen's Fall from Grace, 81 WASH U. L.Q. 917 (2003). The Supreme Court later reversed, holding that the trial court's instructions did not correctly inform the jury of the mens rea required to prove a violation of 18 U.S.C. [section] 1512(b). Arthur Andersen, LLP v. United States, 125 S. Ct. 2129, 2136–37 (2005). The government ultimately decided not to retry the now-defunct firm and did not object to a motion made by David Duncan, the government's star cooperating witness in the Andersen case, to withdraw his guilty plea. John R. Emshwiller, Andersen Figure Files to Withdraw His Guilty Plea, WALL ST. J., Nov. 23, 2005, at C3.

16.   Scrushy has since been indicted on unrelated federal political bribery charges and is now awaiting trial. Milt Freudenheim, Scrushy Faces New Charges of Bribing State Officials, N.Y. TIMES, Oct. 27, 2005, at C18.

17.   An earlier version of the complete data set was published in Brickey, Enron to WorldCom and Beyond, supra note 13, app. A, at 382–401. The earlier iteration, which tracked nearly sixty prosecutions arising out of fraud scandals at seventeen major corporations, covered the period March 2002–August 2003. As many of the cases charged multiple defendants, the database tracked charges against more than ninety defendants. I updated and analyzed much of that data in a more recent article, Enron's Legacy. See Brickey, Enron's Legacy, supra note 13, at 225–28, 245–75.

18.   A table containing the extrapolated data appears infra Appendix 1.

19.   See Brickey, Enron to WorldCom and Beyond, supra note 13, app. A, at 382–401.

20.   Four defendants were on trial in the Adelphia and Qwest trials. See United States v. Rigas, infra Appendix 1, at Adelphia; United States v. Graham, id. at Qwest. In the three Enron-related trials that had multiple defendants, six defendants were jointly tried in one case, see United States v. Bayly, id. at Enron, five went to trial in another, see United States v. Rice, id., and two went to trial in the other, see United States v. Causey, id.

21.   Table 1 does not include retrials following mistrials, see infra Table 6 and text accompanying notes 95–97, but includes other trials currently in progress.

22.   Three of the four Enron-related trials had multiple defendants. See United States v. Bayly, infra Appendix 1, at Enron; United States v. Rice, id.; United States v. Causey, id.

23.   Only one of the ImClone trials had multiple defendants. See United States v. Stewart (Martha), id. at ImClone.

24.   Tyco is the only state prosecution included in the trial data base.

25. This figure excludes two trial defendants whose juries had deadlocked.

26. The defendants included in Table 2 who pled guilty but did not enter into cooperation agreements are ImClone President and CEO Sam Waksal, see United States v. Waksal, infra Appendix 1, at ImClone; Enron Treasurer Ben Glisan, see United States v. Glisan, id. at Enron; and two executives in the NewCom prosecutions, see United States v. Kahn, id. at NewCom. Enron's Glisan, who is serving a five-year term, is reportedly cooperating from prison. Mary Flood, The Fall of Enron: Prisoner Goes to See Grand Jury; Enron ExOfficial Likely Cooperating, HOUS. CHRON., Mar. 5, 2004, Bus. Sec., at 1.

27. For a more extended discussion of how prosecutors have used cooperating witnesses to build cases against higher-ups in the corporation, see Brickey, Enron's Legacy, supra note 13, at 263–75.

28. The two defendants in the NewCom case who entered guilty pleas did not enter into cooperation agreements. See United States v. Khan, infra Appendix 1, at NewCom. Similarly, the defendant who pled guilty in the Impath case does not appear to have agreed to cooperate. See United States v. Adelson, id. at Impath.

29. Table 2 includes criminal charges in the following fraud investigations: Adelphia, Cendant, Charter Communications, Credit Suisse First Boston, Dynegy, Enron, Health-South, Homestore, ImClone, Kmart, McKesson HBOC, NewCom, NextCard, Purchase-Pro, Qwest, Rite Aid, Symbol Technologies, Tyco (federal charge only), and WorldCom (federal charges only). Table 2 was originally published as Table 6 in Brickey, Enron's Legacy, supra note 13, at 264.

30. By number of defendants affected. Includes partial acquittal accompanied by hung jury on other charges; does not include or reflect disposition after mistrial was declared.

31. Only two of the Enron prosecutions that have gone to trial (United States v. Rice, see infra Appendix 1, at Enron, and United States v. Causey, id.) had co-defendants who became cooperating witnesses. But, in another, Enron Treasurer Ben Glisan, who pled guilty in a separate case but did not enter into a cooperation agreement, was granted immunity in exchange for his testimony in United States v. Bayly, see id.; 10 Enron Players: Where They Landed After the Fall, N.Y. TIMES, Jan. 29, 2006, [section] 3, at 10, and in the trial of Skilling and Lay. Alexei Barrionuevo, Ex-Treasurer Testifies Skilling Left Enron in Weak Shape, N.Y. TIMES, Mar. 22, 2006, at C3.

32. United States v. Arthur Andersen, LLP. See infra Appendix 1, at Enron.

33. United States v. Rice, id.

34. United States v. Bayly, id. Enron Treasurer Ben Glisan, who pled guilty in a separate case but did not enter into a cooperation agreement, was granted immunity in exchange for his testimony in Bayly.

35. United States v. Scrushy, id. at HealthSouth.

36. United States v. Thomson, id.

37. United States v. Crumpler, id. These numbers are derived from reports of others who pled guilty and testified against the defendant. Because the underlying fraud in this case is intertwined with the overall fraudulent scheme, it is possible that other defendants who were cooperating witnesses in United States v. Scrushy (Case 1), id., also assisted in developing the case against the defendant in Crumpler.

38. United States v. Stewart (Martha), id. at ImClone.

39. United States v. Stewart (Larry), id.

40. This conclusion is fully consistent with an earlier sampling from the data base that was not limited to defendants who elected to go to trial. See Brickey, Enron's Legacy, supra note 13, at 255–56.

41. Those in this group were high level executives at Adelphia, Cendant, Enron Broadband Services, HealthSouth, Impath, Martha Stewart Living Omnimedia, Ogilvy & Mather

(Senior Partner and Executive Group Director), Tyco, Westar, and WorldCom. See infra Appendix 1.

42. They were CFOs of Adelphia, McKesson HBOC, NewCom, Ogilvy & Mather, and Qwest. See infra Appendix 1.

43. Among the accounting and financial executives were three vice presidents, a controller and an assistant controller, and officers who held the titles of Director of Internal Reporting, Accountant and Senior Division Director, and Senior Director of Transactional Accounting. The breakdown and affiliations of these defendants is shown in fuller detail infra Appendix 1.

44. The breakdown and affiliations of these defendants is shown in fuller detail infra Appendix 1. The remaining defendants who are not mentioned in the previous enumeration of defendants who went to trial include two vice presidents and a Secret Service Lab employee who was charged with lying when he testified as an expert witness for the government in Martha Stewart's trial.

45. See supra note 15.

46. See, e.g., Kathy M. Kristof & Josh Friedman, KPMG Tax Case Grows: Ten More People Are Indicted over Alleged Fraudulent Shelters Promoted by the Firm, L.A. TIMES, Oct. 18, 2005, at C1 (reporting that one defendant's lawyer said the prosecutors were "seriously overreaching in this case"); Andersen Mar. 14 Press Release, supra note 9 (asserting that prosecution of the accounting firm would be unjust and "an extraordinary abuse of prosecutorial discretion"); John R. Emshwiller, An Ambitious Enron Defense: Company's Moves Were All Legal; with $40 Million War Chest, Skilling Calls on Lawyer with Business Expertise; Hiring a Sociology Professor, WALL ST. J., Jan. 20, 2006, at A1 (reporting that defense lawyers will argue that the indictment of Skilling and Lay targets what in reality are ordinary business and accounting decisions); Lay Speech, supra note 6 (claiming that the Enron Task Force failed to meet its projected time table for bringing all Enron-related indictments, not because the cases were complicated, but "because it is complicated to find crimes where they do not exist").

47. Table 5 does not include verdicts obtained in retrials following a mistrial. Nor does it include United States v. Causey (Enron Case 4), see infra Appendix 1, at Enron, which began while this article was in press and was expected to last another three months.

48. United States v. Arthur Andersen, LLP, id.

49. United States v. Rice (Enron Broadband Services prosecution), id.

50. United States v. Bayly (Nigerian barge deal prosecution), id.

51. United States v. Scrushy, id. at HealthSouth.

52. United States v. Thomson, id.

53. United States v. Crumpler, id.

54. United States v. Stewart (Martha), id. at ImClone.

55. United States v. Stewart (Larry), id.

56. State v. Kozlowski, see infra Appendix 1, at Tyco.

57. State v. Belnick, id.

58. United States v. Rice (Enron Case 3), id. at Enron; State v. Kozlowski (Tyco Case 1), id. at Tyco; United States v. Wittig (Westar Energy), id. at Westar Energy Inc.

59. These and other related factors that appear to have contributed to mistrials in corporate fraud prosecutions are considered in Part III.

60. Reed Abelson & Jonathan Glater, A Style That Connected with Hometown Jurors, N.Y. TIMES, June 29, 2005, at C1; Kyle Whitmire, Jurors Doubted Scrushy's Colleagues, N.Y. TIMES, July 2, 2005, at C5 [hereinafter Whitmire, Jurors Doubted Scrushy's Colleagues].

By the time Scrushy went to trial, fifteen HealthSouth executives, including all five former CFOs, had pled guilty and become cooperating witnesses.

61.   Abelson & Glater, supra note 61; Dan Morse et al., HealthSouth's Scrushy Is Acquitted. Outcome Shows Challenges for Sarbanes-Oxley Act: SEC Suit Still Ahead; No Job Offer from Company, WALL ST. J., June 29, 2005, at A1; Kyle Whitmire, Determined to Find Guilt, but Expecting Acquittal, N.Y. TIMES, June 29, 2005, at C5.

62.   Morse et al., supra note 62; Whitmire, Jurors Doubted Scrushy's Colleagues, supra note 61.

63.   See supra note 61.

64.   Morse et al., supra note 62.

65.   Id.; Whitmire, Jurors Doubted Scrushy's Colleagues, supra note 61.

66.   Abelson & Glater, supra note 61.

67.   Morse et al., supra note 62.

68.   Whitmire, Jurors Doubted Scrushy's Colleagues, supra note 61. For the latest bizarre twist on the public relations front, see Evan Perez & Corey Dade, Scrushy Denies Trying to Buy Support: HealthSouth Ex-CEO Paid PR Firm, Writer and Pastor During His Criminal Trial, WALL ST. J., Jan. 20, 2006, at A12, and Simon Romero & Kyle Whitmire, Writer Says Scrushy Paid Her to Write Favorable Articles, N.Y. TIMES, Jan. 20, 2006, at C3.

69.   Abelson & Glater, supra note 61; Morse et al., supra note 62; Simon Romero & Kyle Whitmire, Former Chief of HealthSouth Acquitted in $2.7 Billion Fraud. Case Fails to Sway Jury in Scrushy's Hometown, N.Y. TIMES, June 29, 2005, at A1; Chad Terhune & Dan Morse, Why Scrushy Won His Trial and Ebbers Lost, WALL ST. J., June 30, 2005, at C1; Kyle Whitmire, Determined to Find Guilt, but Expecting Acquittal, N.Y. TIMES, June 29, 2005, at C5; Whitmire, Jurors Doubted Scrushy's Colleagues, supra note 61; cf. Linda Deutsch, "CSI" and "Law & Order" Lead Jurors to Great Expectations, ST. LOUIS POSTDISPATCH, Jan. 30, 2006, at D1 (describing how "CSI" effect has given jurors unrealistic expectations of high-tech forensic evidence in run-of-the-mill cases where such evidence is rare).

70.   Andrew Ross Sorkin, Hung Jury Ends Trial of Banker: Setback for Prosecution of Misconduct on Wall St., N.Y. TIMES, Oct. 25, 2003, at A1.

71.   John R. Emshwiller, Federal Jury Declines to Convict at an Enron Trial, WALL ST. J., July 21, 2005, at C4.

72.   Mary Flood, Broadband Trial: The Outcome; No Guilty Verdicts in Latest Enron Case; Results of Fraud Case Spell Trouble for Prosecutors in Future Trials, Legal Experts Say, HOUS. CHRON., July 21, 2005, at A1 [hereinafter Flood, No Guilty Verdicts].

73.   See supra note 15.

74.   The defendants were accused of treating the company like a "private piggy bank." Peter Grant et al., Prosecutors Say Rigases Stole from Adelphia, WALL ST. J., Mar. 2, 2004, at C4.

75.   CUC merged with HFS Inc. to form Cendant. Both defendants were high-level executives at CUC as well.

76.   Michael Graczyk, Jury Acquits Former Enron Execs of Some Charges and Deadlocks on Others, ST. Louis POST-DISPATCH, July 21, 2005, at C3 (noting that the jury's inability to reach a verdict "tells us something of the government's use of its resources in this case" (quoting Barry Pollack, a lawyer for one of the defendants)); Thor Valdmanis, Quattrone Mistrial Doesn't Bode Well for Future Cases, USA TODAY, Oct. 26, 2003, available at http://www.usatoday.com/money/industries/brokerage/2003-10-26-quattrone_x.htm (predicting that the government's decision whether to retry Quattrone would signal that prosecutors would be "less aggressive" in pursuing questionable cases (quoting Jack Sylvia, a panner at Mintz Levin, who was not involved in the case)).

77.   David Carr & Adam Liptak, In Tyco Trial, an Apparent Gesture Has Many Meanings: Publicity to Prompt Mistrial Motion, N.Y. TIMES, Mar. 29, 2004, at C1; Mark Maremont & Kara Scannell, Tyco Jury Resumes Deliberating: Defense Fails in Mistrial Bid Based on Media Coverage of Juror, but Incident Could Fuel Appeal, WALL ST. J., Mar. 30, 2004, at C1.

78.   Mark Maremont et al., Mistrial Scuttles Possible Guilty Verdicts in Tyco Case: Jurors Criticize Prosecution, Defense for Clumsy Tactics; Lessons Learned for Retrial, WALL ST. J., Apr. 5, 2004, at A1.

79.   Andrew Ross Sorkin, Juror No. 4 Says No O.K. Sign and No Guilty Vote, N.Y. TIMES, Apr. 7, 2004, at A1.

80.   Mark Maremont & Chad Bray, Tyco Trial Jurors Say Defendants Weren't Credible: Conviction of Kozlowski, Swartz Highlights Risk of Executives' Testifying, WALL ST. J., June 20, 2005, at A1 [hereinafter Maremont & Bray, Tyco Defendants Weren't Credible]. The evidence included video tapes of a bacchinale-like birthday bash in Sardinia (underwitten in part by Tyco) and a virtual tour of a posh New York apartment (also paid for by Tyco) equipped with exotic furnishings that included a now notorious $6,000 shower curtain. John Schwartz, I Don't Want to Calculate the Cost to Matriculate, N.Y. TIMES, Oct. 9, 2005, [section] 3, at 26.

81.   Pete McEntegart, One Angry Man: A Juror Gives an Inside Account of Why the Tyco Trial Fell Apart, TIME, Apr. 12, 2004, at 47 (noting that the jury heard testimony from 48 witnesses, that more than 700 exhibits had been introduced, and that the testimony produced more than 12,000 pages of transcript). Maremont & Bray, Tyco Defendants Weren't Credible, supra note 81. Both men were later sentenced to lengthy prison terms. Andrew Ross Sorkin, Ex-Tyco Officers Get 8 to 25 Years: 2 Sentenced in Crackdown on White-Collar Crime, N.Y. TIMES, Sept. 20, 2005, at A1 (reporting that Kozlowski and Swartz were both sentenced to serve 8 1/3 to 25 years in prison). The two men were remanded to custody immediately after they were sentenced, and the judge refused to release them on bail pending appeal. Bail Denied to Two Tyco Executives, N.Y. TIMES, Oct. 4, 2005, at C2.

82.   John R. Emshwiller, Federal Jury Declines to Convict at an Enron Trial, WALL ST. J., July 21, 2005, at C4. Not surprisingly, the prosecutors strenuously objected to such an early end to the deliberations.

83.   Flood, No Guilty Verdicts, supra note 73 (quoting Robert Mintz, a frequent legal commentator on high profile white collar trials). But see Vioxx Case Leads to Hung Jury: Retrial Planned in 2001 Death, WASH. POST., Dec. 13, 2005, at A10 (mistrial declared in first federal Vioxx trial after jury had just begun fourth day of deliberations; judge had admonished jury to reach a verdict in a "reasonable time" and declared that "[i]t has now been a reasonable time [and w]e cannot get a verdict"); Alex Berenson, A Mistrial Is Declared in 3rd Suit Over Vioxx, N.Y. TIMES, Dec. 13, 2005, at C1 (mistrial declared in first federal Vioxx trial after jury deliberated eighteen hours over three days).

84.   Flood, No Guilty Verdicts, supra note 73 (quoting defense lawyer Ed Tomko, who represented one of the defendants in the case).

85.   Randall Smith & Kara Scannell, Inside Quattrone duty Room, Discord Culminates in Mistrial, WALL ST. J., Oct. 27, 2003, at A1.

86.   Id.

87.   Andrew Ross Sorkin, Quattrone Juror Says Three Wouldn't Budge, N.Y. TIMES, Oct. 27, 2003, at C11. Credibility was also a factor in the retrial of Tyco's Kozlowski and Swartz. Maremont & Bray, supra note 81.

88.   Evidently believing that—like the prosecutors in the Tyco case—he had learned from his mistakes, Quattrone testified again in his second trial. This strategic move came at a price, however, because his admission of knowledge of the contents of the e-mails produced in the first trial also served to undermine the fundamental basis for his claimed

innocence. To the surprise of his supporters, the jury returned guilty verdicts after less than a day of deliberations. Randall Smith, In Quattrone Case, 'Nice' Prosecutor Wins: Jurors Checked Emotions at the Door, WALL ST. J., May 4, 2004, at C1; Randall Smith, Quattrone Found Guilty on 3 Counts in Big U.S. Win: Former CSFB Star Banker Could Face 2 Years in Jail; A Case Built on E-Mail, WALL ST. J., May 4, 2004, at A1; Andrew Ross Sorkin, Wall St. Banker Is Found Guilty of Obstruction, N.Y. TIMES, May 4, 2004, at A1. The decision whether to put the defendant on the stand may, of course, be pivotal in trials in which juries reach unanimous verdicts. In the prosecution against WorldCom CEO Bernie Ebbers, for example, his decision to testify hurt more than it helped. Jesse Drucker & Li Yuan, 'How Could He Not See?': Documents Swayed Ebbers Jury, WALL ST. J., Mar. 17, 2005, at C1; Jonathan D. Glater & Ken Belson, Ebbers, on Witness Stand, May Have Lost His Case, N.Y. TIMES, Mar. 16, 2005, at C1. And jurors in the retrial of Tyco executives Dennis Kozlowski and Mark Swartz concluded that neither defendant was a credible witness and that Swartz came across as "a really good liar" on the stand. Maremont & Bray, Tyco Trial Defendants Weren't Credible, supra note 81.

In contrast, post-verdict comments after the Martha Stewart trial suggested that the decision not to put the defendants on the stand was a "serious mistake." Jonathan D. Glater, Defense Gambled, and Lost, With a Minimal Presentation, N.Y. TIMES, Mar. 6, 2004, at B1. As one juror put it, "How could we tell anything about how smart either of them was if they never took the stand?" Id. And then there was the possibility that her failure to tell the jury her side of the story created the impression that she was arrogant or aloof. As another juror posited, "[By not testifying, Stewart] seemed to say: 'I don't have anything to worry about. I fooled the jury. I don't have anything to prove.'" Memorandum of Law in Support of Martha Stewart's Motion for New Trial Pursuant to Federal Rule of Criminal Procedure 33, at 14, United States v. Stewart, S1-03-Cr-717 (MGC) (S.D.N.Y. Mar. 31, 2004) (on file with author).

89.   Carrie Johnson, For Prosecutors, Shorter Is Sweeter: Government Got Chance to Analyze, Fix Mistakes, WASH. POST, June 18, 2005, at D1.

90.   Shawn Young & Dionne Searcey, Qwest's Ex-CEO Is Charged in Probe of Insider Trading, WALL ST. J., Dec. 21, 2005, at A3.

91.   Ken Belson, U.S. Tries Simpler Tack Against Ex-Chief of Qwest, N.Y. TIMES, Jan. 20, 2006, at C3.

92.   Id.; Young & Searcey, supra note 91.

93.   Christopher Palmeri, The Case Against Qwest's Nacchio: The Telecom's Former CEO Has Finally Been Indicted—For Fraud and Insider Trading. Getting a Conviction Will Be No Slam Dunk, BUSINESSWEEK ONLINE, Dec. 24, 2005, http://www .businessweek.com/technology/content/dec2005/tc20051221_927069.htm.

The prosecutors have also streamlined their cases for the retrial of defendants in the Enron Broadband Services case (see Mary Flood, Five Former Enron Execs Reindicted, HOUS. CHRON., Nov. 10, 2005, at B1) and the trial of Enron's Skilling and Lay. Alexei Barriounuevo, Prosecutors Shift Focus on Enron, N.Y. TIMES, Jan. 11, 2006, at C1; Kurt Eichenwald, Big Test Looms for Prosecutors at Enron Trial, N.Y. TIMES, Jan. 26, 2006, at A1; Mary Flood, Government Plans to Trim Witness List, HOUS. CHRON., Dec. 2, 2005, at B4.

94.   When the mistrial was declared in the Duke Energy case, it was uncertain whether the remaining defendant would be retried, see Mistrial in Case of Former Duke Energy Executive, N.Y. TIMES, Dec. 10, 2005, at B2, but the prosecutor ultimately decided to drop the remaining charges. Peter Geier, A Defense Win in the Heart of Enron Country, NAT'L L.J., Jan. 23, 2006, at 6.

95.   Retrials of the Enron Broadband Services defendants are scheduled for 2006.

96.   Stacey Stowe, Cendant's Ex-Chairman Faces His Third Trial, N.Y. TIMES, Feb. 15, 2006, at C15; Cendant Juror Says Most Favored a Conviction, ST. LOUIS POST-DISPATCH, Feb. 15, 2006, at C2.

13

Prison Time, Fines, and Federal White-Collar Criminals: The Anatomy of a Racial Disparity

Max M. Schanzenbach and Michael L. Yaeger

I. INTRODUCTION

Do criminals of different races, sexes, or socio-economic status receive different sentences? If so, why? For decades, these have been among the predomi-
nant questions in the academic and political discussion of sentencing. There
was at least one study of sentencing disparity conducted in the 1920s, (1) and
many other studies were undertaken over the next six decades. (2) The Federal
Sentencing Guidelines (the "Federal Guidelines" or the "Guidelines") arose in
part from a desire to eliminate unwarranted sentencing disparity between
judges, (3) and the focus on disparity has not abated since the Guidelines took
effect in 1987. (4) Indeed, the recent Supreme Court decision in United States
v. Booker, (5) which arguably grants greater discretion to district courts in
criminal sentencing by making the Guidelines "advisory," will heighten interest in disparity.

We examine racial disparities in white collar criminal sentencing using a
large dataset provided by the United States Sentencing Commission. We also

"Prison time, fines, and federal white-collar criminals: The anatomy of a racial disparity,"
by Max M. Schanzenbach and Michael L. Yaeger from *Journal of Criminal Law and
Criminology*, 96(2): 757 (2006). Reprinted by special permission of Northwestern
University School of Law, The Journal of Criminal Law and Criminology.

discuss sex disparities at some length, in part because they provide an interesting contrast to racial disparities. We focus on white collar crimes (non-violent, economic crimes) for several reasons. First, it is perhaps surprising that racial disparities persist for such crimes, which would not appear to be as racially tinged as those involving violence or drug trafficking. Second, the presence of significant alternative punishments, such as fines, leaves more room for judicial discretion than in the case of more serious crimes. Finally, there are fewer sources of disparity in white collar crimes. For example, in the case of drug crimes, legislatures make distinctions between crack and powder cocaine and mandate minimum sentences. (6) In addition, the crimes are likely reported in different ways: drug traffickers are likely caught in sting operations, whereas those who commit fraud or embezzlement are likely more often sought after due to victim complaints.

We find large racial disparities using standard regression techniques. In other words, when controlling for as many relevant characteristics as possible, blacks and Hispanics receive longer prison sentences than whites. This is consistent with previous studies. However, careful consideration of the nature of white collar crimes reveals that a large portion (up to one-third) of the estimated disparity is driven by the ability to pay a fine. Similarly, income is also shown to be an important factor, and it is poorly measured in the data. In addition, we find that the calculation of the Guideline's sentencing range may actually work in favor of minorities, and determining the sentencing range is one of the most important elements of Guideline's sentencing scheme. Our results call into question traditional studies of sentencing disparities, and we conclude that the estimation of racial disparities, even under a determinant sentencing framework like the Guidelines, is more complicated than previous work indicates.

This paper is organized as follows: Part II discusses how prison sentences and fines are calculated under the Federal Sentencing Guidelines. Part III discusses the empirical and theoretical literature on fines and white-collar sentencing. Part IV discusses the data and the methodology of our study with a particular focus on the problems of identifying racial bias empirically. Part V describes and interprets the results of our study. Part VI concludes.

II. THE FEDERAL SENTENCING GUIDELINES

For most of American history, federal district court judges had vast discretion over sentencing. Some statutes prescribed a maximum fine or time of imprisonment for a particular crime, and a handful prescribed minimums. Otherwise, trial judges were basically free to impose the sentences they thought appropriate. The law gave them almost no guidance in the exercise of their discretion, and their judgments were virtually never subject to appellate review. (7)

All of this changed when Congress passed the Sentencing Reform Act of 1984. (8) The law established the Sentencing Commission, a bipartisan, independent agency within the judicial branch, and charged it with "promulgating detailed guidelines prescribing the appropriate sentences for [federal] offenders." (9) The Sentencing Act also "direct[ed] the Commission to periodically review and revise the Guidelines" and "authorize[ed] the Commission to submit amendments to Congress." (10) Accordingly, from the time the Guidelines took effect on November 1, 1987 until the Booker decision, sentencing in federal courts has been controlled by a comprehensive set of rules created by an administrative agency. Prior to Booker, the Guidelines were mandatory and were treated as such by the courts. (11) Except for special circumstances in which "departures" are authorized, a trial judge must sentence a criminal in accordance with the Guidelines or risk a reversal on appellate review. (12) Booker, discussed in greater detail below, made the Guidelines "advisory" but still requires district court judges to consult them.

A. Prison Sentences Under the Guidelines

Although complex in application, the Guidelines are fairly straightforward in theory. As one commentator has observed, the Guidelines can be understood as "nothing more than a set of instructions for one chart—the Sentencing Table." (13)

Under the Guidelines, a defendant is sentenced by determining in which of the 258 boxes of the Table he or she belongs. (14) A judge uses the Guidelines to calculate the defendant's "offense level," a figure intended to measure the gravity of the crime currently, and the defendant's "criminal history category," a figure intended to measure the gravity of the offender's past criminal conduct. The offense level is the position on the vertical or y-axis of the grid (expressed in Arabic numerals), and the criminal history category is the position on the horizontal or x-axis of the grid (expressed in Roman numerals). The intercept of the two factors provides a sentencing range expressed in months. For example, a defendant with an offense level of 9 and a criminal history category of I can be sentenced from four to ten months. Because all sentences are expressed on the chart in terms of months of imprisonment, sentences consisting solely of probation, fines, or non-prison confinement (the latter category includes house arrest and time in a "half way house") are denoted as sentences of "0" months. This range is the area in which a judge has absolute discretion. If a judge has properly calculated the offense level and criminal history, a sentence within this range is unreviewable. (15)

1. Offense Level Calculations   A defendant's offense level is comprised of several elements: (1) the points assigned to the specific statutory violation at issue (also called the base offense level); (16) (2) adjustments to the base offense level that reflect relevant conduct specific to the crime of conviction ("relevant conduct" is a term of art under the Guidelines and can include size of the loss, other crimes committed by the defendant, and even other crimes committed by his accomplices); (17) and (3) the points assigned to general offense adjustments that apply equally to all offense categories, such as the offender played an aggravating role in the offense. (18)

The points assigned to the specific statutory violation at issue take two forms: the "base offense level" of the crime, meaning the amount of points the commission assigned to conviction for a particular statutory violation, and the "specific offense characteristics" of the crime, meaning the particular aspects of a crime that make it more or less blameworthy than other violations of the same statute. (19) Examples of specific offense characteristics include the amount of money stolen in a fraud and the amount of violence involved in the course of a robbery. (20) So far, then, the system appears relatively simple in application as well as theory: Every criminal who commits a robbery receives the base level of points, and those who commit an especially violent robbery receive additional points for specific offense characteristics. However, the precise number of special points given for specific offense conduct depends not only upon the conduct—such as possessing a weapon—but also upon the underlying statutory crime. For example, a robber receives five extra points for possessing a firearm, while a drug trafficker receives just two points for possessing any dangerous weapon (including a firearm). (21)

As noted above, "relevant conduct" can include other crimes by the defendant and other crimes committed by his accomplices. A court is supposed to take "relevant conduct" into effect if it is proved by a "preponderance of the evidence" (a lower standard than "beyond a reasonable doubt") at the sentencing hearing, irrespective of whether the defendant had been charged with the conduct in the indictment. A judge is even supposed to consider some "relevant conduct" if that conduct underlies charges for which a defendant has been acquitted. (22)

General offense adjustments are applied for aspects of crimes that are not confined to particular statutory violations. Moreover, while the number of points allotted for specific offense characteristics varies depending on the underlying statutory violation, general offense adjustments carry the same weight regardless of the underlying statutory violation. For example, the "vulnerable victim" adjustment is applied for all crimes in which the defendant knew or should have known that the victim was unusually vulnerable due to his age, mental condition, or physical condition; and in all crimes it raises the base offense level by two points. (23)

2. Criminal History Calculations   Criminal history calculations are somewhat more straightforward than offense level calculations. Defendants are assigned criminal history points on the basis of their nominal sentence length, not actual time served, and irrespective of how long ago a conviction occurred. It is also irrelevant whether a defendant's previous conviction has any relation to her current offense. Thus, as Professor Kate Stith and Judge Jose Cabranes note, "a defendant convicted of white collar fraud who recently served a short prison sentence for a previous fraudulent scheme receives the same criminal history enhancement as does the white collar defendant who ten years ago served a sentence for drug possession." (24)

3. Departures from the Guidelines   In most cases a judge must sentence a defendant within the applicable range of the Sentencing Table. However, a judge is authorized to "depart" from the Sentencing Table if, in the words of the Sentencing Reform Act and the Guidelines, "there exists an aggravating or mitigating circumstance of a kind, or to a degree, not adequately taken into consideration by the Sentencing Commission in formulating the Guidelines." (25) Given the comprehensive nature of the Guidelines, this standard weighs against departures. Moreover, a decision to depart can be appealed to a higher court, whereas a decision not to depart cannot be appealed. (26) The basic result of the current system is that departures in general are discouraged and downward departures are especially discouraged. (27) When they occur, it is usually at the prosecutor's prompting. (28) That is, most downward departures are usually given for "substantial assistance," meaning that the prosecutor has recommended that the defendant's sentence be reduced because the defendant has substantially assisted in the prosecution of another individual. (29)

4. United States v. Booker   On January 12, 2005, the Supreme Court held in United States v. Booker that the provisions of the Federal Sentencing Act that made the Guidelines binding violated the Sixth Amendment. (30) Despite the severance of the binding provisions, however, the Guidelines remain important. First, the data on Guidelines-era sentences collected by the United States Sentencing Commission (the "Sentencing Commission" or the "Commission") is the richest source of information we have on federal sentences in any era. Second, Booker itself provides that "[t]he district courts, while not bound to apply the Guidelines, must consult those Guidelines and take them into account when sentencing." (31) Exactly what "consult" means in the context of the Booker and the Guidelines is not yet clear, (32) but at a minimum the Guidelines will probably serve as a sort of treatise or Restatement of Sentencing. (33) Under Booker, the circuit court likewise relies on the existing guidelines to review the "reasonableness" of the district court's sentence. (34)

How these changes affect sentencing will not be clear for some time, and important questions remain unanswered. For example, do the circuit courts now review departures with greater deference than before? What is a reasonable sentence? Do the Guidelines ranges still represent a safe harbor for sentencing judges? When, as now, the entire legal community is considering wide-ranging reforms and reevaluating the sentencing regime at the federal and state levels, it is especially important that we understand what the actual effects of the Guidelines have been.

B. Fines Under the Guidelines

The Guidelines specify that a court must impose a fine in all cases, "except where the defendant establishes that he is unable to pay and is not likely to become able to pay any fine." (35) In determining the amount of the fine, a judge is expressly directed to consider "the burden that the fine places on the defendant and his dependents relative to alternative punishments" (36) and "any . . . pertinent equitable considerations." (37) In the case of fines, then, the court is not only permitted to consider the personal characteristics of a defendant, but is commanded to consider them. The Sentencing Commission's usual fear of disparity is muted. In addition, even if a large fine is imposed, judges are required to apply the Sentencing Guidelines for prison time as they would have otherwise. (38)

If a defendant is ordered to pay a fine, that fine is calculated by reference to the Fine Table found at Section 5E1.2(c)(3) of the Sentencing Guidelines (Figure 1).

The Fine Table is trumped only when "the defendant is convicted under a statute authorizing (a) a maximum fine greater than $250,000, or (b) a fine for each day of violation." (39) In those cases a court "may impose a fine up to the maximum authorized by statute." (40) The range of fines in each cell of the Fine Table is remarkably broad. For example, the fine range for an offense level of 4 to 5 is between $250 and $5,000, and the fine range for an offense level of 18 to 19 is between $6,000 and $60,000. In general, the sentencing judge assesses fines after the probation officer (an officer of the court who advises the judge on the appropriate level of sentence) investigates the offender's financial situation. (41) Fines can also be incorporated into a plea bargain.

C. Sentencing Disparities and the Guidelines

The Guidelines were implemented primarily to reduce unwarranted sentencing disparities. However, post-Guidelines studies find that irrelevant factors such as race and sex continue to affect sentencing. David Mustard conducted one of the most comprehensive studies of sentencing under the Guidelines. (42) Mustard found that unexplained race, sex, and income disparities in length of prison sentence exist even after accounting for an offender's position in the Guidelines sentencing grid (explained in greater detail below), offense type, education, and age. (43) While Mustard found that much of the racial disparity was due to departures from the Guidelines, he found that blacks sentenced under the Guidelines still had an average prison sentence more than two months longer than similarly situated whites. (44) In addition to studying the length of sentence, Mustard also found that (1) whites were more likely to receive a sentence of no prison term than similarly situated blacks and Hispanics, and that (2) they were also more likely to receive a downward departure. Women fared better than men in all specifications.

Apart from Mustard, a number of other post-Guideline studies have also found racial disparities. Celesta Albonetti, examining only drug offenders in

---

FIGURE 1 Guidelines for Fines

[section] 5E1.2. Fines for Individual Defendants

(a) The court shall impose a fine in all cases, except where the defendant establishes that he is unable to pay and is not likely to become able to pay any fine.

(b) The applicable fine guideline range is that specified in subsection (c) below. If, however, the guideline for the offense in Chapter Two provides a specific rule for imposing a fine, that rule takes precedence over subsection (c) of this section.

(c) (1) The minimum of the fine guideline range is the amount shown in column A of the table below.

(2) Except as specified in (3) below, the maximum of the fine guideline range is the amount shown in column B of the table below.

(3)

	Fine Table	
Offense Level	**A** **Minimum**	**B** **Maximum**
3 and below	$100	$5,000
4–5	$250	$5,000
6–7	$500	$5,000
8–9	$1,000	$10,000
10–11	$2,000	$20,000
12–13	$3,000	$30,000
14–15	$4,000	$40,000
16–17	$5,000	$50,000
18–19	$6,000	$60,000
20–22	$7,500	$75,000
23–25	$10,000	$100,000
26–28	$12,500	$125,000
29–31	$15,000	$150,000
32–34	$17,500	$175,000
35–37	$20,000	$200,000
38 and above	$25,000	$250,000

1991–92, found that blacks, men, and those with lower educations received longer sentences. (45) Douglas McDonald and Kenneth Carlson concluded that disparities between blacks and whites increased after the Guidelines, but that these differences were largely due to the policy choices of the Sentencing Commission, not the biases of prosecutors or judges. (46) This finding, of course, is in contrast to Mustard's later conclusion that most of the disparity between blacks and whites was due not to the policy choices embedded in the Guidelines, but to departures from the Commission's strictures. (47)

While important, these studies fail to identify the source of the sentencing disparity. A racial disparity could arise because of prejudiced prosecutors and judges, but other sources are possible as well. For example, wealth, quality of legal counsel, and the seriousness of the crime may not be fully controlled for and these factors may be correlated with race. To directly address whether judges are at the root of racial disparities, Schanzenbach examined whether racial disparities were correlated with judicial characteristics. (48) He was unable to identify the actual sentencing judge, so his study used variation in the percent Democrats, black, Hispanic, and female judges at the district level. (49) He found no consistent correlations between any of these judicial characteristics and racial disparities, and concluded that it is unlikely that judges are the primary cause of racial disparities in sentencing. (50)

In addition to racial disparities, the literature has also focused on inter-judge disparities: in other words, how much do individual judges matter? The literature is divided as to whether inter-judge disparities increased or decreased after the Guidelines. Hofer et al. have argued that the Guidelines decreased inter-judge sentence disparities. (51) Anderson et al. found a decrease in inter-judge disparities in sentence length after the Guidelines, yet argued that the advent of mandatory minimum sentences for drug offenses might have contributed to the decline. (52) On the other hand, Lacasse and Payne found that the Guidelines made no difference. In a unique approach, they measured inter-judge disparity by examining whether plea bargains changed after the Guidelines. (53) If inter-judge disparities truly decreased under Guidelines, Lacasse and Payne reasoned, the judge assigned to a case should have less influence on the decision to plea and on the substance of the plea agreement than she did before. (54) Yet Lacasse and Payne found the contrary: the judge assigned to a case influenced plea decisions as much after the Guidelines as before. (55) Schanzenbach and Tiller have recently shown that Democrats give lighter sentences than Republicans in the case of violent and drug crimes, and that these differences increase when circuit courts are aligned (in other words, Democrats in a Democratic circuit give lower sentences than Democrats in a Republican circuit). (56) These findings, taken together, are consistent with the notion that judges still have substantial discretion under the Sentencing Guidelines.

Our paper contributes to the disparity literature by examining racial disparities in the sentencing of white-collar criminals. Despite the abundance of disparity studies since the Guidelines were enacted, none have focused on white-collar crime in particular.

Those studies that have examined white-collar crime have merely included it in a larger study without detailed comment or investigation. This is a significant gap in the literature because white-collar crime has a few traits that make it an especially fertile source of insight into sentencing.

First, because fines are used against those who are convicted of white-collar crime more often than those who are convicted of violent crimes, drug crimes, or immigration crimes, white-collar crime offers an opportunity to examine the use of fines and their effect on prison sentence disparities. This feature of white-collar crime is especially pertinent because law and economics scholars have championed fines as a cheaper alternative to imprisonment. (57)

Second, some notable empirical work on federal sentencing before the Guidelines has focused on white-collar crime. (58) White-collar crime therefore provides a place for comparison between the pre- and post-Guidelines world.

Third, if there is disparity in the sentencing of white-collar crime, bias might be more plausibly ascribed to judges or prosecutors than in other types of crimes. Legislators and police have not exercised as much influence over white-collar crime as they do over other types of crime, leaving prosecutors and judges with more discretion. (59) Anti-drug criminal law provides an illustrative contrast. Defendants sentenced for possessing or trafficking in crack cocaine are disproportionately black, (60) and possession and distribution of crack is punished much more severely than possession and distribution of powdered cocaine. (61) There is no obvious legislative thumb on the scale creating this kind of racial disparity in white-collar crime. Likewise, because credit card, bank, and securities fraud are likely to be reported by victims or institutions instead of resulting from sting operations, police may exert less control over the investigations and arrests of white-collar criminals than they do violent criminals or drug criminals. Investigations and arrests of white-collar criminals spring from victim complaints more often than from beat-cop observations, and complaints may be investigated by prosecutors before the police ever make an arrest. (62) In fact, the complaints may be made directly to prosecutors, bypassing the police entirely until the prosecutors decide they have enough evidence to make an arrest, and only then do the police show up and arrest the fraudster. (63)

III. PREVIOUS WORK ON FINES
AND PRISON TIME

There is a large amount of theoretical literature on fines, particularly on optimal fines and the trade-off between prison and fines. (64) The theoretical literature goes far beyond the scope of this paper. There is, however, an important argument from the law and economics literature that fines are an underused form of punishment. (65) If a defendant is not judgment-proof, fines are a comparatively inexpensive way to deter and punish because imprisonment, the most likely alternative, is so costly to society. This may lead to inequitable prison sentences between rich and poor, but, the argument goes, so long as fines are severe enough, the actual level of punishment should be equated. We consider the relevance of this argument in greater detail when we discuss our results.

We are aware of three detailed quantitative (66) studies on fines and imprisonment in the United States, all of which examine only pre-Guidelines cases. Joel Waldfogel used pre-Guidelines sentencing data to determine whether or not judges traded prison time for fines in white-collar cases. (67)

He concluded that there was strong evidence that courts (or possibly prosecutors in plea bargains) "traded" fines for prison time, particularly for wealthier
defendants. When defendants were poorer, judges imposed a mix of fines and
imprisonment. As part of the Yale studies on white collar crime, David
Weisburd, Stanton Wheeler, Elin Waring, and Nancy Bode also studied pre-
Guidelines sentencing data, and while their study did not consider whether
fines were traded for prison time, they did find that fines depend on net worth,
which is consistent with Waldfogel's result. (68) John Lott, in another pre-
Guidelines study, also found that fines correlate to income. Lott did not, however, find a significant relationship between income and prison terms. (69)
Waldfogel suggests that this discrepancy between his study and Lott's may be
due to Lott's much smaller sample size. (70)

It is possible, however, that the Guidelines have changed some of the conditions Waldfogel observed. Specifically, they seem to have reduced the ability
of judges to impose fines in lieu of imprisonment—in at least three ways. First,
the Guidelines do not permit judges to use fines as an independent sanction
unless a defendant is in "Zone A" of the Sentencing Table. (71) In all other
cases fines must be coupled with some form of detention. Second, fines do not
justify departures from the Guidelines, although judges still have some sentencing room within the Guidelines. Third, the Guidelines increased the
mandatory prison sentences for white-collar crimes, and departures from these
sentences are subject to appellate review.

IV. DATA AND METHOD

A. The Data

The data used are collected and maintained by the Office of Policy Analysis of
the Sentencing Commission. (72) The judicial terms 1992–93 through
2000–2001 are examined. Earlier judicial terms are not used because they contain a large number of pre-Guidelines cases. In this period 105,917 people
were sentenced under the Guidelines for white-collar offenses, which we
define as fraud, embezzlement, forgery/counterfeiting, bribery, tax offenses,
and money laundering. (73) We forgo examining later cases because of the
increased prominence of white collar crimes after 2001, the introduction of
the Feeney Amendment in 2003, and Booker.

Eliminating those for whom necessary variables (age, race, fine amount,
prison sentence, etc.) were missing reduced the sample by about 9,000 offenders for a total of 97,208. When we refer to the "full sample" this culled data is
the number we mean. The culled data are quite detailed, and include the
offenders' education, race, exact sentencing grid position, offense level, and
criminal history. The Office of Policy Analysis only collected income data
between 1991–92 and 1993–94. Income data is still collected by probation
officers and included in the Pre-Sentencing Reports ("PSRs") given to the

sentencing judge, but after 1994 the Office of Policy Analysis dropped the income variable as too unreliable. Thus, when income is used in our analysis, the sample size is reduced from 97,208 to 22,208.

Table 1 presents the means and percentages of descriptive variables in the sample. When means are reported, the standard error is included below the mean in parentheses. The first thing to note is that nonwhites make up roughly 45% of the sample. This is sufficient representation to allow us to identify any disparities between different ethnic groups. In addition, only 57% of those convicted receive prison time, and 24% receive downward departures from the Guidelines.

Nearly 94% of the cases were resolved in plea bargains. The use of pleas is important to any interpretation regarding where racial discrepancies originate. Bias can enter the system at the judicial level or via the prosecutors, who have a great deal of discretion regarding what cases to bring, the level of the offense, and what to agree to in a plea bargain. (74)

TABLE 1   **Means and Proportions (Standard Errors in Parentheses)**

Variable	Mean or Proportion
Total Prison Sentence	11.34 (21.32)
Prison Time Given	58%
Sentence Within Range	76%
Downward Departure	24%
Downward Departure (Substantial Assistance)	14%
Downward Departure (Judge Initiated)	8%
Upward Departure	.88%
Age	38.52 (11.99)
Male	64%
Female	27%
White	54%
Black	29%
Hispanic	44%
Asian	4%
Other	1%
Citizen	88%
Jury	6%
Bench	.098%
Less Than High School	29%
High School	55%
College	12%
Advanced Degree	5%
No Dependents	38%
One Dependent	21%
Two Dependents	18%
Three or More Dep.	23%
N	97,208

B. The Methodology

Three different measures are used to estimate the severity of the punishment: length of sentence in months, whether any prison time was imposed, and whether a downward departure was made. When the length of prison sentence is the dependent variable, the equation is estimated as a tobit because 42% of the sample received a prison sentence of zero months. The estimated equation takes the form:

$$\text{Sentence}_{ijt} = \alpha\ \text{Race}_{ijt} + \pi\ X_{ijt} + \theta\ \text{Guideline}_{ijt} + \delta\ \text{District}_{jt} + \beta\ \text{Term}_t + \omega\ \text{Offtype}_{ijt} + \beta\ \text{TrialType}_{ijt} + \varepsilon_{ijt} \tag{1}$$

Here, i indexes individual, j indexes district, and t indexes judicial term. Epsilon (ε) is the error term. Race is a vector of racial dummy variables (white being the excluded category); X is a vector of demographic characteristics including age, education, sex, citizenship status, and the number of dependents. Guideline is a matrix of dummy variables indicating where precisely the convict falls in the sentencing grid. Thus, there is a dummy variable for each box of the grid (following Mustard's approach). This technique should control simultaneously for offense level, criminal history, and any offense level adjustments. District is a matrix of dummy variables for judicial district (e.g., the Southern District of New York, the Eastern District of Texas) and Term is a matrix of dummy variables for judicial term. Offtype is a matrix of dummy variables accounting for the offense type (e.g., fraud versus tax). TrialType are dummy variables accounting for whether there is a plea, jury, or bench trial, with plea being the excluded category. Restitution is required under the Guidelines when possible and is entered as a quadratic. It may influence the amount of the fine paid and also helps control for the severity of the offense (the amount of restitution is positively correlated with prison sentence).

Next, we used a probit specification on whether or not a prison sentence was imposed. Probits are used when the dependent variable takes on zero or one, and they allow us to measure how various traits affect the probability of observing the punishment.

$$\Pr(\text{Any Pris}_{ijt}) = \psi\ \text{NoPrisPoss}_{ijt} + \alpha\ \text{Race}_{ijt} + \pi\ X_{ijt} + \theta\ \text{Guideline}_{ijt} + \delta\ \text{District}_{jt} + \beta\ \text{Term}_t + \omega\ \text{Offtype}_{ijt} + \beta\ \text{TrialType}_{ijt} + \varepsilon_{ijt} \tag{2}$$

Any Pris takes on the value 1 when a positive prison sentence was imposed and zero otherwise. The other variables remain as before, with the addition of NoPrisPoss, which is a dummy variable taking on the value 1 if the Guidelines permit a prison sentence of zero months, and 0 otherwise. All coefficients are reported as marginal effects, taking the other variables at their means.

Finally, downward departures are considered:

$$\Pr(\text{DownwrdDept}_{ijt}) = \alpha\ \text{Race}_{ijt} + \pi\ X_{ijt} + \theta\ \text{Guideline}_{ijt} + \delta\ \text{District}_{jt} + \beta\ \text{Term}_t + \omega\ \text{Offtype}_{ijt} + \beta\ \text{TrialType}_{ijt} + \varepsilon_{ijt} \tag{3}$$

Downwrd Dept takes on 1 if the judge imposes a sentence less than the Guidelines recommend and 0 otherwise. The sample excludes cases in which downward departure is impossible (because the Guidelines already permit a sentence of no prison time).

C. The Identification and Interpretation
of Unexplained Racial Disparities

The coefficients on racial dummy variables must be interpreted cautiously. Unobservable factors that are correlated with race and the dependent variable (sentence length) can cause a racial dummy variable to be statistically significant even if there is no "true" discrimination. If those unobservable factors are legally relevant considerations in sentencing, such as unaccounted victim harm or the dangerousness of the convict then "true" racial bias in sentencing may not exist.

The economics literature gives one a flavor of the difficulty in linking racial disparities to discrimination or a particular form of discrimination. Large wage disparities are found between blacks and whites. Wage disparities, albeit much smaller in magnitude, are also found between white ethnic groups. (75) Discrimination between white ethnic groups is a dubious explanation for these disparities. In addition, whether or not wage disparities between blacks and whites are the result of bias in the labor market, or earlier discrimination in schooling, health care, and other human capital investments is controversial and difficult to identify empirically. (76) Racial disparities in hiring are easier to trace because they are open to randomized experiments. For example, a recent study using traditionally black names on applications and race neutral names on others (but with equivalent credentials) found that applicants with black names were much less likely to receive an interview. (77) This is strong evidence of racial bias in the labor market, but unfortunately we cannot employ a similar methodology when it comes to sentencing.

Another example of the problem of interpreting racial disparities comes from examinations of the mortgage market. A number of studies have found that blacks are more likely than similarly situated whites to be rejected for home loans. (78) A widely noted contradiction, however, is that blacks are actually slightly more likely to default on home loans. If blacks truly faced greater hurdles in borrowing due to discrimination, then, presumably, only blacks that were especially low credit risks would be lent money, thereby producing a lower default rate for black borrowers. (79) How can these disparate results be explained? The seeming contradiction is actually consistent with at least two different interpretations. The first is that there are some characteristics that are correlated with race yet which independently contribute to loan risk, and the bank observes these characteristics but the econometrician does not. The bank is not discriminating on the basis of race in this scenario. Another possibility, however, is that lenders observe what the econometrician observes but engage in "rational discrimination," meaning that they have an idea of which unobserved risk factors are correlated with race, but cannot observe them directly, and so they consciously take account of race in order to avoid these unobservable factors. (80)

The point of this discussion is simply to emphasize that the source of racial biases must be investigated very carefully and all possible interpretations of the outcomes considered. Independent factors correlated with race must somehow be ruled out.

V. THE RESULTS

Table 2 begins the analysis by presenting raw averages by race for some relevant variables. However, these are unadjusted averages that do not control for a variety of factors such as offense level, criminal history, and crime category. They are merely taken as a starting point for the discussion.

On average, prison sentences for all groups in the sample are low: between 10 and 13 months. No sizeable racial disparities are evident based on the raw data. Blacks in the sample have lower average prison sentences than whites and are no more likely to be incarcerated. They are much less likely to be granted downward departures, however, and this difference was significant at less than the 1% level. Hispanics receive longer average prison sentences than whites

TABLE 2 Variables by Race and Fine Status

	White	Black	Hispanic
Average Prison Sentence	11.47	10.28	12.83
	(20.08)	(19.29)	(22.42)
Average Prison Sentence (if fined)	8.09	7.16	12.09
	(18.56)	(16.98)	(24.02)
Average Prison Sentence (if not fined)	12.67	10.85	13.08
	(21.14)	(19.16)	(21.09)
Downward Departures	27%	18%	25%
Prison Time	57%	55%	61%
Income < 10 K	31%	52%	47%
Income between 10 K and 20 K	23%	26%	26%
Income between 20 K and 35 K	16%	11%	13%
Income > 35 K	30%	9%	14%
Any Fine Paid	26%	16%	19%
Amount of Fine (if any)	$10,793	$2,850	$6,522
	(38,266)	(11,547)	(27,062)
N	62,322	28,077	10,049

(1.36 months longer), but are given prison time and downward departures at a comparable rate.

The starkest finding is that prison time is less for those who pay a fine versus those who pay no fine, and these differences are all statistically significant at the 1% level. We do not formally consider the effect of fines on prison time, as other studies have, but these averages provide some evidence that the amount of prison time is in part determined by the fine.

The income data, a subset of the full data, are provided for comparison purposes. Although whites in the sample are clearly wealthier as a group than blacks and Hispanics in the sample, all offenders in the sample tend to have low incomes irrespective of their race. For example, 70% of whites make less than $35,000 per year, and only 46% of whites make more than $20,000 per year.

A. Disparities by Demographic Group: Dependents, Education, Age, U.S. Citizenship, Female Sex, and Being White Associated with Lower Prison Term

Table 3 presents tobit estimates of Equation 1. In each of these regressions, the dependent variable is total prison sentence in months. Tobits are run to account for the large number of zero prison sentences. The sample is subdivided

TABLE 3   Tobits on Total Prison Sentence

Variable	1 Full Sample	2 No Fine	3 Fine Payers
Black	.98 ***	.63 ***	1.83 ***
	(.13)	(.14)	(.38)
Hispanic	1.11 ***	.63 ***	2.36 ***
	(.21)	(.23)	(.53)
Asian	−.58 *	−.64 *	.054
	(.30)	(.34)	(1.28)
Other	.33	.072	−.43
	(.54)	(.59)	(1.41)
Citizen	−4.40 ***	−4.568 ***	−3.05 ***
	(.19)	(.20)	(.46)
Male	2.72 ***	2.84 ***	3.06 ***
	(.13)	(.14)	(.39)
Age	.29 ***	.27 ***	.36 ***
	(.029)	(.032)	(.071)
Age Squared/ 100	−.42 ***	−.39 ***	−.40 ***
	(.032)	(.042)	(.082)

Continued

TABLE 3 *Continued*

Variable	1 Full Sample	2 No Fine	3 Fine Payers
Restitution/ 10,000	.53 ★★★ (.043)	.047 ★★★ (.0027)	.74 ★★★ (.089)
Restitution Squared/10,000	−.59xe−7 ★★★ (.44e−9)	−.51xe−8 ★★★ (.72e−9)	−.98xe−8 ★★★ (.92e−9)
Income < 10 K			
Income between 10 K and 20 K			
Income between 20 K and 35 K			
No Dependents	1.38 ★★★ (.19)	1.40 ★★★ (.35)	1.11 ★★★ (.35)
One Dependent	.51 ★★ (.21)	.67 ★ (.37)	.28 (.51)
Two Dependents	−.002 (.21)	.015 (.23)	−.052 (.52)
Three Dependents	−.26 (.22)	−.19 (.25)	−.54 (.55)
High School	−1.39 ★★★ (.13)	−1.20 ★★★ (.13)	−1.61 ★★★ (.34)
College	−1.82 ★★★ (.19)	−1.41 ★★★ (.22)	−2.39 ★★★ (.45)
Advanced	−1.74 ★★★ (.27)	−1.44 ★★★ (.31)	−1.83 ★★★ (.56)
Trial	9.53 ★★★ (.22)	9.14 ★★★ (.38)	12.31 ★★★ (.47)
Sample Size	97,208	75,138	22,070

Variable	4 Income Sample	5 Income Sample	6 Base Level Controls
Black	1.43 ★★★ (.23)	.93 ★★ (.23)	−2.00 ★★★ (.19)
Hispanic	1.74 ★★★ (.6l)	1.37 ★★ (.60)	−.87 ★★★ (.31)
Asian	1.26 (.82)	1.05 ★ (.54)	−1.82 ★★★ (.54)
Other	.72 (1.72)	.089 (1.07)	−1.36 ★ (.77)
Citizen	−3.72 ★★★ (.51)	−3.00 ★★★ (.51)	−4.30 ★★★ (.51)

TABLE 3 *Continued*

Variable	4 Income Sample	5 Income Sample	6 Base Level Controls
Male	3.98 ★★★	4.18 ★★★	6.22 ★★★
	(.36)	(.35)	(.19)
Age	.47 ★★★	.58 ★★★	.80 ★★★
	(.083)	(.079)	(.042)
Age Squared/ 100	−.64 ★★★	−.72 ★★★	−.87★★★
	(.091)	(.091)	(.041)
Restitution/ 10,000	.13 ★★★	.12 ★★★	.24 ★★★
	(.0080)	(.008)	(.0037)
Restitution Squared/10,000	−.15e–8 ★★★	−.15e–8 ★★★	−.15e–8 ★★★
	(.13e–9)	(.13e–9)	(.13e–9)
Income < 10 K		6.19 ★★★	
		(.14)	
Income between 10 K and 20 K		1.19 ★★★	
		(.43)	
Income between 20 K and 35 K		1.25 ★★	
		(.63)	
No Dependents	1.48 ★★★	.38	.95 ★★★
	(.51)	(.50)	(.28)
One Dependent	.22	.012	.29
	(.51)	(.53)	(.30)
Two Dependents	−.46	−.71	−.14
	(.54)	(.54)	(.30)
Three Dependents	−.32	−.29	−48
	(.57)	(.56)	(.32)
High School	−.94 ★★★	−.38	.10
	(.34)	(.35)	(.18)
College	−1.68 ★★★	−.79 ★	1.39 ★★
	(.43)	(.48)	(.28)
Advanced	.83	−1.53 ★★	2.53 ★★
	(.68)	(.67)	(.39)
Trial	14.45 ★★★	14.47 ★★★	14.47 ★★★
	(.53)	(.52)	(.52)
Sample Size	22,208	22,208	96,556

Standard errors in parentheses. Total Prison Sentence in months is the dependent variable. All regressions include dummy variables for sentencing grid position, offense type, judicial term, and district.
★ Coefficient statistically significant at the 10% level.
★★ Coefficient statistically significant at the 5% level.
★★★ Coefficient statistically significant at the 1% level.

in a number of ways: first, the full sample is used, then the sample is divided between fine payers and non-fine payers, and then we reestimate Equation 1 using the income sample. Finally, we consider the effect of controlling for base offense level instead of final offense level on the estimated race and sex disparities.

Column 1 in Table 3 estimates Equation 1 using the full sample. A number of legally irrelevant or discouraged factors are correlated with the length of the sentence, even after accounting for the offender's position in the sentencing grid, type of offense, district court, and judicial term. Having more dependents, higher levels of education, being older, U.S. citizenship, being female, and being white are all associated with lower prison terms. For example, having no dependants (versus having three or more) is associated with a 1.38 month longer prison sentence. Having a high school education (versus failure to graduate) is associated with a 1.39 month shorter prison sentence. (81) Age is positively, though decreasingly, associated with a longer prison sentence. Citizens receive sentences on average 4.40 months shorter than non-citizens. As is commonly found in the sentencing disparity literature, a large unexplained sex disparity exists (and remains quite large regardless of specification). The point estimate in column 1 implies that men receive a prison sentence of an average 2.72 months longer than women.

Finally, there are unexplained differentials based on race and ethnicity. The point estimates imply that blacks receive roughly .98 months and Hispanics 1.11 months longer sentences on average than whites after accounting for all observable variables. This corresponds to roughly a 10% longer prison sentence than average. The magnitude of this disparity is not huge, but that it persists under the Guidelines is troubling. In addition, it corresponds in magnitude to estimated disparities in the case of more serious crimes, such as drug crimes. (82) Having established the existence of a racial disparity under a typical regression specification, we examine how sensitive the racial disparities to alternate specifications.

B. The Effect of Fines: Paying to Get Out of Prison

Because judges have broad discretion over fines, we do not incorporate them directly into the analysis. As discussed, fines are likely endogenous. In other words, they are determined by the judge simultaneously with the amount of prison time and each element of the total sentence, fine and prison time, has an influence on the other. However, we have strong reasons, a priori, to suspect that fines reduce prison time and that the ability to pay a fine is correlated with race. Thus, we divide the sample into those who paid fines and those who paid no fine and consider the estimated racial disparities within the two groups. If our hypothesis is correct, the estimated racial disparity among those who pay a fine should be larger than the estimated racial disparity among those who do not pay a fine.

Columns 2 and 3 of Table 3 split the sample into those who paid no fines (column 2) and those who paid a fine (column 3). Among those who paid no fine, both blacks and Hispanics have .63 months longer prison sentences than whites, which are roughly two-thirds of the corresponding estimates in column 1 and represent only a 5% disparity compared to the average sentence. When racial disparities are estimated using the fine-paying sample, the estimated disparities are much larger for blacks and Hispanics. For blacks, the disparity is 1.83 months among fine payers versus .63 months among non-payers. Likewise, for Hispanics, the disparity is 2.36 months among fine payers versus .63 months among nonpayers. Because the average prison sentence if fined is only eight months, the racial disparities estimated here are nearly 25% relative to the average sentence, a substantial relative and absolute increase. In sum, racial disparities are three to four times larger among fine payers than non-payers, and roughly one-third of the overall disparity among the races estimated in column 1 is due to disparities between fine payers.

We do not interpret the larger racial disparity estimated in the fine-paying sample as evidence that those who pay fines face more discrimination. Instead, we interpret our result as evidence that whites who pay fines get out of more prison time than blacks and Hispanics who pay fines. This is likely because the more one pays, the more time is forgiven, and blacks and Hispanics tend to pay less than whites. A back-of-the-envelope calculation makes this clearer. According to Table 2, blacks who paid fines paid $8,000 less than whites who paid fines. If we ascribe all of the racial disparity among fine payers—all 1.83 months—to the extra fines paid by whites, then a white collar offender can buy out prison time at $4,371 per month.

Admittedly, this quick estimate most likely goes too far. We believe it is incorrect to ascribe the racial disparity among fine payers entirely fines. After all, a disparity exists (albeit much smaller) among those who did not. Nonetheless, it demonstrates that sentencing is a complicated process, and the size of the racial disparity can swing widely between different subsamples. In addition, the increase in the disparity between sub-samples is potentially explainable by factors other than judicial prejudice. This is not to say that the increase in the disparity is no cause for concern. That would depend on whether one thinks that the fines traded in lieu of prison are adequate and whether we could be certain that judges are charging the same "price" across racial groups, something we are not able to discern.

C. The Effect of Income: More Money, Less Prison Time

Columns 4 and 5 of Table 3 limit the sample to the three years for which income data were collected. Column 4 is provided as a means of comparison for column 5, and does not include income controls. As can be seen, the estimated racial disparities are a higher for the income sub-sample.

The coefficient on the dummy variable for less than $10,000 of income in column 6 is significant at less than the .0001 level and implies that those in this income level receive sentences roughly six months longer than those in the excluded ($35,000 or more) category. We presume that some of this difference arises because income determines what quality of legal services the defendant retains and perhaps the greater ability to trade fines for prison time. The socio-economic status of the defendant is undoubtedly proxied by income as well. This effect rapidly decreases for our higher income categories to 1.19 months for $10,000 to $20,000 of income and 1.25 months for $20,000 to $35,000.

More important for our purposes is the effect of income controls, even crude ones, on the estimated racial disparities. The inclusion of income in column 5 reduces the coefficients on the black and Hispanic dummy variables by roughly one-third. Thus, income differences may explain up to one-third of the estimated disparity. More accurate measures of income or assets would undoubtedly reduce this further. As noted above, we have reason to believe that income is poorly measured. First, a sizeable portion of the sample (37%) reports little or no income. This is strange, considering that the nature of the crimes reported here (embezzlement, fraud, larceny, tax offenses) almost require higher income levels and a position of responsibility. Second, apart from any oddities of the actual data collected, we know that offenders have incentives to underreport income and assets. Underreporting is a way to avoid paying fines and restitution, and sizeable income and assets may be evidence of an offender's degree of wrongdoing.

D. The Offense Level Calculations

Column 6 of Table 3 conditions sentences on base offense level instead of final offense level. As discussed, judges have some discretion over the calculation of the final offense level. It is possible that biases and prejudices could be masked or reflected in its calculation. Thus, conditioning on the final offense level could potentially understate the biases reflected in race and sex disparities. For example, biased judges could be more willing to find that a Hispanic man played an aggravating role than a white woman, which increases the offense level and hence the sentencing range. Adjustments to the base offense level are generally reviewed deferentially because they are highly fact-bound. Previous empirical work indicates that judges exercise a substantial degree of discretion in these areas. (83) Conditioning on this increased offense level could then understate the scope of an unwarranted disparity.

On the other hand, the base offense level is an incomplete measurement of the severity of the crime. For example, the offense level is enhanced in the case of fraud to account for the size of the loss, whether a banking institution was affected, or whether sophisticated means were used. Thus, some disparities between sentences at the base offense level are justified because they may disappear once various aspects of the different offenders' conduct are accounted for.

Column 6 of Table 3 reveals that, when sentences are conditioned on base offense level, blacks and Hispanics actually receive shorter sentences than whites. In other words, when sentences are compared without accounting for before judicial discretion, blacks and Hispanics receive shorter sentences relative to whites. After adjustments are made—after judicial discretion is accounted for—blacks and Hispanics receive longer sentences relative to whites. This means that when sentences are conditioned on base offense level, our findings regarding race and ethnicity are actually reversed. For blacks, sentences are two months shorter, and for Hispanics, sentences are .87 months shorter. Our findings regarding sex, however, are similar even when sentences are conditioned on base offense level; men continue to receive longer sentences relative to women. In fact, the coefficient on the sex dummy variable doubles in size relative to column 1, rising from under three months to over six months.

Table 4 takes on the offense level calculation directly and the findings are consistent with those of Table 3's column 6. First, blacks and Hispanics have lower calculated offense levels—blacks by .90 levels and Hispanics by .61 levels. For most crimes in our sample, this would reduce the minimum Guideline prison sentence by roughly two months. Thus, it is not surprising that conditioning on base offense level versus final offense level in the prison sentence regressions changes the results significantly. Also note that men have higher calculated offense levels and whether or not a fine was paid has no influence on the estimated race and sex disparities.

What should one make of this? The case of the sex disparity is easy because the sex disparities work against men in both cases: men have higher calculated final offense levels and higher prison sentences conditional on the final offense level. In the case of racial disparities, however, the interpretation becomes tricky because the racial disparities work in opposite directions: minorities have lower calculated final offense levels but, conditional on the final offense level, higher prison terms. It is possible that whites commit larger and more complicated frauds on average, requiring higher calculated offense levels, and hence conditioning on the base offense level instead of the final offense level omits important independent variables. However, the size of the fraud should be controlled for based on the amount of restitution ordered, which we include as an independent variable. Estimates controlling for total loss due to the fraud, which was a variable collected in some years, while not reported, yielded similar results. Interestingly, the payment of a fine, in the case of final offense levels (see columns 2 and 3 of Table 4), does not affect the size of the disparity by much. This stands in contrast to the prison sentence results. However, these disparities are now working in favor of nonwhites, so the results are not inconsistent. (84)

On balance, we suspect that much of the reversal here is due to omitted variable bias given the inadequacy of the base offense controls, and relevant sentencing factors such as sophistication of a fraud may well be correlated with race. This, however, is only an educated guess. We would suspect similar factors to be at work in the sex disparity, which, contrary to the race results, increased.

TABLE 4 OLS Regressions on Final Offense Level

Variable	1 Full Sample	2 No Fine	3 Fine Payers
Black	−.90 ★★★	−.87 ★★★	−1.01 ★★★
	(.029)	(.029)	(.056)
Hispanic	−.61 ★★★	−.65 ★★★	−.59 ★★★
	(.041)	(.051)	(.096)
Asian	−.42 ★★★	−.22 ★★★	−.43 ★★★
	(.062)	(.073)	(.13)
Other	−.41 ★★★	−.41 ★★★	−.26
	(.11)	(.11)	(.23)
Citizen	−.20 ★★★	.11 ★★★	.44 ★★★
	(.045)	(.046)	(.084)
Male	.68 ★★★	.78 ★★★	.65 ★★★
	(.027)	(.029)	(.057)
Age	.13 ★★★	.10 ★★★	.16 ★★★
	(.009)	(.009)	(.011)
Age Squared/100	−.11 ★★★	−.078 ★★★	−.15 ★★★
	(.016)	(.012)	(.013)
Restitution/10,000	.55 ★★★	.53 ★★★	.63 ★★★
	(.043)	(.0043)	(.014)
Restitution Squared/ 10,000	−.61xe−7 ★★★	−.57xe−7 ★★★	−76xe−7 ★★★
	(.94e−9)	(.94e−9)	(.26e−9)
No Dependents	−.082 ★	−.071 ★	−.013
	(.042)	(.046)	(.079)
One Dependent	−.005	.012	.083
	(.045)	(.049)	(.084)
Two Dependents	−.011	.022	.11
	(.045)	(.048)	(.084)
Three Dependents	−.0075	.064	.14
	(.048)	(.053)	(.089)
High School	.41 ★★★	.52 ★★★	.45 ★★★
	(.027)	(.029)	(.027)
College	.88 ★★★	1.11 ★★★	.91 ★★★
	(.042)	(.047)	(.079)
Advanced	1.16 ★★★	1.41 ★★★	1.20 ★★★
	(.072)	(.072)	(.11)
Trial	3.80 ★★★	3.79 ★★★	3.45 ★★★
	(.052)	(.052)	(.092)
Sample Size	96,522	74,837	22,070

Standard errors in parentheses. Total Prison Sentence in months is the dependent variable. All regressions include dummy variables for sentencing grid position, offense type, judicial term, and district.
★ Coefficient statistically significant at the 10% level.
★★ Coefficient statistically significant at the 5% level.
★★★ Coefficient statistically significant at the 1% level.

E. Incarceration and Downward Departures

Mainly for comparison purposes, Tables 5 and 6 perform probits on whether a prison sentence was imposed and whether a downward departure from the Guidelines was made. In Tables 5 and 6, just as in Table 3, large racial disparities are estimated, and racial disparities are greater among those who paid fines.

The prison probit results in Table 5 (Y = 1 if there is some prison time imposed, 0 otherwise) parallel the results using total prison sentence in months as the dependent variable. The reported coefficients should be interpreted as the increase in the proportion going to prison based on being black, Hispanic, etc. relative to those who are white. In column 1, for example, the coefficient on the black dummy is .035, suggesting that 3.5 percentage points more blacks go to prison than observationally equivalent whites. Given that 55% of the sample are not sentenced to any prison time, this represents a slight disparity. As in the case of prison sentences, however, the disparities for fine payers are much larger than disparities among nonpayers. For example, for nonpayers the black–white disparity is 2.2 percentage points versus 4.7 percentage points for fine payers.

Table 6 performs a probit analysis on downward departures (Y = 1 if there is a downward departure, 0 otherwise). The sample is limited in two important ways. First, all substantial assistance departures are removed. Such departures must be requested by the prosecution, and cannot be unilaterally granted by the judge. Second, we exclude all cases in which no prison time was a possibility because it was in the Guideline range or available as an alternative sentence (this excludes cases in the A and B range of the sentencing table).

As in the case of the prison probits, sizeable disparities are estimated, and these disparities are much larger within the group that paid a fine than within the group that did not. In the case of blacks, the disparity for fine payers is nearly twice as large, and in the case of Hispanics it is nearly five times as large.

F. Comparisons to Past Studies

In many respects our results are consistent with past studies of white-collar crime. Like Mustard, who examined fraud cases under the Guidelines as part of his broad study, and Michael Benson and Esteban Walker, who examined pre-Guidelines white-collar crime cases in a single federal district court, we find that in white-collar cases, when sentences are conditioned on final offense levels, nonwhites were both more likely to be incarcerated and more likely to receive longer sentences than whites. (85) Like Waldfogel, we find evidence suggesting that defendants are able to trade fines for reductions in prison time.

In some respects, however, our results diverge dramatically from the last book in the series of Yale Studies, Weisburd et al.'s Crimes of the Middle Classes, which examined federal white-collar crime sentences meted out between 1976 and 1978 (roughly ten years before the Guidelines took effect). When we condition sentences according to final offense levels, we find that blacks and Hispanics are both more likely to be incarcerated and more likely

TABLE 5   Probit on Prison (Y = 1 If Prison Imposed, 0 Otherwise)

Variable	1 Full Sample	2 No Fine	3 Fine Payers
Guidelines Permit no	−.26 ★★★	−.26 ★★★	−.21 ★★
Prison	(.018)	(.012)	(.028)
Black	.035 ★★★	.022 ★★★	.047 ★★★
	(.005)	(.024)	(.012)
Hispanic	.064 ★★★	.058 ★★★	.071 ★★★
	(.007)	(.008)	(.017)
Asian	−.018 ★	−.021 ★	.003
	(.011)	(.012)	(.019)
Other	−.023	.014	−0.012
	(.019)	(.019)	(.041)
Citizen	−.19 ★★★	−.20 ★★★	−.11 ★★★
	(.005)	(.006)	(.015)
Male	.10 ★★★	.10 ★★★	.091 ★★★
	(.004)	(.021)	(.010)
Age	.007 ★★★	.007 ★★★	.009 ★★★
	(.001)	(.001)	(.002)
Age Squared/100	−.012 ★★★	−.012 ★★★	−.013 ★★★
	(.001)	(.001)	(.003)
No Dependents	.048 ★★★	.050 ★★★	.023
	(.007)	(.008)	(.014)
One Dependent	.019 ★★	.024 ★★★	.004
	(.007)	(.007)	(.015)
Two Dependents	.005	.013	−.023
	(.007)	(.008)	(.015)
Three Dependents	−.0007	−.006	−.019
	(.008)	(.008)	(.016)
High School	−.052 ★★★	−.042 ★★★	−.033 ★
	(.005)	(.005)	(.001)
College	−.078 ★★★	−.065 ★★★	−.059 ★★★
	(.007)	(.008)	(.013)
Advanced	−.046 ★★★	−.035 ★★★	−0.023
	(.012)	(.012)	(.017)
Trial	.25 ★★★	.21 ★★★	.34 ★★★
	(.007)	(.048)	(.019)
Sample Size	97,095	74,937	21,971

Standard errors (the numbers in parentheses) are Huber-White robust estimates. Total Prison Sentence in months is the dependent variable. All regressions include dummy variables for sentencing grid position, offense type, judicial term, and district. Coefficients reflect marginal effects.
★ Coefficient statistically significant at the 10% level.
★★ Coefficient statistically significant at the 5% level.
★★★ Coefficient statistically significant at the 1% level.

TABLE 6   Probit on Downward Departure from Guidelines (Y = 1 If Downward Departure, 0 Otherwise)

Variable	1 Full Sample	4 No Fine	5 Fine Payers
Black	−.041 ★★★	−.037 ★★★	−.071 ★★★
	(.004)	(.008)	(.013)
Hispanic	−.022 ★★★	−.013 ★	−.065 ★★★
	(.007)	−.013 ★	(.016)
Asian	−.039 ★★★	−.016	−.074 ★★★
	(.009)	(.011)	(.021)
Other	−.032 ★	−.042 ★★★	.029
	(.017)	(.017)	(.057)
Citizen	.029 ★★★	.031 ★★★	−.003
	(.006)	(.006)	(.019)
Male	−.083 ★★★	−.077 ★★★	−.098 ★★★
	(.005)	(.006)	(.018)
Age	−.008 ★★★	−.006 ★★★	−.016 ★★★
	(.001)	(.001)	(.002)
Age Squared/100	.011 ★★★	.011 ★★★	.022 ★★★
	(.001)	(.001)	(.003)
No Dependents	−.041 ★★★	−.031 ★★★	−.049 ★★★
	(.006)	(.007)	(.017)
One Dependent	−.022 ★★★	−.019 ★★★	−.031 ★★
	(.007)	(.007)	(.017)
Two Dependents	−.005	−.005	−.024
	(.007)	(.007)	(.019)
Three Dependents	−.003	−.013 ★	(.019)
	(.008)	(.008)	(.021)
High School	.015 ★★	.012 ★★	.039 ★★★
	(.004)	(.0049)	(.013)
College	.038 ★★★	.034 ★★★	.067 ★★
	(.007)	(.007)	(.018)
Advanced	.029 ★★	.023 ★★	.055 ★★
	(.009)	(.011)	(.022)
Trial	−.064 ★★★	−.028 ★★★	−.10 ★★★
	(.006)	(.0066)	(.011)
Sample Size	41,822	35,237	6,515

Standard errors (the numbers in parentheses) are Huber-White robust estimates. Total Prison Sentence in months is the dependent variable. All regressions include dummy variables for sentencing grid position, offense type, judicial term, and district. Coefficients reflect marginal effects.
★ Coefficient statistically significant at the 10% level.
★★ Coefficient statistically significant at the 5% level.
★★★ Coefficient statistically significant at the 1% level.

to receive long sentences relative to whites. When we condition sentences according to base offense levels, thereby eliminating the effect of adjustments, we find that the results flip; blacks and Hispanics are less likely to be incarcerated and more likely to receive shorter sentences relative to whites. Both techniques revealed disparities, but opposing ones. In contrast, Weisburd et al.'s pre-Guidelines study found no statistically significant racial disparity (though the estimated race coefficient in their prison sentence regression is 12%, roughly in line with ours). Several possible explanations for these discrepancies between our study and the Yale Studies come to mind.

First, our sample sizes are different. The Yale Studies use a sample of 1,094 cases; because of the mechanization of data collection under the Sentencing Commission, we were able to obtain a sample size of 97,208. (86) Second, some unobserved aspect of the Guidelines might have created a disparity where once there was none. This could have happened any number of ways. To give just one example, the Guidelines might have altered the "paradox of leniency and severity" identified by one of the earlier Yale Studies, Sentencing the White Collar Offender: Rhetoric and Reality. (87) The severity occurs, the study claimed, because judges hold defendants with high social status to a higher moral standard than other defendants, and so punish high-status defendants more when they transgress. The leniency occurs because high social status is usually tied to what the study calls "impeccability," meaning a record free of previous criminality and full of magnanimity, and this record supposedly prompts the judge to be lenient. Together these elements combined to pull judges in two directions. The severity element is at the fore when judges are deciding whether to sentence people to prison, and the leniency element is at the fore when judges are deciding how long a prison term should be. (88) According to the theory, then, high status offenders are imprisoned more than other offenders, but among those who are imprisoned, they have the shorter prison terms.

Perhaps the Guidelines altered the paradox for actual sentences, examined in this study as sentences conditioned on final offense levels, by taking many in/out decisions, meaning decisions of whether or not to impose any prison time, away from judges. The severity effect may be less powerful under the Guidelines because judges have less discretion than before in choosing whether to sentence offenders to prison, yet the leniency effect may be just as strong as it was before the Guidelines were enacted. Given that whites tend to be wealthier and of higher status than blacks and Hispanics, the attenuation of the severity effect may have created the disparity in our results. On the other hand, this theory has at least one major weakness: as a practical matter, judges have retained a great deal of discretion in white-collar cases. After all, a large portion of the criminals in our sample (roughly 42%) fall into "Zone A," the section of the Sentencing Table in which judges have a choice as to whether to imprison an offender. Judges also retain a great deal of discretion in meting out fines because the ranges on the Fine Table are so wide. (89) Still, it may deserve further consideration.

The Yale Studies' hypothesis of the leniency and severity paradox might also shed some light on why conditioning sentences on base offense levels reverses our findings. Perhaps base offense level does not account for the factors that, pre-Guidelines, the Yale Studies found encouraged severity against high status defenders. And perhaps final offense level, which incorporates adjustments for amount of money stolen or leadership roles in the offense, etc., does account for the factors that, Pre-Guidelines, the Yale Studies found encouraged severity. This might explain why sentences conditioned on base offense level differ so dramatically from sentences based on final offense level.

VI. CONCLUSIONS

Despite the Sentencing Guidelines' focus on reducing unwarranted sentencing disparities, unexplained racial and ethnic differentials persist even for non-violent, white-collar crimes. We find, however, that the disparities are highly sensitive to sub-samples and to the specification of the model. When the dependent variable is the total prison sentence conditional on the final offense level, the disparities are roughly three times larger among those offenders who paid a fine. This result is nearly as stark in the prison and downward departure probits. When income is considered, the prison sentence disparities decrease by roughly one-third. In addition, when we condition sentences on base offense levels instead of final offense levels, the estimated racial disparities actually flip signs. Whites, not blacks and Hispanics, are on the losing side of the disparity. The sex disparity, on the other hand, consistently disfavors men.

We conclude that observed racial disparities in prison sentences for white-collar criminals are due in large part to the ability of different groups to pay fines and other factors which are often not controlled for or are poorly controlled for (such as wealth). Paying fines reduces the prison time imposed, and thus it seems that whites receive shorter sentences, in part, because they have a disproportionate ability to pay fines. This does not imply that there are no other sources of racial disparities, however, because disparities remained even within the group that did not pay a fine.

There are a couple of important policy implications to be drawn from the analysis. First, if fines are more heavily relied upon, the analysis suggests that racial disparities in prison sentences, particularly those between black and whites, might increase. Second, if racial disparities in white-collar sentences and fines are driven partly by income levels and unobserved assets, then a more creative system of fining and ascertaining the ability of offenders to pay fines might actually reduce observed racial disparities. If fines are made proportionate to wealth and a system of payment options is created, prison time may be forgiven in a more equitable fashion.

APPENDIX 1 Sentencing Table (in Months of Imprisonment) (90)

Offense Level	Criminal History Category (Criminal History Points)		
	I (0 or 1)	II (2 or 3)	III (4, 5, 6)
1	0–6	0–6	0–6
2	0–6	0–6	0–6
3	0–6	0–6	0–6
4	0–6	0–6	0–6
5	0–6	0–6	1–7
6	0–6	1–7	2–8
7	0–6	2–8	4–10
8	0–6	4–10	6–12
9	4–10	6–12	8–14
10	6–12	8–14	10–16
11	8–14	10–16	12–18
12	10–16	12–18	15–21
13	12–18	15–21	18–24
14	15–21	18–24	21–27
15	18–24	21–27	24–30
16	21–27	24–30	27–33
17	24–30	27–33	30–37
18	27–33	30–37	33–41
19	30–37	33–41	37–46
20	33–41	37–46	41–51
21	37–46	41–51	46–57
22	41–51	46–57	51–63
23	46–57	51–63	57–71
24	51–63	57–71	63–78
25	57–71	63–78	70–87
26	63–78	70–87	78–97
27	70–87	78–97	87–108
28	78–97	87–108	97–121
29	87–108	97–121	108–135
30	97–121	108–135	121–151
31	108–135	121–151	135–168
32	121–151	135–168	151–188
33	135–168	151–188	168–210
34	151–188	168–210	188–235
35	168–210	188–235	210–262
36	188–235	210–262	235–293
37	210–262	235–293	262–327
38	235–293	262–327	292–365
39	262–327	292–365	324–405
40	292–365	324–405	360–life
41	324–405	360–life	360–life
42	360–life	360–life	360–life
43	Life	Life	Life

Zone A: Offense Levels 1–8
Zone B: Offense Levels 9–10
Zone C: Offense Levels 11–12
Zone D: Offense Levels 28+

APPENDIX 1 *Continued*

	Offense Level	Criminal History Category (Criminal History Points)		
		IV (7, 8, 9)	V (10, 11, 12)	VI (13 or More)
	1	0–6	0–6	0–6
	2	0–6	0–6	1–7
	3	0–6	2–8	3–9
Zone A	4	2–8	4–10	6–12
	5	4–10	6–12	9–15
	6	6–12	9–15	12–18
	7	8–14	12–18	15–21
	8	10–16	15–21	18–24
Zone B	9	12–18	18–24	21–27
	10	15–21	21–27	24–30
Zone C	11	18–24	24–30	27–33
	12	21–27	27–33	30–37
	13	24–30	30–37	33–41
	14	27–33	33–41	37–46
	15	30–37	37–46	41–51
	16	33–41	41–51	46–57
	17	37–46	46–57	51–63
	18	41–51	51–63	57–71
	19	46–57	57–71	63–78
	20	51–63	63–78	70–87
	21	57–71	70–87	77–96
	22	63–78	77–96	84–105
	23	70–87	84–105	92–115
	24	77–96	92–115	100–125
	25	84–105	100–125	110–137
	26	92–115	110–137	120–150
	27	100–125	120–150	130–162
Zone D	28	110–137	130–162	140–175
	29	121–151	140–175	151–188
	30	135–168	151–188	168–210
	31	151–188	168–210	188–235
	32	168–210	188–235	210–262
	33	188–235	210–262	235–293
	34	210–262	235–293	262–327
	35	235–293	262–327	292–365
	36	262–327	292–365	324–405
	37	292–365	324–405	360–life
	38	324–405	360–life	360–life
	39	360–life	360–life	360–life
	40	360–life	360–life	360–life
	41	360–life	360–life	360–life
	42	360–life	360–life	360–life
	43	Life	Life	Life

Max Schanzenbach, *Assistant Professor of Law, Northwestern University School of Law.*

Michael Yaeger *is an attorney with the law firm of Cahill Gordon & Reindel LLP in New York City. The views expressed in this article do not necessarily represent the position of his firm or of the clients of the firm, and should not be imputed to them.*

NOTES

1.   See Thorsten Sellin, The Negro Criminal: A Statistical Note, 140 ANNALS AM. ACAD. POL. & SOC. SCI. 52 (1928).

2.   See John Hagan, Extra-Legal Attributes and Criminal Sentencing: An Assessment of a Sociological Viewpoint, 8 LAW & SOC'Y REV. 357 (1974) (surveying the literature); see also DOROTHY CAMPBELL TOMPKINS, SENTENCING THE OFFENDER— A BIBLIOGRAPHY (1971) (same); Edward Green, Research on Disparities, in THE CRIMINAL IN THE ARMS OF THE LAW 529 (Leon Radzinowicz & Marvin E. Wolfgang eds., 1971) (same); Andrew Overby, Discrimination Against Minority Groups, in THE CRIMINAL IN THE ARMS OF THE LAW 569 (same); Gary Kleck, Racial Discrimination in Criminal Sentencing: A Critical Evaluation of the Evidence with Additional Evidence on the Death Penalty, 46 AM. SOC. REV. 783 (1981) (same).

3.   See KATE STITH & JOSE A. CABRANES, FEAR OF JUDGING: SENTENCING GUIDELINES IN THE FEDERAL COURTS 38–77, 104, and accompanying notes (1998).

4.   See Sentencing Reform Act, Pub. L. No. 98–473, 98 Stat. 1837 (1984).

5.   125 S. Ct. 738, 767 (2005).

6.   To trigger mandatory minimum drug sentences, powdered cocaine trafficked must be one hundred times that of crack. 21 U.S.C. [section] 841(b)(1)(A)(iii)-(B)(iii) (2000). For a discussion and critique, see Albert Alschler, Disparity: The Normative and Empirical Failure of the Federal Guidelines, 58 STAN. L. REV. 85, 102–04 (2005).

7.   STITH & CABRANES, supra note 3, at 9–11. The structure and language of our description of the Sentencing Guidelines owes much to Stith and Cabranes's book and to an essay by Frank Bowman. See Frank O. Bowman, III, The 2001 Federal Economic Crime Sentencing Reforms: An Analysis and Legislative History, 35 IND. L. REV. 5 (2001).

8.   See Sentencing Reform Act.

9.   28 U.S.C. [section] 991(b)(1)(b) (2000). For a brief description of the Commission's composition, see Ami L. Feinstein et al., Eighth Survey of White Collar Crime Procedural Issues: Federal Sentencing, 30 AM. CRIM. L. REV. 1079, 1080 (1983).

10. Feinstein et al., supra note 9, at 1083 (citing 28 U.S.C. [section] 994 (o), (p) (1980)).

11. 28 U.S.C. [section] 3553 (2000) (invalidated by United States v. Booker, 125 S. Ct. 738, 745–46 (2005)).

12. A sentence within a properly calculated Guidelines range is not reversible. 18 U.S.C. [section] 3742 (2000).

13. See supra note 7, at 9.

14. See infra Appendix 1.

15. 18 U.S.C. [section] 3742.

16. Base offense levels are specified in the United States Sentencing Guidelines Manual, Chapter Two—Offense Conduct. For example, price fixing has a base offense level of 10. U.S. SENTENCING GUIDELINES MANUAL [section] 2R1.1(a) (2006).

17. These are often called "Specific Offense Characteristics" and are specified for each crime in Chapter Two of the Guidelines Manual. For example, price-fixing has a base offense level of 10, but adjustments are made based on the "value of commerce" affected. See id. [section] 2Rl.1(b)(2). For a discussion, see STITH & CABRANES, supra note 3, at 70.

18. These are detailed in the Guidelines Manual, Chapter Three—Adjustments. For example, if the judge at the sentencing hearing finds that the offender played an "aggravating role" in the offense, the offense level may be increased by as much as four levels. U.S. SENTENCING GUIDELINES MANUAL [section] 3B1.1(a).

19. See supra, notes 15–16.

20. Bowman, supra note 13, at 10.

21. STITH & CABRANES, supra note 3, at 68 n.199 (citing U.S. SENTENCING GUIDELINES MANUAL [subsection] 2B3.1(G)(2) (1996), 2D1.1(b)(1) (1996)).

22. See United States v. Watts, 519 U.S. 148, 157 (1997) (conduct underlying charges for which defendant has been acquitted may be relied on in sentencing); U.S. SENTENCING GUIDELINES MANUAL [section] 1B1.3 cmt.

23. See U.S. SENTENCING GUIDELINES MANUAL [section] 3A1.1(b).

24. STITH & CABRANES, supra note 3, at 72.

25. 18 U.S.C. [section] 3553(b) (2000); U.S. SENTENCING GUIDELINES MANUAL [section] 5K2.0 policy statement.

26. The judge's mechanical calculation of offense level and criminal history category can be appealed even when the sentence is within the Guidelines. 18 U.S.C. [section] 3772.

27. See STITH & CABRANES, supra note 3, at 72–77, for a general discussion of departures under the Guidelines.

28. U.S. SENTENCING COMM'N, DOWNWARD DEPARTURES FROM THE FEDERAL SENTENCING GUIDELINES (IN RESPONSE TO SECTION 401 (M) OF PUBLIC LAW 108–21) iv–v (2003), available at http://www.ussc.gov/departrpt03/departrpt03.pdf (noting that recently the government initiates 40% of non-substantial assistance downward departures). Substantial assistance departures have also become increasingly common, and in 2003 outpaced non-substantial assistance departures. Id. at 32 tbl.1.

29. 18 U.S.C. [section] 3553(e).

30. United States v. Booker, 125 S. Ct. 738, 767 (2005).

31. Id. at 767.

32. Compare United States v. Wilson, 350 F. Supp. 2d 910 (D. Utah 2005), and United States v. Wilson, 355 F. Supp. 2d 1269 (D. Utah 2005), with United States v. Ranum, 353 F. Supp. 2d 984 (E.D. Wis. 2005).

33. Cf. United States v. Mueffelman, 327 F. Supp. 2d 79, 96 (D. Mass 2004) (holding the Guidelines unconstitutional after the Supreme Court issued Blakely v. Washington, 124 S. Ct. 2531 (2004), but before it issued Booker):

> [T]here will never be a return to truly indeterminate sentencing. The Guidelines have dramatically changed the way judges and parties think about sentencing; it has created a common vocabulary in terms of which we can compare cases and like or unlike defendants. I, along with all of the other judges who have declared the Guidelines as a whole unconstitutional under Blakely, will recognize and surely be guided by their provisions.

Id.

34. Booker, 125 S. Ct. at 770.

35. U.S. SENTENCING GUIDELINES MANUAL [section] 5E1.2(a) (2006).

36. Id. [section] 5E1.2(d)(3).

37. Id. [section] 5E1.2(d)(8).

38. There is nothing permitting a departure from the Guidelines on the basis of payment of a fine or an adjustment in the offense level to reflect fine payment. However, the Guidelines provide that fines should be imposed in a manner such that the "combined sentence" reflects the seriousness of the offense. Id. [section] 5E1.2(d)(l). Of course, the judge retains discretion within the confines of calculating the offense level and sentencing within the range.

39. Id. [section] 5E1.2(c)(4).

40. Id.

41. The Guidelines authorize the judge to consider the ability to pay a fine and the impact of a fine on the offender's dependents and ability to pay restitution. See generally 18 U.S.C. [section] 3572 (2000).

42. David B. Mustard, Racial, Ethnic, and Sex Disparities in Sentencing: Evidence from the U.S. Federal Courts, 44 J.L. & ECON. 285 (2001).

43. Id. at 299–305. This disparity was present for nearly all types of offenses, but ranged from almost 10.5 months for drug trafficking to 0.91 months for fraud. Id. at 306 tbl.8.

44. Id. at 297 tbl.6.

45. Celesta A. Albonetti, Sentencing under the Federal Sentencing Guidelines: Effects of Defendant Characteristics, Guilty Pleas, and Departures on Sentence Outcomes for Drug Offenses, 1991–1992, 31 LAW & Soc'v REV. 789, 817 (1997).

46. DOUGLAS C. MCDONALD & KENNETH E. CARLSON, BUREAU OF JUSTICE STATISTICS, SENTENCING IN THE FEDERAL COURTS: DOES RACE MATTER? 177 (1993).

47. Mustard, supra note 42, at 311–12.

48. Max Schanzenbach, Racial and Sex Disparities in Prison Sentences: The Effect of District-Level Judicial Demographics, 24 J. LEGAL STUD. 57 (2005).

49. Id. at 65.

50. There were some differences within particular crime categories. For example, Schanzenbach found that black white-collar offenders were sentenced more lightly in districts with more black judges. There was some evidence that having more Hispanic judges reduced sentences for black and Hispanic drug offenders, but no similar effect was found for having more black judges. Id. at 80–81.

51. Paul J. Hofer et al., The Effect of the Federal Sentencing Guidelines on Inter-judge Sentencing Disparity, 90 J. CRIM. L. & CRIMINOLOGY 239, 240 (1999).

52. James M. Anderson et al., Measuring Interjudge Sentencing Disparity: Before and After the Federal Sentencing Guidelines, 42 J.L. & ECON. 271, 273 (1999).

53. Chantale Lacasse & A. Abigail Payne, Federal Sentencing Guidelines and Mandatory Minimum Sentences: Do Defendants Bargain in the Shadow of the Judge?, 42 J.L. & ECON. 245 (1999).

54. Id. at 247–50.

55. Id. at 267–68.

56. Max Schanzenbach & Emerson Tiller, Strategic Judging Under the Sentencing Guidelines: Positive Political Theory and Evidence, 23 J.L. ECON. & ORG. (forthcoming spring 2007).

57. The seminal article is Gary S. Becker, Crime and Punishment: An Economic Approach, 76 J. POL. ECON. 169, 193 (1968) (contending that "social welfare is increased if fines are used whenever feasible"). For a concise overview, see RICHARD A. POSNER, THE ECONOMIC ANALYSIS OF LAW [section] 7.2 (5th ed. 1998).

58. The most influential studies—and justly so—are probably those conducted under the direction of Stanton Wheeler and published in book form as the Yale Studies on White-Collar Crime. The quantitative work is published in various books and articles (the articles being essentially preliminary findings), including DAVID WEISBURD ET AL., WHITE-COLLAR CRIME AND CRIMINAL CAREERS (2001); DAVID WEISBURD ET AL., CRIMES OF THE MIDDLE CLASSES: WHITE-COLLAR OFFENDERS IN THE FEDERAL COURTS (1991) [hereinafter WEISBURD ET AL., CRIMES OF THE MIDDLE CLASSES]; David Weisburd et al., Class, Status and the Punishment of White-Collar Criminals, 15 LAW & SOC. INQUIRY 223 (1990); Stanton Wheeler et al., White Collar Crimes and Criminals, 25 AM. CRIM. L. REV. 331 (1988); and Stanton Wheeler et al., Sentencing the White-Collar Offender: Rhetoric and Reality, 47 AM. Soc. REV. 641 (1982) [hereinafter Wheeler et al., Sentencing the White-Collar Offender]. In addition to their quantitative work, the Yale researchers also published three other books, the most pertinent to this Paper being STANTON WHEELER ET AL., SITTING IN JUDGMENT: THE SENTENCING OF WHITE-COLLAR CRIMINALS (1988), which summarizes and discusses extensive interviews of federal district court judges. Other researchers (that is, researchers outside the Yale project) have also conducted useful quantitative studies. See, e.g., Michael L. Benson & Esteban Walker, Sentencing the White-Collar Offender, 53 AM. Soc. REV. 294 (1988) (in-depth study of a single federal district court in a Midwestern state); John Hagan & Ilene Nagel, The Differential Sentencing of White Collar Offenders in Ten Federal District Courts, 45 AM. SOC. REV. 802 (1980); John Hagan & Patricia Parker, White-Collar Crime and Punishment: The Class Structure and Legal Sanctioning of Securities Violations, 50 AM. SOC. REV. 302 (1985) (examining securities violations in Canada); Ilene H. Nagel & John Hagan, The Sentencing of White-Collar Criminals in Federal Courts: A Socio-legal Exploration of Disparity, 80 MICH. L. REV. 1427 (1982); Ilene H. Nagel & John L. Hagan, White-Collar Crime, White-Collar Time: The Sentencing of White-Collar Offenders in the Southern District of New York, 20 AM. CRIM. L. REV. 259 (1982).

59. For example, there are no mandatory minimum sentences in the case of federal white collar crimes, but mandatory minimums are common in drug crimes. For a discussion of how this may contribute to disparity between crimes post-Booker, see M.K.B. Darmer, The Federal Sentencing Guidelines After Blakely and Booker: The Limits of Congressional Tolerance and a Greater Role for Juries, 56 S.C.L. REV. 533, 565 (2005). Post-Enron, Congress has shown a greater willingness to tinker with white collar crime. See Sarbanes-Oxley Act of 2002, Pub. L. 107–204, [subsection] 902–06, 116 Stat. 745 (enhancing penalties for white collar crime); [section] 805 (directing the Commission to amend the Guidelines to ensure that the punishments for obstruction of justice are "sufficient to deter and punish that activity"). These amendments are not covered by the time span of the sample.

60. See Carol A. Bergman, The Politics of Federal Sentencing on Cocaine, 10 FED. SENT'G REP. 196, 196 (1998) ("In 1993, 88.3 percent of those sentenced for trafficking crack were African American; 4.1 percent were white.").

61. For example, "a ten-year mandatory minimum sentence is triggered by trafficking fifty grams of crack, but one must traffic five thousand grams of powder cocaine to trigger the same sentence." Id.

62. WEISBURD ET AL., CRIMES OF THE MIDDLE CLASSES, supra note 58, at 97 tbl.5.1. The data are from the 1980s, but conform to common intuition: fraud and embezzlement cases are usually detected because of reports by victims or employers

(with securities fraud being an exception). Id. In fact, victim/employer complaints or "routine audits or investigations" detect nearly 80% of white collar crimes prosecuted. Id.

63. Some white-collar crimes, however, such as tax crimes, might resemble street crime in that they are initially investigated by tax officials who are not prosecutors and are therefore only selectively referred for prosecution. These types of white-collar crime therefore resemble street crime in that they have another level where bias can creep in.

64. See, e.g., POSNER, supra note 57, at 244–48; James Andreoni, Reasonable Doubt and the Optimal Magnitude of Fines: Should the Penalty Fit the Crime?, 22 RAND J. ECON. 285 (1991); David D. Friedman, Reflections on Optimal Punishment," or, Should the Rich Pay Higher Fines?, 3 REV. L. & ECON. 185 (1981); Louis Kaplow, The Optimal Probability and Magnitude of Fines for Acts That Definitely Are Undesirable, 12 INT'L REV. L. & ECON. 3 (1992); Steven. D. Levitt, Incentive Compatibility Constraints as an Explanation for the Use of Prison Sentences Instead of Fines, 17 INT'L REV. L. & ECON. 179 (1997); John R. Lott, Should the Wealthy Be Able to "Buy Justice"?, 95 J. POE. ECON. 1307 (1987); A. Mitchell & Daniel Rubinfeld, A Model of Optimal Fines for Repeat Offenders, 46 J. PUB. ECON. 291 (1991); A. Mitchell Polinsky & Steven Shavell, A Note on Optimal Fines When Wealth Varies Among Individuals, 81 AM. ECON. REV. 618 (1991); A. Mitchell Polinsky & Steven Shavell, The Optimal Tradeoff Between the Probability and Magnitude of Fines, 69 AM. ECON. REV. 880 (1979); A. Mitchell Polinsky & Steven Shavell, The Optimal Use of Fines and Imprisonment, 24 J. PUB. ECON. 89 (1984); Steven Shavell, Specific Versus General Enforcement of Law, 99 J. POE. ECON. 1088 (1991); George Stigler, The Optimum Enforcement of Laws, 78 J. POE. ECON. 526 (1970); cf. Becker, supra note 57, at 169 (developing a "market model" of crime); Isaac Ehrlich, Crime, Punishment, and the Market for Offenses, 10 J. ECON. PERSP. 43 (1996) (same, with a useful bibliography on economic models of crime); Ann D. Witte, Estimating the Economic Model of Crime with Individual Data, 94 Q. J. ECON. 57 (1980) (same).

65. See, e.g., POSNER, supra note 57, at 244–48 (suggesting that the best way to get convicts to pay fines is to impose heavy non-pecuniary sanctions as alternatives).

66. We found a fourth study which could be described as empirical, but not quantitative: SALLY T. HILLSMAN ET AL., U.S. DEP'T OF JUSTICE, FINES IN SENTENCING: A STUDY OF THE USE OF THE FINE AS A CRIMINAL SANCTION (1984). Hillsman and her colleagues provide valuable information on sentencing practices in the federal and state courts, as well as courts of foreign jurisdiction. They present the state of the law as captured in statutes and case law, and they also researched ongoing practice by conducting "a national telephone survey of one hundred twenty-six courts in twenty-one states; on-site visits to thirty eight courts of various types in seven states; and an in-depth, case record study of fine use and collection in New York City's five limited and five general jurisdiction courts." Id. at 10. However, Hillsman and her colleagues did not analyze disparities in race, socio-economic class, or sex, or conduct much quantitative research beyond tallying fine amounts. Although the study is related to the questions posed in this Article, it is not directly responsive.

67. Joel Waldfogel, Are Fines and Prison Terms Used Efficiently? Evidence on Federal Fraud Offenders, 39 J.L. & ECON. 107 (1995).

68. WEISBURD ET AL., CRIMES OF THE MIDDLE CLASSES, supra note 58, at 150–57 (discussing the fines results and observing that "[t]hose with the most money available are most likely to be fined").

69. John R. Lott, Do We Punish High Income Criminals Too Heavily?, 30 ECON. INQUIRY 583 (1992).

70. Waldfogel, supra note 67, at 131.

71. See the commentary section of U.S. SENTENCING GUIDELINES MANUAL [section] 5E1.2 cmt. (2006) ("A fine may be the sole sanction if the [G]uidelines do not require a term of imprisonment.").

72. We obtained the data from the website of the Inter-University Consortium for Political and Social Research, http://www.icpsr.umich.edu (last visited Mar. 28, 2006).

73. We are therefore adhering to the definition of white-collar crime offered by Herbert Edelhertz: "[A white-collar crime is] an illegal act or series of illegal acts committed by nonphysical means and by concealment or guile, to obtain money or property, or to obtain business or personal advantage." HERBERT EDELHERTZ, U.S. DEP'T OF JUSTICE, THE NATURE, IMPACT AND PROSECUTION OF WHITE COLLAR CRIME 3 (1970).

74. See STITH & CABRANES, supra note 3, at 105.

75. For a recent treatment, see George J. Borjas, Ethnicity, Neighborhoods, and Human Capital Externalities, 85 AM. ECON. REV. 365 (1995).

76. For a recent discussion, see Pedro Carneiro et al., Labor Market Discrimination and Racial Differences in Premarket Factors, 48 J.L. & ECON. 1 (2005).

77. Marianne Bertrand & Senhil Mullainathan, Are Emily and Brendan More Employable Than Latoya and Tyrone? Evidence on Racial Discrimination in the Labor Market from a Large Randomized Experiment, 94 AM. ECON. REV. 991 (2004).

78. See, e.g., Alicia Mundell et al., Mortgage Lending in Boston: Interpreting HMDA Data, 86 AM. ECON. REV. 25 (1996).

79. See Helen Ladd, Evidence on Discrimination in Mortgage Lending, 12 J. ECON. PERSP. 41 (1998).

80. For an excellent treatment of the difficulty in identifying the source of a racial disparity, see IAN AYRES, PERVASIVE PREJUDICE? 45–87 (2001).

81. Those with less than a high school education are the excluded category in the education dummy variables.

82. See Schanzenbach & Tiller, supra note 56, tbl.3.

83. Id.

84. We acknowledge the possibility that prosecutorial discretion leaves whites with lower level offenses to slip past while minorities do not. This would cause the average adjustment for whites to be larger than the average adjustment for minorities, which could explain the result.

85. See Benson & Walker, supra note 58, at 298–99 ("Contrary to Wheeler et al., we find that nonwhites are more likely to be incarcerated than their white counterparts. . . . As with the In/Out decision, race has a significant effect on the length of sentence: Nonwhite defendants received longer sentences than white defendants."); Mustard, supra note 42, at 312 ("The differences by race . . . exist across offense types. . . . Blacks and males not only receive longer sentences but also are less likely to receive no prison term when that option is available.").

86. See supra Part IV.A.

87. See Wheeler et al., Sentencing the White-Collar Offender: Rhetoric and Reality, supra note 58, at 645.

88. See id. at 651, 653.

89. See supra Table 2.

90. The "zones" mark areas of the table in which judges have the same amount of discretion.

14

Prosecutions Drop for US White-Collar Crime; They're Down 28 Percent from Five Years Ago, as Homeland Security Cases Rise in Priority

Alexandra Marks, *Staff Writer*

NEW YORK—It's the kind of announcement that should put white-collar criminals on notice. The Securities and Exchange Commission (SEC) is now investigating more than 80 companies in the growing stock-option scandal.

The government has charged officials at two companies for backdating options—a practice that funneled guaranteed profits to executives. More indictments are expected.

But far from ratcheting up the fight against financial wrongdoing, the federal government is actually shifting resources away from it. The number of white-collar crime prosecutions is down 28 percent from five years ago,

"Prosecutions drop for US white-collar crime; They're down 28 percent from five years ago, as homeland security cases rise in priority," by Alexandra Marks reproduced with permission from the August 31, 2006 issue of *The Christian Science Monitor* (www.csmonitor.com). Copyright © 2006 The Christian Science Monitor.

according to an analysis of federal data by the Transactional Records Access Clearinghouse at Syracuse University.

The reason? The government's focus on homeland security, experts say. In the same period white-collar crime prosecutions fell, for instance, immigration prosecutions more than doubled.

"There's been a shift of priorities since Sept. 11 at the FBI [Federal Bureau of Investigation], in the sense that they've moved bodies from fraud and white-collar crime units to terrorism units," says James Sanders, a partner at McDermott Will & Emery in Los Angeles and a former federal prosecutor. "At the same time, the [white-collar crime] cases have gotten bigger and more complex."

During the 1980s and 1990s, many of the white-collar crime cases involved things like bank fraud, insider trading, and stock manipulation, many of which were not document-intensive. Trials could take as little as four or five days, says Mr. Sanders. But cases like Enron and WorldCom involved complex financial manipulations at high levels. Prosecutors had millions of documents to wade through, which in some cases took years to do.

"Those are very, very complex, document-intensive cases," says J. Boyd Page, senior partner at Page Perry LLC in Atlanta, which was involved in some civil litigation connected to the WorldCom case. "The documents that were made available for our review were something like 1,250 boxes packed one end to the other."

The Enron and WorldCom convictions, as well as the passage of the Sarbanes-Oxley Act in 2002, which holds CEOs directly accountable for their public financial statements, may have had a deterrent effect on some wrong-doers in corporate America, say experts. But they doubt that the drop in white-collar prosecutions reflects an equivalent drop in financial wrongdoing.

Instead, they say, the drop is a reflection of changed priorities. One key factor: The staff available to investigate such cases has shrunk. According to the Justice Department's Office of the Inspector General, the FBI had 2,385 agents engaged in fighting financial crimes in 2000. By 2004, that number had dropped to 1,882.

"There's always been a serious limitation of resources that has caused the government to focus on only the most egregious, large-scale fraudulent schemes," says Christopher Bebel, former federal prosecutor and specialist in securities fraud. "This continuing diversion of resources toward perceived immigration and terrorism threats greatly heightens the dilemma associated with that problem."

That's become particularly apparent in the current stock-option scandal, say experts, because of the scandal's extensiveness. Corporate lawyers say the SEC is relying on companies themselves to do independent investigations, to act as screeners of a kind, and then share with government lawyers if any egregious behavior turns up.

"The US Attorneys offices don't have the prosecutorial resources to truly investigate each one of these cases separately themselves," says Sanders. "They're basically saying to law firms like mine, 'We want you to be independent and come back to us and tell us if there's been an offense here.' "

If an offense is found, Sanders says, the government will do its own investigation.

A spokesman for the SEC declined to comment on the nature of its investigations. But he did note that the number of agents working on the "prevention and suppression of fraud" increased from 981 in 2001 to 1,232 in 2005.

The Justice Department also defends its success in fighting corporate crime, noting that it's cyclical in nature. "We had an extremely high number of convictions from 2001 to 2004, which rose from years prior to 2001 and is typical of these kinds of investigations and prosecutions because they are cyclical," says Brian Roehrkasse, a Department of Justice spokesman. "Since July of 2002, we've had 1,063 corporate fraud convictions, which is a significant amount of work in a four-year period."

White-collar crime experts don't fault the Justice Department for lack of zeal in its work, but do worry about the shrinking resources devoted to keeping corporate America on its ethical toes.

"People can steal a much greater amount of money with a pen than they can with a gun," says Mr. Page. "If we don't take a stand to say, 'Look, this is wrong' . . . then we turn our head, and it results in a lot of people thinking it's OK."

InfoMarks: Make Your Mark

What Is an InfoMark?

It is a single-click return ticket to any page, any result, or any search from InfoTrac College Edition.

An InfoMark is a stable URL, linked to InfoTrac College Edition articles that you have selected. InfoMarks can be used like any other URL, but they're better because they're stable—they don't change. Using an InfoMark is like performing the search again whenever you follow the link, whether the result is a single article or a list of articles.

How Do InfoMarks Work?

If you can "copy and paste," you can use InfoMarks.

When you see the InfoMark icon on a result page, its URL can be copied and pasted into your electronic document—web page, word processing document, or email. Once InfoMarks are incorporated into a document, the results are persistent (the URLs will not change) and are dynamic.

Even though the saved search is used at different times by different users, an InfoMark always functions like a brand new search. Each time a saved search is executed, it accesses the latest updated information. That means subsequent InfoMark searches might yield additional or more up-to-date information than the original search with less time and effort.

Capabilities

InfoMarks are the perfect technology tool for creating:

- Virtual online readers
- Current awareness topic sites—links to periodical or newspaper sources
- Online/distance learning courses
- Bibliographies, reference lists
- Electronic journals and periodical directories
- Student assignments
- Hot topics

Advantages

- Select from over 15 million articles from more than 5,000 journals and periodicals
- Update article and search lists easily
- Articles are always full-text and include bibliographic information
- All articles can be viewed online, printed, or emailed
- Saves professors and students time
- Anyone with access to InfoTrac College Edition can use it
- No other online library database offers this functionality
- FREE!

How to Use InfoMarks

There are three ways to utilize InfoMarks—in HTML documents, Word documents, and Email

HTML Document

1. Open a new document in your HTML editor (Netscape Composer or FrontPage Express).
2. Open a new browser window and conduct your search in InfoTrac College Edition.
3. Highlight the URL of the results page or article that you would like to InfoMark.
4. Right-click the URL and click Copy. Now, switch back to your HTML document.
5. In your document, type in text that describes the InfoMarked item.
6. Highlight the text and click on Insert, then on Link in the upper bar menu.
7. Click in the link box, then press the "Ctrl" and "V" keys simultaneously and click OK. This will paste the URL in the box.
8. Save your document.

Word Document

1. Open a new Word document.
2. Open a new browser window and conduct your search in InfoTrac College Edition.
3. Check items you want to add to your Marked List.
4. Click on Mark List on the right menu bar.
5. Highlight the URL, right-click on it, and click Copy. Now, switch back to your Word document.
6. In your document, type in text that describes the InfoMarked item.
7. Highlight the text. Go to the upper bar menu and click on Insert, then on Hyperlink.

8. Click in the hyperlink box, then press the "Ctrl" and "V" keys simultaneously and click OK. This will paste the URL in the box.
9. Save your document.

Email

1. Open a new email window.
2. Open a new browser window and conduct your search in InfoTrac College Edition.
3. Highlight the URL of the results page or article that you would like to InfoMark.
4. Right-click the URL and click Copy. Now, switch back to your email window.
5. In the email window, press the "Ctrl" and "V" keys simultaneously. This will paste the URL into your email.
6. Send the email to the recipient. By clicking on the URL, he or she will be able to view the InfoMark.